RESPONDING TO LITERATURE

MULTICULTURAL PERSPECTIVES

Teacher's Guide

RESPONDING TO LITERATURE

MULTICULTURAL PERSPECTIVES

Teacher's Guide

Senior Consultants

ARTHUR N. APPLEBEE
State University of New York at Albany

JUDITH A. LANGER
State University of New York at Albany

Authors

DAVID W. FOOTE

MARGARET GRAUFF FORST

MARY HYNES-BERRY

JULIE WEST JOHNSON

BASIA C. MILLER

BRENDA PIERCE PERKINS

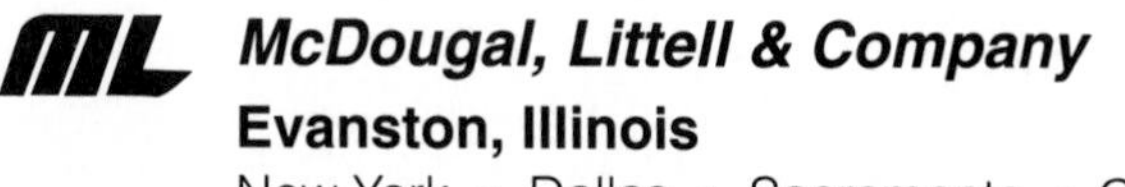

McDougal, Littell & Company
Evanston, Illinois
New York • Dallas • Sacramento • Columbia, SC

ISBN 0-8123-7648-X

Box 1667, Evanston, Illinois 60204

1 2 3 4 5 6 7 8 9 10 – MAM – 95 94 93 92 91

Contents of the Teacher's Guide

A All aspects of this text reinforce a student-centered, response-based approach to literature study.

B Arthur Applebee and Judith Langer, Director and Co-Director of the National Center on Literature Teaching and Learning, serve as Senior Consultants for the McDougal, Littell literature programs.

C These essays discuss seven classroom approaches that reflect current research into effective teaching practices.

D Reading and writing are integrated throughout the text. Students use journals before, during, and after reading as a place to record their responses and as a source of ideas for responding in writing.

E A sample test is accompanied by an explanation of test structure and of the thinking processes required by each section of the test. Also given are instructions on how to introduce these unique tests to students and how to score the tests.

F The literature in *Multicultural Perspectives* is organized thematically by author purpose, a structure that enables students to make connections between literary works and to consider how different writers have responded to the same impulses to communicate.

G An introduction at the beginning of every unit provides a context for reading the works and defines literary terms taught in the unit. Students further develop their literary vocabulary as they discuss the techniques utilized in particular works.

H A survivor of the Vietnam war, Le Ly Hayslip now lives in Los Angeles. Her gripping account of traditional rural life and of the horrors of war, published in 1989, exemplifies the immediacy and relevance of the nonfiction selections in this book.

I Students often study poems in pairs, which enriches understanding of both poems and encourages students to see individual works in broader contexts.

J Through the unit reviews, students synthesize their understandings of major concepts and then express their understandings in a variety of writing formats. The reviews integrate graphic organizers into the prewriting process, to support students in rethinking unit material.

K Those works that typify authors' recognized styles are featured in this text: for example, this powerful poem illustrates Langston Hughes's mastery of imagery and diction.

F Unit 1 CELEBRATING HERITAGE

Unit 2 OPPOSING INJUSTICE

The blank pages in this Guide allow maximum flexibility. A teacher may remove all the materials for a selection and re-file these materials in file folders or in a three-ring notebook.

Unit 3 AFFIRMING IDENTITY

L This essay and other works in this text such as "I Have a Dream" and *A Raisin in the Sun* are African-American literary classics.

M This entertaining account of a young Native American's attempts to win a maiden's heart and hand provides a perspective on Native American life before the devastation caused by Caucasian and African-American settlement.

Unit 4 EXPLORING CULTURAL CONFLICTS

N Among the highly contemporary works in the book is this short story, which was later incorporated into Tan's best-selling novel, *The Joy Luck Club.*

O Mark Mathabane explores the reality of apartheid in a nonfiction work that opens students' eyes to contemporary political realities. Like Le Ly Hayslip, Jamaica Kincaid, and Rosario Ferré, Mathabane now resides in the United States.

Unit 5 ENGAGING THE IMAGINATION

P García Márquez, Borges, and Neruda—foremost among twentieth-century Latin American writers—are well known among readers in the United States.

Q At the end of every unit, one or two selections without full study apparatus allow students to practice the skills of an independent reader.

Unit 6 EXAMINING LIFE EXPERIENCES

R Studying multiple poems by Gwendolyn Brooks deepens students' appreciation for this contemporary American writer and provides opportunities for students to make well-founded generalizations about voice, style, and theme.

S This classic play deals with themes that remain as relevant today as when the play was written: generational conflict, racial tensions, thwarted dreams, cultural values, the importance of self-respect. Showing the film version of this work can insure maximum classroom impact.

T A research-based approach to vocabulary-building is implemented throughout *Multicultural Perspectives.* Words essential to understanding a selection are presented in context on the prereading page. Within the selection itself, words are underscored and defined. Vocabulary worksheets provide students with a second and often a third opportunity to work with the words in different contexts.

Overview of *Multicultural Perspectives*

Multicultural Perspectives is a collection of works that reflect the rich multicultural mix of American society. The anthology includes the works of writers who were born in or emigrated to the United States as well as Caribbean and Latin American writers whose works are well known among American readers. This anthology, along with *Contemporary Short Stories*, is part of McDougal Littell's *Responding to Literature* series, an innovative program based on reader response theory. All the texts in this series combine fine literature with study materials that support the student's reading, thinking, and writing processes. Each anthology is accompanied by a Teacher's Guide, which includes Vocabulary Worksheets and Tests in copy master form.

Student Book

Literature. *Multicultural Perspectives* provides a sample of the literary richness of minority cultures: African American, Hispanic and Latin American, Asian American, and Native American. The anthology contains works by major contemporary writers (Gabriel García Márquez, Gwendolyn Brooks, Jamaica Kincaid, Pablo Neruda, Alice Walker, Mark Mathabane) as well as works now regarded as classics (for example, *Narrative of the Life of Frederick Douglass*, poems by Langston Hughes, Lorraine Hansberry's *A Raisin in the Sun*, Martin Luther King, Jr.'s "I Have a Dream," Zora Neale Hurston's "How It Feels to Be Colored Me"). Approximately half the selections are by women writers. This text provides a rich mix of fiction, nonfiction, and poetry as well as a full-length play. Teachers can use *Multicultural Perspectives* as a core text or as a supplement to traditional anthologies, which may not give sufficient coverage to the contributions of minority cultures.

Organization. The literature is organized thematically, according to purpose for writing. The titles of the six units focus on concerns common among both minority and mainstream writers:

Unit 1. Celebrating Heritage
Unit 2. Opposing Injustice
Unit 3. Affirming Identity
Unit 4. Exploring Cultural Conflicts
Unit 5. Engaging the Imagination
Unit 6. Examining Life Experiences

Each unit begins with an introduction that provides a context for the selections that follow and defines the literary terms taught in conjunction with the literature. Each unit ends with a review that requires students to make connections among the selections in the unit and then to write about these connections. Within each unit are one or two Insight features, brief pieces that enrich the study of a main selection.

Study Materials. The study materials that accompany the selections include both prereading and postreading support.* The prereading page prepares students to read in three ways:

- **Approaching the Selection** gives students necessary background information.
- **Building Vocabulary** presents essential words that are later defined in footnotes or sidenotes.
- **Connecting Writing and Reading** introduces a major issue that is later examined in the postreading questions.

The postreading material is divided into three parts:

- **Thinking About the Selection** presents open-ended discussion questions that address major issues, encourage a range of responses, extend ideas introduced in prereading, and make connections between literatures and cultures. Students build personal interpretations as the basis for further exploration of the literature and for thinking critically about literary issues.
- **Analyzing the Writer's Craft** gives an explanation and an activity that focuses on one literary technique exemplified in the selection. Skills are introduced at the beginning of a unit and explained in greater detail in Analyzing the Writer's Craft.
- **Connecting Reading and Writing** presents analytical and creative assignments with specified audiences and optional formats.

Throughout the study materials, students are encouraged to explore ideas in their journals, to work collaboratively, to think divergently, and to rely on the text as the basis for informed responses.

Scaffolding. The concept of scaffolding—structured support for student reading and thinking—is apparent in the carefully crafted lessons throughout the anthology. The prereading page for selections establishes a framework for reading. Questions after selections are supported by "think abouts," which are points to consider when answering the questions. In the most challenging selections, footnotes or sidenotes explain confusing or obscure references and passages.

In contrast to challenging selections, which have extensive scaffolding, are selections labeled "Responding on Your Own." These selections, which are easier for students to comprehend, are presented with only a brief introduction and essential footnoting. Students function as independent readers, applying the reading and analytical skills developed in preceding lessons.

* An exception is the "Responding on Your Own" feature, in which a selection is presented with abbreviated prereading support and no postreading questions.

Teacher's Guide

The Teacher's Guide offers a wealth of ideas and resources from which teachers can choose according to their own teaching styles and the needs of their students. The Guide is divided into two basic parts. The first part (pages 1–37) is addressed to the teacher as professional educator and includes articles on research-based instructional strategies and recommendations for extended reading. The second part (which begins on page 38) addresses the needs of the teacher as classroom facilitator and presents lesson materials for the selections in the student book.

Part One: Background and Long-Term Planning

Research and Philosophy. In a six-page essay, Arthur Applebee and Judith Langer, senior consultants to the McDougal, Littell literature programs, explain the learning theory that is the basis for the instructional material in the student book. The consultants discuss their research findings and current classroom practices and describe effective approaches for implementing response-based literature instruction.

Teaching Strategies. A series of essays introduces seven classroom approaches that reflect current research into effective teaching practices. Topics covered include journals, logs, and notebooks; cooperative and collaborative learning; instruction in the heterogeneous classroom; the teaching of writing in a classroom community; integrating the language arts; multimodal learning; and assessment options, including portfolio assessment. Following the last essay is a sample *Multicultural Perspectives* test, accompanied by an explanation of test structure and of the thinking processes required by each section of the test. A bibliography of professional resources supplements each essay.

Part Two: Lesson Planning and Implementation

The selections in the student book have corresponding lessons in the Teacher's Guide, which consist of teaching ideas, suggested answers to the questions in the student book, and a test. Most lessons also include a one-page or two-page Vocabulary Worksheet, which features the essential vocabulary words introduced on the prereading page of the student book and other useful words that appear in the selection.

Tests include essay questions, graphic organizers, and objective questions, all of which challenge students' higher level thinking skills. (See page 36 of this Guide for a sample test with accompanying explanation.) Vocabulary Worksheets are designed to teach vocabulary words through multiple exposures in a variety of contexts. Creative formats include crossword puzzles, humorous poems and stories, and word games. Tests and Vocabulary Worksheets are in copy master form and may be reproduced for classroom use.

Teaching Ideas. The idea pages present teachers with a variety of teaching options: motivation activities and graphics; multimodal activities; suggestions for teaching learning disabled students, limited English proficient students, and gifted and talented students; collaborative and cooperative learning activities; suggestions for making connections across literature, across the language arts, across the humanities, and across the curriculum; and teaching tips from classroom teachers. In addition to these options, the idea pages contain standard features such as objectives; plot summaries; literary, historical, and biographical information; bibliographies for teachers and students; and content quizzes.

Answers to questions are framed as suggested responses. Teachers are encouraged to accept all answers that can be supported with textual evidence. For those selections in the student book that do not have postreading questions (Responding on Your Own), the Guide includes discussion questions with suggested answers.

For the writing assignments in the student book, the Guide includes suggestions for modeling the formats, for collaborative approaches to planning and revision, and for integrating grammar and composition lessons into the instructional process.

Unit Materials. At the beginning of each unit is a Unit Preview, a scope and sequence chart showing the essential vocabulary words, literary skills, writing formats, and writing modes covered in the study materials for each selection. At the end of the unit, after the selection lessons, are the suggested answers for the Reviewing Concepts graphic in the student book and guidelines for evaluating the writing assignment.

Instructional Features of the Student Book

Before a work of literature:

Approaching the Selection
- Gives students necessary background

Building Vocabulary
- Introduces essential words

Connecting Writing and Reading
- Stimulates thinking about a key issue in the work

Within a work of literature:

Definitions of Essential Words
- Facilitate vocabulary acquisition

Explanatory Footnotes
- Help students meet the challenge of difficult works

After a work of literature:

Thinking About the Selection
- Guides students in responding personally, in building interpretations, in thinking creatively, and in thinking critically about the work

Analyzing the Writer's Craft
- Teaches literary techniques within the context of specific works

Connecting Reading and Writing
- Presents options for exploring meaning through analytical and creative writing

In every unit:

The Unit Introduction
- Creates context by introducing themes and literary terms

The Insight Feature
- Enriches the study of one or two selections

Responding on Your Own
- Provides students with an opportunity to apply the skills of an independent reader

Reviewing Concepts
- Supports students in making and describing connections among the selections in a unit

Objectives

The primary goals of *Multicultural Perspectives* are to expose students to fine multicultural literature and to provide students with a framework that enables them to respond to this literature in personal, critical, and creative ways. An important related goal is to draw students into the literary experience through literature and study materials that pique their interest, that are appropriate to their abilities, and that motivate them to participate actively in the process of reading and understanding literature. Throughout the text, students are encouraged to offer opinions, to make choices, and to explore connections, with their own ideas and experiences and between literature and the real world. Students respond both individually and collaboratively, both orally and in writing.

All instruction in *Multicultural Perspectives* is literature-based. Students master new vocabulary through the context of literature. Students explore literary techniques as illustrated in the selections. Students write *about* literature and *from* literature in a variety of modes and formats, always for authentic audiences and purposes.

Enjoyment, knowledge, appreciation, and a lifelong habit of reading: these goals can be achieved by using *Multicultural Perspectives* in a response-based English program.

Objectives for each selection are presented at the beginning of the corresponding lesson in the Teacher's Guide.

Features of the Teacher's Guide

Resources for the Response-Based Literature Classroom

Information

Journals, Logs, and Notebooks

- for encouraging active response to literature

Collaborative and Cooperative Learning

- for structuring interactive response

The Heterogeneous Classroom

- for supporting response on many levels

A Community of Writers: Classroom Techniques

- for teaching effective written response

Integration in the English Classroom

- for implementing literature-based instruction

Multimodal Learning

- for guiding nonverbal response

Assessment Options

- for measuring growth in response capabilities

Literary, Historical and Biographical Notes

- for enhancing the background for the teacher/facilitator

Teaching Ideas

Activity Options

Motivation Activities
Tips from Classroom Teachers
Multimodal Activities

Suggestions for Teaching

Limited English Proficient Students
Learning Disabled Students
Gifted and Talented Students

Suggestions for Cooperative and Collaborative Learning

Connections

Across Literature
Across the Language Arts
Across the Humanities
Across the Curriculum

Copy Masters

Vocabulary Worksheets

- for building vocabulary through context

Selection Tests

- for assessing comprehension of key concepts

Overview of Skills: ***Multicultural Perspectives***

Literature and Literary Skills

Literary Genre

Drama
Fiction
- Fantasy
- Magical Realism
- Oral Literature

Nonfiction
- Aphorism
- Autobiography
- Essay
- Historical Writing
- Memoir

Poetry
- Ode

Literary Elements and Techniques

Alliteration
Assonance
Character
- Cultural Hero
- Foil

Characterization
Conflict
- External Conflict
- Internal Conflict

Consonance
Description
Dialogue
Diction (Word Choice)
Epigraph
Experimental Form
Figurative Language
Flashback
Foreshadowing
Hero
Humor
Imagery
Irony
Metaphor
Meter
Mood
Narrator

Writing Modes and Formats

Expressive and Personal Writing

Anecdote
Aphorisms
Autobiographical Essay
Autobiographical Sketch
Cartoon Strip
Collage
Diary Entry
Free-Verse Poem
Haiku
Journal
Letter
Memoir
Oral History
Outline for Personal Speech
Personal Essay
Personal Response
Poem
Sonnet

Informative (Expository) Writing: Analysis

Annotation
Director's Notes
Explanation
Expository Essay
Guest Column
Instructions
Introduction
Letter
Note
Notes, Explanatory
Pamphlet
Playbill
Review
Speech

Informative (Expository) Writing: Classification

Booklet
Chart
Comparison Chart
Cookbook
Diagram
Family Tree
Graph
Graphic Representation
List
Program
Program Notes
Time Line

Informative (Expository) Writing: Synthesis

Booklet
Captions
Cue Cards
Essay
Eulogy
Expository Essay
Evaluation
Guidelines
Handbook
Headlines
Interpretative Essay
Letter
List of Questions
Newspaper Column
Notes, for Oral Presentation
Obituary
Outline
Press Release
Question/Answer Column
Questions
Report
Report Card
Review
Summary
Transcript
Verdict

Literature and Literary Skills

Literary Elements and Techniques *continued*

Paradox
Personification
Persuasion
Plot
- Climax
- Exposition
- Falling Action
- Rising Action

Point of View
- First-Person
- Limited
- Omniscient
- Third-Person

Repetition
Rhyme
Setting
Simile
Speaker
Stage Directions
Structure
Style
Symbol
Theme
Title
Tone

Response to Literature

All the writing in *Multicultural Perspectives*, whether writing about literature or writing from literature, is based on student response to literature.

Writing Modes and Formats

Narrative and Imaginative Writing

Ballad
Comic Strip
Conversation
Dialogue
Dramatic Monologue
Dramatic Scene
Dramatic Skit
Episode
Human Interest Story
Letter
Monologue
Narrative Poem
Notes
Poem
Rap Song
Scene
Script
Sequel
Song Lyrics
Story
Storyboard

Observation and Description

Biographical Sketch
Book Review
Captions
Catalog
Catalog Copy
Character Sketch
Descriptive Essay
Eulogy
Eyewitness Account
Introductory Speech
Obituary
Pamphlet
Personality Profile
Poem
Poster
Profile
Tribute
TV Commercial
Word Search Puzzle

Persuasion

Campaign Poster
Campaign Speech
Editorial
Grant Proposal
Handbill
Introduction
Letter
Letter of Complaint
Letter of Recommendation
Memo
Nomination
Persuasive Speech
Petition
Proposal
Publicity Slogans
Recommendation
Sermon
Slogans
Speech

Reports (Research)

Essay
Expository Essay
Guidelines
Informational Footnotes
Notes, for Class Presentation/Report
Notes, for Panel Discussion
Oral Presentation
Report
Research report
Summary

Response-Based Literature Instruction: Theory and Application

JUDITH A. LANGER AND ARTHUR N. APPLEBEE

Senior Consultants

Literature instruction has long been at the center of the secondary curriculum of every state and school district, and literature continues to be the focus of instruction in most English classrooms. However, although the past twenty-five years have seen major changes in the teaching of writing and reading, there has been little systematic improvement in literature instruction during this period, even during the recent period of reform. This benign neglect has occurred despite crucial advances in the understanding of thinking and reasoning, reading and writing relationships, and "thought provoking" instructional approaches. English teachers need instructional programs and materials that reflect these new understandings, and that are integrated so that the theories of student thinking that now drive the writing instruction are related to those that drive the literature instruction. Teachers need new approaches that acknowledge the role of literature in the development of the sharp and critical mind.

The English Curriculum. Recent studies of the secondary school English curriculum have highlighted a number of problems in most programs: 1) Teachers' goals for the teaching of literature stress student response and understanding, but the questioning strategies in most programs treat literature as a source of "right answers." 2) In part as a result, the teaching of literature has remained a teacher-centered and text-centered activity, in contrast to an increasingly student-centered approach in composition. 3) The literature program is often completely separate from the writing program; writing is not treated as a context for enriching and extending student response to literature. 4) The selections chosen for study remain unnecessarily narrow; generally, they do not represent the many rich and diverse traditions that are part of the students' literary heritage. Even when a broader range of materials has been included in literature anthologies, teachers have avoided these materials because they are unfamiliar and often because the accompanying teaching support has been less than satisfactory.

Text-Based and Reader-Based Approaches. During the twentieth century, the major debates about the teaching of literature have centered on the relative contributions of the text and the reader's own understanding to "good" reading. New critical approaches, which dominated decades of instruction, involve close and careful textual analyses. They focus on the text as a source of knowledge, and by and large, emerge from a more generalized view that the text has a "message" that needs to be extracted by a reader following certain procedures. Recent studies indicate that the analytical procedure itself too often becomes the focus of instruction rather than a support for the reading process.

Another text-based approach to literature relies upon standard critical interpretations of works and urges teachers to rely on those interpretations as the focus of instruction. Rather than learning to develop their own responses, students are asked to learn the interpretations of others.

In contrast, approaches that focus on the reader—reader response theory, for example—consider meaning to reside in the reader or in the transaction between the reader and the text, with the reader's interpretations as evidence of good reading. Reader-based approaches are

Reader-based approaches are the views most consonant with current research on reading comprehension as an interactive and constructive process and with process-oriented research on reading, writing, and reasoning.

the views most consonant with current research on reading comprehension as an interactive and constructive process and with process-oriented research on reading, writing, and reasoning. Reader-based approaches also underlie the theoretical framework of *Multicultural Perspectives*, which builds upon current theories of writing, literature, and the teaching of literature. This text is designed to remedy the problems that have been identified in recent studies of the English curriculum.

Multicultural Perspectives: Conceptual Framework

For the past few years, Judith Langer has been developing a theory for the teaching of literature, which describes the process of coming to understand literature and the contribution that the teaching of literature can make to the intellectual and cultural development of the growing student. Langer's theory is based on research that has shown the following:

- The meaning-making processes used in reading literature are not necessarily the same as those used in other coursework.
- The special contribution of literary understanding to the developing intellect needs to be acknowledged.
- The teaching of critical thinking in literature—the kinds of questions asked and the kinds of responses sought—needs to differ from the teaching of critical thinking in other subjects.

The Process of Reading Literature. A process view of reading suggests that making sense of a work of literature involves building envisionments, with understanding changing and growing over time. The term *envisionment* refers to the world of understanding a reader has about a text. When you read *A Raisin in the Sun*, for instance, what you read in Scene 1 (when Walter and Ruth quarrel over his late-night conversations with friends) provides you with only the scantest hints of what will unfold later in the play. The conversation is important at that time because it provides you with the necessary information to begin building an understanding of what will happen later. Thus the conversation is only of momentary importance, soon disappearing from your awareness, replaced with a deepening and ever-changing understanding of the relationship between Walter and Ruth.

Meaning-Making Through Envisionment-Building. An envisionment includes what a reader understands about a text, the questions the reader has, and the reader's hunches about how the piece will unfold. A reader has a different envisionment at each point in a reading; the envisionment changes as the reading progresses. As more is read, some details are dropped from the envisionment as no longer important (for example, Travis's request to carry groceries in front of the supermarket), and new details are added. The effect is a continuing elaboration upon the reader's knowledge: for example, upon the reader's awareness of the sources of the conflict between Walter and Ruth. Meaning gained from one portion of the reading is shaped by earlier interpretations and continues to change in light of interpretations developed later in the reading. This changing understanding is at the heart of the reader's response to literature, and needs to be at the heart of meaningful reader-based instruction.

Envisionment as Response. Envisionment is the way in which a reader experiences a text, the reader's total understanding or response at any point in time. During the reading of a novel, story, play, or poem, a reader's envisionment changes as new information from the text and new inferences from the reader influence the reader's response. This evolving envisionment might be thought of as a series of envisionments, which leads to an envisionment at the end of a reading. This end point is not the sum total of all the other envisionments, but rather a result of all the changes and modifications in understanding that have occurred along the way.

The envisionment at the end of a reading—the text world of ideas, questions, and quandaries that every reader comes away with after reading a work of literature—is a reader's starting point for contemplation and discussion. This envisionment can become the basis for further modification, as other readers offer alternative ways of making sense of a text.

The concept of envisionment as response is a critical one for instruction. The belief that when students read they continually modify their understandings demands questions that are not structured according to traditional hierarchies. These hierarchies, based on distinctions such as literal questions and inferential questions or on Bloom's taxonomy, are text-based and do not reflect the reader's process of sense-making. Words "on the page," for instance, are quite different from the ways in which those words are combined in a reader's mind at any given point in time. Talking about particular words from the text outside of the reader's text world disregards the response-building process the reader has engaged in. Rather than helping readers, discussions that begin by focusing on the "literal" meaning of the text rather than on what sense students have made of the text can actually get in the way of students' understanding. Similarly, retracing the plot line to check understanding ignores the envisionment-building process that led to the readers' response to the text as a whole. Rather than building on what students already understand, such activities force them to retreat from their understandings to focus on details out of context. Focusing on details may be helpful at a later point, however, as readers begin to sort out why their interpretations of the same text differ.

The belief that when students read they continually modify their understandings demands questions that are not structured according to traditional hierarchies.

Readers naturally want to discuss their envisionments (or initial responses). Recall, for example, the experience of finishing a good book, a mystery perhaps. You probably ended up with ideas and questions you wanted to talk about with others who had read the same book. What you experienced was a desire to share your envisionment.

The best reader-based questions teachers can ask immediately after students have read a selection are questions that tap students' envisionments. These questions might be similar to the following: What were you thinking as you finished the story? Is there anything you'd like to talk about? What did the poem mean to you?

Stances in the Process of Envisionment-Building. As a reader builds an envisionment, he or she adopts a series of changing relations toward a text, with each relation, or stance, adding a somewhat different dimension to the reader's developing response. Rather than being linear, stances have the potential to recur at any point in the reading. They describe the active reader's use of different knowledge sources in interaction with the text.

The stances provide a helpful way to think about the process of responding to a text. The four major stances are as follows:

1. **Being Out and Stepping Into an Envisionment.** In this stance, readers attempt to make contacts with the world of the text by using prior knowledge, experiences, and surface features to identify essential elements: for example, genre, content, structure, and language. Readers begin to construct an envisionment.

2. **Being In and Moving Through an Envisionment.** In this stance, readers are immersed in their own understandings, using their previously constructed envisionments, prior knowledge, and the text itself to further the creation of meaning. As students read, meaning-making moves along with the text. Readers are caught up, for example, in the narrative of a story or the imagery of a poem.

3. **Stepping Back and Rethinking What One Knows.** In this stance, readers use their envisionments to reflect on their own previous understandings. Rather than prior knowledge informing their envisionments as in the other stances, in this stance readers use their envisionments to rethink their prior knowledge, feelings, and actions.

4. **Stepping Out and Objectifying the Experience.** In this stance, readers distance themselves from their envisionments, reflecting on and reacting to the content, the text, or to the reading experience itself. Teachers have focused primarily on this stance in the past, but it is only one part of the process of coming to understand literature.

Readers take these stances toward texts not only when they are reading, but also when they are thinking about and discussing what they have read. Thus, literature lessons can become an excellent time to teach students to use the stances as ways to enrich their understandings. Using questions based on the stances rather than on the more traditional hierarchies focuses instruction on the process of understanding. Students clarify what they understand and at the same time learn effective strategies for building meanings on their own.

What Is Unique About Literary Understanding?

While readers use the stances during envisionment-building in both literary and informative contexts, the essential concerns are different for each type of reading. When engaged in informative reading (for example, to get information from social studies and science material), readers early on establish a sense of the topic and of the author's slant, and they use this judgment as a point of reference to monitor new and growing understandings. Once a sense of direction is established, it takes a great deal of countervailing information to change a reader's notion of the whole.

The reading of literature involves a great deal of critical thinking that is different from the kinds of thinking required by informative texts.

In contrast, literary reading abounds with the exploration of possibilities. Readers continually open new possibilities for meaning, for alternative interpretations and changing points of view. The possibilities change over time, growing out of the readers' developing envisionments.

The reading of literature involves a great deal of critical thinking that is different from the kinds of thinking required by informative texts. For example, in social studies or science materials, students must focus on understanding an argument or on learning specific content. As with literary texts, the reader works with a sense of the whole. However, in informational reading the sense of the whole serves as a steady point of reference, while in literary reading it is a constantly changing horizon of possibilities.

Instruction that helps students become competent readers of literature needs to reflect an awareness of these distinctions. Teachers must encourage students to recognize ambiguities, to explore possibilities, and to seek ways of "filling out" meanings, using their knowledge of the text and of human experience to develop deeper insights. The goal is to support students in becoming mature, sophisticated readers, capable of dealing with complex texts in increasingly thoughtful ways.

Putting Theory into Practice

The ideal literature classroom is a literary community where students are active meaning-makers: where they have room to respond, interpret, think critically, and contrast their ideas with those of other readers. To move toward this ideal, the questions asked need to change dramatically, so that they support the process of understanding, from the student's point of view. Rather than seeking right answers and predetermined interpretations, questions need to serve as "thought tappers." Students should respond to these open-ended questions individually, in small groups, or as a class, sharing their initial questions and understandings and then moving beyond into more fully developed interpretations.

The following are guidelines for supporting students through the rethinking process, after they have read a literary selection.

1. **Sharing Impressions.** Begin with a question that encourages students to share their initial responses to the work. For example: What picture lingered in your mind after you read this story? How do you feel about what happened to Gregorio Cortez?
2. **Constructing Interpretations.** Ask open-ended questions that operate as scaffolds, helping students to move beyond their initial understandings toward fuller and more carefully reasoned responses. Students might explore motivations, causes and effects, and implications, and might relate the parts to one another and to their understanding of the whole. Students might also consider how their ideas and feelings have changed as a result of their reading experience. The questions asked might be similar to the following: What do you think motivates the narrator to give the quilts to Maggie rather than Dee? How would you explain the meaning of the last sentence in the story? Who do you think better appreciates her heritage, Dee or Maggie?
3. **Responding Creatively.** Ask questions that help students explore the implications of current understandings or rethink either momentary or previous understandings, feelings, or questions. For example: What might the story be like if Gregorio Cortez had not lived by a heroic code? If Bay Ly had not been the only child left at home, how might her relationship with her father have been different? If Paule Marshall had been male, how might her childhood experiences have been different?
4. **Responding Critically.** After the students have worked through their understandings, ask them to become critics: to analyze, evaluate, argue, and defend, and to compare this work with other works or their own understandings with the interpretations of others. For example:
   - This speech is King's most famous and is considered by critics to be one of the great speeches of the twentieth century. Tell whether you agree with this view and give examples from the speech that influence your opinion.
   - Which of Frederick Douglass's qualities would be most valuable in fighting injustice today? Give reasons for your answer.
   - In what ways does this story resemble tall tales that you have read?

Because of the strength of their own developed interpretations, students by this time are equipped to undertake a critical analysis of a text or to consider the interpretations that their classmates or published critics may offer. Students' own interpretations will continue to evolve in the light of the perspectives that others bring.

In addition to conducting discussions, it is important to involve students in collaborative activities and in writing both before and after reading. The following are guidelines for further analysis and for making writing an integral part of the meaning-making process.

The ideal literature classroom is a literary community where students are active meaning-makers: where they have room to respond, interpret, think critically, and contrast their ideas with those of other readers.

- **Analyzing the Writer's Craft.** After students have spent time thinking critically about a work, they are ready to apply their knowledge of literary elements and analyze the text from a writer's point of view. Students' appreciation of language and structure and of the effects these engender is enhanced when you assign groups of students to work collaboratively on literary analysis: for example, when pairs of students identify metaphorical language and analyze its effects or when groups of students chart a plot and debate the question of climax.
- **Writing and Reading.** Writing offers a powerful context for thinking about literature, for clarifying understandings, and for sharing them with others. Writing before reading helps students connect the reading they will do with what they already know, thus providing a way into a new text or orienting the reader toward that text. Similarly, writing during reading—in reading logs or journals—helps students think about ideas in progress and clarify their changing envisionments. Students can also record puzzlements and questions to return to for later discussion. In related ways, writing after reading provides students with opportunities to connect the reading they have done to other ideas, texts, and experiences. For example, before reading "The Legend of Gregorio Cortez" you might ask students to select a hero and to rank that hero according to certain heroic qualities. During reading students might note similarities and differences between Gregorio Cortez and their own heroes, among other envisionment-building issues. After reading, students might discuss the qualities that make a hero and then choose a writing option that extends the issue into a new context.

Each type of question and activity is likely to tap a different stance, providing students with an array of vantage points from which to reflect upon a text. The guidelines for questions are not meant to imply that only one sequence of question types is effective or that each type of question and activity needs to be addressed during every lesson. However, one guideline is almost always applicable: Begin a discussion with an open-ended question that taps students' initial responses (not the teacher's understandings), thus inviting students to take an active role in building their own understandings of literature.

Effective Instruction: Underlying Principles

A teacher's techniques, and the activities within which they are embedded, are likely to be different in every classroom. The teacher alone has the professional knowledge to tailor instruction to the needs of a particular class. Across classrooms, however, the following principles underlie programs that effectively involve students in learning to develop rich, thoughtful interpretations of literature.

1. **Students are active makers of meaning.** Students are treated as thinkers, as if they can and will have interesting and cogent thoughts about a work of literature, which they will want to discuss.
2. **Literature reading generates questions.** Effective programs assume that after reading a work, students come away with initial responses and with questions that are part of their envisionments. Good instruction acknowledges that the process of understanding literature involves the raising of questions.
3. **Content questions tap student knowledge.** When teachers ask questions about content, they are tapping into student knowledge and understandings. Such questions have no predetermined right answers and are meant to prompt extended thought and sharing of ideas.
4. **Class meetings are a time to develop understandings.** Meaningful class discussions support the process of coming to understand. With the help of the teacher, students develop envisionments by assuming different stances toward the text. Thus, the cognitive behaviors students engage in during discussion are the same envisionment-building behaviors they engage in during reading.
5. **Instruction scaffolds the process of understanding.** All questions, activities, and assignments are designed to help students develop their own understandings, not memorize (or guess) the "right" interpretation of a text.
6. **Control is transferred from teacher to students.** Students work through their ideas alone, in small groups, and in class discussion. While students work, they are encouraged to interact collaboratively, to respond to and communicate with each other.

Multicultural Perspectives is a text designed to help the teacher put into practice these principles for effective instruction. The activities and questions in the program support envisionment-building, build confidence in dealing with literary texts, and encourage active participation in the classroom literary community.

Related Reading

Andrasick, Kathleen D. *Opening texts: Using writing to teach literature*. Portsmouth, NH: Heinemann. 1990.

Applebee, A. N. *The teaching of literature in programs with reputations for excellence in English*. Report Series 1.1, Center for the Learning and Teaching of Literature, State University of New York at Albany. 1989a.

Applebee, A. N. *Literature instruction in American schools*. Report Series 1.4, Center for the Learning and Teaching of Literature, State University of New York at Albany. 1989b.

Applebee, A. N., Langer, J. A., & Mullis, I., *Crossroads in American education*. Princeton, NJ: National Assessment of American Progress, Educational Testing Service. 1989.

Applebee, A. N. & Purves, A. C. Literature and the English Language Arts. In P. Jackson (Ed.) *Handbook of curriculum research*. NY: Macmillan. In press.

Britton, J. *Language and learning*. London: Penguin. 1970.

Britton, J. Writing and the story world. In B. Kroll & G. Wells (Eds.), *Explorations in the development of writing*. New York: Wiley. 1983.

Brody, P., DeMilo, C. & Purves, A. C. *The current state of assessment in literature*. Albany, NY: SUNY Albany, Center for the Learning and Teaching of Literature. 1989.

Bruner, J. S. *Actual minds, possible worlds*. Cambridge, MA: Harvard University Press. 1986.

Close, Elizabeth. How did we get here? Seventh-graders sharing literature. *Language Arts*, December 1990.

Diaz, P. and Hayhoe, M. *Developing response to poetry*. Philadelphia: Open University Press. 1988.

Langer, J. A. Reading, thinking, writing . . . and teaching. *Language Arts*, 59, 336–341. 1982.

Langer, J. A. Literacy instruction in American schools: Problems and perspectives. *American Education Research Journal*, 93, 107–132. 1984.

Langer, J. A. Levels of questioning: An alternative view. *Reading Research Quarterly* 20, 586–602. 1985.

Langer, J. A. *Children reading and writing:* Structures and strategies. Norwood, NJ: Ablex. 1986.

Langer, J. A. How readers construct meaning: An analysis of reader performance on standardized test items. In R. Freedle (Ed.), *Cognitive and linguistic analyses of standardized test performance*. Norwood, NJ: Ablex. 1987.

Langer, J. A. *The process of understanding literature*, Report Series 2.1, Center for the Learning and Teaching of Literature, State University of New York at Albany. 1989.

Langer, J. A. The process of understanding: Reading for literary and informative purposes, *Research in the Teaching of English*, 24, 220-256. 1990.

Langer, J. A. Speaking of knowing: Conceptions of knowing in the academic disciplines. In A. Herrington & C. Moran (Eds.) *Research and scholarship in writing across the disciplines*. NY: Modern Language Association. In press.

Langer, J. A. Understanding literature. *Language Arts*, December 1990.

Langer, J. A. & Allington, R. Curriculum research in writing and reading. In P. Jackson (Ed.), *Handbook of curriculum research.* NY: Macmillan. In press.

Langer, J. A. and Applebee, A. N. Reading and writing instruction: Toward a theory of teaching and learning. In E. Rothkopf (Ed.). *Review of research in education.* Washington DC: American Educational Research Association. 1986.

Langer, J. A. and Applebee, A. *How writing shapes thinking: Studies of teaching and learning.* Urbana, IL: National Council of Teachers of English. 1987.

Langer, J. A., Bartolome, L., Vasquez, O., & Lucas, T. Meaning construction in school literacy tasks: A study of bilingual students. *American Educational Research Journal*. 1990.

Muldoon, P. A. "Challenging students to think: Shaping questions, building community." In *Education Journal*, April 1990.

Probst, R. E. *Response and analysis: Teaching literature in junior and senior high school.* Portsmouth, NH: Boynton/Cook. 1988.

Purcell-Gates, V. On the outside looking in: A study of remedial readers' meaning-making while reading literature. *Journal of Reading Behavior.* In press.

Ravitch, D. & Finn, C. *What do our 17 year olds know? A report of the first national assessment of history and literature*. NY: Harper and Row. 1987.

Rosen, H. *Stories and meanings.* Sheffield, England: National Association for the Teaching of English. 1984.

Rosenblatt, L. *The reader, the text, and the poem.* Cambridge, MA: Harvard University Press. 1978.

Journals, Logs, and Notebooks

Writing enhances understanding, learning, recall, pleasure, and a sense of connecting with literature. Writing helps readers organize their thinking. It helps them make connections between literature and life. It aids them in reaching deeper levels of understanding. It enriches their enjoyment and jogs their memories. Writing fosters active participation in the process of reading literature and the interaction between reader and text that is central to literary understanding.

Journals, logs, and notebooks are three ways students can use writing. Generally, a log is a vehicle for recording somewhat structured responses to literature. In a log, students record their ideas following guidelines that the teacher sets in advance. The journal is more personal, akin to a diary. In journals, students may record responses that no one else will read; or they may record responses to which a teacher or a peer will respond, so that the journal becomes a kind of dialogue. The notebook remains an informal place for recording the points a teacher stresses, for listing chalkboard information, for listing details and describing responses while reading, and for noting connections between literature and life. The term *notebook* or *reader's notebook* sometimes is used interchangeably with *log* and *journal.*

The discussion here will focus primarily on journals, which are used extensively in *Multicultural Perspectives*, as a place to record prereading notes, thoughts while reading, responses to study questions, and prewriting ideas. One section, however, discusses the reading log as a way of structuring response.

Journals in Response-Based Instruction

Each interaction with literature can be an intense, personal, and emotional experience. The interaction can also aid students' cognitive development, a process supported by the use of journals. This vehicle for writing can help students develop the metacognitive awareness necessary to assume responsibility for learning.

Each interaction with literature can be an intense, personal, and emotional experience. The interaction can also aid students' cognitive development, a process supported by the use of journals.

Personal Journals. The journal that is similar to a diary is intensely personal. Here a student's feelings related to a work of literature spill out with abandon; no internal censor monitors what is written. In these journals, students can record the nuggets they mine in literature: the graceful phrase, the striking description, purely idiosyncratic responses. Literature often triggers responses directly related to events in students' lives, events related to their families, friends, joys, and sorrows. A journal can help students capture these feelings as they bubble to the surface in response to literature.

The personal journal is not meant to be read by anyone else. Students must feel safe when they write in such a journal, secure in the knowledge that neither you nor their classmates will read what they have written and that no one will evaluate the content. One of your goals in encouraging students to keep a personal journal is promoting a life-long habit of writing for pleasure and for self-expression. As students begin to feel comfortable with journal writing, the need to prompt them to write should decrease. Students will begin to see the payoff in terms of how such writing enriches their understanding of what they read.

Dialogue Journals. Another kind of journal, also calling for personal response to literature, serves as a repository for a dialogue between teacher and student or between two students. In a dialogue journal, students write personal reactions, questions, predictions, comments—anything, in short, except simple summaries. Then the teacher or peers read and respond to the entries, either individually or as a group. Each response should trigger further cognitive awareness. A reader's question or probe in response to a journal entry can help a student focus, dig deeper, rethink.

A reader's question or probe in response to a journal entry can help a student focus, dig deeper, rethink.

Reading Logs. You may want students to respond to a series of questions in a more structured reading log. The questions may be somewhat generic in nature. That is, the same questions may be asked for all selections within a particular genre. As students read and respond, they can use these questions, as appropriate, to focus their thinking.

The questions used to structure response in a reading log may ask students to respond personally and may guide students in monitoring their thinking. For example: Did you find anything confusing as you began the story? Why do you think you were confused? When was the confusion cleared up? Or wasn't it cleared up? Students can be asked to respond to the title, the characters, and key events within the plot. Entries in a log in response to such questions can serve as springboards for class discussion or for more formal writing assignments. They can also serve as a basis for assessing whether students can handle the materials they are being assigned and for determining when students need extra help.

Sample Responses: Journals and Logs

Suppose that a student has been assigned Alice Walker's short story "Everyday Use." In a personal journal, the student might write comments like the following: *Dee is a little like a girl I know. All she thinks about are her looks and impressing people. Sometimes my friends try to be the center of attention. I guess I do too. But Dee seems so self-centered that she doesn't care at all about her mother or her sister. I remember my mom gave me a special present once, and my brother got angry and said my mom liked me more than him. I know several families in which the children are as opposite as Dee and Maggie. My cousin married a woman like Maggie, extremely shy, but very loving inside.*

If the student were keeping a dialogue journal, a teacher might prod further thinking by expressing his or her own feelings and by asking questions. If a peer responded to the journal entry, he or she might agree with what was said or might disagree. With dialogue journals, both reader and responder grow and learn.

With dialogue journals, both reader and responder grow and learn.

In a reading log, the student's response to questions about key points in the story might include some of the following answers:

- I don't like Dee in the story. She's much too concerned about appearances. That explains why she wants to take the quilts. She can picture them hanging on her wall and people oohing and aahing about them and then complimenting her.
- The way Dee treats her mother reminds me of the high-and-mighty way college students sometimes act toward their parents who didn't have the chance to get a good education. I think that Dee has a lot of growing up to do. Someday, Dee might appreciate her mother for all she did for her. After all, her mother helped raise the money to send Dee to school.
- I liked the ending of this story. I was glad that Maggie smiled a real smile. This may have been the first time that she ever won in a competition with Dee. The author left me with the feeling that Maggie will be more confident from now on. If I were writing this story, I would have ended it the same way.

Guidelines for Journals

Following are basic guidelines for keeping a journal, which you can share with your students at the beginning of the school year. The guidelines apply to personal journals and dialogue journals and also to reading logs.

Guidelines

- Carry a journal with you or keep it in an accessible place.
- Date and label journal entries.
- Record words, passages, and lines that trigger ideas, along with your response to these ideas.
- Designate most of your journal for the journal writing that is suggested throughout *Multicultural Perspectives*.
- Designate a section of your journal for observations, quotations, and imaginative writing that is not tied to a literary selection.

Related Reading

Bode, Barbara A. "Dialogue Journal Writing." *The Reading Teacher*. April 1989.

Elbow, Peter, and Belanoff, Pat. *Sharing and Responding*. New York: Random House, 1989.

Myers, Kris L. "Twenty (Better) Questions." *English Journal*. January 1988.

Rosenblatt, Louise M. *Interactive Writing in Dialogue Journals: Practitioner, Linguistic, Social, and Cognitive Views*, edited by Marcia Farr. Norwood, NJ: Ablex, 1988.

Rosenblatt, Louise M. "Language, Literature, and Values." *Language, Schooling, and Society*, edited by Stephen N. Tchudi. Upper Montclair, NJ: Boynton/Cook, 1985.

Collaborative and Cooperative Learning

Collaborative and cooperative learning are not fads. They are not even new, having had their promoters and adherents for many years. For purposes of this discussion *collaborative learning* is defined as any relatively unstructured group activity, with the group being as large as the entire class or as small as a pair of students. *Cooperative learning,* on the other hand, is a highly structured small-group activity, which results in a group product for which all members are responsible. Most of the discussion here focuses on cooperative learning, although many of the guidelines and benefits apply equally to collaborative learning.

Cooperative Learning: An Overview

Cooperative learning is not the traditional small group situation common in classrooms, in which students work in proximity toward individual goals. Nor is cooperative learning just a group of students working together in which one or two students do all of the work and the others ride on their coattails.

In cooperative learning:

- Students work interdependently to ensure that all of the group's members master the assigned material.
- Individuals are accountable, and each student's mastery is assessed.
- All members are held responsible for each other's learning.
- The membership of the group is heterogeneous in ability.
- All members participate actively in the group.
- Students are encouraged to develop the social skills needed to work cooperatively.
- The teacher monitors behavior and learning and gives feedback to groups on their effectiveness.
- Members of the group evaluate their own effectiveness.

About the middle of this century, Morton Deutsch formulated a theory of three ways in which students can interact as they learn, identifying the styles as cooperative, competitive, and individualistic. In the last two modes of interaction, no relationship exists between the attainments of individuals. Only in a cooperative situation is the success of one individual linked to that of other individuals. Students are still responsible for their own learning, but they are also responsible for helping others in their group to learn.

Advocates of cooperative learning assert that it motivates students to learn, improves social skills, promotes self-esteem in students of all abilities, and lessens dependence on the teacher. Recent classroom research appears to validate claims about the effectiveness of the cooperative learning experience. Research even suggests that students in cooperative classrooms do better on standardized tests than those taught by other methods.

Perhaps one of the most appealing aspects of cooperative learning is its applicability across the curriculum, from literature to mathematics to computer literacy.

Recent classroom research appears to validate claims about the effectiveness of the cooperative learning experience. Research even suggests that students in cooperative classrooms do better on standardized tests than those taught by other methods.

Some applications to the study of English include cooperative research, vocabulary study, panel discussions, and plays and skits. Even writing, always one of the loneliest tasks, responds to the cooperation of partners.

The Cooperative Learning Group

No more than three students in a group are recommended for the class that does not have much experience with cooperative learning. Six is probably the most members a group can have and still be effective. In a cooperative group all members have agreed-upon management tasks, such as those described below. When a group has fewer than five members, each student may assume more than one role. When a group has six members, two students may assume one role.

Materials Manager: Gets materials from the teacher or elsewhere and passes them out to the group.

Discussion Leader: Guides the exchange of ideas.

Recorder: Takes notes during the discussion.

Reporter: Shares the results of the discussion with the class.

Maintenance Director: Takes charge of cleanups.

The make-up of a cooperative learning group depends on its purpose. Grouping by interests and by a cross-section of ability are just two possibilities. Grouping might also be random: for example, students might count off to create groups in which no one has the same number. Then, when an assignment is made, the task may be divided into parts. All the students with the same number then become experts on one part and are held responsible for reporting on it. This technique is sometimes called jigsawing. All the pieces of the puzzle are put together so that everyone in a group sees the whole picture.

A similar example would be three-person groups assigned to read three separate selections on the same topic or with the same theme. Students read their selections silently and then retell them in their own words to the rest of the group. The others in the group may interrupt to comment on similarities and differences they note in the selections.

In another situation, the students in a group may be reading to understand a key concept. All members of the group read the same material but one person may be responsible for explaining the concept to the class, while other members clarify, elaborate, or illustrate, using visual material. The next time the group reports, the members switch roles.

While the groups are working, the teacher circulates and observes for appropriate behavior and also listens for any misunderstandings. Sometimes a teacher may intervene by asking a question that directs the students' thinking toward a solution. Even then, the emphasis should be on having the group, rather than the teacher, work through the problem. At other times, especially if more than one group is having difficulty, teachers may interrupt to discuss the point of confusion with the entire class.

Accountability and Assessment

When a group has completed an assignment, there remains the issue of accountability for both the group and the individuals in it. Some ways of assuring accountability are as follows:

1. Have the group produce a single report, paper, or other end result. Every member signs off on the final product to indicate agreement with its conclusions or answers. Then choose individual students at random to respond to questions.
2. If members produce individual products, randomly choose one to evaluate as representative of the group, or have the group make the choice.
3. Keep a progress chart on which the performance of each group and its individuals is charted, or have each group keep the chart. Hold students responsible for improving the performance of the group and its members.
4. Divide the tasks so that each member completes a different one. However, don't accept any work until all the group's members have completed their individual tasks and have compiled the results.

To reinforce the understanding in students' minds that they are responsible for all members of the group, encourage them to edit each other's work, to give themselves practice tests, and to assess their own progress.

An important element of cooperative learning is evaluating how well the group functioned. This evaluation might include discussion of what went especially well and what could be improved. Members might report on problems they worked through. This is also a good time for the teacher to offer feedback for a group or for the entire class on ways of improving cooperative skills.

It is important to structure cooperative learning groups to encourage interdependence. The following are useful techniques for fostering cooperation.

1. Distribute the resources among the members of a group: for example, allow only one person to have a necessary reference tool.
2. Assign tasks in jigsaw fashion: for example, divide the responsibility for writing a paper so that each member writes about a particular period. Then the members put the parts into the proper sequence.
3. Before a general discussion of a topic, issue each member several chips, or pieces of art paper, of different colors. When students have used up their chips, they must remain silent. The absence of some colors will also make it clear which students have not contributed.

Grades, the most obvious rewards in most classrooms, can be used to encourage cooperative learning. A teacher might average individual scores; give a group score for a product, which all members receive; randomly score one member's paper or exam; or give individual scores plus bonus points for successful group performance.

Beyond grades, though, there is the greater reward of students who work well with others, learn more, and feel better about themselves as a result of well-conceived and well-executed learning activities.

Related Reading

Johnson, D. W., and Johnson, R. *Cooperation and Competition*. Hillsdale, NJ: Lawrence Erlbaum, 1987.

Johnson, D. W., and Johnson, R. "Cooperative, Competitive, and Individualistic Learning." *Journal of Research and Development in Education*. December 1978.

Johnson, D. W., and Johnson, R. *Learning Together and Alone: Cooperation, Competition, and Individualization* (2nd edition). Englewood Cliffs, NJ: Prentice Hall, 1987.

Johnson, D. W., Johnson, R., Roy, P., and Holubec, E. J. *Circles of Learning: Cooperation in the Classroom* (rev.). Alexandria, VA: Association for Supervision and Curriculum Development, 1984.

Johnson, R., and Johnson, D. W. *Warm-ups, Grouping Strategies, and Group Activities*. New Brighton, MN: Interaction Book Company, 1985.

Wood, Karen D. "Fostering Cooperative Learning in Middle and Secondary Level Classrooms." *Journal of Reading*. October 1987.

The Heterogeneous Classroom

As gardeners with their eye for beauty know, the mix of flowers—with their variety of colors, heights, and textures—is the challenge and the reward of a garden. Gardeners know that each plant will thrive or fail, depending on how its special needs (for soil, water, light, and care) are met.

As teachers with a feeling for learning know, the mix of students—with their variety of abilities, learning styles, and cultural experiences—is the challenge and reward of classroom teaching. Teachers know that each student will thrive or fail, depending on how his or her special needs (for motivation, self-esteem, and appropriate learning experiences) are met.

How can teachers meet the diverse needs of their students while simultaneously creating an atmosphere of community and cooperation? The essay "Multimodal Learning" on pages 32–33 of this Guide addresses the issue of different learning styles. The essay here confronts the issues of cultural and language differences among limited English proficient (LEP) students, of students with learning disabilities, and of the gifted and talented student. The strategies suggested are designed to be consistent with methods and outcomes suggested in other parts of this Guide, including "Collaborative and Cooperative Learning" (pages 20–21) and "A Community of Writers" (pages 26–29).

Many students are faced with the challenge of living in at least two cultures— the predominant culture of the classroom and the culture of their homes and communities.

General Strategies

Limited English Proficient Students. Many students are faced with the challenge of living in at least two cultures—the predominant culture of the classroom and the culture of their homes and communities. Students for whom English is a second language (ESL) may have difficulties both in expressing themselves and in integrating new concepts. There may also be attitudinal differences toward learning that are carried over to the classroom. In order to capitalize on and compensate for the differences, teachers need to acquaint themselves as much as possible with the students' backgrounds and expectations.

Before making any assumptions about either experience or attitude, you as a teacher should learn more about all your students. In a class discussion, encourage students to share their individual backgrounds in and expectations for literature; share your own. Share also your goals for the class and elicit student discussion. Make note of which goals cause apprehension, so that you can plan strategies to help students develop more positive attitudes.

Use community resources or home visits to learn more about students' home environments and cultures. For the ESL student, you might seek answers to the following questions: Are family members literate in their native language? Are any of them fluent and literate in English? Is reading in either language a part of home activities?

Awareness of the diversity of background and the cultural assumptions of your students need not limit your goals for the literature class. Instead, the knowledge can be incorporated into your teaching. What follows are some general strategies for overcoming the language difficulties of LEP students. Many of the suggestions can be implemented either in a small-group situation or as whole-class activities.

1. Start by examining your teaching presentation, making note of any assumptions you have made based on your own cultural attitudes or expectations. Isolate any terms you use that students may not understand. You may need to supply additional background preparation for these concepts.
2. Use a variety of modes to present concepts and to check comprehension: for example, visual prompts such as pictures, signs, advertisements, and videos.
3. Precede every reading and writing activity with a related and similarly structured oral activity. Encourage discussion to reinforce vocabulary and develop comprehension.
4. Read some selections aloud as students follow the reading; or group students with peers who can read selections aloud. Use commercially produced audio tapes when possible or have tapes made in class, using student readers. Students can then listen to the tapes as often as necessary.
5. Read study questions aloud yourself or pair students with partners who can do so. Allow time for explanations and examples.
6. Create a mentoring system in which one student serves as a source of information and assistance for several others. The mentor would be responsible for explaining directions or terms needed to understand an assignment.

7. Define abstract concepts as concretely as possible, giving specific examples. An example would be the use of the term *opinion* in a study question.
8. Build into any activity as many concrete aids as possible, such as sketches, diagrams, and symbols, to clarify meaning. In some cases, create an alternate set of directions, with simplified instructions.
9. Encourage students to express themselves in other media, such as painting, dance, photography, clay sculpture, film, and music.
10. Introduce key concepts before reading, using such techniques as cognitive mapping.

Unfamiliarity with cultural references may make it difficult for some students to understand and fully relate to a selection. The following strategies may be useful in crossing cultural barriers.

1. Preteach any concepts in a selection for which students may not have a cultural reference. These may include historical references to people, events, or settings; mythological references; archaic or obscure terms; or dialect.
2. Be aware of special holidays and events in various communities. Use them as opportunities to invite students to share songs, dances, and customs. Encourage special displays of reading materials and related artifacts.
3. Whenever appropriate and possible, develop concepts using a mix of photographs, slides, films, and videos.
4. Develop (and encourage students to develop) cross-cultural analogies for concepts, characters, plots, and literary themes.

Learning Disabled Students. Learning disabled (LD) students typically have average or above-average potential but have specific difficulties that hinder the processing of information and the acquisition of skills. Areas of dysfunction include auditory memory and discrimination, visual memory and discrimination, fine and gross motor coordination, and written and oral expression. (These difficulties are caused by physical impairment resulting from brain damage, central nervous system dysfunction, mild cerebral palsy, or other physical impairment.) Whenever possible, the literature teacher should work in conjunction with counselors and special-education teachers to develop a program that utilizes the students' strengths and compensates for their disabilities. The following general strategies may also be used to counter learning disabilities. They may be implemented at the class level or within a small group situation.

1. Seat LD students in the front of the room or wherever there are the fewest visual and auditory distractions.
2. Present essential information, including assignments, both orally and in writing.
3. Whenever possible, supply audio or visual aids to reinforce material from the text.
4. Repeat important ideas frequently, and begin each lesson with a summary of material covered the preceding day.
5. Demonstrate the correct way to complete an assignment. Work a sample on the board. Break down the assignment into manageable steps.
6. Avoid making long-term assignments. Assign reading and exercises on a step-by-step basis.
7. Simplify assignments or allow students to select a few of several questions. For writing assignments, allow students to work with partners or to put first drafts on tape.
8. Draw students' attention to titles, subtitles, captions, and illustrations before they read a selection. Encourage students to make predictions and generate questions about the material to be read.
9. Provide students with sufficient time to generate ideas in the prewriting phase of the writing process. Provide for both peer and teacher feedback in the writing, revising, and proofreading phases.

Strategies for Teaching Literature

Students with special needs face unique problems in the study of literature. Limited English proficient students must learn concepts and skills that assume a familiarity with and easy access to cultural symbols. Learning disabled students may have the cultural background and the language but need to process it at their own pace and in the ways best suited to them.

Teachers with special populations also face the challenge of presenting material in such a way as to make it accessible to all students and of doing so in a way that gives all students the opportunity for success and development of self-esteem.

The following strategies should be helpful to teachers in meeting the needs of students with special learning needs.

1. Assign some selections as oral reading exercises within small, heterogeneous groups.
2. Tape record, or have students record, portions of selections to reinforce correct pronunciation and phrasing and to aid comprehension. Include, as part of the tape, instructions that create direct reading/listening activities. For example, telling the student to listen for the main idea in the next paragraph provides a specific goal for completion of the listening exercise.
3. Divide longer reading assignments into several parts, following each part with appropriate comprehension questions.
4. For each section of a longer literary work, explain the main concepts, paraphrasing when necessary. Whenever possible, connect the concepts to the students' own experiences.
5. Check students' comprehension of the discussion questions by asking them to restate the questions in their own words. Where necessary, simplify wording.

6. Where possible, use student tutors. Tutors do not necessarily have to be the students with the best grades. Sometimes the students with special needs of their own are best able to break down a concept into learnable parts for another student.

Discussion Questions. The questions in *Multicultural Perspectives* are especially suited to the heterogeneous classroom because they invite students to offer opinions and to construct personal meanings. Questions do not have "right answers" in the traditional sense. Therefore, every student's answer is a valuable contribution to the process of understanding.

Students with language difficulties have particular problems with questions relating to sequence, relationships and inferences, and irony. The following are suggestions of ways to help these students.

- **Sequence.** Have students create timelines or story sequence maps as they read narrative selections.
- **Relationships and Inferences.** To help students understand abstract terms, provide concrete examples when possible. Identify specific paragraphs and sentences from which inferences and generalizations can be made. Plan brainstorming and clustering activities that aid students in visualizing relationships among events, characters, and ideas.
- **Irony.** One common type of irony involves an anticipated outcome. Students must be able to recognize the probable outcome before they can see the irony or surprise in the actual outcome. For all types of irony, ask students to contribute examples from their experiences or from sports or news stories. An example is the fact that Dr. Martin Luther King, Jr., worked for peaceful existence among all people, but he was killed by a man with a gun.

Vocabulary Skills. As students read, they will be exposed to many new words. You may find it useful to review frequently the following strategies for figuring out the meaning of these new words.

- **Context Clues.** To help students recognize various types of context clues, reproduce the following chart of types of context clues:

  Comparison and Synonym Clues: *like*, *as*, *same*, *same as*, *similar to*, *other*

  Contrast and Antonym Clues: *although*, *but*, *though*, *on the other hand*, *however*, *yet*, *unlike*, *different from*, *in contrast to*, *not*, *as opposed to*

  Example Clues: *for example*, *such as*, *especially*, *for instance*, *like*, *and other*, *one kind*

  Definition or Restatement Clues: *is*, *who is*, *which is*, *that is*, *in other words*, *or* (also commas, colons, dashes, or parentheses)

To help students infer meaning from general context, remind them repeatedly to think about main ideas and the overall meaning of what they are reading.

- **Word Parts.** Review base words, prefixes, and suffixes frequently. Develop or copy charts that give examples of prefixes and suffixes and their meanings. Stress how recognizing the meanings of affixes can help students understand structurally related words.
- **Dictionary.** Be alert to the need to review alphabetizing, especially of words that begin with the same three or four letters.

Study and Research Skills. Introduce students to research strategies such as taking notes, using a library, and looking up words in a dictionary. First explain the strategy and then provide for practice activities. Ask specialists from other subject areas to reinforce the practice activities.

Assign each special-populations student a partner for homework assignments that require research tools such as dictionaries, encyclopedias, and the thesaurus.

The SQ3R method (survey, question, read, record, review) is especially useful to the special-populations student. Providing students with short assignments and requiring the use of the SQ3R method will give them a means of organizing study to improve comprehension.

Speaking and Listening Skills. Some students may be hesitant to read orally or to interpret a reading in class. Allow these students extra time to prepare the material by working with a partner. When students do participate in classroom discussions, do not correct pronunciations or erroneous patterns of intonation. Instead, provide for separate practice in these skills.

Making eye contact with an audience may be difficult for some students because their native cultures consider this act to be impolite. The teacher should explain that in the American culture, it is acceptable and even desirable to make eye contact with an audience when speaking.

Literary Genre. Students with language deficiencies may become particularly frustrated by the figurative language, stress patterns, and nonstandard syntax characteristic of poetry. The following are strategies for making poetry more accessible to these students.

1. Make an audio recording for individual reading and study.
2. Have students work with partners.
3. Present poetry orally, with students working in groups. Let competent readers model correct pronunciation, phrasing, dialect, and intonation.
4. Paraphrase the wording or restructure the sentences as needed to increase comprehension.
5. Explain similes, metaphors, and other figures of speech as students encounter them.

Gifted and Talented Students

Studies show that students identified as gifted and talented have above-average abilities, creativity, and productivity. The following strategies can help those students make use of their special gifts.

1. To highlight the scope and nature of the literature to be covered, utilize any related audio or video tapes and make field trips to related exhibits and performances.
2. Involve students in the planning, preparation, and presentation of lessons. Activities may include collecting lesson materials, developing project ideas, scheduling events, and preparing presentations. Allow class time for students to brainstorm, plan, and prepare their presentations.
3. When students have demonstrated mastery of a skill, provide them with different and more challenging materials. Avoid overteaching subject matter that students have already mastered.
4. Suggest that students acquaint themselves with research methods such as surveys, interviews, and firsthand observations, and with the kinds of information available through local, state, and federal agencies.
5. Take advantage of community resources to locate experts from fields in which students express an interest. Invite experts to speak and work with students.

Throughout the Teacher's Guide for *Multicultural Perspectives* are suggestions for presenting the material to limited English proficient students, to learning disabled students, and to gifted and talented students. These suggestions, in addition to those for cooperative learning and for multimodal activities, will enrich the learning environment for students of diverse capabilities and will ensure your success in meeting the needs of everyone in your classes.

Related Reading

Beyer, Barry K. "Improving Thinking Skills: Defining the Problem." *Phi Beta Kappan*. March 1984.

Celci-Murci, M., and McIntosh, L., eds. *Teaching English as a Foreign Language*. Newbury, MA: Newbury House Publishers, Inc., 1979.

Gaies, S. *Peer Involvement in Language Learning*. Orlando, FL: Harcourt Brace Jovanovich, Inc., 1985.

Gremmo, Marie-Jose. "Learning a Language—Or Learning to Read?" *Discourse and Learning: Papers in Applied Linguistics*, edited by Philip Riley. New York: Longmans Group, Ltd., 1985.

Kessler, C., and Quinn, M. "Cooperative Learning in ESL Science Classes." Paper presented at TESOL Annual Conference, Chicago, IL, 1988.

Kim, Elaine. "Defining Asian American Realities Through Literature." *Cultural Critique Special Issue: The Nature and Context of Minority Discourse*. Spring 1987.

Pugh, Sharon L. "Literature, Culture and ESL: A Natural Convergence." *Journal of Reading*. January 1989.

Spack, Ruth. "Literature, Reading, Writing and ESL: Bridging the Gaps." *TESOL Quarterly*. Vol. 19, 1985.

West, William W. *Teaching the Gifted and Talented in the English Classroom*. Washington, D.C.: National Education Association, 1980.

A Community of Writers: Classroom Techniques

Once there was a fractured kingdom of Literature. A barrier divided it in half. On one side of the barrier was the domain of the Readers; the other side was dominated by the Writers. Whatever commerce existed between the two domains was funneled through a narrow, guarded gate. Then one day the barriers fell, and the people on both sides looked across the dividing line and recognized on the other side people very much like themselves. They began, tentatively at first, the process of uniting a Community of Writers: writers who, as they read, discover reflections of themselves in what those other writers are trying to communicate; writers who, when they write, discover ideas about themselves, the world, and what they read.

In recent years, a new optimism has emerged about the possibility of educating readers and thinkers who are able to express their thoughts in writing. Innovative approaches to the integration of all the language arts have encouraged a sense of community among writers, who recognize and respond to their shared identity.

Writing more, writing more about literature, and writing from literature are characteristics of this new community. The new emphasis on writing gives students more opportunities to communicate ideas that are important to them. It gives teachers more opportunities to nourish student strengths and to recognize and remedy weaknesses.

Inevitably, two concerns of the classroom teacher arise: What happens to instruction in grammar, punctuation, organization, and the other traditional focuses of the English composition class? And doesn't more writing mean more paperwork and even less time for interacting with students on an individual basis? The essay "Integration in the English Classroom" in this Guide (pages 30–31) addresses the first question by suggesting practical methods for teaching those skill areas within the context of literature study. This essay concentrates on different kinds of written responses to literature and provides practical suggestions for handling the paper load.

Writing Ideas

Some creative uses of written responses to literature are discussed in "Journals, Logs, and Notebooks" (pages 18–19) and "Assessment Options" (pages 34–35). The writing exercises described here expand upon the ideas in these essays. The exercises all involve responding to literature in another form or genre of writing. Students write to learn, for in the process of transformation, they will gain insights about both the original work and the new form.

1. Students could bring a character in a story to life through a courtroom dramatization. Trying the guilty party from a story—whether the charge is minor or major—involves exercising judgment, recognizing conflict, following sequence of events, understanding characters' motives, and visualizing events. The role playing should be based on direct information in the story, inferences from the story, and the use of imagination to fill in the gaps. Writing takes place before the dramatization, as students create the script.
2. Students could write a news article that recounts the turning point in a narrative. The article would involve "interviewing" the characters, summarizing the steps leading to the event, and recognizing the elements of conflict and resolution.
3. Students could write a conversation that might take place with a character who is facing a moral dilemma. The conversation should reveal the conflict in the character's mind and should be consistent with the character created by the author.
4. Students could transform prose into poetry, as a response to a character, the theme, or the writer's style.

The following writing ideas encourage students to recognize similar currents of thought in both visual and verbal forms of art. All of the writing ideas involve creative written responses to some art form (slides, videos, prints, museum visits). Many of the suggested techniques can also be applied to music.

1. Have students view the work of an artist who is contemporaneous to a writer under study. Ask students to put themselves in the role of the writer, who composes a letter to the artist after viewing the work.
2. Have students view art to which writers have responded in poetic form. Read the poetry to students. Then have students browse through other art works and choose ones to which they can react poetically, either in a personal or a descriptive way.
3. Have students view strongly emotional art and respond to that emotion in freewriting, as in stream-of-consciousness writing.
4. Have students view portraits of a particular period. Ask students to put themselves into the minds of the models and explain their thoughts and emotions in a written monologue.
5. Have students view paintings of subjects common to art and to the literature under study, such as historical or mythological scenes. Ask students to relate the themes in the art to those in the selection: for exam-

ple, a struggle for glory, the horrors of war, the innocence of children.

6. Have students view detailed scenes of a social situation removed in time and/or distance from students' own experiences. Ask students to observe the scenes for details and then to relate the scenes to experiences in their own lives. As an alternative, you might have the students use the scenes as the basis of fictional narrative.
7. Have students view scenes of a social situation in which two or more people are interacting. Have students write a dialogue between them.
8. Have students view art in which there are powerful visual symbols and metaphors. Encourage students to study the art work for ideas that go beyond the real or familiar and to write their understandings—and their questions—in their journals.

Writing Portfolios

Key to the assessment of a wide variety of written response is the writing portfolio, which may include samples of a student's best work as chosen by the student. Another possibility is for the teacher or student to select one project and have the student collect in a portfolio all stages of the writing: sketches of ideas, drafts, responses (from teacher and peers), revisions, final draft.

The use of portfolios supports the teacher in evaluating and assisting in the development of students as writers. The teacher can compare recent efforts with earlier ones, focusing on such dimensions as effective use of language, organization and development, and improvements after revision. The use of portfolios encourages students to recognize writing as a process and helps develop the ability to evaluate their own writing.

Teacher involvement in the process of selecting the work to be presented in the portfolio includes establishing criteria for inclusion. These criteria can range from the very open (whatever the student selects) to the very specific. Specific criteria might stipulate the exact number of items to be included: for example, specific assignments (for instance, essays, homework assignments, book reports, journal entries, letters, freewriting) and work that illustrates specific skills (for instance, dialogue, opinion, description, argument, use of sensory details). A less restrictive approach might allow the student, with teacher guidance, to choose the areas that need the most development. Another approach would be to specify some of the categories, while leaving at least one unspecified for the student's choice.

The writing portfolio is flexible and can include work from other disciplines; a student's comments on his or her own writing, for example, an explanation of why certain pieces were included, a self-analysis of weaknesses and strengths, a critical comparison of the strongest and the weakest pieces, end-of-year letters in which students introduce and assess the contents of the portfolio; and peer and teacher responses at different stages of development (prewriting, drafting, revising, editing, and publishing).

Crucial to the management of a writing community is the concept of the writing workshop: an atmosphere in which student writers share their work—in class or outside of it—and support one another in their writing endeavors.

The Writing Workshop

Crucial to the management of a writing community is the concept of the writing workshop: an atmosphere in which student writers share their work—in class or outside of it—and support one another in their writing endeavors. Not all students are able to provide meaningful help immediately. Before they can offer useful criticism, they must have a model to work from. The first step then is to teach students how to respond to each other's writing and how to use such responses.

Begin with an assignment such as a simple essay. Take students through the stages of the writing process, but do not become part of the process yourself by giving revision suggestions. Instead, ask students to rewrite on their own. Discuss with each student, or have the student write a paragraph describing the types of changes made in the revision. To guide students, ask them: Did you change the content? Rewrite entire paragraphs? Or did you just correct some spelling and punctuation errors?

The next time you give an assignment, make your comments on each student's paper, pointing out both the weaknesses and strengths of the writing. Then have students revise. Again, have students evaluate the revision process. Before giving another assignment, address some of the weaknesses you have observed. Repeat the discussion of the types of changes made in revision.

Continue this process until you think that students have begun to feel comfortable with the writing process. They should then be ready to learn to respond to each other's writing. Make transparencies of several student papers. (If you have more than one group, you can use examples from the work of a student in another class.) Display the papers one at a time and ask students to respond to them. The responses should be in writing and should be no more than fifty words. Limit the responses to specific points that are relevant to the kind of writing displayed. For example: Did the writer have an exciting opening for this narrative? What other facts might this writer have included to support the argument? The questions should reflect previously given instruction and should mirror the types of comments you have been making on other assignments.

Next, allow students to respond to their classmates' papers. Group students in pairs or in threes. Again, have students respond in writing and attach the response to the original piece so that the writer can read the responses privately. Have the students turn in their original pieces, the responses to their pieces, and the pieces as revised. Discuss, as a group, the types of responses that students found most helpful.

After students have mastered the basics, you will want to teach the revision process, concentrating on specific ways in which students can improve their papers. Areas to focus on might include using appropriate dialogue, writing closing sentences, sequencing the details of events, and choosing exact words. An important understanding to convey is that revising for content is different from proofreading. Explain too that three separate read-throughs may be necessary to check capitalization, punctuation, and spelling.

Peer Editing: Benefits to Student and Teacher

Once students understand the revision process, they are ready to work in peer-editing groups. Research indicates that the untrained student will make most revisions at the word level, often correcting only spelling and punctuation errors. The number of corrections at the phrase, sentence, multi-sentence, and text level will be higher in a class in which students are accustomed to peer-group response. Those students are also more likely to follow suggestions for revision, including those of the teacher.

When the teacher grades assignments, it is time consuming for the teacher and a passive process for the students. The teacher's comments, no matter how carefully and laboriously framed, may not always be meaningful to the student. Both research and pragmatic evidence shows that a teacher's suggestions are often not applied to other writings even when understood.

With peer editors, both the writing and the editing processes are learning experiences. As editors, students apply criteria to evaluate the writing. They also learn the mechanics of revision. This knowledge can be transferred to their own work. Since peer editing is both a written and an oral interaction between partners, there is time and space for explanation and discussion. It is an active process for both parties.

Research indicates that students who are trained to evaluate writing show the following benefits:

1. They learn new ideas, vocabulary, styles, and strategies of organization. They may become more adventurous in their use of these and other aspects of writing such as mood, tone, and voice.
2. Having a responsive peer audience gives students immediate feedback and helps students put themselves in the reader's place.
3. Students can, when engaged in the critical process, relate more easily to the writing of their peers than to that of published authors.
4. Students become mature writers with the ability to apply self-discipline to their own work.

Less tangible perhaps, but no less real, are the changes that come from cooperative learning of this sort: improved motivation, more positive attitudes toward learning, and increased self-esteem.

Equally important are the benefits to teachers:

1. Since peer editing goes on during drafting and revision, the teacher's work load is considerably reduced.
2. The students can understand issues of revision and can respond to a teacher's comments on a different level than they might have if they had not themselves engaged in the critical analysis of writing.
3. The quality of the writing and of the grammar, mechanics, and spelling will be higher.

Peer-Editing Groups

You can expect that a classroom with peer-editing groups will be somewhat noisier than a traditional classroom. The noise level is perhaps no worse than the sound of any group of workers engaged in productive communication. As in the workplace, rules of courtesy can be developed and followed. Voices can be kept low, space can be left between groups, rules can be made about interrupting or talking over another person trying to make a point. For students engaged in a cooperative venture such as peer editing, extending the attitude of cooperation to others should be a natural step.

Cooperative groups are usually heterogeneous and should, at least initially, be pairs of students or groups of no more than three students. (See also "Collaborative and Cooperative Learning" on pages 20–21 of this Guide). The groups should be flexible, that is, the membership should change frequently. If group work is new to your students, allow them to choose their partners the first time. When students are more comfortable with working in groups, regroup to get a different mix.

Grouping may be done randomly. Sometimes grouping depends on the assignment and the types of tasks involved. Other times you may want to consider writing ability when you group. For example, putting two poor writers together may result in two editors who lack the confidence—and the ability—to suggest changes to the other's work. Two good writers working together may result in competition and conflict.

Next, you must establish the goals of peer editing. Keep in mind that, at first, some students may not want to share their writing. Once they understand the positive goals of the group, they may be able to accept the idea. Some examples of goals are as follows:

- To give students feedback from other students and the opportunity to revise their papers before turning them in to the teacher.
- To develop in students editing and proofreading skills so that they can read their own papers more critically.

- To develop a sense of audience by sharing writing and getting an immediate response.

The evaluation criteria for each assignment will vary. You may want to create a checklist, posting it prominently in the room. Evaluation guidelines should be made clear before each assignment. For example, if you are working on paragraph development, you might tell editors to ask themselves these questions as they read: What is the main idea of the paragraph? Is the idea supported? Does the paragraph have a strong closing sentence? Are there any sentences unrelated to the main idea? For some assignments you may want more open-ended questions: Do images help you visualize the scene? Is the use of dialogue appropriate? Your guidelines may also change from the draft stage to the editing stage, as you change the emphasis. For example, in the drafting stage you may be more concerned with issues such as organization, and later your attention might turn to effectiveness of language.

A checklist of criteria for each assignment may be helpful when you are grading papers. A checklist is also useful when implementing a system of holistic evaluation for the assessment of writing. In holistic evaluation, a team of at least two teachers evaluates the same paper based on agreed-upon guidelines. The guidelines usually include criteria related to composition skills that reflect performance at different levels of writing. The evaluation is quite rapid and involves ranking papers as high, medium, or low or rating them on a scale of 1 to 5, with no more than a few minutes spent on each paper. Teacher-evaluators do not analyze details in the writing or stop to correct or comment on strengths or weaknesses. The final grade is an average of the scores awarded by the individual teachers.

Your room now is buzzing with self-disciplined activity. The interaction began with students exchanging ideas. As they drafted their papers they stopped to exchange papers and to read them aloud to each other. The interaction continued through the editing and proofreading stages. It is the publishing stage now, and the students are sharing their work with a larger audience. You and they can feel a certain satisfaction at how far you have come since the barriers came down. Welcome to the Community of Writers.

Related Reading

Christenbury, L. "Three Techniques of Student Evaluation." *Classroom Practices in Teaching English: How to Handle the Paper Load,* edited by G. Stanford. Urbana, IL: National Council of Teachers of English, 1979.

Cussler, Elizabeth B. "Art in the Literature Class." *English Journal.* March 1989.

Dudley, Martha. "The Writing Workshop: Structuring for Success." *English Journal.* January 1989.

Elbow, Peter, and Belanoff, Pat. *Sharing and Responding.* New York: Random House, 1989.

Holdzkom, D. "Using Peer Groups to Improve Writing Classes." *Peer Facilitator Quarterly.* January 1985.

Huot, Brian. "The Literature of Direct Writing Assessment: Major Concerns and Prevailing Trends." *Review of Educational Research,* AERA. Summer 1990.

McManus, Ginger, and Kirby, Dan. "Using Peer Group Instruction to Teach Writing." *English Journal.* March 1988.

Mitchell, Sandra Powell. "Before the Search: Genuine Communication and Literary Research." *English Journal.* September 1989.

Integration in the English Classroom

A question often asked is: What happens to traditional instruction in grammar, usage, mechanics, and spelling when the emphasis in an English classroom is put on literature and writing about literature? Formal, discrete lessons in each area are likely to be curtailed. Instead, instruction in those skill areas becomes an integral part of the study of literature and the resulting classroom writing activities. Literature, for example, may become the model to teach an aspect of grammar, while a lesson on usage may grow out of errors that appear in a number of student compositions.

Instruction in grammar, usage, mechanics, and spelling can be presented in a variety of ways: for example, mini-lessons (a whole-class activity) directed toward a particular problem area; teacher-student conferences when individual students misapply learning; peer-group activities in which students analyze the nature of their errors; and journals or notebooks in which students record correct models of troublesome spellings or usages. Practice exercises and worksheets do not have to be left out of the learning experience if they are an outgrowth of the classroom literature or writing experience.

The goal of integrated instruction is to have students take on more responsibility for revising and editing their own work and the work of their peers.

Students should understand that their major goal in writing is to communicate the ideas that are most important to them. One way to improve their ability to communicate is to study how other writers have used form and language to communicate effectively. Students can then analyze their own work for effectiveness and can apply what they learn during their revision process.

The goal of integrated instruction is to have students take on more responsibility for revising and editing their own work and the work of their peers. Integrated instruction makes the revision and editing processes more active and therefore more powerful learning experiences.

An Integrated Approach to Mechanics

Handled correctly, punctuation is hardly noticed. Improperly used, punctuation can change the writer's meaning and distract the reader. The goal of writers should be to use punctuation to help them communicate clearly. To demonstrate the importance of punctuation, choose a fairly complex passage from a work of literature —for example a passage that includes appositives, definitions, a series, or dialogue—and omit all commas, periods, and capital letters. Then ask students to insert the punctuation and compare it to the writer's. Follow this activity by showing photocopies or overhead transparencies of student papers. Ask students to insert whatever punctuation is necessary to make the writer's meaning clear. (This activity is also appropriate for a word processor.)

Going beyond the period, comma, and capital letter, find literary passages that demonstrate the effective use of semicolons, dashes, exclamation points, quotation marks, parentheses, italics, and ellipses. You should restrict this type of activity to modern writers, since the conventions of punctuation have changed over the years. Create assignments in which students can use the passages as models.

Matters of Style

Literature can be used when teaching sentence variety: for example, you can use as models a number of sentences that do not begin with the subject. Have students analyze the sentences for structure. Encourage discussion about why sentence variety is important in effective writing. Also point out the use of punctuation in those constructions, such as the use of a comma to set off an introductory clause. Then assign students to write their own sentences in imitation. This exercise can be expanded to longer forms, such as paragraphs or essays. Later, students can analyze their own writing, keeping track of the number of similar patterns. If they find that the same patterns are repeated too often, they can revise for sentence variety.

A similar exercise can be used to teach sentence combining. Rewrite a literary passage, breaking up the sentences. Then have students combine the sentences and compare their versions to the original. Encourage students to use the literary passage only as a reference and to analyze their own versions for effectiveness. This activity can then be extended to students' own writing.

To demonstrate distinctions in style, have students rewrite a literary selection in a different style: for example, a humorous essay written in an informal style might be translated into more formal language. Then discuss why one style is more appropriate for a specific purpose than another. A follow-up writing assignment might involve using different styles to present the same information.

Vocabulary and Spelling

Vocabulary development and improvement in spelling are closely related and can both be an outgrowth of the study of literature. Probably nothing is more inhibiting to young writers than worrying about spelling during the drafting process. Many students avoid newer, more adventurous words in order to avoid misspelling them. Looking a word up in the dictionary is difficult without a good idea of how to spell the word. The only way students can gain ownership of new words, though, is for them to use the words.

> ***Vocabulary development and improvement in spelling are closely related and can both be an outgrowth of the study of literature.***

One way to build vocabulary is to have students keep track of new and interesting words as they are encountered in reading. Encourage students to incorporate the words in discussions and in their writing. Have them record the words in their personal dictionaries. Each entry in such a dictionary should include an accurate spelling, a definition (which can be the student's paraphrase of a dictionary entry), and a sample sentence. Students can draw upon the words with some confidence when drafting and revising and can refer to their dictionaries to check spelling when they are proofreading.

Instead of using formal spelling lists, base any tests on the words culled from literature selections. Make your own choices or ask students to suggest words that they feel are especially challenging or interesting. Other activities can be developed around the words as well, such as skits and games. The popular parlor game Dictionary can be adapted to classroom vocabulary study. When a student finds a challenging word, he or she looks it up in a dictionary and then asks several classmates to define the word as it might be defined in a dictionary. Each student then reads his or her definition with outward confidence.The group decides which definition is correct. Finally, the person who presented the word initially either confirms the finding of the group or gives the correct definition.

New words can be taught in families. For example, if students encounter the word *penumbra* in their reading, present a mini-lesson on other words with the same root (*umbrella, umbrage, adumbrate*) to extend meaning.

An important part of learning to correct one's spelling is being able to recognize when a word just doesn't look right. One common spelling problem is the confusion of homophones and near-homophones, such as *stationery* and *stationary*. Some spelling errors concern matters of usage, as with making the correct choice between *affect* and *effect*. A useful activity is to choose passages from literary selections that include homophones and near-homophones. In place of each, insert both forms of the word in parentheses. Ask students to choose the correct word in each case. Then have students compare their versions with the original. The same kind of exercise may be used for other pairs of words that are often confused.

The activities suggested in this essay take nothing away from the study of any literary work (though no one work should be overly used as the basis for integrated instruction). Instead, such activities can illustrate for students the importance of all the elements of a selection to achieving a writer's purpose.

Related Reading

Dodd, Anne Wescott, "Demons, Dictionaries, and Spelling Strategies." *English Journal*. December 1988.

Hodges, Richard. *Improving Spelling and Vocabulary in the Secondary School*. Urbana, IL: National Council of Teachers of English, 1982.

Jostad, Karen. "Connecting Literature with Writing at the Intermediate and Secondary Level." *The Writing Notebook: Creative Word Processing in the Classroom*. April/May 1987.

Riddell, Carol Bartlett. "Towards a More Active Vocabulary." *English Journal*. December 1988.

The Round Table. "Teaching Sentence Variety." *English Journal*. October 1989.

Schafer, John C. "Punctuation and Process: A Matter of Emphasis." *English Journal*. December 1988.

Shaughnessy, Mina. *Errors and Expectations*. New York: Oxford University Press, 1977.

Multimodal Learning

We are all unique. We have different sets of characteristics, abilities, and needs. It should not be surprising, therefore, to learn that we have different learning styles as well. Yet it is only recently (the early 1980's) that this theory of learning gained acceptability, based largely on the research of Harvard psychologist Howard Gardner. Gardner recognizes seven types of intelligence: linguistic, logical-mathematical, spatial, musical, bodily-kinesthetic, interpersonal, and intrapersonal. Everyone has all seven intelligences, but in different proportions.

Research indicates that the different kinds of intelligences are located in different parts of the brain. There seems to be a correlation between behavior and hemisphericity (the dominance of either the right or the left side of the brain). The various parts of the brain do cooperate with each other, which suggests that the seven types of intelligence interact as well.

Different environments favor and encourage the development of specific intelligences. From the chart of the characteristic strengths of each intelligence, shown below, you can infer how certain environments are likely to be more favorable to some intelligences than to others. As Gardner points out, when we address the notion of high intelligence in our society, we are usually talking about only two or three: linguistic, logical-mathematical, and sometimes intrapersonal. Other researchers have suggested that because of the emphasis on formal testing, schools tend to favor students who are strong in linguistic and logical-mathematical intelligences and discriminate against those who are weak in those areas though strong in others.

Linguistic	Is verbal; thinks in words; has highly developed auditory skills; likes to read and write
Logical-Mathematical	Thinks conceptually; capable of highly abstract thinking, logic, reasoning
Spatial	Thinks in visual images and pictures; enjoys drawing, designing, building, daydreaming, inventing
Musical	Is sensitive to music, nonverbal sounds, rhythm; enjoys listening to, singing, moving to, playing music
Bodily-Kinesthetic	Processes knowledge through bodily sensations; has fine-motor coordination; communicates through body language
Interpersonal	Understands other people; organizes, communicates, socializes
Intrapersonal	Prefers working alone; intuitive, independent, private, self-motivated

The theory of multiple intelligences is the basis for recognizing that not only do all learners have different abilities but, because they do, they also have different styles of learning. Biological and development characteristics can determine how students learn, what they learn most easily, and what they have the most difficulty with. The same teaching method is not equally effective with all students. Student performance does improve markedly when learning styles are accommodated.

Learning style encompasses five elements: environmental, emotional, sociological, physical, and psychological. Studies show that the individual needs of students are best met when classrooms are organized and teaching approaches are developed with learning styles in mind. These needs include the physical conditions of the classroom as well as interpersonal and pedagogical considerations.

Elements	Stimuli
Environmental	Sound, Light, Temperature, Design
Emotional	Motivation, Persistence, Responsibility, Structure
Sociological	Peers, Self, Pair, Team, Adult, Varied Perceptual, Intake, Time, Mobility
Physical	Analytic/Global, Hemispheric
Psychological	Preference, Impulsive/Reflective

[Rita Dunn and Kenneth Dunn. "Can Students Identify Their Own Learning Styles?" *Educational Leadership,* February 1983, p. 61.]

Within every group a significant number of students have needs that are different enough from the standard to inhibit learning. Classroom design, for example, can affect students' achievement. Students tend to need more light as they grow older. The need for sound also tends to increase during adolescence. Yet often a class includes a minority of students who require less light and some who need complete silence—to the point of needing ear plugs—when they work. Temperature variations may also affect some students more than others. And while a majority of adolescents show a preference for sitting casually in soft chairs, some require the more formal support of a desk.

To accommodate these varying physical needs, a classroom might include an informal area with cushions, couches, and carpeting; quiet areas for some; and an area where students can work while listening to music with a headset on. Loosening a bulb in one corner of the classroom creates an area for those who prefer low light.

The older students get, the less teacher motivated they become, preferring peer learning. By the ninth grade, there also is a greater need to learn and study alone. At all levels, though, some students have needs that are contrary to the general tendencies of the age group. Allowing for variation can accommodate the different styles. Thus, students might set mutual objectives within a small group under teacher guidance, go off to study by themselves, and then return to share their findings with the group and the class.

Not all students learn verbally. If a student's modality is kinesthetic, for example, he or she will learn more if at least the initial instruction is presented through manipulatives. The students who require more mobility than others need to be able to move around the classroom. Instruction can be organized so that different learning takes place in different parts of the room, requiring students to move from one part to the other.

Students with kinesthetic learning styles benefit from activities such as performing skits and observing the natural world. Students with a spacial orientation enjoy building models and sketching illustrations. Students who have musical style respond well to activities such as composing ballads and choosing music to reflect the mood of a literary selection.

The majority of teachers teach analytically, reaching students with linguistic and logical-mathematical strengths. Teachers need to become aware of their own learning and teaching styles so that they can better meet student needs and thus improve classroom performance. One goal should be for teachers to integrate multimodal activities into their lessons. Another goal should be to help all students move from their single, favored modes to a mix of instructional modes from which they might benefit. Activity ideas are suggested throughout this Guide.

Related Reading

Dunn, Kenneth, and Dunn, Rita. "Dispelling Outmoded Beliefs About Student Learning." *Educational Leadership*. March 1987.

Dunn, Kenneth, and Dunn, Rita. "Can Students Identify Their Own Learning Styles?" *Educational Leadership*. February 1983.

Dunn, Rita. *In Their Own Way: Discovering and Encouraging Your Child's Personal Learning Styles*. Los Angeles: Tarcher, 1987.

Dunn, Rita, Beaudry, Jeffrey S., and Klavas, Angela. "Survey of Research on Learning Styles." *Educational Leadership*. March 1989.

Assessment Options

Historically, the term *assessment* has been almost synonymous with testing and with pencil-and-paper testing in particular. The question that naturally arises is, what does such testing accomplish? If a test is valid, it should reflect, by means of a numerical score or letter grade, an accurate picture of students' ability to answer questions about a limited area of knowledge. What it may, or may not, do is ascertain how well students have learned the comprehension, thinking, and problem-solving skills they must be able to carry over to other learning situations.

In recent years, many attempts have been made to extend the concept of assessment to other strategies that may be more reliable in measuring student growth. They include portfolio assessment and interactive assessment, as well as other strategies that go beyond the traditional pencil-and-paper methods. This essay examines contemporary thinking about a few of these nontraditional methods of assessment. Many of these methods do apply to the evaluation of student writing, but strategies for the assessment of writing is discussed in a separate essay, "A Community of Writers: Classroom Techniques," on pages 26–29 of this Guide.

Portfolio Assessment

One of the most popular new assessment tools is the portfolio. Much like the portfolios of artists and writers, assessment portfolios are collections of the students' best work. Limiting portfolios to students' best work allows teacher and students together to monitor the students' progress in a particular subject or skill area. The significant factor is that students have a voice in what goes into the folder. The teacher may establish certain broad criteria for what goes in, such as requiring a certain number of pieces during a set period or specifying that certain areas of study (for example, reading, writing, or research) be represented. The students, however, evaluate their own work and make their own decisions.

The teacher may ask students to document their choices, explaining, for example, why they chose certain pieces. A student may document the development of a chosen piece by including everything that contributed to the final form— sketches, drafts, revisions—and by explaining how he or she solved the problems in the original version.

At various times in the year students can be asked to study their portfolios, concentrating on a particular skill, such as understanding character development. They then reflect, in writing, on their growth in that area. The students' comments become part of their portfolios. Another option is for students to arrange their writing from the most effective to the least effective and then to explain their ranking and evaluate how their skills have improved. Unlike traditional written tests, self-assessment is not objective. Also unlike traditional tests, the teacher can be sure that students are engaged in thinking about their work, in analyzing and evaluating it, and in monitoring their own understandings.

Also unlike traditional tests, the teacher can be sure that students are engaged in thinking about their work, in analyzing and evaluating it, and in monitoring their own understandings.

Interactive Assessment

Unlike a written test, interactive assessment goes beyond just asking a question and getting a response. This method allows the questioners/evaluators to follow the students' thinking processes. After hearing responses, they can ask students to clarify or justify what they have said, give reasons for their conclusions, or explain why they think as they do. For example, if students have been presented with a paragraph and asked to identify the writer's tone, the questioner/evaluator (who may be the teacher or a peer) can ask what clues students used to decide on an answer. If the student has difficulty answering, one or two incisive questions can direct the students' thinking toward a solution or can pinpoint an area of weakness.

Monitoring Classroom Discussions

The classroom discussion is similar to interactive assessment in that it allows teachers to monitor students' thinking. For example, if students' answers vary widely, the teacher may infer that students are having difficulty in interpreting the task. He or she may wish to intervene with a guiding question or two. Through classroom discussion, teachers can also observe how well students interact with their peers. Are they open-minded about accepting alternative answers? Do they raise important issues suggested by the questions? Do they stick to the main point of the discussion, indicating that they recognize what is relevant to it? Using an observation form or a simple checklist that lists no more than six criteria allows the teacher to observe a number of students in one discussion period.

Journals, Logs, and Other Written Responses

Journals and logs can be used in a directed manner as a place where students are asked to comment or report on particular issues. A complete discussion of journals, logs, and notebooks appears on pages 18–19 of this Guide.

The teacher can evaluate the responses written in journals and logs on the basis of general qualities, such as critical thinking or open-mindedness, and of specific understandings of skills, such as recognizing literary genre or literary techniques.

Another source of information is the teacher's own daily journal or log, in which entries may report examples that can be used to assess student growth.

Many other kinds of creative written responses can be used to evaluate student progress. Following is just a sampling of ideas.

1. **Rewriting.** Changing one element tests students' ability to think about the structure and details of the original. Example: making a minor character into a major one or changing the point of view.
2. **Changing the setting.** Transferring a classic text into a different time and place tests students' ability to summarize and to recognize the important elements of a story. Example: telling the story of Julius Casear's assassination as an item on the evening news.
3. **Analogies.** Creating analogies tests students' ability to recognize connections between texts. Example: Huckleberry Finn: river:: Bilbo Baggins: road.

Drama and Art

Improvisation and role playing are two additional ways students can experience literature. Before being able to act out a dramatic scene, the actors must develop the context and the characters through reading and through calling on their own experiences. The scene can be based on what happens in the original text, as when the teacher outlines a situation involving the characters and asks students to supply dialogue and action. Or the scene can be an extension or variation of the work, as a trial for the wicked Uriah Heep or a detective's interview of the principals in the death of Mercutio.

Visually and musically oriented students can incorporate the arts into their responses in such a way as to demonstrate their understanding of a work of literature. Shakespeare's plays, for example, have been extensively explored and clarified in paintings, opera, and dance. A comparison of the characters of Romeo and Juliet as they appear in literature, drama, and dance might be accompanied by graphics or by video or audio tapes. Similarly, students may choose to create their own illustrations for stage settings and costumes to demonstrate their insight into the work.

Although the field of assessment is opening up to innovative ideas that get students more involved in the assessment process, no doubt teachers will continue to use more traditional testing devices to evaluate students' skills. Multiple choice and short-answer tests will still be the principal tools. However, if teachers use these tools in conjunction with the other evaluation techniques described here, they can form a more complete picture of students' skills and progress.

Related Reading

Costa, A. L. "Re-assessing Assessment." *Educational Leadership*. April 1989.

Gardner, Howard. "Assessment in Context: The Alternative to Standardized Testing." Paper prepared for the National Commission on Testing and Public Policy, Berkeley, CA, 1988.

Haney, Walter, and Madaus, George. "Searching for Alternatives to Standardized Tests: Whys, Whats, and Whithers." *Phi Delta Kappan*. May 1989.

Hoge, Robert D., and Coladarci, Theodore. "Teacher-Based Judgments of Academic Achievement: A Review of the Literature." *Review of Educational Research*, AERA. Fall 1989.

Liftig, R. A. "Feeling Good About Student Writing: Validation in Peer Evaluation." *English Journal*. February 1990.

Valencia, Sheila. "Alternative Assessment: Separating the Wheat from the Chaff." *The Reading Teacher*. September 1990.

Wasserman, Selma. "Reflections on Measuring Thinking, While Listening to Mozart's Jupiter Symphony." *Phi Delta Kappan*. January 1990.

Annotated Test

This test appears in the Teacher's Guide on pages 183 and 184. The annotations here explain the test construction and give suggestions for administering and scoring all of the tests included in the Guide.

A Part 1 tests the student's understanding of major issues in the selection. The section includes questions on theme and character as well as questions on central concepts that are narrower in scope. Because the nature of broad interpretation is to deal with issues that are open to interpretation, objective questions are rare in this section and are only used when they serve a particular purpose. Graphics are commonly used.

B Each test begins with from two to four essay questions that test broad understanding of the text without impinging on the student's personal experience of the work. Most of the essay questions require interpretive skills. Responses will commonly vary.

C On essay questions and graphics, the indicated points for each question reflect the maximum points that are earned by a thoughtful, thorough response. Fewer points may, of course, be earned.

NAME ______________________ DATE ____________

Two Kinds (page 198)

Test

Part 1 Broad Interpretation **A**

A. Answer the following essay questions based on your understanding of the story. Write your answers on a separate sheet of paper. *(12 points each)* **B**

1. Why do you think that "Pleading Child" and "Perfectly Contented" seem to be two halves of the same song to the narrator?
2. Why do you think the narrator feels both strong and frightened when she fights with her mother over the piano lessons?
3. Why do you think the mother wants her daughter to be a prodigy? What does she hope this will achieve for her daughter? What do you think she hopes it will achieve for herself?
4. The mother thinks that her daughter can learn to be a prodigy. Do you think there is anything wrong with her reasoning? In other words, do you think it is possible to learn to be a prodigy? Why or why not?

B. Think about what the piano means to the mother and what it means to the daughter. Then, in the boxes below, write what you think the piano means to each of them at the beginning of the piano lessons and, years later, when the mother gives the piano to her daughter. *(12 points)* **C**

MOTHER	DAUGHTER
At the beginning of the piano lessons	**D** At the beginning of the piano lessons
When the mother gives the piano to the daughter	When the mother gives the piano to the daughter

Test Exploring Cultural Conflicts 183

Introducing the Tests

Using the test for "Two Kinds" as a sample, follow these steps when introducing the testing approach to the class.

Part 1

1. Explain that the purpose of Part 1 is to examine the students' understanding of the major issues raised in the selection.
2. Point out that question 3 and question 4 have more than one part. The second part of question 4 requires that students support their answers to the first part.
3. Explain that in some essay questions students are asked to discuss two or more related issues. Remind students that they must deal with all parts of every question.
4. Point out that answers will be evaluated on the clarity and soundness of the ideas presented, the detail with which the ideas are supported, and the correctness of grammar, usage, and mechanics.
5. Make sure students understand that they should supply only enough information in the graphic to communicate the points they want to make.

Part 2

1. Explain that the purpose of Part 2 is to test the students' understanding of more specific aspects of the selection.
2. Point out that questions in this part often require inferences, that is, knowledge not directly stated but clearly implied.
3. Note the instruction line for question 6, which indicates that more than one answer may be correct. Explain that this instruction, wherever it appears, means that more than one answer is either acceptable or required. When answering such questions, students should always look for more than one correct answer and indicate *all* answers they believe to be correct.
4. Note that a second graphic is included in this test. Explain that this graphic requires information inferred from the text.

NAME ______________________ DATE ____________

Part 2 Close Interpretation E

A. Write **R** if the event shows that the daughter is rebelling against her mother. Write **N** if it does not. *(4 points each)* F

____ **1.** The daughter watches Shirley Temple movies on television.

____ **2.** The daughter tries to predict daily temperatures in Los Angeles, New York, and London.

____ **3.** The daughter counts the foghorn bellows during her mother's tests.

____ **4.** The daughter practices her curtsy for the talent show.

____ **5.** The daughter refuses to practice the piano anymore.

B. Write the letter of the best answer. Where noted, there may be more than one answer. *(6 points each)*

____ **6.** What does the narrator fear in her relationship with her mother? *(You may choose more than one answer.)* G

a. That her mother will leave her.

b. That her mother loves her too much.

c. That her mother will be disappointed in her.

d. That her mother doesn't love her for who she is.

____ **7.** After which of the following events does the narrator finally decide to stop trying to be a prodigy?

a. The talent show.　**c.** The first piano lesson.

b. The mother's death.　**d.** Seeing Shirley Temple on television.

C. One sentence in the following quotation from the story contains a simile. Circle that sentence, and then, in the boxes below, tell what two things are compared in the simile. *(8 points)* H

"I was a dainty ballerina girl standing by the curtains, waiting to hear the right music that would send me floating on my tiptoes. I was like the Christ child lifted out of the straw manger, crying with holy indignity. I was Cinderella stepping from her pumpkin carriage with sparkly cartoon music filling the air."

[ ] is compared to [ ]

D Each test contains at least one graphic, which may serve any of several purposes: to make test-taking less daunting, to allow students to apply their understandings of the text, and to reach students who may not have a highly verbal learning style.

E This section focuses on more specific elements of the selection. Most questions measure inferential skills. The questions deal with subordinate issues related to the main point. Part 2 may be made up of objective questions and/or graphics.

F On objective questions, the indicated points reflect the percentage points that are earned by the correct answer or answers.

G This instruction line appears only when more than one answer is either acceptable or required. Students should be told to note this line whenever it appears.

H Graphics should be filled in with words or phrases or otherwise marked according to directions.

Answer Key

An Answer Key appears at the back of this Guide. The Key gives guidelines for scoring the essay questions and graphics and correct answers for objective questions.

Scoring Essays and Graphics

For essay questions, the Answer Key provides a suggested breakdown of points for usage and mechanics, clarity and coherence, soundness, and detail, followed by guidelines for scoring. Some guidelines for both essays and graphics are extensive and are meant to provide help in scoring a range of responses—not to indicate the minimum requirements.

The introductory statement for each guideline, or set of guidelines, indicates whether the response or responses *should* be found in highly-scored answers or whether they may *possibly,* and acceptably, be found in highly-scored answers.

Scoring Objective Questions

The Answer Key for objective questions indicates the answer choice or choices that are required for each response to be considered correct and, when applicable, lists additional, supportable answers. An answer choice indicated as "possible," although allowable, is not in itself a complete answer and need not be included for the answer to be considered correct. Multiple answer choices of equal value must all be indicated for full credit. If fewer than all are indicated by the student, he or she should receive partial credit.

Note: The tests for poetry are designed to be administered as open-book tests; the tests are marked as such. Other tests may be given as open-book tests, if the needs of the students or the difficulty of the material warrants this approach.

UNIT 1 Celebrating Heritage

Selections	Essential Vocabulary	Literary Skills	Writing Formats	Writing Modes
The Legend of Gregorio Cortez				
Student Book page 6 **Teacher's Guide** Lesson, pages 40–42 Test, pages 43 and 44		cultural hero	journal obituary eulogy comic strip diary entries proposal press release narrative poem rap song	expressive and personal writing observation and description narrative and imaginative writing informative (expository) writing: analysis persuasion
***from* When Heaven and Earth Changed Places**				
Student Book page 22 **Teacher's Guide** Lesson, pages 45–47 Test, pages 49 and 50		theme	journal nomination guest column chart letter handbill song lyrics book review biographical sketch	expressive and personal writing observation and description narrative and imaginative writing informative (expository) writing: classification informative (expository) writing: synthesis persuasion writing about literature
From the Poets in the Kitchen				
Student Book page 31 **Teacher's Guide** Lesson, pages 51 and 52 Vocabulary Worksheet, page 53 Test, pages 55 and 56	adversity encompass exhorting infuse aesthetic voraciously indiscriminately testimony legacy	aphorism theme	journal diary entry letter dramatic skit cartoon strip list booklet	expressive and personal writing narrative and imaginative writing informative (expository) writing: classification
The Way It Is **Mother to Son**				
Student Book page 40 **Teacher's Guide** Lesson, pages 57 and 58 Vocabulary Worksheet, page 59 Tests, pages 61 and 62	commercial inaudible dominant	simile extended metaphor speaker	journal	expressive and personal writing writing about literature
Lineage **Women**				
Student Book page 46 **Teacher's Guide** Lesson, pages 63 and 64 Tests, pages 65–67		alliteration repetition	journal family tree poem letter storyboard character sketch oral history autobiographical sketch recommendation memo	expressive and personal writing observation and description narrative and imaginative writing persuasion

Selections	Essential Vocabulary	Literary Skills	Writing Formats	Writing Modes
Everyday Use				
Student Book page 51 **Teacher's Guide** Lesson, pages 69–71 Vocabulary Worksheet, page 72 Test, pages 73 and 74	furtive sidle	foil	journal review dialogue informational footnotes captions memo press release booklet sequel	expressive and personal writing informative (expository) writing: analysis narrative and imaginative writing report (research) observation and description persuasion
My Mother Pieced Quilts **My Father's Song**				
Student Book page 61 **Teacher's Guide** Lesson, pages 75 and 76 Test, pages 77 and 78		sound devices: alliteration, consonance, assonance	journal	expressive and personal writing
Sweet Potato Pie				
Student Book page 67 **Teacher's Guide** Lesson, pages 79 and 80 Vocabulary Worksheet, page 81 Test, pages 83 and 84	apex entities ubiquitous	The student book does not contain discussion questions, analysis of literary techniques, or writing assignments for this story. These materials appear in the Teacher's Guide lesson.		
Reviewing Concepts				
Student Book page 75 **Teacher's Guide** page 85				

The Legend of Gregorio Cortez

Américo Paredes
(ä mā′ rē kō pä rā′ thās)

page 6

■ **Test,** TG pages 43 and 44

Objectives

1. To respond to a story that presents the exploits of a hero.
2. To understand the literary concept of cultural hero.
3. To express ideas in a variety of writing formats: journal, obituary, eulogy, comic strip, diary entries, proposal, press release, narrative poem, rap song.

Plot Summary

Gregorio Cortez, a hero of the past, is remembered in song for his marksmanship, values, and skills as a cowboy and farmer. His prankster brother, Román, tricks an American by exchanging a lame horse for a sorrel mare. Later the American accuses Román of cheating him, and when Román answers back, the sheriff shoots him and fires at Gregorio Cortez. In the ensuing gun battle, Cortez kills the sheriff and then escapes on the sorrel mare. Sheriffs and rangers all over Texas try to capture Cortez, who eludes them, outwitting some and killing others. Finally, El Teco, a man greedy for the reward money, betrays Gregorio Cortez, who surrenders to spare his family persecution. At his several trials, Cortez defends himself so cogently that he is about to be set free. However, questioned by his enemies, he admits taking the sorrel mare and is sentenced to prison for horse stealing. A daughter of President Lincoln falls in love with Cortez and arranges to have him released. Before leaving prison, however, he is poisoned and dies less than a year later.

IdeaBank

✱ Limited English Proficient Students
"The Legend of Gregorio Cortez" uses some vocabulary and diction that may be difficult for students with limited English proficiency. Examples are phrases such as "thirty-thirty," "sorrel mare" (page 9); "it was from the big bunches that he ran" (page 12); "he was given to eat and drink" (page 12); and "a dam where the vaqueros watered their stock" (page 14). Compile a list of tricky phrases and have students work in pairs with proficient readers to decipher the meanings. ✱

IdeaBank

▲ Motivation. As an alternative to the Connecting Writing and Reading activity, ask students to list heroes from movies or television shows of the past or present. Next to each hero's name, students should identify his or her outstanding qualities. As students read the story, they can compare these heroes with Gregorio Cortez. ▲

InformationBank

Literary Note. Two brief paragraphs were cut from this story. The deletions involved the Mexicans' misinterpretation of the expletive "son of a bitch" as an Anglo saint, "Sanavabiche."

IdeaBank

✤ Multimodal Activities

1. Students who play the guitar might find and perform a corrido or another ballad for the rest of the class. Possibilities include traditional ballads, such as "Pretty Polly," "Tom Dooley," or "Casey Jones," or more contemporary ballads, such as Woodie Guthrie's "Pretty Boy Floyd" or "Deportees," Bob Dylan's "Lily, Rosemary, and the Jack of Hearts" or "The Lonesome Death of Hattie Carroll," or Leonard Cohen's "Suzanne."
2. Students could draw a mural, on newsprint, depicting the heroic exploits of Gregorio Cortez.
3. Have students design a wanted poster that the sheriffs might have used in attempting to capture Cortez.
4. Students might draw a design and then write a suitable epitaph for Gregorio Cortez's tombstone. ✤

IdeaBank

✾ Learning Disabled Students. The Spanish word *corrido* means "running" or "continuous" as well as "generous" or "full." Paredes's retelling of this corrido is episodic and eventful. Have students plot the events of the corrido on a time line, first filling in events that they remember, then referring to the story to identify any events they may not recall. ✾

IdeaBank

❧ **Gifted and Talented Students.** Have students compare Gregorio Cortez with a hero from a different culture—for example, Odysseus as portrayed in *The Odyssey*. They might present their comparisons by adding to the chart made for the activity under Analyzing the Writer's Craft. ❧

InformationBank

Historical Note. After President Lincoln's daughter has proposed marriage, Gregorio Cortez sees himself "like a German . . . with a half-dozen little blond cockroaches" in the yard. Toward the end of the 1800's, many German immigrants settled in Texas, especially in the area around San Antonio, lured by inexpensive, fertile land for farming. Town names such as New Braunfels, Fredericksburg, and Bergheim reflect Texas's German heritage.

ResourceBank

For the Student. Dobie, J. Frank. *A Vaquero of the Brush Country*. Boston: Little, Brown, 1949.

Gilpin, Laura. *The Rio Grande: River of Destiny*. New York: Duell, Sloan and Pearce, 1949.

IdeaBank

★ **Interactive Assessment.** Encourage students to perform their rap songs (assignment 4 in Connecting Reading and Writing) in small groups or for the class as a whole. Listeners might concentrate on (1) whether the song sounds like a real rap song and (2) whether it conveys the heroic qualities of its subject. ★

⌘ Connections

Across the Humanities. Have students find out about the life of a vaquero and identify some skills involved in tending cattle and riding the range. Students also might research the Texas Rangers and their involvement in the struggle between Mexicans and Anglos.

❷ Content Quiz

1. Who talks Gregorio Cortez into moving north of the border? his brother Román
2. What does Cortez do to the Major Sheriff who has shot his brother? Cortez shoots and kills him.
3. Why does El Teco betray Cortez to the sheriffs? for a $1000 reward
4. For what crime is Cortez sentenced to prison? for stealing a horse
5. How does Gregorio Cortez die? from slow poison

Guidelines for Response

Thinking About the Story, page 19

1. Opinions will vary. Students who enjoyed the story may have found it entertaining and suspenseful. Students who did not enjoy the retelling may say it was long, repetitive, or predictable.

2. Some students may assert it is inappropriate for a brave man to die by such a cowardly, underhanded method. These students might add that it would have been fitting if Cortez had died while fighting his enemies, with his pistol blazing, or while performing some deed characteristic of his noble life. Other students may say that poisoning is appropriate because it shows that Cortez's enemies consider him so formidable that they dare not risk an open confrontation. Students may note that only through foul play can such a noble man be vanquished.

3. Responses will vary. As examples of realistic events, students may list the confrontation in which Román is shot (page 10) and the persecution of Cortez's family and people who have helped him (page 15). Students may find exaggerated the number of sheriffs Cortez kills, events in which hundreds of sheriffs chase Cortez but are afraid to face him (page 14), Cortez's crossing of the San Antonio River (page 13), his legal trials in town after town (page 16), and the offer of marriage from President Lincoln's daughter (page 17).

4. Responses will vary. Some students may say that Gregorio Cortez is equally skilled as a vaquero and as a farmer and is unsurpassed with his pistol. These students may note that his skills as a fighter earn him great respect and that posses of ten or more men cower before him. Other students may point out that Cortez defends himself admirably in the courtroom, arguing convincingly for the justice of his cause. Still other students may admire the love of family that prompts Cortez to avenge his brother and later to surrender. These students may add that he exemplifies a definition of manhood that values courage and self-sacrifice as ideals of conduct. Finally, students may cite respect for elders, a willingness to work hard, and quiet modesty as admirable qualities.

5. Some students may answer that had Gregorio Cortez not lived by a heroic code, the sheriffs might have feared him less and might have succeeded in killing or capturing

him. Other students may say that Cortez might not have had the courage to take on hundreds of sheriffs and to ride five hundred miles. Some students may assert that had Cortez chosen to bend rather than to break, he would have lied about the sorrel mare and thereby escaped jail and, ultimately, an early death. Still other students may suggest that he might have accepted the marriage proposal from President Lincoln's daughter.

6. Students may note that in this version a Mexican hero scores victory after victory over the Americans: pursued by hundreds of Americans, Cortez kills as many as dare to confront him; he convinces the American judges with his irrefutable arguments on the side of justice; and he symbolically conquers the United States by rejecting President Lincoln's daughter, who wants to marry him. Finally, by poisoning him, the Americans again act cowardly and perpetuate yet another injustice. Students may note that the changes made in the corrido depict a larger-than-life champion, a paragon of bravery, intelligence, and honesty who fights against ignoble enemies. They may point out that in the corrido Cortez surrenders to save his people and chooses prison rather than tell a lie.

7. Answers to this question will vary greatly but should reflect knowledge of Cortez's qualities. Some students may find qualities such as honesty, stamina, and resourcefulness admirable. Other students may say that Cortez's loyalty to his family and his people is a quality still considered heroic today. Still other students may suggest that Cortez's courage in fighting alone against overwhelming odds is a timeless heroic quality.

Analyzing the Writer's Craft, page 20

Students' charts may be similar to the following:

Cortez	Values he represents
killing the sheriff who shoots Román	bravery, loyalty
jumping into the river canyon	bravery, cleverness, strength
turning himself in	responsibility, self-sacrifice, compassion
self-defense in court	intelligence, articulateness
admitting he stole the mare	honesty, responsibility

Connecting Reading and Writing, page 20

1. For assignment 1, have students read several obituaries from a local newspaper and identify the characteristics of this format.

2. To help students with assignment 2, bring in comic strips for them to examine.

3. For assignment 4, you might have students read narrative poems such as "The Ballad of John Henry."

NAME ______________________ DATE ____________

The Legend of Gregorio Cortez (page 6)

Test

Part 1 Broad Interpretation

A. Answer the following essay questions based on your understanding of the story. Write your answers on a separate sheet of paper. (*20 points each*)

1. How does Gregorio Cortez compare with a tall tale hero such as Paul Bunyan or Pecos Bill?
2. What or who do you think contributes most to Cortez's downfall? Explain your answer.

B. Put a check next to one of the quotations. Then, in the box on the right, briefly explain whether you think the quotation supports the message of the story. (*28 points*)

☐	"The courage we desire and prize is not the courage to die decently, but to live manfully." —Thomas Carlyle
☐	"Courage ought to be guided by skill, and skill armed by courage."—Sir Philip Sidney
☐	"Heroism feels and never reasons and therefore is always right." —Ralph Waldo Emerson
☐	"Heroism . . . is endurance for one moment more." —George Kennan
☐	"Fortune helps the brave." —Terence
☐	"Every hero becomes a bore at last." — Ralph Waldo Emerson

NAME ______________________ DATE ______________

Part 2 Close Interpretation

Think about the cultural values evident in the story of Gregorio Cortez. What values are revealed in his everyday life before Román's death? What values are revealed in the crisis after Román's death? Identify these values in the appropriate boxes below, choosing from those values listed and/or using your own. (*32 points*)

courage	loyalty	honesty	peaceableness
modesty	trickiness	courtesy	respectfulness
cleverness	hard work	shrewdness	
skill	quietness	endurance	

Cultural values revealed in everyday life	Cultural values revealed in the crisis

from When Heaven and Earth Changed Places

Le Ly Hayslip
(lā lē hā′ slip)

page 22

■ **Test,** TG pages 49 and 50

Objectives

1. To respond to an autobiographical excerpt set in Vietnam.
2. To identify themes in a selection.
3. To express ideas in a variety of writing formats: journal, nomination, guest column, chart, letter, handbill, song lyrics, book review, biographical sketch.

Summary

In this excerpt from her autobiography, Le Ly Hayslip describes her childhood in wartime Vietnam. She recalls a time when her father cared for her during her mother's trip to Da Nang and shared stories with her about getting his land and hiding from enemy soldiers. Her father told her to honor her ancestors and to tell what she has seen to the next generation so that her family's tradition of survival and love of their land can continue.

IdeaBank

▲ **Motivation.** As an alternative to the Connecting Writing and Reading activity, have students recall a special childhood memory of their own. To help students begin, suggest the following ideas:

- hearing a favorite family story about the past
- experiencing a family crisis
- having a memorable holiday celebration
- sharing a special time with a family member

Ask students to describe their memories in their journals. Then have them compare their memories with Hayslip's as they read. ▲

IdeaBank

❧ **Gifted and Talented Students.** Ask students to read "Seventeen Syllables" in Unit 4 (page 210). Have students compare the father-daughter relationships in these two works. ❧

IdeaBank

✲ **Collaborative Learning.** Have small groups of students work together to create charts comparing Bay Ly's (bī lē) daily life with their own and listing details about customs, food, chores, songs, and beliefs. ✲

IdeaBank

✤ **Multimodal Activities**

1. Have students create or find appropriate music for the song lyrics on page 23. Ask students to sing the songs and discuss their importance to Bay Ly's family.
2. Have students work collaboratively to create a scrapbook of illustrations to show different aspects of the Vietnam War.
3. Have students create a comic strip based on an incident Hayslip describes. ✤

● *Tips from the Classroom* ●

I like to use this story to explore the concept of courage. Before students read the selection, write the word *courage* on the board and ask students to provide a definition and examples. List students' responses on the board. After students have read the selection, ask them to evaluate the definition and examples, and ask them how they would expand their definition or even redefine the word *courage* in light of what they have read. Encourage students to discuss what aspects of the story changed their perceptions of courage.

Chrysanthe LaRosa
Commack High School
Commack, NJ

IdeaBank

✱ **Limited English Proficient Students**
There are frequent references to events in the distant past in this excerpt. To help LEP students grasp the order of events that take place after Bay Ly's mother travels to Da Nang, draw a time line on the board and have students supply the excerpt's major events in chronological order. As an alternative to the time line, have students create a story-sequence map as they read. ✱

InformationBank

Historical Notes

1. The first Vietnamese rebellion against Chinese colonial rule took place in A.D. 39. A Vietnamese noble was executed after the revolt, and his wife, Trung Trac, and sister-in-law, Trung Nhi, sought revenge. The Trung sisters, along with the legendary heroine Phung Thi Chinh, led troops against the Chinese and later established a kingdom that lasted about three years.

In the 1400's, the Vietnamese hero Le Loi led a victorious revolt against the Chinese Ming Dynasty rulers. He organized a guerrilla army, planned ambushes, and used elephants instead of horses to defeat Chinese troops.

Another leader, Gia Long, gained control of southern Vietnam in 1802 and later defeated a Vietnamese ruler to gain control of northern and central Vietnam. Gia Long had dikes, canals, and granaries constructed in order to help unify and rebuild Vietnam after years of warfare.

The names of these and similar leaders were frequently invoked during the war years of the 1950's–1970's.

2. Help students understand that in the Vietnam War civilians were involved, both as targets of United States and South Vietnamese relocation activity and as supporters of rebel guerrillas. Frances FitzGerald's *Fire in the Lake* deals extensively with Vietnamese village life during the war.

IdeaBank

★ Interactive Assessment

1. To assess students' understanding of the literary concept of theme, have pairs of students discuss the following literary elements:

1. the difference between theme and subject
2. the major themes of literary works they have already read

2. After students have completed the letter for optional assignment 2 of Connecting Reading and Writing, have pairs of students exchange papers and evaluate each other's letters according to the following criteria:

- Does the writer provide information that will interest the reader?
- Does the information relate to similarities and differences between American and Vietnamese cultures?
- What questions still linger in your mind? ★

⌘ Connections

Across the Humanities

1. Have students research an element of Vietnamese culture such as religion, customs, art, music, or food. Ask students to plan a multicultural festival featuring events or exhibitions related to the culture of Vietnam and the other cultures celebrated in Unit 1.

2. Ask students to research the history of the Vietnam War, focusing on the involvement of the United States. Have them create a television news report, a map, or a time line to present their findings.

ResourceBank

For the Teacher. Golub, Jeff, ed. *Activities to Promote Critical Thinking*. Urbana, Ill.: National Council of Teachers of English, 1988.

Paulson, F. Leon, Pearl R. Paulson, and Carol A. Meyer. "What Makes a Portfolio a Portfolio?" *Educational Leadership* (February 1991): 60–63.

❓ Content Quiz

1. Name one of Bay Ly's father's qualities. [Students may name any one.] handsome; easygoing; hardworking; honest; kind; funny

2. How does Bay Ly's father make the children feel better during the war? He sings comical songs.

3. Bay Ly's father gets angry at her mother for causing him to lose face. What did Bay's mother do to make him feel this way? She contradicted him in front of the refugees.

4. What does Bay Ly's father do to stop his daughter's crying? He gives her a rice cookie.

5. What does Bay Ly's father teach his daughter that is unusual to teach a girl in that culture? how to make things; how to use tools

6. Who is Phung Thi Chinh? a legendary Vietnamese woman warrior who fought against the Han during the Chinese wars

7. How does Bay Ly's father say he got his land? His parents gave him the biggest share of land because his wife proved to be the hardest working daughter-in-law.

8. How did Bay Ly's father escape from two jungle patrols? He stayed in the river for two days.

9. What does Bay Ly think her job is? to avenge her family

10. What does Bay Ly's father tell her one of her jobs is? [Students may name any one.] to stay alive; to marry and have a family; to live in peace; to tend the shrine of her ancestors; to bear witness

Guidelines for Response

Thinking About the Selection, page 29

1. Most students will respond positively to Bay Ly's father, noting that he is an affectionate father and husband. Some students may, however, be disturbed that he slapped his wife when she contradicted him.

2. Students will probably say that Bay Ly's family maintains its unity fairly well, but it also suffers heartbreaking losses. The relationships among Bay Ly, her father, and her mother seem emotionally secure despite the war. The father is especially comforting to Bay Ly; his tale of the military exploits of the ancestor Phung Thi Chinh inspires Bay Ly to feel brave. In addition, students may note that the father regards it as his duty to "take care of my family and my farm" (page 26), and when the Moroccan soldiers destroy the village, he takes great risks in order to save some of the family's possessions. However, most students will also mention the war-related losses suffered by Bay Ly's extended family (pages 26–27).

3. In their cluster diagrams, many students may have recorded associations that relate primarily to the Vietnam War and that are predominantly negative. While the selection will reinforce some of these associations, it may also help students see Vietnam as a country whose people have bravely endured hardship and have struggled to maintain the values associated with family and culture.

4. Some students may think that the father feels as he does about fighting because he has seen the suffering caused by the factions that have battled for control of his country; he may have come to believe that stability is impossible and that no ideology is worth dying for. Many students may suggest that the continuity of the family and their culture is overwhelmingly important to the father, which is why he wants Bay Ly to survive, have children, and "tend the shrine of our ancestors" (page 27). Individual students may react differently to the father's advice. Some may agree that survival is more important than fighting, but others may insist that certain values are worth going to war for.

5. Many students may think that if other children had been living at home, the father's affection and attention would have been divided among all the children and that he would not have had time to develop so close a relationship with Bay Ly. However, other students may think that Bay Ly's father is the type who would have made all his children feel special and that their relationship would have been essentially no different.

6. Students will probably say that they are aware of Bay Ly's attitude toward her father because she writes about him affectionately and with admiration. In her description of her father at the beginning of the selection, all of his attributes are favorable—he is "good-looking," "easy-going," and "a hard and diligent worker" (page 23). Students may mention that almost all the incidents in the selection reveal positive characteristics of the father—for example, he shows a sense of humor when he tells Bay Ly not to tell her mother about the roast duck; he is brave when he outwits the Moroccan soldiers. His only serious lapse—slapping Bay Ly's mother—is placed in perspective by the mother.

7. Students will probably say that the Vietnamese people attach great importance to their families, the capacity for hard work, and their survival as a people. The father's affection for his daughter, plus his repeated references to family members—including ancestors such as Phung Thi Chinh—show the importance of family. The father's admiration for his wife's ability to work hard—and the fact that, as a reward for her diligence, his parents left the couple the biggest share of farm land—attest to the significance of hard work. Many students may note that the father's account of the struggle with the Chinese, in which he says that "freedom . . . must be won and won again" (page 26), shows that the Vietnamese will make great sacrifices to ensure the survival of their culture.

8. Some students may assert that Bay Ly's father showed greater courage. These students may point out that he risked his life for the sake of his family. Instead of fleeing from the village, he hid from Moroccan patrols and remained in the river for two days to save a few tools and belongings from the enemy soldiers. Other students may say that Gregorio Cortez, a legendary hero, performed almost superhuman feats of courage in fighting single-handedly against hundreds of sheriffs and Texas Rangers intent on capturing him. These students also may point out that Cortez showed great courage in surrendering when he discovered that his family and those loyal to him were being persecuted on his behalf.

Analyzing the Writer's Craft, page 30

The following are some explicit statements of theme that students may cite: "One's country is as sacred as a father's grave" (page 25); "Freedom is never a gift. . . . It must be won and won again" (page 26); "Your job is . . . to live in peace and tend the shrine of our ancestors" (page 27). Some themes expressed indirectly are the importance of family and the necessity for hard work.

Connecting Reading and Writing, page 30

For assignment 2, suggest that students work in pairs to devise a way to organize their charts.

The assignment 3 option asks students to compose song lyrics. Suggest that students also try to set their lyrics to music.

For assignment 4, provide examples of book reviews for students to examine.

NAME ______________________ DATE ______________

from When Heaven and Earth Changed Places (page 22)

Test

Part 1 Broad Interpretation

Answer the following essay questions based on your understanding of the selection. Write your answers on a separate sheet of paper. *(15 points each)*

1. In his advice at the end of the selection, is Bay Ly's father asking her to be a hero? Explain your answer with reference to your understanding of what a hero is.
2. In what ways has Bay Ly's family been affected by war? How have they adapted their lives to war? Support your answer with details from the selection.
3. How do you think that Bay Ly's relationship with her father would have been different if he had been a more traditional Vietnamese? Explain your answer.

Part 2 Close Interpretation

A. This selection gives many clues to what was expected of women in Vietnam during the time Bay Ly was growing up. It also tells about the actions and personalities of the women in Bay Ly's family. In the box on the left, write brief notes describing the behavior expected of women. In the box on the right, write brief notes describing the behavior of Bay Ly and her female relatives. (*22 points*)

BEHAVIOR EXPECTED OF WOMEN	BEHAVIOR OF WOMEN IN BAY LY'S FAMILY

NAME ______________________________ DATE ______________

B. Write **T** if the quotation reflects one of the themes of the selection. Write **N** if it does not. (*3 points each*)

____ **1.** "A woman should be good for everything at home, but abroad good for nothing."—Euripides

____ **2.** "A man's village is his peace of mind."—Anwar el-Sadat

____ **3.** "What a pity is it/That we can die but once to save our country!" —Joseph Addison

____ **4.** "He that fights and runs away/May turn and fight another day." —James Ray

____ **5.** "Every noble deed dieth, if suppressed in silence."—Pindar

C. Think about how the writer's descriptions of her father convey information about the things that he holds important and the qualities he values in himself and others. Then fill in the bar graph below. (*18 points*)

	Not important to him	Very important to him
Tradition		
Material wealth		
His plot of land		
His own happiness		
His family's happiness		
A sense of history		
A sense of community		
The Republicans' political rhetoric		
The communists' political rhetoric		

From the Poets in the Kitchen

Paule Marshall

page 31

- **Vocabulary Worksheet,** TG page 53
- **Test,** TG pages 55 and 56

Objectives

1. To respond to an essay in which a writer describes her early experiences with language and with the narrative art.

2. To understand how the use of aphorism supports the theme of a literary work.

3. To express ideas in a variety of writing formats: journal, diary entry, letter, dramatic skit, cartoon strip, list, and booklet.

Summary

Paule Marshall describes how, as a small child, she listened to the long, colorful conversations of her immigrant mother and her mother's women friends—conversations in which Marshall's own sense of the power of language was first nurtured. She notes how their special variety of English—with its Caribbean and African influences—gave these women a sense of identity and self-worth. She describes how, as an adolescent, she devoured standard works of English and American literature. When she discovered that there were black poets, novelists, and dramatists, she was encouraged to become a writer herself. Although Marshall has been influenced by all the writers she has read, she always gives credit to the women who gathered in her mother's kitchen and spun a web of words, exploring a world of ideas.

InformationBank

Historical Note. Marshall mentions that her father left home to become a follower of Father Divine. Father Divine (1880?–1965) was an African-American religious leader whose real name was George Baker. Although controversial because of his indulgence in luxuries, Father Divine was generous and inspired his followers throughout the United States to fight racial prejudice and poverty. In 1915 in New York City, he founded the Peace Mission, a movement that was dedicated to ending war as well as discrimination. During the the period of the Great Depression, the Peace Mission helped to feed and clothe many poor people.

IdeaBank

▲ **Motivation.** As an extension of the Connecting Writing and Reading activity, have students ask family members and other adults what unusual words or expressions they can recall from their youth or their national heritage. Have the class compile a list of words and phrases with accompanying paraphrases or definitions. ▲

“*I try to catch every sentence, every word you and I say, and quickly lock all these sentences and words away in my literary storehouse because they might come in handy.*”

— Anton Chekhov, *The Seagull*, 1896

IdeaBank

❧ **Gifted and Talented Students.** Have students use a reference book of quotations to collect aphorisms about the power—or weakness—of words. After students have collected several quotations that appeal to them, have them write a short essay about an experience of their own that demonstrates the accuracy or inaccuracy of one of the aphorisms they have collected. Index entries that students may wish to refer to include language, literature, dialect, vernacular, and talk. ❧

⌘ Connections

Across the Curriculum. Have students research and prepare brief oral reports for the class on the literary and historical figures mentioned in Marshall's essay: Paul Laurence Dunbar, James Weldon Johnson, Langston Hughes, Zora Neale Hurston, Frederick Douglass, Harriet Tubman, and Sojourner Truth.

ResourceBank

For the Student. Marshall, Paule. *Soul Clap Hands and Sing*. Washington, D.C.: Howard University Press, 1988.

Black on White. The Story of English, Episode 4. Library Video Classics Project. Chicago: Films, Inc., 1986. Videocassette.

For the Teacher. Dillard, J. L. V. *Black English: Its History and Usage in the United States*. New York: Random House, 1972.

❷ Content Quiz

1. According to a male novelist who lectured to Marshall's students, what experience do women writers have that gives them an advantage over male writers? They spend more time in the kitchen as children, listening to the language of their mothers and their friends.

2. From what place had Marshall's mother and her mother's friends emigrated? the island of Barbados

3. What did Marshall's mother and her friends do for a living? They worked as maids or cleaning women.

4. When she was eight or nine, Marshall says she "graduated" from the corner table in the kitchen to what new place? the neighborhood library

5. What type of literature specifically led Marshall to believe that she could become a writer? books by and about black people

Guidelines for Response

Thinking About the Essay, pages 38–39

1. Some students may identify with Marshall's early love of reading and the library. Others may admire the way Marshall used reading and education to move from poverty to a position as a prominent writer. Some may recall experiences similar to those Marshall relates.

2. Students may suggest that the women in this essay are hard-working, creative people who use language as a means of expressing their opinions and frustrations and of reaffirming their self-worth. Students may note that the women, who are all poor, black, and foreign-born, work long hours cleaning other people's homes and that they earn very little money for their labors. Some students may recognize that the women feel powerless in the outside world but that when they gather in the kitchen, they take control of their lives through language by discussing everything from neighborhood gossip to politics and economics. Students may suggest that the women are poets not only because they use metaphors, aphorisms, and parables but also because they use language creatively, mixing Bajan terms with English words and inventing new expressions, like "beautiful-ugly." Students may also observe that these women, like many poets and writers, try to give new depth and meaning to ordinary language.

3. Some students may note that Marshall implies that her ability to "enter fully into the lives of the characters" in the books she reads helped her to handle the "storm" of adolescence (page 36). Students may suggest that her discovery of African-American writers made her realize that she, too, could become a writer. Students may note that Marshall says it was the women around the kitchen table who taught her how to tell stories, who trained her to listen to language, and who helped her set standards of excellence.

4. Some students may suggest that Marshall would have been treated differently as a boy: a boy might have been pushed out of the kitchen, talked to differently, and encouraged to play and socialize outdoors, away from the kitchen. Students may also note that even if Marshall's mother would have encouraged a boy to listen to kitchen talk, his peers would have pressured him to pursue more male-oriented activities. Other students may think that Marshall's situation would not have been any different if she had been male; a boy would still have been exposed to the women's language as he sat at the table.

5. Some students may point out that the women's job experiences typify the difficulty immigrants face when they arrive in a new country. Students may say that the essay demonstrates the importance of maintaining cultural connections through language and networking with other immigrants for moral support; listening to the women use Bajan expressions taught Marshall to appreciate her West Indian heritage. Some students may suggest that the schools Marshall attended were not sensitive to the cultural needs of immigrant children; Marshall learned to read and write, but her teachers did not expose her to African-American literature and culture.

6. Students who share Marshall's interest in reading or who enjoy creative language may express interest in reading more of her work. Students who are immigrants may find Marshall's writing relevant to their own lives and may hope to gain additional insight into the immigrant experience by reading more of Marshall's work.

7. Some may feel that an experience such as Marshall's would be difficult to duplicate today since family life is more disjointed in contemporary society. They may say that adults are busier and have fewer opportunities to gather and talk and that children seldom sit and listen to adults, preferring instead to watch television or do some other activity. Some may argue that in very close families, children still have an opportunity to absorb the language of adults or older siblings.

Analyzing the Writer's Craft, page 39

Students may suggest that the quote from Grace Paley emphasizes the beauty of everyday language and that the quote from Czeslaw Milosz points out the importance of language in maintaining connections to cultural identity. In discussion, students may note that these two ideas come together as the theme of Marshall's essay.

Connecting Reading and Writing, page 39

For assignment 1, suggest that students share their letters or diary entries with the class.

If the grammar and composition book you use has a lesson on autobiography, you may want to refer to this lesson.

NAME ________________________________ DATE ______________

From the Poets in the Kitchen (page 31)

Vocabulary Worksheet

Essential Vocabulary

adversity *n.* Poverty and trouble.
aesthetic *n.* Artistic viewpoint.
encompass *v.* To bring within; comprehend.
exhort *v.* To urge; warn with advice.
indiscriminately *adv.* Not making careful choices; randomly.
infuse *v.* To impart; inspire.
legacy *n.* Anything handed down from, or as from, an ancestor.
testimony *n.* Evidence; indication.
voraciously *adv.* Greedily; eagerly.

Useful Word

apprenticeship *n.* The period of time that one spends learning his or her craft.

Fill in each set of blanks with the correct word from the word list. (Clue: The boxed letters will spell things these poets are surrounded by.)

1. A human being has the ability to do this; an ant can't. _ _ _ _ _ [ ] _ _ _
2. "Stop that or you'll put somebody's eye out!" is meant to do this. _ _ _ [ ] _ [ ]
3. This is the set of standards that guides what and how a painter paints or a writer writes. _ _ [ ] _ _ _ _ _ _
4. This is how the waitress will expect you to eat if you order everything on the menu. _ _ _ [ ] _ _ _ _ _ _ _
5. This is how you picked what to have for dinner if you closed your eyes and stuck a pin into the menu. _ _ _ _ _ _ _ _ _ _ [ ] _ _ _ _ _
6. A person who goes from rags to riches has overcome this. _ [ ] _ _ _ _ _ _ _
7. This is a name for the time you spend in trade school or the minor leagues. _ [ ] _ _ _ _ _ _ _ _ _ _ _ _
8. This could be money, property, or red hair. _ _ _ [ ] _ _
9. The "I Have a Dream" speech by Martin Luther King does this with idealism. _ [ ] _ _ _ _
10. Did you study last night? How you do on the test today will provide this. _ _ [ ] _ _ _ _ _ _

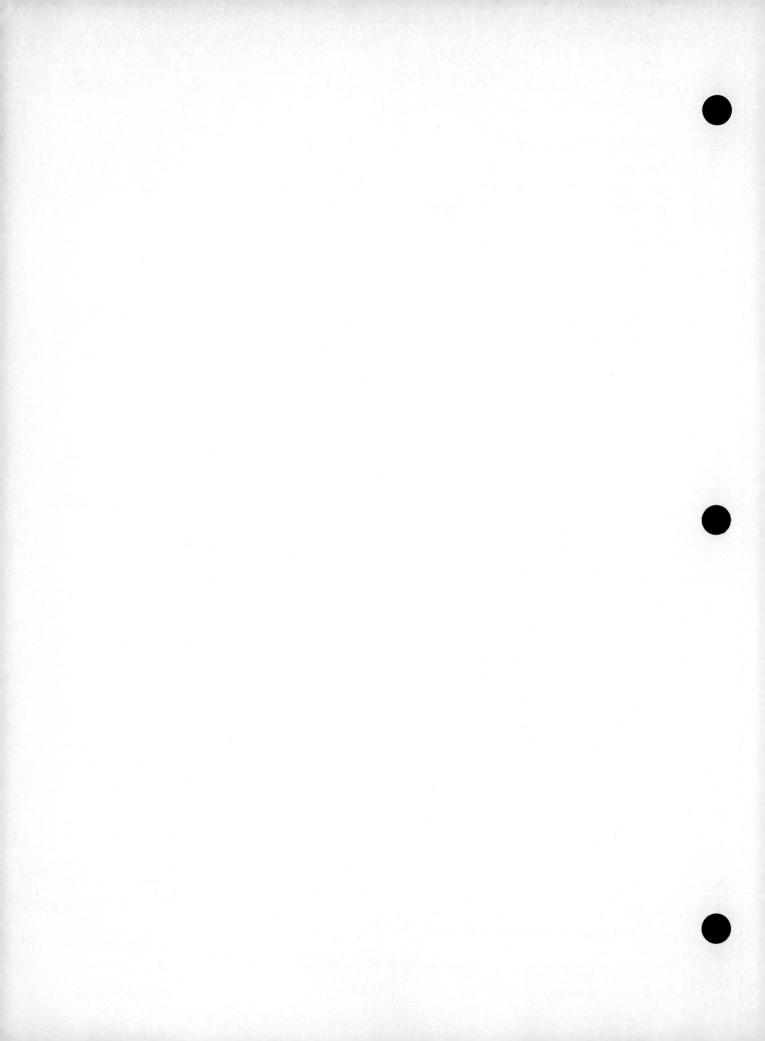

NAME ______________________________ DATE ______________

From the Poets in the Kitchen (page 31)

Test

Part 1 Broad Interpretation

A. Answer the following essay questions based on your understanding of the essay. Write your answers on a separate sheet of paper. (*16 points each*)

1. What does talking together do for the women in the kitchen? Explain your answer.
2. Why do you think the writer calls her mother and her mother's friends poets? What does this say about how the writer views poets and poetry? Use details from the essay to support your answers.
3. What does the writer find when she begins reading the works of Paul Laurence Dunbar, James Weldon Johnson, Langston Hughes, and Zora Neale Hurston? In what ways is that discovery like the talk of the women in the kitchen?

B. Write **T** next to the aphorisms below that support the theme of the essay. Write **N** next to those that do not. (*1 point each*)

	4. "Speech is civilization itself. The word, even the most contradictory word, preserves contact—it is silence which isolates."—Thomas Mann
	5. "Inject a few raisins of conversation into the tasteless dough of existence."—O. Henry
	6. "But let your communication be, Yea, yea; Nay, nay; for whatsoever is more than these cometh of evil."—Matthew 5:37
	7. "It is good to rub and polish our brain against that of others."—Michel de Montaigne
	8. "I never found the companion that was so companionable as solitude."—Henry David Thoreau
	9. "A vein of poetry exists in the hearts of all men."—Thomas Carlyle
	10. "The author who succeeds in his work is he who describes interesting and significant things which it has been given to him to observe and experience in his own life."—Leo Tolstoy
	11. "I would venture to guess that Anon, who wrote so many poems without signing them, was often a woman."—Virginia Woolf
	12. "Talkers are no good doers."—William Shakespeare
	13. "[Words] are the cry of our hunger for reality and our means of signifying the strange table spread for us."—Babette Deutsch

NAME ______________________________ DATE ______________

Part 2 Close Interpretation

A. In the boxes in the middle, make brief notes telling whether you think the aphorisms on the left agree with the sayings on the right, taken from the essay. Briefly explain your answers. (*18 points*)

Aphorism	Do the two express the same idea?	Saying
"You are not obliged to put on evening clothes to meet God."—Austin O'Malley		"God don' love ugly and He ain' stuck on pretty."

Aphorism	Do the two express the same idea?	Saying
"Speech is power."—Ralph Waldo Emerson		"In this man world you got to take yuh mouth and make a gun!"

B. Write **R** if the statement reflects the opinions of the women in the kitchen. Write **N** if it does not. (*3 points each*)

_____ **1.** Franklin Delano Roosevelt is ruining the country.

_____ **2.** You can't scrub the floor on an egg and cheese.

_____ **3.** Hitler is a fiend.

_____ **4.** The war in Europe is terrible but necessary.

_____ **5.** Marcus Garvey is a great man.

_____ **6.** Some people don't know what to do when the going gets rough.

_____ **7.** The authorities will get you if you beat "New York children."

_____ **8.** A person can't make a dollar in America.

The Way It Is

Gloria Oden

Mother to Son

Langston Hughes

page 40

■ **Vocabulary Worksheet,** TG page 59

■ **Tests,** TG pages 61 and 62

Objectives

1. To respond to two poems that explore how mothers are role models for their children.

2. To understand how poets use extended metaphors to enhance meaning.

InformationBank

Historical Note. Gloria Oden's subject in "The Way It Is" is more than just her mother; she also celebrates the spiritual strength and beauty of an entire generation of African-American women. During the 1960's and 1970's, there was a cultural movement for black pride in which black artists celebrated their rich African heritage and revolted against assimilation into white culture. Other literature on this theme includes *Roots* by Alex Haley, an essay by Alice Walker called "In Search of Our Mothers' Gardens," and the play *A Raisin in the Sun* by Lorraine Hansberry.

IdeaBank

❧ **Gifted and Talented Students.** Ask students to write poems celebrating their ideas of beauty. Have them begin by making cluster diagrams in which *beauty* is the central word. Encourage them to use concrete, sensory images and to include strong, fresh metaphors. Encourage volunteers to read their poems aloud. ❧

IdeaBank

▲ **Motivation.** Before students chart resemblances between themselves and an adult, it may help them to list specific characteristics of the adult. You may want to offer questions such as these to get students started: What does the adult look like? Describe his or her hair, skin, face, height, and weight. What does he or she do for fun? For work? What does he or she do when angry? When sad? When happy? What is he or she especially good at? What does he or she value most in life? ▲

" . . .when poems stop talking about the moon and begin to mention poverty, trade unions, color, color lines and colonies, somebody tells the police. "

— Langston Hughes,
from Anita King, ed., *Quotations in Black,* 1981

IdeaBank

✤ **Multimodal Activity.** Students might paint or draw portraits of the mother in "The Way It Is." Have students find illustrations or photographs that show the kind of stairs described in "Mother to Son."✤

⌘ Connections

Across the Language Arts. Dialect is a form of speech spoken by the people in a particular region, country, or social class. "Mother to Son" is written in an African-American dialect. Explain to students that dialect includes vocabulary, grammar, and pronunciation that differs from standard English. Have students cite examples of dialect in the poem ("kinder," "ain't been no," "set down," "I'se," "climbin' "). Then have students read the poem aloud to convey the nature of this dialect when it is spoken. You might ask students to find examples of this dialect in other poems or short stories they have read. What effect does dialect have upon a work of literature?

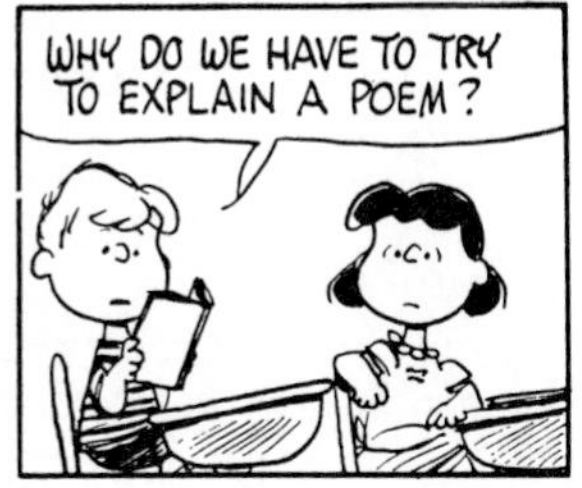

ResourceBank

For the Student. *Langston Hughes*. Annenberg/CPB Project. New York: New York Center for Visual History, 1988. VHS videocassette.

For the Teacher. Danielson, Susan. "Langston Hughes Curriculum Packet: Dig and Be Dug in Return." Portland, OR: Oral History Program, Inc., 1981.

Miller, R. Baxter. *The Art and Imagination of Langston Hughes*. Lexington, KY: University Press of Kentucky, 1989.

Content Quiz

1. To what minority group does the speaker in "The Way It Is" belong? She is African-American.
2. Whom does the speaker in "The Way It Is" celebrate? her mother
3. How does the speaker in "The Way It Is" describe this person—as beautiful, stern, or funny? beautiful
4. To what part of a building does the speaker in "Mother to Son" compare her life? a staircase
5. In which direction has the speaker been moving all her life? She has been climbing upward.

Guidelines for Response

Thinking About the Poem, page 42

1. Responses will vary. Some students may find that the poem reminds them of admiration they have felt for an adult who is important in their lives. Others may resent the stereotyped idea of beauty in the media.

2. Students may suggest that the speaker realizes that her mother has given her a firm sense of herself and pride in her blackness; the phrase "commercial virtues" implies that the speaker belittles the blond-haired, blue-eyed white concept of beauty, seeing it as the product of advertising. Since her mother, who is beautiful, has black skin, the speaker associates black skin with beauty; therefore, since the speaker is black, she feels positive about herself.

3. The speaker compares physical characteristics of herself and her mother. Her skin is brown but her mother's is browner (line 20). The mother is apparently taller than the speaker (line 28). Since the speaker feels like a scarecrow—"toothed, boned, and angled"—when she stands next to her mother, apparently her mother possesses physical gracefulness that the speaker feels she lacks.

4. Most students will probably think that the mother is a good model because she makes her daughter proud to be African-American. Other students may cite the daughter's feelings of awkwardness to support their opinion that the daughter is somewhat intimidated by her mother's beauty; the mother may not be a good model because the daughter cannot really emulate her.

5. Students may note that the simile "skin white as the unicorn's" suggests that the conventional white standard of beauty is just as much a myth as the unicorn. Others may note that the simile "as May morning on the lips of a rose" suggests something fragile and easily spoiled. In contrast, the simile comparing the mother's skin to an oak tree suggests that the mother's beauty is more substantial.

6. Students may surmise that the poet feels that positive, realistic role models are important in a society where the images in the media are false and unattainable.

Thinking About the Poem, page 44

1. Many students may agree that life is not always easy; some may suggest that life is much more difficult for some people than for others.

2. Students may surmise that the speaker's comparison suggests that her life has been a struggle; climbing a stairway is always a struggle against gravity, but this particular climb is made even more difficult by the presence of tacks and torn boards. Crystal is sparkling and delicate, and may be associated with affluent people; in contrast, the speaker is a tough woman with the endurance to go on.

3. Students may suggest that the difficulties of the speaker's life have not defeated her; she has kept "climbin' on/And reachin' landin's" (lines 9-10). Her advice to her son shows that she is a determined woman who has not grown bitter or self-pitying.

4. Students may think that the woman's perseverance in spite of difficulties makes her a good role model. Others may suggest that the mother seems too good to emulate and that the son might need a more realistic role model.

5. Students may suppose that the mother's dialect makes her seem direct and down to earth. Some may feel that sympathy for the woman's struggle may make readers more willing to accept her advice.

6. Responses may vary. Some students may admire the perseverance of the mother in "Mother to Son." Others may enjoy the pride and beauty of the mother in "The Way It Is."

Analyzing the Writer's Craft, page 45

The students' further interpretation of the extended metaphor may be similar to these examples:

Parts of the metaphor	Interpretation
3. turnin' corners	finding new solutions
4. goin' on in the dark	struggling when answers do not seem clear

NAME ______________________________ DATE ______________

The Way It Is (page 40)

Vocabulary Worksheet

Essential Vocabulary

commercial **inaudible**
dominant

Useful Words

billow **seizure**

Read the following story fragment and use the context clues to figure out the meanings of the underlined words. Then, use these meanings to help you work the exercise below. If you like, you may use a dictionary to check the meaning of a word.

Four things kept Jan "Jigger" Johnson from plunging to the jagged rocks below and ending her mission: the four fingers of her right hand that grasped the small ledge. Her left arm dangled at her side, broken. Her pressurized spacesuit, shredded by the blast of wind that had pushed her off the cliff, was useless now against the icy, **dominant** wind that ruled this planet like a dictator. Worse, her helmet mask was shattered and the radio destroyed. Now each burst of wind brought waves of a strange green snow that **billowed** around her, stinging her eyes and cutting into her skin.

Between gusts, Jigger desperately strained to hear human sounds, but the almost animal-like howl of the wind in the canyon below made anything else **inaudible.** One boot brushed against a root. Applying a little weight, Jigger raised herself enough to grab hold of an ugly, stunted tree. The wind's next blast, miraculously, lifted her onto the ledge that held the tree.

Trying not to jar her left arm, Jigger settled against the tree to catch her breath. Her employees would be wondering about her by now. She pictured them at the base, among the machines—the weather controllers and planet refinishers—who would soon conquer this seemingly ceaseless wind. Her group planned to take over this planet quickly, completely. Their **seizure** would be permanent. And profitable.

The changes they would make would all be very **commercial**—restaurants, entertainment, golf courses. Earth was so crowded and dirty that it would be easy to get people to come here. Thousands had signed up already. There was room for two hundred million. She and her partners would make billions. *That wind* couldn't stop them.

A blast of wind seemed to shake the very planet, and the ugly little tree shifted slightly. The tree whose roots had embraced that cliff for a hundred centuries, whose blossoms opened once every hundred years to gather and reflect the radiance of its sun—the tree shifted. Jigger tried to jump back, but the wind carried her over the side before she knew what had happened. (To be continued.)

Match each underlined word in the story fragment with the correct definition below.

______________________ **1.** Designed to have wide popular appeal.

______________________ **2.** That cannot be heard.

______________________ **3.** Having superior force or influence; ruling.

______________________ **4.** Surged or swelled in a large wave.

______________________ **5.** A sudden taking.

NAME ______________________ DATE ____________

The Way It Is (page 40)

Open-Book Test

Part 1 Broad Interpretation

A. Answer the following essay questions based on your understanding of the poem. Write your answers on a separate sheet of paper. *(16 points each)*

1. At the end of the poem, the speaker says, "I am so pleased with myself." Why do you think she feels this way?
2. Think about the difference between the media's portrayal of physical beauty in a woman and the speaker's sense of beauty. What effect has the speaker's own sense of beauty had on her self-esteem?
3. Think about the title of the poem. What connection do you see between the title and the ideas expressed in the poem?

B. Think about the ways in which the speaker compares herself to her mother. Then, in the boxes below, make notes about how the speaker is like her mother and how she is different. *(16 points)*

HOW SHE IS LIKE HER MOTHER	HOW SHE IS DIFFERENT

Part 2 Close Interpretation

Write the letter of the best answer. *(12 points each)*

____ 1. The speaker believes that she is less beautiful than

a. her mother. **b.** other black girls. **c.** both strangers and friends.

____ 2. The lines "Walnut/like the satin leaves of the oak" describe the skin of

a. the speaker. **b.** the speaker's mother. **c.** women in advertising.

____ 3. The lines "the scarecrow child of/yesteryear" describes how the speaker sees herself when compared to

a. her mother. **b.** white strangers. **c.** women in advertising.

NAME ______________________________ DATE ______________

Mother to Son (page 40)

Open-Book Test

Part 1 Broad Interpretation

Answer the following essay questions based on your understanding of the poem. Write your answers on a separate sheet of paper. *(20 points each)*

1. What advice does the mother give to her son?
2. What do you think life has been like for the speaker? Support your answer with examples from the poem.
3. The speaker says that life, for her, has been "no crystal stair." What would a crystal stairway be like? How does the choice of these specific words give the metaphor its meaning?

Part 2 Close Interpretation

A. Think about the poet's comparison between life and a stairway. Then, in the box next to each part of the extended metaphor, note your interpretation of what it says about life. *(20 points)*

PART OF THE METAPHOR	INTERPRETATION
"It's had tacks in it,/And splinters,/And boards torn up"	
"turnin' corners"	
"Don't you set down on the steps"	
"sometimes goin' on in the dark"	

B. Write the letter of the best answer. *(10 points each)*

1. The attitude of the speaker toward her son is one of
   a. pity. **b.** scorn. **c.** amusement. **d.** encouragement.
2. The attitude of the speaker toward life is one of
   a. fear. **b.** gratitude. **c.** resentment. **d.** determination.

Lineage

Margaret Walker

Women

Alice Walker

page 46

■ **Tests,** TG pages 65–67

Objectives

1. To respond to a pair of poems in which speakers express admiration for their female ancestors.

2. To express ideas in a variety of writing formats: journal, poem, letter, storyboard, character sketch, oral history, autobiographical sketch, recommendation, memo.

InformationBank

Biographical Note. Alice Walker was born into a family of sharecroppers. Before devoting her full attention to writing, she worked at a number of different occupations, including teaching at a Head Start program in Mississippi and working on staff in the New York City welfare department. She was inspired to write *Once*, her first published volume of poetry, after a trip to Africa. Later, her interests shifted to fiction, resulting in the publication of *Meridian*, *The Color Purple*, and *The Temple of My Familiar*. She based *The Color Purple* on true stories about her great-grandmother and research she conducted at Spelman College.

IdeaBank

▲ **Motivation.** To help students find information that they can use when they write about the relative or ancestor they most admire, have them interview a relative who remembers some time-honored family stories. ▲

InformationBank

Historical Note. In spite of hardship, black women have contributed significantly to American culture. Writers of fiction include Zora Neale Hurston, Gloria Naylor, and Toni Morrison. Black singers such as Marian Anderson, Ella Fitzgerald, and Bessie Smith have enriched American music. Educator Mary McLeod Bethune influenced New Deal policies in the 1930's.

IdeaBank

❃ **Learning Disabled Students.** You might want to help students understand the ideas expressed in "Women" by listing key questions on the board: Who do "we" and "they" refer to? What do the words *books*, *desks*, and *page* suggest about the goals the mothers have for their children? Then read the poem aloud, pausing every few lines so that students can take notes. ❃

"Everything I have ever written or hoped to write is dedicated . . . to our hope of peace and dignity and freedom in the world; not just as black people, or as Negroes, but as free human beings in a world community."

Tips from the Classroom

These are two of my favorite poems because they deal with women's issues. Although the poems seem simple, they require maturity on the part of the students. Therefore, I usually prepare the class for the poems by asking students to suggest adjectives describing older (female) relatives. This list of adjectives can serve as a point of reference as students read.

Sheila G. Vaughan
Surrattsville High School
Clinton, MD

IdeaBank

★ **Interactive Assessment.** If students did the autobiographical sketch called for in the option for writing assignment 3, have pairs act as peer reviewers for each other's writing. The reviewer might use the following questions as guidelines for evaluating the writing: Does the writer compare himself or herself to an ancestor? Is the comparison clear? Is the ancestor described vividly enough so that the reader gets a sense of what he or she was like? Is the writer's autobiographical sketch interesting? If not, what might make it more interesting?

Reviewers might also consider these questions: What's good about the writing? What two things should be changed? ★

ResourceBank

For the Student. *The American Prose Library Presents an Interview with Alice Walker.* Kay Bonetti, interviewer. Columbia, MO: American Audio Prose Library, 1981. Sound cassette.

For the Teacher. Worthington, Pepper. "The Color Purple." *English Journal 74* (January 1985): 48–52.

❷ Content Quiz

1. What relatives of the speaker is the poem "Lineage" about? her grandmothers
2. Of the three adjectives frail, strong, and brilliant, which best describes these relatives in "Lineage"? strong
3. Does the speaker in "Lineage" think that this adjective describes herself? no
4. In the poem "Women," what were the women trying to get for their children? an education
5. Did they succeed in achieving their goal? yes

Guidelines for Response

Thinking About the Poem, pages 47–48

1. The poem may cause students to re-examine their own ancestors' accomplishments and feel pride in them. Some students may mirror the speaker's feelings of inadequacy. However, other students may feel that they are going to accomplish more than their ancestors have.

2. Students may suggest that in the last line, which reveals the speaker's feelings of inadequacy, the poem shifts emphasis from the ancestors to the speaker. Some students may question the speaker's feelings, suggesting that she might have a different type of strength to face the challenges of the modern world.

3. *Strong* may mean physical strength developed by hard work in the fields. The word also suggests strength of character.

4. Responses may vary. Students may suggest that the challenges that the ancestors faced and the hardships they endured made them strong. Others may suppose their great desire to succeed made them strong.

5. Like the poem's speaker, students may feel awe for their relatives or ancestors. Some students may also feel inadequate as they compare themselves to the subjects of their admiration.

6. Students will probably suggest that if the speaker knew nothing about her lineage, she could not admire her grandmothers and her grandmothers could not serve as role models. However, because she would not have heroic ancestors to compare herself to, she might feel less inadequate.

7. Students may cite the alliteration of the *s* sound in lines 3, 5, and 8; the *g* sound in line 4; the *r* sound in line 9. As examples of repetition, students might note the word "They," which begins lines 2, 3 ,4, 5, and 9, and the line "My grandmothers were strong," which appears three times in the poem. Students may suggest that the alliteration and repetition help establish the rhythm of the poem; both devices—especially repetition—also emphasize and unify ideas in the poem.

Thinking About the Poem, pages 49–50

1. Responses will vary. Students may picture these women as formidable, their strength reflected in their faces. They may see them walking with a determined gait.

2. Some students may cite the determination of these women and how hard they worked to improve their children's lives. Others may admire the way they could be strong but gentle, and have "fists as well as/Hands."

3. The military metaphors may impress many students as being especially appropriate for conveying the hardships these women faced and the obstacles they had to overcome to better their children's lives. In addition, the comparison to generals—who provide armies with crucial leadership and strategic planning—shows additional aspects of the mothers' roles.

4. Responses will vary. Some students may think that fathers would also fight for education. Others may think that fathers would focus on different battles, such as voting rights, fair housing, or battles in wartime.

5. Students may cite similarities in the reverence and respect of the speakers for their ancestors. They may also point out that both speakers admire the strength of their ancestors. Students may contrast the speaker's feelings of inadequacy in "Lineage" with the speaker of "Women," who expresses no inadequacy.

Connecting Reading and Writing, page 50

A book on filmmaking or some issues of *Premiere* magazine should have an example of a storyboard. Have those students who wish to create a documentary storyboard (assignment 3) find such an example to use as a model.

Students may find it helpful to tape their oral history interviews. Encourage students to share their oral history project with members of their families.

If the grammar and composition book you use has a lesson on character sketch, you may want to refer to this lesson.

NAME ______________________ DATE ____________

Lineage (page 46)

Open-Book Test

Part 1 Broad Interpretation

A. Answer the following essay questions based on your understanding of the poem. Write your answers on a separate sheet of paper. *(15 points each)*

1. What is the speaker's attitude toward the grandmothers? How does the speaker feel that she compares with the grandmothers?
2. Why do you think the speaker's grandmothers were so strong?
3. The speaker in the poem associates work with singing. What does this suggest to you about the speaker's attitude toward work? Explain your answer.

B. Think about the kind of people the grandmothers are. Then, draw a line from the picture of the hands to the things that the speaker says or implies that the grandmothers have. *(15 points)*

Energy	Fame
Capability	Enjoyment
Sophistication	Common sense
Satisfaction in work	Rich, full lives
Sense of purpose in life	Connection to nature

Part 2 Close Interpretation

A. Write the letter of the best answer. *(10 points each)*

_____ **1.** Which of the following is *not* true of the grandmothers?
- **a.** They are no longer alive.
- **b.** Nowadays, they often smell of soap.
- **c.** In the past, they worked hard.
- **d.** In the past, they worked cheerfully.

_____ **2.** What does the line "They touched earth and grain grew" suggest about the grandmothers?
- **a.** They were good farmers.
- **b.** They knew how to use magic.
- **c.** They found their work effortless.
- **d.** They used modern equipment and methods.

NAME ______________________ DATE ______________

B. In the poem, Margaret Walker uses alliteration, or repetition of initial consonant sounds. Choose one of the lines below and find the alliteration in the line. Notice the effect of the alliteration and think about the possible reasons that Walker chose to use that technique. Then, follow the directions to complete the chart below. *(20 points)*

- **a.** "They moved through fields sowing seed"
- **b.** "They touched earth and grain grew"
- **c.** "Smelling of soap and onions and wet clay"
- **d.** "With veins rolling roughly over quick hands"

In the box, write the letter of the line that you have chosen.		a, b, c, d
In the box, name the repeated initial consonant sound.		r, s, gr
In the box, write the word or words that describe the sound.		Explosive, hissing, popping, breaking through, rolling, sharp, smooth, gentle, soothing, or pounding.

How do you think the alliteration reinforces the meaning of the line?

NAME ______________________________ DATE ______________

Women (page 46)

Open-Book Test

Part 1 Broad Interpretation

A. Answer the following essay questions based on your understanding of the poem. Write your answers on a separate sheet of paper. *(30 points each)*

1. How does the speaker feel about the women of his or her mother's generation? Why do you think the speaker feels that way?
2. Why do you think the speaker refers to the women as generals? Explain.

B. Think about what the women described in the poem are like. Then, in the box on the left, write brief notes describing any obstacles the women might have faced as they sought opportunities for their children. In the middle box, write the letters of the qualities that you think might have helped them overcome the obstacles. *(20 points)*

OBSTACLES

a. boldness
b. strength
c. timidity
d. hesitancy
e. imagination
f. forcefulness
g. determination
h. other: ______________

QUALITIES

GOAL: EDUCATION FOR THEIR CHILDREN

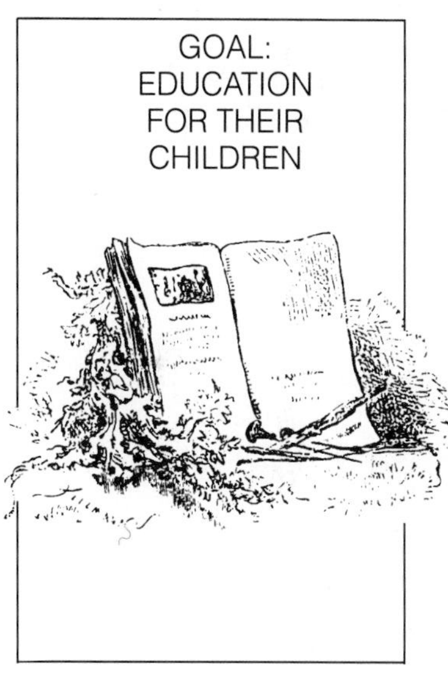

Part 2 Close Interpretation

Write the letter of the best answer. *(20 points each)*

_____ 1. The "Armies" that the women led were
a. other mothers. **b.** federal troops. **c.** the women's families.

_____ 2. The speaker believes that education is
a. a waste of time. **b.** absolutely necessary. **c.** helpful, but not essential.

Everyday Use

Alice Walker

page 51

- **Vocabulary Worksheet,** TG page 72
- **Test,** TG pages 73 and 74

Objectives

1. To respond to a story that explores the different ways a mother and two daughters value their family's heritage.

2. To understand the literary concept of foil.

3. To express ideas in a variety of formats: journal, review, dialogue, informational footnotes, captions, memo, press release, booklet, sequel.

Plot Summary

Outside their primitive farmhouse, a mother and her younger daughter, Maggie, anxiously await the visit of the educated, sophisticated older daughter, Dee. Simple and uneducated, Maggie is especially self-conscious about her burn scars, which are the result of a fire that destroyed the family's first home. Dee arrives in a car with a man; both are dressed and groomed in trendy African-inspired styles. Maggie and the mother, on the other hand, are dressed plainly. Dee announces that she has taken the name Wangero because she could not bear being named after her oppressors —even though she is actually named after a beloved relative. Dee (Wangero) quickly begins going over objects in the house, claiming the butter dish and parts of the butter churn to take home with her. However, when she says she wants to take two family quilts with her, the mother resists, saying that the quilts are Maggie's, for when she gets married. Dee becomes angry, saying that Maggie will subject the quilts to "everyday use" rather than treat them as art objects. Perceiving that it is Maggie, not Dee, who values the quilts for their family association, the mother still refuses Dee's demand. Angry, Dee leaves with her companion in their car.

InformationBank

Historical Note. The black pride movement of the 1960's sought to make African Americans aware of their rich heritage. Leaders such as Stokely Carmichael and H. Rap Brown urged African Americans to define their own standards and stressed that "black is beautiful." African Americans asserted black pride in several ways, such as hair styles, fashion, and names emphasizing African descent. For example, the heavyweight boxing champion of the world, formerly known as Cassius Clay, changed his name to Muhammad Ali.

IdeaBank

▲ **Motivation.** Ask students to think of aspects of their family's heritage that are especially important to them. Have them copy in their journals a chart similar to the one that follows. For each of the categories shown, they should fill in one or more examples relating to their heritage. For example, under the category of language, they might write expressions that they have heard their parents and grandparents use. As they read, have students compare what they value in their heritage with what the characters in the story value.

Family treasures	Traditional foods
Holidays	Language

IdeaBank

✲ **Collaborative Learning.** Have students form groups of four and suppose that Dee (Wangero) sues for possession of the quilts. One pair of students should take the part of Dee and her lawyer; the other pair should take the part of Maggie and her lawyer. Each pair of students should present a written argument advancing the claim of each woman. The arguments should address the question of how a family's heritage should be passed down to future generations. Award the quilts to the most accurate, most clearly thought out, and most compelling argument. ✲

InformationBank

Biographical Note. Like Maggie in "Everyday Use," Alice Walker has experienced acute self-consciousness because of scarring that resulted from a childhood injury. When she was eight years old, a brother accidentally shot her in the right eye with his BB gun. The wound blinded her in that eye and left a "glob of whitish scar tissue, a hideous cataract." Even though most of the scar tissue was removed surgically when she was fourteen, leaving only a "bluish crater," Walker still hated the appearance of her eye and was very reluctant to have her picture taken. Then one day her tiny daughter noticed the scar but thought it looked beautiful, like the earth as seen from space: "Mommy, there's a *world* in your eye." Her daughter's perception reconciled Walker to her scar: "I saw that it was possible to love it."

InformationBank

Literary Note. In her essay "Saving the Life That Is Your Own" (whose title is an allusion to the short story "The Life You Save May Be Your Own" by Flannery O'Connor), Walker describes her difficult search for African-American women writers to use as role models: "Mindful that throughout my four years at a prestigious black and then a prestigious white college I had heard not one word about early black women writers, one of my first tasks was simply to determine whether they had existed. After this, I could breathe easier, with more assurance about the profession I had chosen." Walker discovered her first model in Zora Neale Hurston, who, she explains, "provided . . . more than one of the greatest novels America had produced." Walker goes on to say, "she had provided, as if she knew someday I would come along wandering in the wilderness, a nearly complete record of her life. And though her life sprouted an occasional wart, I am eternally grateful for that life, warts and all."

IdeaBank

❧ **Gifted and Talented Students.** Ask students to imagine themselves returning to their parents' home at one of the following points in the future:

- after their first few weeks in college
- after they have gotten a job and are living independently
- shortly after their marriage
- after the birth of their first child
- after their parents have become elderly and perhaps somewhat infirm

After envisioning how they and their parents would react to each other during such a visit, students should write about it in some appropriate format, such as a letter, cartoon strip, journal entry, dialogue, or short story. ❧

⌘ Connections

Across Literature. Other works in this text that explore the feelings between mothers and their children include the following:

"Mother to Son," Langston Hughes

"My Mother Pieced Quilts," Teresa Palomo Acosta

A Raisin in the Sun, Lorraine Hansberry

"A Visit to Grandmother," William Melvin Kelley

IdeaBank

✣ Multimodal Activities

1. Have students use objects with family associations to create collages, mobiles, or sculptures. In addition to pieces of cloth, they might use toys, household objects, recipe cards, and mementos such as invitations and graduation programs.

2. Students might draw a family tree for the family of the mother in the story, using their imaginations as well as details from the story.

3. In "Everyday Use," the mother serves a meal of traditional family foods. Ask students to compose a menu for a meal that features foods that are traditional in their own families. They should also create a design for the menu, using calligraphy and possibly illustrations. ✣

ResourceBank

For the Student. *The American Prose Library Presents an Interview with Alice Walker.* Kay Bonetti, interviewer. Columbia, Mo.: American Audio Prose Library, 1981. Sound cassette.

The Author Speaks: Selected PW Interviews 1967–1976 (Publisher's Weekly Editors and Contributors). New York: R. R. Bowker Company, 1977.

Walker, Alice. *Horses Make a Landscape Look More Beautiful: Poems*. New York: Harcourt Brace Jovanovich, 1986.

For the Teacher. Evans, Mari, ed. *Black Women Writers (1950–1980): A Critical Evaluation*. Garden City, N.Y.: Anchor Press/Doubleday, 1984.

Walker, Alice. *In Love and Trouble: Stories of Black Women*. New York: Harcourt Brace Jovanovich, 1974.

❓ Content Quiz

1. What is the yard of the narrator's house like? It consists of hard clay bordered with sand; there is an elm tree.

2. How did Maggie get her scars? from the fire that burned the family's first house to the ground

3. How did Dee feel about the family's first house? She hated it and was glad to see it burn.

4. Why has Dee changed her name? She didn't want to be named after her oppressors.

5. Why doesn't Dee feel that Maggie should be allowed to keep the handmade quilts? They are priceless, and Dee thinks that Maggie will just use them as quilts.

Guidelines for Response

Thinking About the Story, page 58

1. Reactions will vary. Many students may respect the mother for her sympathetic understanding of Maggie. Others may feel angry at Dee for putting down her mother and her sister. Still others may feel relieved that Maggie's self-image has improved.

2. Students may like the mother best and Dee the least because the mother is an entertaining storyteller who portrays Dee in a negative light. Others may like her for defending Maggie. Some students may like Maggie best for her direct, sincere reactions and because at the end of the story she gains self-confidence and smiles "a real smile." Others may dislike Maggie for being so fearful and compliant. Students who agree with Dee's ideas may like her despite her selfishness. Others may admire her determination to improve herself.

3. Students who agree may say that Maggie deserves to have the things that are important to her because she has had a hard life, or that Maggie is as entitled to family treasure as Dee. Students may suggest that Dee is not necessarily right in saying that Maggie will put the quilts to everyday use or that as the owner of the quilts, Maggie can do whatever she wants with them. Students also may question whether Dee's interest in the family heritage is just a passing phase, an interest that she will abandon the way she has abandoned her family. Students who disagree may say that the quilts should be preserved and that the strong-willed Dee is the best person to do it. Others may believe that Dee's interest in her heritage is sincere and that she should keep the quilts.

4. Students may answer that Maggie knows more specific facts about her heritage in that she knows who whittled the dasher and she knows how to quilt. Some may say that there is no evidence that Maggie really understands her heritage and its connection to her life. Others may answer that Maggie lives her heritage and that by doing so, she will pass it on to her children. Some students may believe that Dee is developing an understanding of what a heritage consists of, such as her African name, the snapshot she takes of the cow representing the family's rural background, and the quilting tradition. Others may say that Dee seems to be interested in her heritage only because it is fashionable and artistic. She still has the same contempt for her family—her true heritage—that she always had.

5. Students may say that they would be disappointed if the narrator had given in to Dee's fury. Some may answer that they would have found the story depressing because it would show the underdog, Maggie, suffering an injustice. Others may say that they would have felt angry at the unfairness of life. Some students, however, may state that they would prefer Dee to have the quilts. These students may feel relieved that the quilts were preserved.

6. Students may answer that the quilts symbolize the family's heritage and way of life. The decision about who gets the quilts determines whether that heritage will remain a part of everyday life (Maggie's everyday use) or become a lifeless artifact (Dee's wall-hanging). Students may say that Maggie wants the quilts because they are personally important to her; she remembers the patchwork of family history behind the patchwork quilts. With her possession, the personal and intimate win out over the intellectual and sophisticated. Some students may note the irony that despite Dee's African clothes, she has a Western attitude about collecting artifacts and transforming them into art; Maggie's attitude is closer to non-Western oral traditions.

7. Some students may answer that Alice Walker pities Dee as a person who has cut herself off from her roots in an effort to escape the poverty and oppression her people have suffered and who is now desperately trying to build her own heritage. Some may believe that Walker likes her determined persistence at self-improvement but does not like her attitude of superiority toward her mother and sister: "You just don't understand . . . your heritage" (page 57). These students may add that Walker would judge Dee for trying to preserve things at the expense of family relationships. Some may say that Walker has little sympathy for people who want to romanticize and glorify a heritage that they have refused to make a part of their daily lives. Others may think that Walker shows Dee as a person who has the potential to preserve African-American heritage but who still has to learn the right way to go about it.

Analyzing the Writer's Craft, page 59

Students' charts may be similar to the following:

	Dee	Maggie
Physical Traits	attractive	plain
Personality	assertive	shy and unassuming
Values	being fashionable and impressive	love of family
Education	college educated	uneducated
Lifestyle	superficial and unemotional	genuine and affectionate

Connecting Reading and Writing, page 60

For assignment 2, show students samples of informational footnotes.

NAME ________________________________ DATE ______________

Everyday Use (page 51)

Vocabulary Worksheet

Essential Vocabulary

furtive *adj*. Stealthy; sneaky.
sidle *v*. To move sideways, especially in a way that does not draw attention.

Useful Words

clabber *n*. Thickly curdled milk.
oppress *v*. To keep down by the cruel or unjust use of power.
recompose *v*. To calm or quiet oneself again.

Using context clues, fill in each blank with the correct word from the word list. (Clue: The words will fit the rhythm and rhyme scheme of the poem.)

Advice to a Tearful Kitchenmaid

The people that you work for
Are not your ideal bosses.
You're just about to leave them,
Pack your bags, and cut your losses.

I know that they __________________ you.
They are cruel and overbearing.
But __________________ yourself. Don't cry.
Just plan a vengeance daring.

Before you give them notice
And tell them that you're quitting,
Prepare yourself to leave behind
Some food that's only fitting.

Don't tell the world your troubles,
But be __________________. Do not blabber.
Just __________________ over to the churn
And add some soap suds to the __________________.

NAME ______________________________ DATE ______________

Everyday Use (page 51)

Test

Part 1 Broad Interpretation

A. Answer the following essay questions based on your understanding of the story. Write your answers on a separate sheet of paper. (*12 points each*)

1. Why do you think Maggie smiles at the end of the story? Explain your answer.
2. In your opinion, who should get the quilts? Explain your answer.
3. What do you think Hakim-a-barber thinks of the narrator and Maggie? Explain your answer.
4. What are some possible meanings of the title of the story? Explain your answer and support it with details from the story.

B. Think about the ways in which Maggie and Dee relate to their heritage. In the boxes below, write words or phrases describing the things that each woman values in that heritage. (*12 points*)

Dee values	Maggie values

Part 2 Close Interpretation

A. Write the letter of the best answer. (*5 points each*)

_____ **1.** The narrator calls her daughter "Dee (Wangero)" and "Wangero (Dee)" because she thinks her name change is

a. silly. **c.** only temporary.
b. not legal. **d.** an insult to Big Dee.

_____ **2.** How does the narrator feel about Hakim-a-barber?

a. She pities him. **c.** She is afraid of him.
b. She admires him. **d.** She thinks he is foolish.

NAME ______________________________ DATE ______________

B. Think about how Dee contrasts with Maggie and the narrator in the story. In the boxes on the left and right, briefly note how the two other women contrast with Dee in each of the aspects listed. (*30 points*)

How Maggie contrasts with Dee	Aspects of Dee	How the narrator contrasts with Dee
	She is well educated.	
	She is outgoing.	
	Her figure is slender but womanly.	
	She feels superior to others.	
	She hated the old house and all it represented.	
	She wants to display the evidences of her heritage.	

My Mother Pieced Quilts

Teresa Palomo Acosta

My Father's Song

Simon Ortiz

page 61

■ **Test,** TG pages 77 and 78

Objectives

1. To respond to two poems that capture meaningful memories from childhood.

2. To identify sound devices—alliteration, consonance, and assonance—in a poem.

IdeaBank

▲ **Motivation.** To help students recall a vivid childhood memory, have them create cluster diagrams around the name of an adult who was important to them as a child. Ask them to list associations and impressions relating to this person in some of the following areas: physical characteristics, personality traits, hobbies or activities, values, special occasions shared, skills or talents. ▲

IdeaBank

✱ **Limited English Proficient Students**
To help students understand the structure of "My Mother Pieced Quilts," read each stanza aloud. Point out each stanza that presents a different aspect of how to piece together a quilt. For example, help students to recognize that the second stanza mentions the fabrics used and the third stanza explains the way the mother created patterns from the fabrics. Ask volunteers to speculate about why the poet uses this structure. ✱

IdeaBank

✤ **Multimodal Activity.** Have students design their own quilt squares in order to illustrate a meaningful childhood moment. Ask them to draw a simple picture and to describe the colors and fabrics they would use. Encourage students who can sew to actually make their squares. ✤

InformationBank

Literary Note. "My Father's Song" appears in the "Preparation" section of Ortiz's collection of poems, *Going for the Rain*. The speaker of the poems seeks the meaning of life and undergoes a physical and spiritual journey, which includes preparation, leaving home, and returning home. The result of his quest is self-knowledge. In the book's prologue, Ortiz describes the preparation: "A man makes his prayers; he sings his songs. He considers all that is important and special to him, his home, children, his language, the self that he is. He must make spiritual and physical preparation before anything else. Only then does anything begin."

"What I do is listen and watch as carefully as I am able and then tell what happens."

— Simon Ortiz

IdeaBank

✲ **Collaborative Learning.** Ask the class to find out more about quilts. Some students can locate examples of traditional patterns, such as cathedral window, card trick, log cabin, or Ohio star. Others can research the following topics: materials and techniques used to make quilts, famous quilts, contemporary quilt exhibits, the uses of quilts, and quilts from different cultures. Still other students can contact a local crafts shop for further information. Have each student prepare a written report and give a brief oral presentation. ✲

⌘ Connections

Across the Humanities. To help students understand the father's actions in "My Father's Song," ask them to research Acoma attitudes toward nature. Then have them write an essay explaining how the events in the poem illustrate these attitudes.

ResourceBank

For the Teacher. Bozo, Maria del Carmen, Beverly Silva, and Carmen Valle, eds. *Nosotras: Latin Literature Today*. Binghamton, N.Y.: BRP, 1986.

Ortiz, Simon. *Fightin'—New and Collected Stories*. New York: Thunder's Mouth, 1983.

"Women and Literature." (Symposium). *English Journal* 78 (October 1989): 29–60.

IdeaBank

✏ **Self-Assessment.** To help students evaluate their understanding of sound devices, have them do the following:

1. Write a sentence that contains alliteration.
2. Write a sentence that contains consonance.
3. Write a sentence that contains assonance.

Have them compare their sentences to poems in this text in which alliteration, consonance, or assonance appear. ✏

❷ Content Quiz

1. In "My Mother Pieced Quilts," the mother uses the cracked linoleum floor as a drawing board.

2. The black silk comes from a garment that the mother wore to the grandmother's funeral.

3. One of the pictures the mother makes in "My Mother Pieced Quilts" is [Students may name either one.] a little boy reclining; a swallow flying.

4. In "My Father's Song," the speaker recalls when he and his father were planting corn one spring.

5. The speaker and his father in "My Father's Song" accidentally disturb the burrow nest of a mouse.

Guidelines for Response

Thinking About the Poems, pages 65 and 66

1. In responding to the first poem, students might describe their admiration for the mother's artistry, their curiosity about the family in the poem, their recollection of their own parents' love, or a memory of something a family member made by hand, such as a toy or embroidery. Students may say that the second poem elicits sadness, gratitude, or reverence; it may conjure up memories of loss, pride in helping adults, or learning an important lesson.

2. Students may suggest that the speaker in "My Father's Song" appreciates the wonder and beauty of life when he touches the mice and the soft, damp sand. Students may suggest that the speaker values his father's effort to teach him reverence for life and misses his father's wisdom and tenderness. Students may suggest that the speaker in "My Mother Pieced Quilts" realizes that the quilts were more than warm blankets. The speaker seems to appreciate the love and skill that went into making the quilts as well as the scraps of the past they contain. Students may include the fact that the quilts remind the speaker of different seasons, homes, and events from childhood.

3. Students may suggest that a song is a work of art that expresses deep emotions and can be passed to other generations. They may perceive a connection between the mother's impulse to create quilts, the father's role in teaching his son about life, and a joyous song that celebrates life. Students might also note that as artifacts of a family's life, the quilts continue to "sing on," to communicate their message to future generations. Some students may interpret "My Father's Song" to mean that the son himself is his father's "song" in that he, like the quilts, can carry lessons he learns from his father into adulthood and pass them on to others.

4. Some students may feel that the first poem would not be as joyous, uplifting, or poignant. They might feel that unhappy memories would undercut the happy memories depicted on the quilts. Others may feel that they would react unsympathetically to the son in the second poem, or they would view the father as less kind or gentle. Some students may feel that they would not react differently, since the poems address the basic issues of life.

5. Students who feel that Acosta is successful may cite her appeal to sight, sound, and touch, and her use of figurative language in comparing the quilts to weapons, canvases, and faces. They may note the speaker's feelings—respect, admiration, wonder, amazement, love—and identify similar feelings in themselves. Students who feel that Ortiz is successful may note his appeal to sight, sound, and touch. They may appreciate the fact that the speaker misses his father but has gained a respect for nature and for his father's life experience. Students who do not find Acosta or Ortiz successful may indicate that their own childhood experiences were very different from those of the poets and that the poems did not help them understand or appreciate the poets' memories.

6. Students who believe that the mother created quilts out of necessity may mention lines 1–4; those who believe she desired a means of expression may cite lines 13–17, lines 27–36, and lines 39–40. Some students may also suggest that the mother made quilts to pass the time, to relax, to use up old scraps of fabric, or to give as gifts of love.

7. Students may identify evidence of "parent-reverence" in the poem, including the speaker's comment about missing his father (stanza 1), and the fact that the speaker seems to cherish this memory of his father from his childhood.

Analyzing the Writer's Craft, page 66

Students' examples of alliteration might include *star, somber, silk* (first poem, lines 35–36) and *tiny, told, touch* (second poem, lines 18–20). Students' examples of consonance might include *fields, wards, braids* (first poem, lines 47–50) and *shade, sand, clod* (second poem, lines 22–23). Students' examples of assonance might include *river, five, spinach* (first poem, lines 46–47) and *furrow, plowshare, burrow* (second poem, lines 14–16). Students' responses about the overall effect of the sound devices will vary, depending on the examples they identify.

NAME ______________________ DATE ______________

My Mother Pieced Quilts (page 61)

My Father's Song (page 61)

Open-Book Test

Part 1 Broad Interpretation

Answer the following essay questions based on your understanding of the poems. Write your answers on a separate sheet of paper. (*20 points each*)

1. How would you explain the significance of the quilts to the speaker? to her mother? Explain your answers.
2. What do you think is revealed about the father of the speaker in "My Father's Song"? Explain your answer.
3. How do the speakers of these two poems seem to feel about their parents? Support your answer with details from the poems.

Part 2 Close Interpretation

A. In the boxes below, mark the sense or senses to which the imagery in each quotation appeals. (*4 points each*)

	Sight	Hearing	Taste	Touch	Smell
1. "october ripened canvases"					
2. "passed my hand across their cloth faces"					
3. "our cracked linoleum floor the drawing board"					
4. "His voice, the slight catch, / the depth from his thin chest"					
5. "Very gently, he scooped tiny pink animals / into the palm of his hand"					
6. "the very softness / of cool and warm sand and tiny alive mice"					

NAME ______________________________ DATE ______________

B. In each box write the words from the quotation that illustrate each technique—alliteration, assonance, and consonance—and underline the letters that make the sound. For the last item, choose a quotation that you like from one of the poems. If there are no words in a quotation that illustrate a technique, write None in the appropriate box. (*4 points each*)

	Alliteration (the repetition of consonant sounds at the beginnings of words)	Assonance (the repetition of vowel sounds within words)	Consonance (the repetition of consonant sounds within and at the ends of words)
7. "then cemented them / with your thread / a steel needle / a thimble"			
8. "you were the river current / carrying the roaring notes"			
9. "the plowshare had unearthed / the burrow nest of a mouse"			
10.			

Sweet Potato Pie

Eugenia Collier

page 67

- **Vocabulary Worksheet,** TG page 81
- **Test,** TG pages 83 and 84

Objectives

1. To respond to a short story that explores a family reminiscence.

2. To practice the reading and thinking techniques of an independent reader.

Plot Summary

Buddy is in New York City to attend a professional meeting and, with feelings of deep love, watches his brother from his hotel window and begins to reminisce. As the youngest child of sharecroppers, he recalls his parents as shadowy figures whose presence was clear only on special occasions, such as paydays and church on Sundays. His strongest memories revolve around his siblings, especially Lil and Charley who helped raise him. As Buddy reminisces, he remembers that the family's hopes for education centered on him; indeed, he completed high school as class valedictorian and later went to college and became a professor. That afternoon, Buddy had left the meeting to surprise Charley at his Harlem home. After dinner, Charley's wife, Bea, had given Buddy the remains of a delicious sweet potato pie to take with him, and Charley had driven him back to his hotel in his cab. At the hotel Charley had insisted that Buddy give him back the pie because carrying a brown paper bag would have been undignified. Buddy had handed back the pie in resignation and entered the hotel. At the elevator he had glanced back and seen Charley, proudly carrying the sweet potato pie.

IdeaBank

▲ Motivation. Have students recall an incident from their past—one that they feel helped form their character today. Suggest that they complete this sentence to help them gather their ideas: "I am the person I am today because when I was a child, . . ." Have students record this incident in their journals, explaining its contribution to their character. Now have students read the story and notice how incidents from the narrator's childhood have influenced him. ▲

IdeaBank

❖ Cooperative Learning. Have small groups of students use a round-table format to find examples of characterization in "Sweet Potato Pie." Assign each group a major or minor character from the story (Mama, Pa, Charley, Lil, Buddy, Alberta, Jamie, Bea, Mary, Lucy). Then have each group show how Eugenia Collier uses physical description; speech, thoughts, feelings, or actions; or the narrator's direct comments to characterize its assigned character. Assign one student to act as recorder for each group and another to report the group's examples to the class. ❖

"The fact of my blackness is the core and center of my creativity."

— Eugenia Collier

InformationBank

Historical Note. Sharecropping arose after the Civil War and was a farm-tenancy system, common in southeastern states where cotton plantations provided a demand for labor. In the sharecropping system a family worked the fields in return for a share of the profits from the crop they produced. The farm owner provided equipment, animals, seed, and living quarters for these sharecroppers. As more modern, mechanized forms of farming were invented, sharecropping became unprofitable for the farm owners.

IdeaBank

✱ Limited English Proficient Students

1. To help LEP students understand the structure of "Sweet Potato Pie," point out the flashback that begins with the third paragraph of the story and ends on page 71. Explain that a flashback is an interruption in the continuity of a story by a description of events that happened at an earlier time.

2. To help LEP students understand the different dialects of English used in dialogue, create a chart on the board and list examples of nonstandard English (for example, *whyn't, ax, git, out'n, gon*). Assist students in "translating" these words into standard English (*why didn't, ask, get, out of, going to*). ✱

IdeaBank

✤ **Multimodal Activity.** Have students create a sixty-second TV or radio commercial that shows Buddy urging high-school students to stay in school. Direct students to use details from the story to create antidropout slogans and messages. ✤

Tips from the Classroom

The sweet potato pie in the story serves as a symbol. Ask students to describe in their journals what the pie symbolizes to each brother. Then ask students to think of a symbol from their own youth and describe it in their journals.

Nancy Schultz Potter
Shorecrest High School
Seattle, WA

ResourceBank

For the Student. Scanlon, P. M. "Reading Fiction with Structure (alism)," *English Journal* 72 (October 1988): 57–59.

Guidelines for Response

Discussion Questions

1. Why do you think it was so important to Charley that Buddy not be seen carrying a paper bag through the lobby?

[Students may point out that Charley is very proud that Buddy is "somebody," an important person whom people respect and admire. They may suggest that for Charley, the brown bag is a symbol of the poverty and the rural, simple life that Buddy has left behind. Other students may feel that Charley shares Buddy's successes vicariously.]

2. How would you describe the relationship that Buddy and Charley share?

[Since Charley was the oldest child and responsible for raising Buddy, students may point out that the two nearly share a father-son relationship. Other students may suggest that these two brothers share a deep love and mutual respect for each other, and Buddy feels gratitude for all that Charley has done for him.]

3. Of what importance was family life in the shaping of Buddy's and Charley's lives and characters?

[Some students may suggest that even though Buddy and Charley's family was poor, they shared a close-knit, loving relationship in which everyone looked out for everyone else. Students may feel that this sense of family supported Buddy in his efforts and motivated him to do his best in school. Others may believe that Charley's lack of bitterness towards his brother's success stems from his strong family ties and the feeling that the success of any family member reflects on all the others.]

4. If you were Charley, how would you feel if you compared your life to Buddy's?

[Students' answers will vary. Some students may suggest that they would be bitter that Buddy had been the one to have all the advantages. As support for these feelings, they may cite the fact that Charley was never able to develop his artistic talent. Other students may believe that they would share in Buddy's success the way Charley does, being proud of the positive influence Charley had on Buddy as a young boy.]

⌘ Connections

Across the Language Arts. Eugenia Collier uses particularly effective modifiers in this story, such as "her *dark* face *stern*," "*well-modeled* features," and "Charley's voice *low* and *terrible*." Ask students to write their own descriptions of someone they know well, using precise modifiers to create a strong characterization.

If the grammar and composition book you use has a lesson on using modifiers, you may want to refer to this lesson.

Across the Humanities. Have students research and present brief lectures on an aspect of black heritage, including the Harlem Renaissance of the 1920's; notable scientists, statesmen, entertainers, musicians, and artists; customs, beliefs, traditions, and practices. Encourage students to use slides, photographs, documents, and other visual aids.

❓ Content Quiz

1. Why did Charley help raise Buddy? Their parents were sharecroppers who worked all day.
2. Buddy remembers his parents clearly only on special occasions. Name one of those occasions. on the day the sharecroppers were paid; at church on Sundays
3. What success of Buddy's did the entire family share? his graduation from high school as class valedictorian
4. What did Bea give Buddy to take back to his hotel? the remains of a sweet potato pie
5. Who carried the brown paper bag into the hotel? Charley

NAME ____ DATE ______________

Sweet Potato Pie (page 67)

Vocabulary Worksheet

Essential Vocabulary

apex *n.* The highest point.
entity *n.* A thing or being that has a real existence, as distinguished from a mere function.
ubiquitous *adj.* Present, or seeming to be present, everywhere at the same time.

Useful Words

edifice *n.* A building, especially one that is large or looks important.
err *v.* To do something wrong; sin.
gaunt *adj.* Thin, bony, and hollow-eyed.
inscrutable *adj.* Mysterious; not easy to understand.
ominously *adv.* Threateningly; sinisterly.

Write on a separate sheet of paper all the words you can find that go from left to right or top to bottom in the puzzle.

A	N	G	R	Y	F	A	D	L
R	P	A	P	E	R	W	U	W
I	F	T	F	N	T	O	P	R
G	E	O	O	D	E	R	N	O
H	A	B	R	I	C	K	F	N
T	R	E	M	L	O	V	E	G
G	A	C	L	E	A	R	H	O

Now, use eight of these words to fill in the sets of blanks in the following sentences. If you cannot find a word that fits, look at the puzzle again.

1. Too much __ __ __ __ can make a person **gaunt**.
2. A style or custom that is **ubiquitous**, but only for awhile, is a __ __ __.
3. One who longs to get to the **apex** yearns to arrive at the __ __ __.
4. Jane's plans call for an **edifice** made of __ __ __ __ __ __.
5. A look, gesture, or message that is **inscrutable** is one with a meaning that isn't __ __ __ __ __ __.
6. As usual, you **erred**. Don't you ever do anything __ __ __ __ __?
7. It is reasonable to feel __ __ __ __ __ in response to someone who speaks **ominously**.
8. Treating emotions as **entities** allows us to speak of them as, for example, "clutching" at us. This way of describing feelings suggests that they have a real, physical __ __ __ __ __.

NAME ______________________ DATE ______________

Sweet Potato Pie (page 67)

Test

Part 1 Broad Interpretation

Answer the following essay questions based on your understanding of the story. Write your answers on a separate sheet of paper. (*20 points each*)

1. Why do you think Charley carries the sweet potato pie into the hotel after the narrator agrees to leave it behind? Explain your answer.
2. How do you think Charley feels about never having had the opportunity to develop his own skills or potential? How do you feel about Charley's lost opportunities? Explain your answers.
3. Eugenia Collier, the author of this story, has said, "The fact of my blackness is the core and center of my creativity." Do you think that Buddy might also say the same of himself? Explain your answer.

Part 2 Close Interpretation

A. Although Buddy and Charley are brothers, they have led very different lives. One basic reason for the differences in their lives centers on the opportunities available to them. In the box on the left, identify the main reasons that Buddy had greater opportunities than Charley did as a child. In the box on the right, identify the main reasons that Buddy has greater opportunities than Charley does as an adult. (*10 points*)

AS A CHILD	AS AN ADULT

B. Think about what sweet potato pie represents to Charley and what it represents to Buddy. Then, in the appropriate boxes, list some of your ideas. (*10 points*)

CHARLEY	BUDDY

NAME ______________________________ DATE ______________

C. Sometimes it is not clear which of two characters in a story is the protagonist—the most important character who usually gains the reader's strongest sympathy or interest. The antagonist is the character or force against which the protagonist is pitted. Think about who might be the protagonist in this story and who or what might be the antagonist. Then write brief notes reflecting your thoughts in the boxes below. *(20 points)*

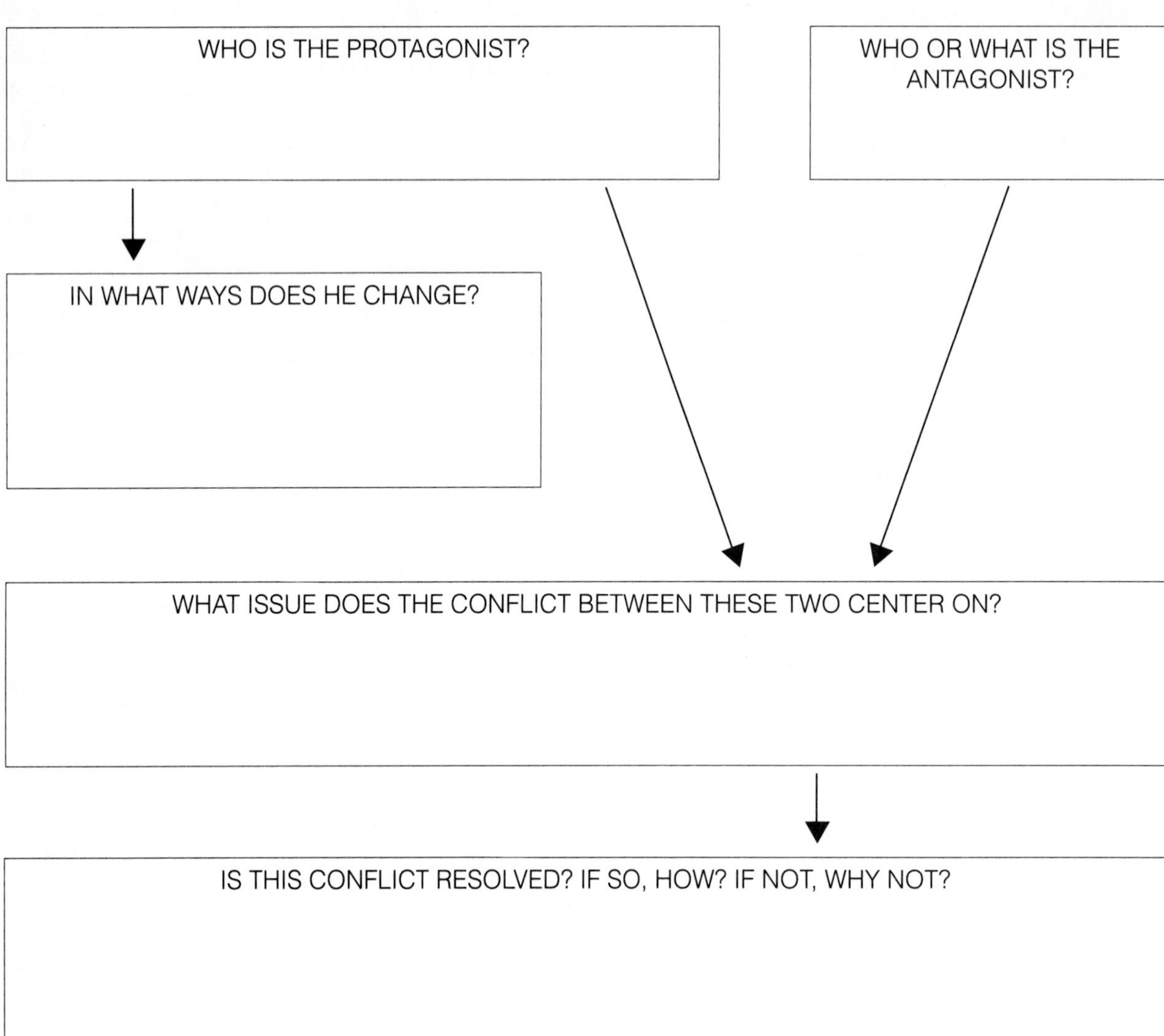
WHO IS THE PROTAGONIST?
WHO OR WHAT IS THE ANTAGONIST?
IN WHAT WAYS DOES HE CHANGE?
WHAT ISSUE DOES THE CONFLICT BETWEEN THESE TWO CENTER ON?
IS THIS CONFLICT RESOLVED? IF SO, HOW? IF NOT, WHY NOT?

Parents and Children: Transmitting Cultural Values

Below are suggested answers for the chart assigned on page 75 of the student book. Listed are the titles of eight other selections, the names of parents or parent figures, and the values transmitted. Accept other answers if students can support them with evidence from the selections.

Title	Parent	Values
The Legend of Gregorio Cortez	Guitarreros	bravery, loyalty, responsibility, honesty, self-sacrifice
From the Poets in the Kitchen	mother and friends	love of language, appreciation of the power of the spoken word and the poetry of everyday speech
The Way It Is	mother	strong sense of self-worth, pride in being black
Mother to Son	mother	determination, perseverance, strength of spirit
Lineage	grandmothers	strength of character, joy in living
Women	mother and others of her generation	determination, sacrifice for children, importance of education
Everyday Use	narrator	personal involvement with heritage, love of family, endurance
Sweet Potato Pie	Charley	responsibility for family members, personal dignity, self-sacrifice

Evaluation Guide for Writing Assignment

The well-developed student essay will meet the following criteria:

- Identifies values portrayed in the selections read
- Provides examples from the selections for the values identified
- Contains a statement of the student's personal values
- Shows parallels between the student's values and those identified in the selections

UNIT 2 Opposing Injustice

Selections	Essential Vocabulary	Literary Skills	Writing Formats	Writing Modes
***from* To Be A Slave**				
Student Book page 80 **Teacher's Guide** Lesson, pages 88 and 89 Vocabulary Worksheet, page 90 Test, pages 91 and 92	susceptible inexhaustible align stupor	historical writing	journal transcript essay monologue poem song notes informal outline	expressive and personal writing observation and description narrative and imaginative writing informative (expository) writing: classification informative (expository) writing: synthesis
***from* Narrative of the Life of Frederick Douglass, an American Slave**				
Student Book page 86 **Teacher's Guide** Lesson, pages 93–95 Vocabulary Worksheet, page 96 Test, pages 97 and 98	elasticity languished epoch	conflict autobiography	journal introduction speech eulogy time line autobiographical sketch oral history recommendation director's notes	expressive and personal writing narrative and imaginative writing informative (expository) writing: synthesis persuasion writing about literature
As I Grew Older **Any Human to Another**				
Student Book page 96 **Teacher's Guide** Lesson, pages 99 and 100 Vocabulary Worksheet, page 101 Test, pages 103 and 104	marrow diverse unsheathed	figurative language	journal	expressive and personal writing
***from* Letter from Birmingham Jail**				
Student Book page 101 **Teacher's Guide** Lesson, pages 105–107 Vocabulary Worksheet, page 108 Test, pages 109 and 110	moratorium rabid anarchy paternalistically	persuasion	journal notes verdict letter editorial booklet captions time line photo essay	expressive and personal writing observation and description narrative and imaginative writing informative (expository) writing: classification informative (expository) writing: analysis informative (expository) writing: synthesis persuasion
***from* Farewell to Manzanar**				
Student Book page 111 **Teacher's Guide** Lesson, pages 111 and 112 Test, pages 113 and 114		setting mood irony	journal memoir poem conversation dramatic scene collage personal essay expository essay report	expressive and personal writing narrative and imaginative writing informative (expository) writing: analysis informative (expository) writing: synthesis persuasion writing about literature report

Selections	Essential Vocabulary	Literary Skills	Writing Formats	Writing Modes
Blues Ain't No Mockin Bird				
Student Book page 119 **Teacher's Guide** Lesson, pages 115 and 116 Test, pages 117 and 118		theme	journal episode dramatic scene guidelines letter of complaint evaluation recommendation	expressive and personal writing narrative and imaginative writing informative (expository) writing: analysis informative (expository) writing: synthesis persuasion writing about literature
November Cotton Flower **A Note of Humility**				
Student Book page 128 **Teacher's Guide** Lesson, pages 119 and 120 Vocabulary Worksheet, page 121 Test, pages 123 and 124	assumed meager	The student book does not contain discussion questions, analysis of literary techniques, or writing assignments for these poems. These materials appear in the Teacher's Guide lesson.		
The Censors				
Student Book page 130 **Teacher's Guide** Lesson, pages 125–127 Test, pages 129 and 130		The student book does not contain discussion questions, analysis of literary techniques, or writing assignments for this story. These materials appear in the Teacher's Guide lesson.		
Reviewing Concepts				
Student Book page 133 **Teacher's Guide** page 131				

from To Be a Slave

Julius Lester

page 80

- **Vocabulary Worksheet,** TG page 90
- **Test,** TG pages 91 and 92

Objectives

1. To respond to an essay on the slave trade and understand the concepts of freedom and slavery.

2. To express ideas in a variety of writing formats: journal, transcript, essay, monologue, poem/song, notes, informal outline.

Summary

Julius Lester describes the historical roots of the African slave trade, first in Europe and then in the New World. He explains that initially the colonists tried unsuccessfully to use Native Americans as a source of cheap labor. Then they attempted to use poor people, prisoners, and debtors from Europe as indentured servants. Eventually, however, the colonists found that black slaves imported from Africa were easier to keep and more adaptable than other laborers. Lester includes excerpts from a first-person narrative by an African who describes his capture and the terrible hardships of his ocean voyage to the colonies.

IdeaBank

▲ **Motivation.** As an extension of the Connecting Writing and Reading activity, ask students to reflect on the kinds of freedoms they enjoy. On the board create two lists under the following headings:

Freedom from . . .	Freedom to . . .

Then have students brainstorm as you write their ideas under the appropriate headings. Finally, have students discuss what they think their lives would be like without these freedoms. ▲

"No man can put a chain about the ankle of his fellow man without at last finding the other end fastened about his own neck."

— Frederick Douglass, Civil Rights Meeting, Washington, D.C., October 22, 1883

IdeaBank

✤ Multimodal Activities

1. Have several students create and perform a dialogue between several captured Africans in the hold of a slave ship during the voyage across the Atlantic.

2. From the early 1700's until the Civil War, antislavery groups in America and England published slave narratives in an effort to shape opinion against the slave trade. Ask students to imagine that they are publishing the first-person narrative in this selection as an abolitionist pamphlet. Ask them to create an illustration for the pamphlet, depicting what they see as the most terrible or frightening moment in the narrative. ✤

InformationBank

Literary Note. This excerpt was taken from the prologue of Lester's history of slavery in the United States. It was cut to delete some graphic descriptions of brutality that Lester includes from other sources and to make a coherent narrative with Charles Ball's autobiography as the only source of quotations.

IdeaBank

✲ **Collaborative Learning.** Help the class compile a list of people who were instrumental in the antislavery movement. Divide the class into groups of three or four students, and have each group choose a figure from the list to report on to the class. Ask students to consider some of the following questions as they research: Do you consider this person a hero? Was this person considered a hero in his or her lifetime? Did this person endure additional hardships due to working for his or her beliefs? Did a particular person or event inspire him or her to participate in the struggle against slavery? Have each group orally present its findings to the class. ✲

InformationBank

Historical Note. In 1750 there were about 200,000 slaves in the colonies. By 1860 the number had grown to about four million, almost all of these in thirteen southern states. Only about one fourth of all the whites in slave states (about 45,000 plantation owners) owned slaves or belonged to a family that owned them.

ResourceBank

For the Student. Lester, Julius. *Do Lord Remember Me*. New York: Holt, Rinehart, and Winston, 1985.

———. *Long Journey Home*. New York: Dial Press, 1972.

Guidelines for Response

Thinking About the Selection, pages 84 and 85

1. Students will have varied impressions of the slave trade. Some will focus mainly on its inhumanity; others will be surprised and perhaps impressed by how extensive and well organized it was. Some may be surprised at the complicity of many African chieftains, and some may find it odd that the first slave ship would sail from Puritan Massachusetts.

2. Responses will vary. Some students may mention particular atrocities, such as the killing of infants (page 83) or the horrendous conditions in the hold of a slave ship.

3. Many students will point out that Africans sold into slavery usually lost their loved ones, including both family and friends, and all their possessions. Moreover, they lost their homeland and in most cases their culture, including their language. Some students may mention that, according to Lester, the cultural losses were greatest for those slaves brought to the United States.

4. Students might mention that the captured slaves needed physical strength and endurance, for the voyage across the Atlantic was long and their living conditions deplorable. Often they arrived sick and malnourished. Some students may stress that the slaves needed courage and spiritual strength to endure separation from homeland and family and the prospect of a life of misery. Other students may note that the slaves also needed adaptability and the hope that somehow things would get better.

5. Some students may think that if Lester had included the point of view of a slave trader, the trader would probably be trying to justify his behavior. This rationalization might increase a reader's sympathy for the captured Africans. Conversely, other students might say that a slave trader might present all slave traders in a less villainous light. The overall effect on the selection would depend greatly on the perspective and sentiments of the particular trader.

6. Many students will find the firsthand account by the captured African very moving and vivid. It adds specificity and immediacy to Lester's analysis. Some students may feel that the slave's account drives home the wretched inhumanity of slavery more than Lester's historical account does.

7. Responses will vary. Some students may mention that the slave trade has had an enormous impact on the history and culture of the United States. These students may note that Americans who have not learned about the system in which tens of millions of Africans were captured, chained, and transported to America are unaware of a formative part of early United States history. Other students may assert that Americans today should know about the terrible injustice endured by African Americans. These students may cite details provided by Lester, such as the horrible ordeal of the slave woman struggling to free herself while watching her child drown. Some students may assert that learning about the slave trade instills a deep appreciation for the strength of spirit that enabled African Americans to survive and eventually triumph over this injustice.

Connecting Reading and Writing, page 85

Make sure that students are familiar with the format of daytime talk shows, such as Oprah Winfrey's and Geraldo Rivera's.

Students might prefer to compose the slave's monologue, poem, or song in small groups.

For assignment 3, suggest that four or five people work together on their oral reports to present a panel discussion.

If the grammar and composition book you use has a lesson on oral history, you may want to refer to this lesson.

❷ Content Quiz

1. At first the colonists tried to use __Indians__ as laborers.

2. Most of the slaves brought to the colonies came from the western part of __Africa__ .

3. According to his firsthand account, the captured African was transported on a __log raft__ down the river to the slave ship.

4. As the slaves were being put in irons, two women __jumped overboard__ in an attempt to save their babies' lives.

5. __The United States__ developed a system of slavery that was more cruel than that of any other country.

NAME ______________________________ DATE ______________

from To Be a Slave (page 80)

Vocabulary Worksheet

Essential Vocabulary

align
inexhaustible
stupor
susceptible

Useful Word

evolve

Read the following poem and use the context clues to figure out the meanings of the underlined words. Then, use these meanings to help you work the exercise below. If you like, you may use a dictionary to check the meaning of a word.

They say I am **susceptible** to l♥ve and all its charms.
They say I'm just a sucker for r♥mance.
I'll listen to old l♥ve s♥ngs for forever and a day,
Or sing them, if you give me half a chance.

I fall into a **stupor** at the thought of valentines.
Upon my silken couch I faint and sigh.
I simply can't begin to get enough of hearts and fl♥wers.
I need an **inexhaustible** supply.

My l♥ve for l♥ve did not **evolve** as I grew through the years—
No, all at once, at ten, I saw the light.
And now I wear these hearts upon my sleeve, my hat, my sh♥es,
And put them into everything I write.

Yes, I **align** with Cupid; I'm his partner and his pal.
The only time I treat him angrily
Is when the person falling into l♥ve (poor, helpless f♥♥l!)—
The one who feels his arr♥w's sting—is me.

Match each underlined word in the poem with the correct definition below.

______________ **1.** Develop gradually over a period of time.

______________ **2.** Incapable of being used up.

______________ **3.** Easily affected; sensitive; unresistant.

______________ **4.** A state in which the mind and senses are numbed.

______________ **5.** Cooperate or take sides with.

from To Be a Slave (page 80)

Test

Part 1 Broad Interpretation

A. Answer the following essay questions based on your understanding of the selection. Write your answers on a separate sheet of paper. (*15 points each*)

1. Do you think there is a possible justification for the colonists' using slave labor? If so, what is it? If not, what else might the colonists have done? Explain your answers.
2. Who do you think was the most despicable of the people involved in the slave trade: the African chieftain, the slave ship's white captain, or the plantation owner? Who do you think was the most responsible for the continuation of the African slave trade? Explain your answers.

B. Think about the account in the selection of the slave's capture in Africa, his ocean passage, and his arrival in America. Then imagine that you were able to interview him. Briefly note his possible responses to the questions given on the chart below. (*18 points*)

	CAPTURE	PASSAGE	ARRIVAL
3. "What was the most terrible thing that happened to you or that you saw?"			
4. "What was your greatest fear, or what did you miss the most?"			

NAME ____________________ DATE ____________

	CAPTURE	PASSAGE	ARRIVAL
5. "What was most important in helping you to survive?"			

Part 2 Close Interpretation

Write the letter of the best answer. Where noted, there may be more than one answer. *(8 points each)*

_____ **1.** According to the selection, in which of the following regions was African slavery first introduced?

a. Europe. **c.** South America.
b. The Caribbean. **d.** North America.

_____ **2.** According to the selection, which of the following is true of Africans in the New World? (*You may choose more than one answer.*)

a. They were the chief source of indentured servants.

b. They were among the first non-Native Americans to explore the New World.

c. They were abused by their African captors as well as by the white slave traders.

d. As slaves in the North American colonies, they were encouraged to maintain their African traditions.

from Narrative of the Life of Frederick Douglass, an American Slave

Frederick Douglass

page 86

- **Vocabulary Worksheet,** TG page 96
- **Test,** TG pages 97 and 98

Objectives

1. To respond to an autobiographical selection that describes the life of a slave.

2. To evaluate subjective and objective writing in an autobiography.

3. To express ideas in a variety of writing formats: journal, introduction, speech, eulogy, time line, autobiographical sketch, oral history, recommendation, director's notes.

Summary

In this excerpt from his autobiography, former slave Frederick Douglass describes his experiences when he is rented by his owner to Mr. Covey, a man who has a reputation as a slave breaker. Douglass relates how his harsh treatment at Covey's hands during the first six months breaks him "in body, soul, and spirit." Fearing for his life, Douglass runs back to his owner to plead for protection, but Douglass's owner forces him to return to Covey. When Covey attempts to tie him up and beat him, Douglass fights him off. Douglass marks this incident as a turning point—one that restores his manhood and self-confidence and makes him again determined to seek his freedom.

Tips from the Classroom

Douglass once said, "I have found that to make a contented slave it is necessary to make a thoughtless one." Write this quotation on the board and challenge students to find illustrations of its truth in the *Narrative.* In what way does slavery also depend upon the ignorance of slave owners? In what other ways are people "enslaved" by their ignorance?

T. R. Kerth
Maine South High School
Park Ridge, IL

IdeaBank

▲ **Motivation.** To extend the Connecting Writing and Reading activity, have students share their ideas in a group discussion, or have them create cluster diagrams for the word *slavery*. Have students add words and phrases to the diagram as they read the selection. ▲

InformationBank

Literary Note. This excerpt is half of a chapter from *Narrative of the Life of Frederick Douglass*. Among the deletions was one paragraph about a woman slave used as a breeder and a long passage that is a tangent from the story.

InformationBank

Biographical Note. When he fled from slavery to Massachusetts in 1838, Frederick Augustus Washington Bailey changed his name to Frederick Douglass in order to avoid being captured and returned to his master. In Massachusetts, however, he found that he had not completely escaped racial prejudice. He lost his first job in a shipyard when the other men, who were white, refused to work with him. During the 1840's, Douglass organized protests in Massachusetts against segregated seating on trains and in churches. Approximately ten years later, in Rochester, New York, he led attacks on discriminatory hiring practices and against segregated schools.

IdeaBank

✤ **Multimodal Activities**

1. Have students act out and tape-record a series of interviews by a reporter from an abolitionist newspaper with the following people: Mr. Covey, Master Thomas, Sandy Jenkins, and William Hughes. What version of the events in this selection would each person offer?

2. Have students design a newspaper advertisement announcing the publication of *Narrative of the Life of Frederick Douglass* in 1845. As an extension to this activity, students might design a dust jacket for a modern edition of this autobiography, including a picture or a design on the front; a synopsis, a photocopy of a picture of Douglass, and a brief biography on the inside flaps of the jacket; and reviewers' comments on the back. ✤

IdeaBank

❃ **Learning Disabled Students.** To help students visualize Douglass's descriptions of men working with oxen or threshing grain, provide pictures or explain how that work was done. For example, oxen are led rather than driven from behind like horses. Thus Douglass was in danger of being trampled by the oxen and run over by the cart. Threshing, or fanning, was done by a machine that separated kernels of grain from stalks. The early machines were powered by horses walking a treadmill, while a revolving cylinder knocked the kernels off the stalks and a fan blew away the husks. The machine was stationary, and the farmhands had to pick up the large bundles of wheat in the fields and carry them to the machine. When Douglass collapsed doing this work, the threshing of the wheat stopped. ❃

InformationBank

Historical Note. In his autobiography, Frederick Douglass records the allotment of clothing given to slaves: two coarse linen shirts, one pair of linen trousers, one jacket, one pair of winter trousers made of coarse "Negro cloth," one pair of stockings, and one pair of shoes, "the whole of which," he writes, "could not have cost more than seven dollars." Children too young to work were given only two coarse linen shirts per year. When these wore out, they went naked.

⌘ Connections

Across Literature. Students may wish to compare and contrast Douglass's view of the African-American experience with the views of Julius Lester (from *To Be a Slave*), Richard Wright (from *American Hunger*), and James Baldwin (from *Notes of a Native Son*).

ResourceBank

For the Student. Davis, Ossie. *Escape to Freedom: A Play About Young Frederick Douglass.* New York: Viking Press, 1978.

Free at Last. A history of black America with a view of Frederick Douglass. Indiana University, 1965. 16mm black/white 30 min. film.

For the Teacher. Foner, Philip S., ed. *Frederick Douglass on Women's Rights.* Westport, Conn.: Greenwood Press, 1976.

McFeely, William S. *Frederick Douglass.* New York: W. W. Norton and Co., Inc., 1990.

IdeaBank

❧ **Gifted and Talented Students.** Have students prepare a proposal to a television network for a show based on this selection to be shown during Black History Month. The proposal should provide reasons for learning about Frederick Douglass and why this episode in his life is particularly important. The proposal can also include a tentative cast of well-known actors. As an alternative, you might suggest that some students read the entire *Narrative* and then pitch a proposal for a miniseries based on the entire book. ❧

IdeaBank

★ **Interactive Assessment.** Have students who did assignment 3 in Connecting Reading and Writing work in pairs as peer reviewers, using the following questions as an evaluation guideline:

- Is enough background information given so that the setting and the story are clear?
- Is there a logical sequence to the events described?
- Are the characters clearly described?
- Is dialogue used effectively?
- Are both objective descriptions and subjective reactions provided?
- Is any part of the autobiographical sketch unclear or hard to understand?
- What details might be added or deleted?
- Are precise verbs, nouns, and modifiers used?
- Is figurative language used, as appropriate? ★

❓ Content Quiz

1. Frederick Douglass receives his first beating from Mr. Covey because an ox cart damages a gate.
2. Mr. Covey is known as the snake among the slaves because he secretly watches them while they work.
3. After collapsing and being hit on the head by Mr. Covey, Douglass runs away to St. Michael's to beg Master Thomas for protection.
4. The slave Sandy Jenkins gives Douglass a root that he believes will protect Douglass from being beaten.
5. After Douglass fights Mr. Covey, Covey never beats him again.

Guidelines for Response

Thinking About the Selection, pages 92–93

1. Responses will vary. Many students will feel admiration for Douglass because of his courage in fighting back against the bullying Mr. Covey. Others will wonder why he did not escape for another four years.

2. Students may observe that Douglass sees the distinction between fighting and being whipped as parallel to the distinction between being a "slave in form" and a "slave in fact" (page 92). If Douglass were whipped, students may argue, he would feel beaten down, subjugated —once more at the mercy of his beater, once more a "slave in fact." Students may conclude that his ability to feel triumph in "a fight" allows him the dignity of a human being instead of the indignity of a slave.

3. Students may see Douglass's choices revealing all or most of the following characteristics: courage, independence, determination, strength of will. Students may see that all his decisions to stand up to Mr. Covey reflect these qualities. His refusal to take off his clothes to be beaten (page 87) foreshadows his later defiant decisions to return to Master Thomas (page 89), to hide from Mr. Covey (page 90), and finally to fight and persevere against the slave breaker (page 91). Students may find Douglass's strength of will evident throughout the excerpt in his ability to endure his situation. Students may point out that Douglass's agreeing to take the root only to please Sandy (page 91) shows his kindness and gratitude toward those who treat him like a human being.

4. Although some students may feel that Master Thomas is kinder than Mr. Covey, others may see his relationship with Douglass as only slightly less antagonistic than Covey's. They may point out that Mr. Covey is a slave breaker, whose task is to reduce Douglass to the state of a brute. Master Thomas, however, is just as determined that Douglass be broken, though he will not dirty his own hands to do it. The students may mention that Thomas sends Douglass to Mr. Covey twice, the second time dispelling any idea Douglass might have about his sense of mercy or fairness. These students may feel that Master Thomas is worse because he is more hypocritical.

5. Students who may have felt that stories of brutality toward slaves were exaggerated may be shocked at this true account. This excerpt will confirm the impressions of other students. Students will most likely empathize with Douglass and understand the terrible dilemma most slaves faced: perform long hours of brutalizing work or be beaten; try to escape and be beaten or worse.

6. Some students may feel that if Master Thomas had not sent Douglass back to Mr. Covey, Douglass might never have faced that moment of truth when he fought for his humanity and thus may have remained a slave. Others may argue that given such strength of character, Douglass would inevitably have rebelled in some way—even at Master Thomas's plantation—gained his freedom, and achieved the same things.

7. Students may suggest that slavery dehumanizes both slave and master. Douglass says, "I was broken in body, soul, and spirit. . . . behold a man transformed into a brute!" (page 88). Students may propose that both masters, Thomas and Covey, have had their own humanity stripped away in their treatment of Douglass as a creature to be "broken." Douglass says that his bloodied appearance would "affect any but a heart of iron" (page 90), yet it fails to move Thomas.

8. Responses will vary. Some students may mention Douglass's strength of will, which enabled him to fight Mr. Covey for nearly two hours rather than submit to a brutal whipping from this slave breaker. These students may state that without this quality, those fighting injustice today might lose heart and not persevere in the struggles that may exact years of work and sacrifice. Other students may say that intelligence, evident in Douglass's analysis of the consequences of brutal discipline upon his character, is the most valuable quality in fighting injustice today. These students may assert that analyzing the consequences of injustice upon its victims and proposing workable strategies to remedy social ills require intelligence. These students may add that without intelligence, those fighting injustice today will be thwarted in their attempts to persuade others to work toward improving society.

Analyzing the Writer's Craft, page 93

Passages that students may choose include these: "He then went to a large gum tree . . . for similar offenses" (page 87); "If at any one time . . . into a brute!" (page 88); and "You have seen . . . let him do his worst" (page 89). Students may find the first passage primarily objective, except for a few words such as "savagely." They will probably find the second passage more subjective, with expressions such as "bitterest dregs" and "the dark night of slavery." The students may note that the third passage is objective in its descriptions of the events but also subjective in its descriptions of Douglass's feelings.

Connecting Reading and Writing, page 94

For samples of introductions to autobiographies, you may direct students to the library.

For eulogies, students may research newspaper accounts of funerals of very famous people; the *New York Times Index* is a useful resource.

If the grammar and composition book you use has a lesson on autobiography, you may want to refer to this lesson.

NAME ____________________ DATE ____________

from Narrative of the Life of Frederick Douglass (page 86)

Vocabulary Worksheet

Essential Vocabulary

elasticity **epoch** **languish**

Useful Words

dregs **singular** **stupor**

Read the following story and use context clues to figure out the meanings of the underlined words. Then use these meanings to help you work the exercise below. If you like, you may use a dictionary to check the meaning of a word.

"What are you doing?" asked Trudy, peering over her roommate's shoulder while quietly slipping a second piece of pizza out of the box beside her.

"A paper for class," said Nan. "American music in the last fifty years. I'm accepting contributions for the pizza."

"Pretty exciting time," said Trudy, pulling a wadded dollar bill from her jeans pocket and dropping it on the table. "All that vitality, that energy!"

"Oh, come on! Everyone knows American music has been **languishing** since the forties. Aaron Copland was probably the last—"

"Nan, you're out of your mind! What about Big Mama Thornton and Sam Cooke, for starters? Of course, Elvis's recording of 'Hound Dog' marked an **epoch**. Rock-and-roll would never be the same. And obviously the **singular** sound of Chuck Berry changed the face of American music. No one had ever heard anything quite like it. I know a lot of what came along in the late seventies was boring and stupid enough to put any music lover into a **stupor**, but even then something from the Grateful Dead would usually wake you up and bring some feeling back. And I have faith that we're heading toward a rebirth. I mean, bad as it gets sometimes, American music has **elasticity**. It bounces right back. I'll admit that some of the musicians are the **dregs** of humanity—who knows what barrel the producers scraped to get them—but you know others are very good people, and even the jerks sometimes make—"

"Stop!" hollered Nan.

"Oh, come on," said Trudy, taking a bite from her third piece of pizza, "I gave you a buck."

"I mean, stop talking about rock-and-roll. My paper is on American *classical* music."

"Oh," said Trudy. "I didn't know there was any. Why'd you get green pepper on this pizza? You know I hate it."

Match each underlined word in the story with the correct definition below.

____________ 1. Solid material left in the bottom of a container of liquid; the worst or least desirable part of something.

____________ 2. Unusual; out of the ordinary.

____________ 3. The quality of being able to recover quickly.

____________ 4. A state in which the mind and senses are numbed.

____________ 5. Becoming weak.

____________ 6. The beginning of a new and important period in the history of something.

NAME ______________________ DATE ____________

from Narrative of the Life of Frederick Douglass (page 86) Test

Part 1 Broad Interpretation

A. Answer the following essay questions based on your understanding of the selection. Write your answers on a separate sheet of paper. (*15 points each*)

1. Why, in your opinion, is the battle with Covey a turning point for Douglass?
2. What actions does Douglass take to try to improve his situation at Mr. Covey's farm? What do these actions say about Douglass as a person?
3. From this short excerpt, what insights do you get into the realities of slavery? Explain your answer.

B. Think about what slavery does to both the slave and the slaveholder, as revealed in this excerpt from Douglass's autobiography. Then read the quotations below. In the boxes note details from the excerpt that seem to support or contradict the quotation. (*20 points*)

	What in the excerpt supports or contradicts the quotation?
"It is observed by Homer that a man loses half his virtue the day he becomes a slave; he might have added, with truth, that he is likely to lose more than half when he becomes a slave-master."—Richard Whately	
"No one is a slave whose will is free."—Tyrius Maximus	
"It is a common law of nature, which no time will ever change, that superiors shall rule their inferiors."—Dyonysius	

NAME ______________________ DATE ____________

Part 2 Close Interpretation

In the excerpt, Douglass uses a combination of unemotional, objective description and passionate, subjective description. For each quotation below, indicate whether Douglass's language is primarily objective or subjective. Then briefly note whether you think the choice of language is effective and why or why not. (*35 points*)

	Objective or subjective language?	Is the language choice effective? Explain.
"I had been at my new home but one week before Mr. Covey gave me a very severe whipping, cutting my back, causing the blood to run, and raising ridges on my flesh as large as my little finger."		
"His comings were like a thief in the night. He appeared to us as being ever at hand. He was under every tree, behind every stump, in every bush, and at every window, on the plantation."		
"My long-crushed spirit rose, cowardice departed, bold defiance took its place; and I now resolved that, however long I might remain a slave in form, the day had passed forever when I could be a slave in fact."		

As I Grew Older

Langston Hughes

Any Human to Another

Countee Cullen

page 96

- **Vocabulary Worksheet,** TG page 101
- **Test,** TG pages 103 and 104

Objectives

1. To respond to two poems that present ideas about dreams and obstacles.
2. To understand the literary concept of figurative language.

IdeaBank

▲ **Motivation.** As an alternative to the Connecting Writing and Reading activity, ask students to think about their goals in one or more of the following pursuits: art, business, science, music, politics, theater, sports, education, family life, and medicine. Ask students to write their goals in their journals. Then have them read "As I Grew Older" and "Any Human to Another" and compare their goals with the dreams of the speakers of these two poems. ▲

InformationBank

Biographical Note. In 1921, Langston Hughes attended Columbia University in New York City. Unhappy, however, with the path his life was taking, he dropped out of college a year later, traveled in Europe and Africa, and wrote in his spare time. On returning to the United States in 1924, he took a job as a busboy in a hotel in Washington, D.C. When the famous poet Vachel Lindsay visited the hotel, Hughes left three of his poems beside Lindsay's plate on a table in the dining room. Lindsay was so impressed with the poems that he read them aloud at a lecture that very night. Thanks to Lindsay's support, Hughes's first poem was published in a magazine in 1925. A year later, his first book of poems was published. Among other things, publication earned Hughes a scholarship to Lincoln University in Pennsylvania, from which he graduated in 1929.

IdeaBank

✤ **Multimodal Activity.** Langston Hughes was one of the first of the "Jazz Poets," poets who preferred to read their poetry aloud in coffeehouses, accompanied by live, improvisational jazz. Suggest students compose a tune for either "As I Grew Older" or "Any Human to Another." Have them consider various types of music, such as gospel, classical, folk, blues, new age, or jazz. Students may want to perform their compositions or make a recording for the class to hear. ✤

IdeaBank

❃ **Learning Disabled Students.** To help students comprehend the figurative language in "Any Human to Another," have volunteers read each of the five stanzas. Help students to paraphrase each stanza after it is read. Discuss the similes in the first and second stanzas ("ills . . . / Like an arrow," lines 1–3; "grief . . . intertwine / Like sea and river," lines 7–9); the metaphor in the third stanza ("A little tent / Pitched in a meadow / Of sun and shadow," lines 16–18); the personifications of joy and sorrow in the fourth stanza; and the two similes in the last stanza ("grief / Like a blade," lines 25–26, and "sorrow . . . like a crown," lines 30–31). ❃

ResourceBank

For the Student. Cullen, Countee. *Color.* (American Negro: History and Literature Series, Number 3). Salem, N.H.: Ayer Company Publishers, Inc., 1970.

From These Roots. William Greaves Productions, 1974. 16mm, 29 min. film reel.

Langston Hughes: Blues Poet. West Hollywood, Calif.: The Center for Cassette Studies. 29 min.

For the Teacher. Bogumil, M. L., and M. R. Molino. "Pretext, Context, Subtext: Textual Power in the Writing of Langston Hughes, Richard Wright, and Martin Luther King, Jr." *College English* 52 (November 1990): 800–11.

Durham, J. R. "The City in Recent American Fiction: Listening to Black Urban Voices." *College English* 52 (November 1990): 764–75.

Paul, A. "Langston Hughes and the Demands of Art, Politics, Race, and Financial Survival." *The Chronicle of Higher Education* 35 (November 2, 1988): A5–A7.

⌘ Connections

Across Literature. Other works by African Americans that deal with dreams and obstacles include the following: from *Narrative of the Life of Frederick Douglass, an American Slave* by Frederick Douglass; from *To Be Young, Gifted, and Black* by Lorraine Hansberry; and "Choices" by Nikki Giovanni.

Guidelines for Response

Thinking About the Poems, page 99

1. Some students may say that both poems make them feel sad, for both address suffering, prejudice, and denied dreams. Other students may find the poems heartening, for both speakers retain hope and strength.

2. Some students may say that the compassion felt by the speaker in "Any Human to Another" reflects their own sentiments. They may agree with the speaker that "Your grief and mine / Must intertwine" (lines 7–8), and that all humans know the experience of sorrow, which "never scorned to speak / To any . . ." (lines 22–23). These students may argue that our world would be a better place if the speaker's dream for humanity were to come true. Other students may suggest that the speaker's views are unrealistic and that very often people who cry, cry alone. Some may argue that humans would all be dragged down to the same depressing level if everyone were to feel the degree of empathy that the speaker wants.

3. Students may notice that the wall in "As I Grew Older" rose "slowly, slowly" and that it became so tall "it touched the sky" (line 15). They may suggest that the wall rose as the speaker became an adult, for the title of the poem implies this, and the speaker apparently was hopeful as a youth. Students may observe that the wall conceals the speaker's dreams, shutting out light and hope. Some may suggest that the wall represents racial prejudice and that if the wall were destroyed, the speaker could experience again "a thousand lights of sun" (line 31). Other students may say that the wall represents any oppression that prevents adults from attaining their early dreams.

4. Students may say that the speaker of "As I Grew Older" is concerned with racial discrimination and that for this speaker, as for many African Americans, racial prejudice has been a tremendous obstacle. Some students may observe that progress has been made toward combating prejudice since Hughes wrote his poem. Students may point out that in "Any Human to Another" the speaker's dream is that all humans will care about each other and feel each other's sorrows. Some students may suggest that achieving this dream would entail eliminating selfishness, something even more difficult to accomplish than eliminating racial prejudice.

5. Students may say that both poems would be depressing if the speakers expressed a defeatist attitude. They may suggest that the speakers' resiliency and strength give these poems their power. Others may say that the poems would be just as moving if the speakers had been dispirited. These students may say that by expressing a defeatist attitude, the poems would seem more true to life.

6. Students may say that Cullen's theme in "Any Human to Another" is close to Dr. King's definition of altruism; for example, in the final stanza the speaker says, "Your every grief / Like a blade / Shining and unsheathed / Must strike me down" (lines 25–28). Students may suggest that the issue of altruism or empathy is treated indirectly in "As I Grew Older." Some may say that if more people were altruistic, the speaker would not need to "lie down in the shadow" (line 19) and that empathy from others would help the speaker "Break through the wall!" (line 26)

7. Some students may say that racial prejudice is still a major problem and that for many African Americans "the thick wall" (line 22) is still a reality. These students may feel that "As I Grew Older" remains painfully relevant. Others may argue that racial discrimination has diminished since Langston Hughes wrote his poem and that the need for brotherhood and empathy expressed in "Any Human to Another" makes this poem more relevant today.

Analyzing the Writer's Craft, page 100

Students may list "like an arrow" (line 3) as a simile, jotting down words such as *painful* and *penetrating* to suggest their impressions. They may list "like sea and river" (line 9) as a simile, suggesting *flowing* and *intermingling* as impression words. Students may list "A little tent / Pitched in a meadow" (lines 16–17) as a metaphor, citing *isolation* and *oasis* as impression words. Some students may list the simile "Like a blade" (line 26), suggesting *cutting* and *wounding* as impression words. Some students may list as personifications "Joy may be shy, unique, / Friendly . . ." (lines 20–21) and "Sorrow never scorned to speak . . ." (line 22) suggesting *aloofness*, *reserve*, and *familiarity* as impression words.

❓ Content Quiz

1. What stands between the speaker and his dream in "As I Grew Older"? a wall

2. In "As I Grew Older," to what does the speaker compare his dream? a sun

3. How will the speaker find his dream again in "As I Grew Older"? He will break through the wall to shatter the darkness.

4. What does the speaker in "Any Human to Another" believe all people share? ills; grief; sorrow

5. Name one comparison the speaker in "Any Human to Another" uses to describe suffering? [Students may name any one.] an arrow piercing the body; a shining, unsheathed blade; a wreath of bitter aloes

NAME ____ DATE ______________

As I Grew Older (page 96)
Any Human to Another (page 96)

Vocabulary Worksheet

Essential Vocabulary

diverse **marrow** **unsheathed**

Read the following scene and use context clues to figure out the meanings of the underlined words. Then use these meanings to help you work the exercise below. If you like, you may use a dictionary to check the meaning of a word.

Scene. Mr. Fellowes *and* Mrs. Moore *are old friends. They thoroughly enjoy their constant arguments, but neither will ever admit it. They go at each other with the swords of wit* **unsheathed**, *not blunted by any covering of tact or false courtesy. Today, because of the occasion, they are being somewhat more mellow than usual.*

Mr. Fellowes (*looking around the hall at the guests, his daughter the bride, his fine new son-in-law, and his own radiant wife*)**.** I feel the happiness of this moment all the way to the **marrow**.

Mrs. Moore. Can't.

Mr. Fellowes. Of course I can. Everything is perfect. Everyone is content. I don't see how I could be happier.

Mrs. Moore. Maybe. But you can't feel happiness in your marrow. Pain. Cold. Fear. Any of those things. Not happiness.

Mr. Fellowes (*looking at* Mrs. Moore *in astonishment*)**.** That's the silliest thing I ever heard of. If I can feel all those **diverse** things in my marrow, why can't I feel happiness?

Mrs. Moore. Aren't all that diverse, are they?

Mr. Fellowes. Well, they're certainly not similar.

Mrs. Moore. Sure they are. All bad.

Mr. Fellowes (*scornfully*)**.** So what you're saying is that you can feel bad things in your marrow, but not good things. Well, where do you feel good things?

Mrs. Moore. Your heart. Heart's bursting with joy, overflowing with happiness, that sort of thing.

Mr. Fellowes. Heart, fiddlesticks. I ought to know what I'm feeling and where. And I say I can feel it in my bones.

Mrs. Moore (*looking around the hall at the guests, the bride,* Mr. Fellowes's *fine new son-in-law, the radiant* Mrs. Fellowes, *and finally her old friend*)**.** Well, maybe some kinds of happiness go deeper than others.

Match each underlined word in the scene with the correct definition below.

__________________ **1.** The soft tissue that fills the cavities of most bones.

__________________ **2.** Different; varying.

__________________ **3.** Removed from a scabbard, or case.

NAME ______________________ DATE __________

As I Grew Older (page 96)
Any Human to Another (page 96)

Open-Book Test

Part 1 Broad Interpretation

A. Answer the following essay questions based on your understanding of the poems. Write your answers on a separate sheet of paper. (*15 points each*)

1. What do you think the wall in "As I Grew Older" represents? Give an example of how this "wall" blocks dreams in the world.
2. What actions might be considered as breaking through the wall in "As I Grew Older"? Explain your answer.
3. Think about the main idea expressed in "Any Human to Another." What do you think would be the overall psychological and social effects on people if this idea were to come true?

B. Write **A** if the quotation expresses a thought that the speaker of "Any Human to Another" would probably agree with. Write **D** if he or she would probably disagree. (*2 points each*)

	4. "I am a man, and whatever concerns humanity is of interest to me."—Terence
	5. "No man is an island, entire of itself; every man is a piece of the continent, a part of the main."—John Donne
	6. "Every man for himself."—John Heywood
	7. "True freedom is to share / All the chains our brothers wear."—James Russell Lowell
	8. "Laugh, and the world laughs with you; / weep, and you weep alone."—Ella Wheeler Wilcox
	9. "Let every man mind his own business."—Miguel de Cervantes
	10. "To withhold from a child some knowledge . . . of the world's sorrows and wrongs is to cheat him of his kinship with humanity."—Agnes Repplier
	11. "It is with sorrows as it is with countries—each man has his own."—François René de Chateaubriand

NAME ______________________ DATE ____________

Part 2 Close Interpretation

A. Think about the different mood conveyed in each stanza of "As I Grew Older." On the lines below, write the letters of those words that describe the mood that you feel in each stanza. (*15 points*)

a. despair	**c.** hope	**e.** joy	**g.** disillusionment
b. anger	**d.** horror	**f.** resignation	**h.** determination

______	______	______	______	______
Stanza 1	Stanza 2	Stanza 3	Stanza 4	Stanza 5

B. Choose one simile or metaphor from each of the two poems. In the boxes below, write down what is described, what it is compared to, and the qualities or ideas that are communicated. (*24 points*)

	"As I Grew Older"	"Any Human to Another"	
Simile or metaphor			Simile or metaphor
Thing described			Thing described
Compared to			Compared to
Qualities or ideas communicated			Qualities or ideas communicated

from Letter from Birmingham Jail

Martin Luther King, Jr.

page 101

- **Vocabulary Worksheet,** TG page 108
- **Test,** TG pages 109 and 110

Objectives

1. To respond to a letter defending the rights of individuals to stand up for their beliefs.

2. To understand the art of persuasion.

3. To express ideas in a variety of writing formats: journal, notes, verdict, letter, editorial, booklet, captions, time line, photo essay.

Summary

From his Birmingham jail cell, King writes a letter to clergymen who have criticized the nonviolent protest he inspired and organized. He gives his reasons for leaving his home to come to Birmingham, reviews the four steps in a nonviolent campaign, and explains why he and his organization have chosen this particular time and Birmingham as the particular place for action. He justifies the nonviolent direct action of his organization in several ways: emotionally, by appealing to his audience's response to the effects of segregation on individuals, especially children; intellectually, by arguing the differences between just and unjust laws and explaining when it is necessary to break unjust laws; and historically, by referring to examples from various times and cultures. King expresses his disappointment at the stance of the white moderates who, despite their verbal support, have allowed injustice to continue through their lack of action. He explains that active protest can creatively channel the anger felt by blacks. King admits that he is an "extremist" but cites many extremists throughout history who are now remembered as great men. Finally, he refers to his connection, by virtue of being a clergyman, to the men he addresses and hopes for a future devoid of misunderstanding and characterized by love.

> *"Man was born into barbarism, when killing his fellow man was a normal condition of existence. He became endowed with a conscience. And he has now reached the day when violence toward another human being must become as abhorrent as eating another's flesh."*
>
> — Martin Luther King, Jr., *Why We Can't Wait,* 1964

IdeaBank

▲ **Motivation.** To help students with the Connecting Writing and Reading activity, have them use the scale shown below to indicate how far they would go to stand up for an issue they believe in, such as animal rights, saving the environment, increased penalties for drunk drivers or drug dealers, or to protest censorship of music/lyrics and rock video performances. Volunteers might draw their scales on the board.

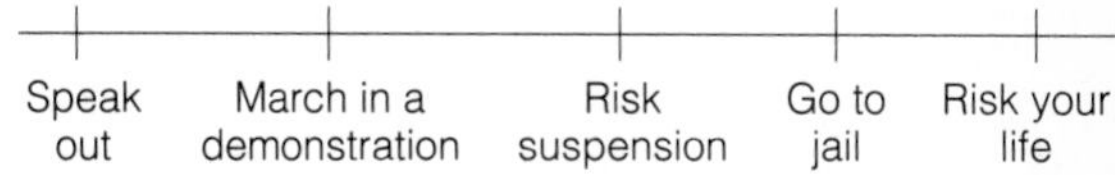

InformationBank

Literary Note. Deletions made in King's letter are specific references to local ministers who would be unknown to students.

IdeaBank

❧ **Gifted and Talented Students.** To further his credibility, support his opinion, and gain the confidence of the audience to whom he addresses his letter, King cites many religious and philosophical leaders, such as Reinhold Niebuhr, St. Augustine, St. Thomas Aquinas, and Martin Buber. Have students locate and list these references. Then assign each of the philosophers to individuals or pairs of students as topics for short research projects in which they investigate the lives and ideas of these men and determine their relevance to King's arguments. Have students present short reports to the class, including excerpts from the writings of these classic thinkers. ❧

InformationBank

Historical Note. King wrote a doctoral thesis on the life and teachings of Mohandas Gandhi of India, another nonviolent social leader. One model for the Birmingham sit-ins and boycotts was a nonviolent demonstration in 1930 in which Gandhi led hundreds of followers on a two-hundred-mile march to the sea. There, they made salt from seawater as a protest against the Indian Salt Acts, which made it a crime to possess salt not bought from the government. Like King, Gandhi was often jailed; he spent seven years in prison for political activity. He, too, believed that it was honorable to be imprisoned for a just cause.

IdeaBank

❋ Learning Disabled Students. The complexity of King's writing will be a challenge to many students. Break the letter into parts and help students make outlines of the ideas that are expressed in each part. The letter might be divided like this:

I. Why King is in Birmingham
II. Four basic steps in a nonviolent campaign
III. Purpose and necessity of direct action
IV. Segregation and its impact on self-concept
V. Issue of breaking laws/civil disobedience
VI. Failure of white moderates
VII. Issue of precipitating violence
VIII. Extremism

Have students note the transitional phrases King uses to move his argument from paragraph to paragraph and the fact that nearly every paragraph has a clearly stated topic sentence. Help students appreciate how this organization allows King to communicate complex ideas. ❋

⌘ Connections

Across the Language Arts. Use "Letter from Birmingham Jail" to teach and/or review the principles of parallel structure. First, help students to find examples of parallel words, phrases, or clauses, such as these:

- " . . . when you have seen vicious mobs *lynch your mothers and fathers at will* and *drown your sisters and brothers at whim* . . ."
- " . . . other than *write long letters*, *think long thoughts*, and *pray long prayers* . . ."

Also help students to see that King often uses a string of parallel clauses (both dependent and independent) to emphasize points and show patterns, such as the series of *when* clauses on page 104, beginning "But when you have seen vicious lynch mobs . . .," and the *who* clauses on page 106, beginning "but the white moderate, who is more devoted . . . ." Finally, encourage students to write several sentences that incorporate parallel structures.

If the grammar and composition book you use has a lesson on parallel structure, you may want to refer to this lesson. The examples and exercises in that lesson can be supplemented with examples drawn from "Letter from Birmingham Jail."

Across the Humanities. Have students investigate, report on, and respond to some of the most recent legislation—both state and federal— affecting civil rights. Suggest or assign topics such as gay rights, fair housing laws, discrimination based on gender, rights of criminals, or racial quotas.

IdeaBank

✤ Multimodal Activities

1. Have students design and create posters for a celebration of the birthday of Martin Luther King, Jr. Encourage them to use quotations from the letter as part of their designs.

2. Help students plan and present a multimedia program in memory of King using tape recordings of his speeches, slides or videotapes of his life, music, original poems, essays, or skits.

3. Ask students who enjoy writing lyrics and music to compose ballads based on stories and ideas from King's letter.

4. Have students represent an idea or ideas from this essay in abstract graphic designs using only black, white, and red. ✤

ResourceBank

For the Student. *The Freedom Movement as Told by Coretta Scott King*. New York: Caedmon, 1972. Sound disk.

King, Martin Luther, Jr. *Why We Can't Wait*. New York: Harper and Row, 1964.

Martin Luther King, Jr.: "I Have a Dream." Oak Forest, Ill.: MPI Home Video, 1986. VHS videocassette.

The Speeches Collection. Oak Forest, Ill.: MPI Home Video, 1989. VHS videocassette.

For the Teacher. Kazemek, F. E. "The Fierce Urgency of Now: Honoring the Life of Martin Luther King, Jr., In and Out of the Classroom." *Journal of Education* 170 (Number 1, 1988): 66–76.

❓ Content Quiz

1. King describes the four steps in any nonviolent campaign. Name one. [Students may name any one.] collection of facts, negotiation, self-purification, direct action

2. What did Birmingham city leaders promise to remove —and then did not? humiliating racial signs in public facilities and services

3. According to King, what kinds of laws are people entitled to disobey? unjust laws

4. What group of citizens does King express his greatest disappointment in? white moderates

5. According to King, what do Jesus, Martin Luther, Abraham Lincoln, and Thomas Jefferson have in common? They were all extremists.

Guidelines for Response

Thinking About the Selection, page 109

1. Students' responses will vary. Some students may say that King's logic and determination impressed them as well as his description of the grief and anger experienced by black people living in the South. Others may have been moved by his comment about the interrelatedness of all people and his hope for a future of brotherhood.

2. For some students, the clergymen may have felt ashamed, since King's letter points out flaws in their thinking and implies that they have not thought deeply enough about the issues: ". . . your statement, I am sorry to say, fails to express . . ." (page 102). Students may suggest that the clergymen may have admired King because of the clarity and inspiration of his writing. For other students, the clergymen may not have changed their thoughts and feelings about the demonstrations, despite King's eloquence.

3. Students who answer that King was wise to criticize the white moderate may feel that he astutely recognizes an important source contributing to segregation in the South. Students who feel that King's criticism was unwise may say that he risked alienating white moderates and that he could have inadvertently provoked them into taking a position opposing that of civil rights activists.

4. Students who agree with King's methods may say that his advocacy of nonviolent protest is admirable and that the four steps he outlines are very logical methods for achieving justice. Students may think that King's nonviolent actions, such as sit-ins and marches, are reasonable, and they may commend King for arguing that negotiation comes often as a result of direct action that had created "tension" in a situation. These students may also indicate their admiration for King's distinction between just and unjust laws and argue that if King is an extremist, then extremism is justified in his case. Students who disagree with King's methods may say that it is never right to precipitate a crisis. Some students may take issue with King's differentiation between justice and injustice and argue that individuals do not have the right to break laws, even by nonviolent means. They may view King as an extremist who believed that the ends always justify the means.

5. Students may find unrealistic King's idea that suddenly "the deep fog of misunderstanding will be lifted" and that everyone will live in love and brotherhood (page 108). However, students who recognize that King is setting forth an ideal toward which people can strive—that he is attempting to define values to live by daily—may deem his vision realistic in that it can be achieved in small ways every day, or in particular times and places.

6. Students may say that had the letter been written today, King would discuss more complex ways in which various groups, especially African Americans, have been excluded from the American dream. Such a letter might refer to the pervasive poverty, unemployment, and crime that plagues urban areas with large minority populations. Students may point out that the remedies for these problems are less clearly defined today.

7. Students may list the following as convincing elements of his argument: his refuting being labeled as an "outsider," because everyone is entitled to the freedoms guaranteed to citizens of the United States and also because he had been invited to Birmingham; his claim that no time is more timely for action than any other, because people who are content with the status quo are never likely to be receptive to public protests; that segregation is unjust because it degrades humanity; his definition of unjust laws as laws enacted by one group of people binding not on them but only on another group who has had no part in enacting those laws.

8. Responses will vary. Students may point out that King as a leader based his ideas on high moral principles, invoking the entire Judeo-Christian tradition, the vision of the early American founders, and the documents on which the United States was built. Some students may argue that the main reason he was effective in opposing injustice in the United States was that he appealed to ideals, values, and beliefs shared by most Americans. These students may conclude that he might have failed utterly by taking the same approach in a totalitarian country, in which the people have little or no freedom. Other students may counter that the force of King's convictions would stir people and improve social conditions even in the most repressive countries.

Analyzing the Writer's Craft, page 110

Examples cited may include the following: Appeals to reason: refutation of the "outsider" idea; why the action took place when it did; refutation of the "untimely" argument. Appeals to emotion: description of the life of an African American who is subject to discrimination and degradation; vision of an America rich with understanding and brotherhood. Appeals to ethics: laws should be applied universally, not by one group to another; the injustice of segregation; justification of breaking laws when one makes known the reason and accepts the penalty.

Connecting Reading and Writing, page 110

For the assignment 2 option, show students examples of newspaper editorials.

For the assignment 4 option, provide copies of popular magazines that contain photo essays.

NAME ______________________ DATE ______________

from Letter from Birmingham Jail (page 101)

Vocabulary Worksheet

Essential Vocabulary

anarchy
moratorium
paternalistically
rabid

Useful Words

oppressor
retaliate

Read the following poem and use context clues to figure out the meanings of the underlined words. Then use these meanings to help you work the exercise below. If you like, you may use a dictionary to check the meaning of a word.

"We're in a state of **anarchy**," the duck said to the goose.
"The cow is in the corn and all the pigs are running loose.
The fox is near the henhouse, and there's no one standing guard.
It seems that losing Rooster Rex has hit the barnyard hard."
"That chicken was a dictator!" the goose returned with heat,
"**Oppressor** of his feathered friends and fellows with four feet.
At last someone **retaliated** for his cruelty
And cruelly declawed him. Now he's harmless as a flea."
"And now we have no leader," said the barn mouse with a sigh.
"I kind of miss Old Paint, a horse with class and quite a guy.
I know they say he ran this farm **paternalistically**,
But I appreciated someone taking care of me."
"Oh, can it for a little while," said Bess, the big brown cow.
"Let's call a **moratorium** on politics for now.
So I went to the field and got a little extra feed!
So sue me! But I tell you, it's no leader that we need.
We don't need Rooster Rex, Old Paint, or any other king.
We sure don't need their **rabid** backers always battling.
(The natives of this barnyard get a little out of hand
Whenever there's a question of who'll rule our little land.)
So cluck and quack and caw all day, if that's what makes you tick,
But quit your squawking, buddies, 'cause you make old Bessie sick."
The others looked at Bess with awe and then sent up a cheer
And next thing that she knew that cow was named Queen for a Year.

Match each underlined word in the poem with the correct definition below.

__________ 1. Extreme.

__________ 2. An authorized delay or stopping of some specified activity.

__________ 3. A person who keeps others down by cruel or unjust use of power or authority.

__________ 4. Political disorder and violence; lawlessness.

__________ 5. Returned like for like, especially paying back injury for injury.

__________ 6. In a manner suggesting a father's relationship with his children.

NAME ______________________ DATE ______________

from Letter from Birmingham Jail (page 101)

Test

Part 1 Broad Interpretation

A. Answer the following essay questions based on your understanding of the letter. Write your answers on a separate sheet of paper. (*16 points each*)

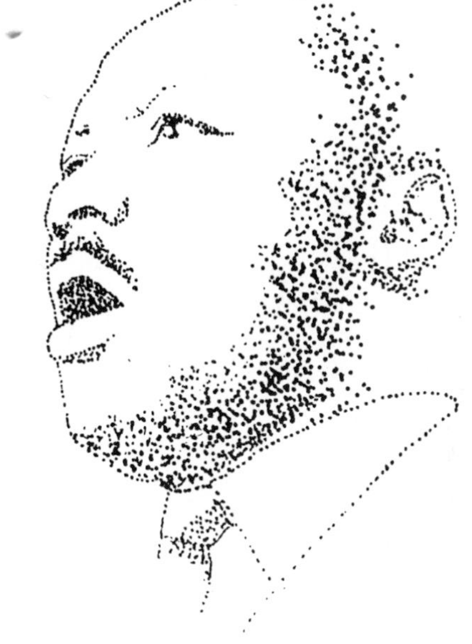

1. Do you agree with King about *whether* one should disobey an unjust law? about *how* one should disobey an unjust law? Explain your answers.
2. King said, "One day the South will recognize its real heroes." What do you think are King's criteria for a hero? Support your answer with details from the letter.
3. Do you agree with King that it can be good to create tension in an unjust situation? Explain your answer.

B. Write **A** if Martin Luther King, Jr., would probably have agreed with the statement. Write **D** if he would probably have disagreed. (*2 points each*)

	4. "Patience is the best remedy for every trouble."—Plautus
	5. "Rigorous law is often rigorous injustice."—Terence
	6. "Moderation is best, and to avoid all extremes."—Plutarch
	7. "Everything comes to those who can wait."—Rabelais
	8. "Laws and institutions must go hand in hand with the progress of the human mind." —Thomas Jefferson
	9. "Men are by nature unequal. It is vain, therefore, to treat them as if they were equal." —James A. Froude
	10. "Freedom is not saved by powerlessness. Freedom is inseparably linked with power and the will and capacity to use it."—Dorothy Thompson
	11. "Those who set themselves the task of making their communities into places in which the average human being may obtain a share, not only of greater physical well-being, but of wider mental and spiritual existence, will lead an active and adventurous life to reach their goal."—Eleanor Roosevelt

NAME ________________________________ DATE ______________

Part 2 Close Interpretation

A. Think about the techniques of persuasion as you read the quotations on the left. Then, in the boxes on the right, indicate whether each quotation appeals primarily to the intellect, the emotions, or the ethics of the reader. Write brief notes explaining your answers. (*12 points each*)

"Several months ago the affiliate here in Birmingham asked us to be on call to engage in a nonviolent direct-action program if such were deemed necessary."	Appeals primarily to ☐ Intellect ☐ Emotions ☐ Ethics Explanation:
"Negroes have experienced grossly unjust treatment in the courts. There have been more unsolved bombings of Negro homes and churches in Birmingham than in any other city in the nation."	Appeals primarily to ☐ Intellect ☐ Emotions ☐ Ethics Explanation:
"As in so many past experiences, our hopes had been blasted, and the shadow of deep disappointment settled upon us."	Appeals primarily to ☐ Intellect ☐ Emotions ☐ Ethics Explanation:

B. Basing your answers on King's explanation, write **T** if the statement describes something that makes a law unjust. Write **F** if it does not. (*3 points each*)

_____ **1.** It applies only to a minority of the population.

_____ **2.** It is expensive for the taxpayer.

_____ **3.** It applies to everyone, regardless of circumstances.

_____ **4.** It applies to people who were denied the right to vote on it.

_____ **5.** It does not agree with moral law.

_____ **6.** It causes tension among the population.

_____ **7.** It demeans and hurts the human personality.

_____ **8.** It separates human beings from one another.

from Farewell to Manzanar

Jeanne Wakatsuki Houston and James D. Houston

page 111

■ **Test,** TG pages 113 and 114

Objectives

1. To respond to an autobiographical excerpt that describes a situation beyond a person's control.

2. To identify irony in a selection.

3. To express ideas in a variety of writing formats: journal, memoir, poem, conversation, dramatic scene, collage, personal essay, expository essay, and report.

Summary

Like thousands of other people of Japanese ancestry living on the West Coast during World War II, the Wakatsuki family attempts to cope with its confinement in a detention camp by keeping busy. Papa cares for pear trees, brews sake and brandy, paints, carves driftwood, and makes a rock garden. Mama works as a dietitian, visiting young mothers and helping people in the camp stay healthy. The residents maintain an aura of normality, trying to carry on their lives as though they are living in a typical American town. The internees' ability to cope, however, is undercut by the tragedy of this inescapable, humiliating situation.

IdeaBank

▲ **Motivation.** To help students with the Connecting Writing and Reading activity, have them first select one of the four listed situations. Then ask them to brainstorm a list of possible ways to cope with that situation, as shown in the partial sample below.

Situation: family loses source of income

What I can do?

1. spend less money
2. look for a part-time job
3. start a babysitting service

When students have completed their lists, have them briefly describe in their journals how well they think they might cope with the situation. As students read the selection, have them notice how Jeanne and her family respond to living at Manzanar. ▲

IdeaBank

❧ **Gifted and Talented Students.** Encourage students to create oral histories by interviewing members of the community who recall the feelings toward Japanese Americans in the early 1940's. ❧

IdeaBank

❖ **Cooperative Learning.** Ask students to imagine that the historical events referred to in this excerpt from *Farewell to Manzanar* are taking place now. Divide the class into three or more groups. Have each group select members to role-play a news anchorperson and a reporter; the rest of the group can role-play the residents of Manzanar. The anchorperson should begin by summarizing the story. Then have the reporters interview the residents, allowing them to share their experiences and feelings about their situation. ❖

IdeaBank

✲ **Collaborative Learning.** Have students work together to find out more about Japanese-American detention camps that existed in the United States during World War II. Suggest that they investigate the book *Manzanar,* by John Armor and Peter Wright, which contains an essay by John Hersey titled "A Mistake of Terrifically Horrible Proportions" in addition to numerous photographs taken at the Manzanar camp. Students could use this resource, along with other items such as newspaper articles from the 1940's, to prepare an oral presentation on this chapter of American history. ✲

ResourceBank

For the Student. *Farewell to Manzanar.* Directed by John Corty. Los Angeles: Corty Films/Universal TV. NBC/TV, March 11, 1976.

Hansen, Arthur A., ed. *Japanese American World War Two Evacuation Oral History Project, Part One: Internees.* Westport, Conn.: The Meckler Corporation, 1990.

For the Teacher. Bosworth, Allan R. *America's Concentration Camps.* New York: Norton, 1967.

IdeaBank

✏ **Self-Assessment.** Have students review their completed Connecting Reading and Writing assignments. Ask them to select the assignment they think is most successful and to offer an explanation for their assessment. Direct them to do the same thing for the least successful assignment. ✏

Guidelines for Response

Thinking About the Selection, page 116–117

1. Some students may find this selection bleak and depressing, leaving them with a sense of loneliness, isolation, sadness, and regret. Other students may feel anger. Still others may see a glimmer of hope in the way the people of Manzanar cope with their internment.

2. Students may suggest that the title of her book, *Farewell to Manzanar,* indicates that Houston wrote this memoir to try to come to terms with her memories. As she describes the yearbook, her family's activities, and the natural surroundings, the reader senses that she had mixed feelings—both sentimental and pained—about Manzanar.

3. Students may feel that the parents had the hardest time coping since they had to give up the property, positions, and respect they had worked hard to earn. Other students may believe that the transition to camp life was most difficult for the older children, who were out of high school and ready to start life on their own. Students also may feel that although it must have been difficult for the teenagers to leave their school friends and activities, their life in the camp was made easier by the recreation available there. Some students may suggest that children adapted best to life in the camp because they were young and resilient.

4. Students may speculate that Japanese Americans became distrustful of the U. S. government and that feelings of alienation were long-lasting. In all likelihood, some students will think that the emotional turmoil produced by such an experience could have left the internees with serious psychological and sociological problems.

5. Since many students will see the desert as a barren, lonely, harsh landscape, they may infer that the setting reinforces the mood of depression and isolation. Other students may note that the people of Manzanar make the desert bloom with parks and gardens; students may connect this fact with a feeling of hope and resilience. Students may also cite the inspirational effect of the Sierras as evidence of the relationship between setting and mood.

6. Responses may vary. Some students may feel that the main reason Jeanne Wakatsuki Houston wrote this memoir was to show her readers what life was like for a typical Japanese American family in an internment camp during World War II. Contrary to some reader's expectations, the members of this family spent most of their time just trying to make the best of a bad situation rather than expressing resentment over the injustice they endured. Life went on much as usual. Though branded by the government as enemies, the internees remained loyal Americans. Other students may say that the main reason for Houston's writing this memoir was her desire to make sense out of a painful, if not traumatic, episode from her childhood. By describing how her family carried on with their lives under terribly distressing conditions, she put her past into perspective and came to terms with it.

7. Some students may feel that there are sufficient legal safeguards to prevent a recurrence of such internment. Others may point to the anti-Arab demonstrations that occurred during the 1991 Gulf War, for example, and may suggest that it is a short step from such demonstrations to the forced internment of people who "look like the enemy."

Analyzing the Writer's Craft, page 117

Students may identify some of the following examples of irony: the author's brother Bill sings popular songs such as "Don't Fence Me In" (page 115); the camp has a hillbilly band made up of Japanese Americans in cowboy hats and jeans; the name of the camp means "apple orchard," but the camp was almost a desert when the internees arrived because the water had been siphoned off for Los Angeles; the author's older brother Woody wanted to volunteer for the army and fight for the country that forced him into the detention camp.

Connecting Reading and Writing, page 118

Suggest that students working on assignment 2 and its option role-play their conversations with a partner.

If the grammar and composition book you use has a lesson on expository writing, you may want to refer to this lesson.

? Content Quiz

1. The Wakatsuki family lives in Block 28 of the Manzanar War Relocation Center in southern California.

2. The Wakatsukis live here because the government has forced Japanese Americans to live in detention camps during World War II.

3. Papa passes the time by gardening, brewing sake and brandy, painting watercolors, and carving driftwood.

4. Jeanne and the eleven members of her family live at Manzanar for three years.

5. Two ways in which Manzanar is like a typical American town is that it has schools; churches; Boy Scouts; beauty parlors; gossip; fire and police departments; glee clubs; softball leagues; films and entertainment; sports; class plays; high school yearbooks. [Students may name any two.]

NAME ______________________________ DATE ______________

from Farewell to Manzanar (page 111)

Test

Part 1 Broad Interpretation

A. Answer the following essay questions based on your understanding of the selection. Write your answers on a separate sheet of paper. (*15 points each*)

1. Do you think the writer felt that her family suffered greatly from being forced to live in a detention camp? Use details from the selection to explain your answer.
2. What do you think is ironic about life in the detention camp? Explain your answer.
3. If you were a Japanese American living in a detention camp during World War II, how do you think you would feel about the fact that neither German Americans nor Italian Americans had been forced into detention camps? Explain.

B. Read the following quotations. Then, in the box on the right, write brief notes about what you think the four quotations say about the Japanese American detainees. (*19 points*)

"Some families would vie with one another for the most elegant floor designs, obtaining a roll of each color . . . , cutting it into diamonds, squares, or triangles, shining it with heating oil, then leaving their doors open so that passers-by could admire the handiwork."	
"He hauled stones in off the desert and built a small rock garden outside our doorway."	
"Near Block 28 some of the men who had been professional gardeners built a small park, with mossy nooks, ponds, waterfalls, and curved wooden bridges."	
"She wore a bright yellow, long-billed sun hat she had made herself and always kept stiffly starched. Afternoons I would see her coming from blocks away, heading home, her tiny figure warped by heat waves and that bonnet a yellow flower wavering in the glare."	

Part 2 Close Interpretation

A. Write the letter of the best answer. (*6 points each*)

_____ 1. According to the selection, where do the Issei receive most of their "spiritual sustenance" while in the detention camp?

a. From music. **c.** From meditation.
b. From nature. **d.** From their families.

_____ 2. According to the selection, which of the following popular sayings best describes most of the detainees' attitudes toward life in the detention camp?

- **a.** All's fair in love and war.
- **b.** It is all for the best anyway.
- **c.** Make the best of a bad situation.
- **d.** I'm mad as heck and I'm not going to take it anymore.

_____ 3. Which of the following does *not* describe the Japanese Americans in this detention camp?

- **a.** Proud.
- **b.** Disloyal.
- **c.** Resigned.
- **d.** Resentful.

B. The information that the writer includes in this selection comes from several sources. In the boxes on the left are facts that she includes. In the boxes on the right, identify what you think the source or sources of that fact might be. Some possibilities are offered below. (*3 points each*)

The writer's own memories	Family stories	The high school yearbook	Other accounts of the time

Fact	Possible source or sources
4. The Owens Valley became a desert after its water was diverted to Los Angeles.	
5. The wind through the pear leaves sounded like the surf.	
6. Papa carved furniture from driftwood.	
7. Papa talked Woody out of volunteering for military service, and Woody waited to be inducted.	
8. Her brother led a dance band called The Jive Bombs.	
9. People who lived in Owens Valley during the war remember seeing the camp gardens from the highway.	

Blues Ain't No Mockin Bird

Toni Cade Bambara

page 119

■ **Test,** TG pages 117 and 118

Objectives

1. To respond to a short story that explores a family's encounter with intrusive strangers.

2. To understand how theme and structure are related in a short story.

3. To express ideas in a variety of writing formats: journal, episode, dramatic scene, guidelines, letter of complaint, evaluation, and recommendation.

Plot Summary

When two men who are making a film about the county food stamp program arrive at Granny Cain's place and ignore her request to cease filming, she gets angry. Granny, a very proud woman, tries to explain her anger to the children who are playing in the yard, but the young twins from next door do not understand. A few minutes later, Granddaddy Cain returns from the woods with a chicken hawk he has captured; he nails it to the toolshed door and then kills its frantic mate with a hammer. Now Granddaddy Cain seems to notice the two men for the first time. He calmly greets the men, but his quiet demeanor is enough to upset them. Granddaddy holds out a hand for the camera and, with a slap of his other hand, breaks it in half. The intruders slowly back away. Granddaddy has restored order to the household.

IdeaBank

❧ **Gifted and Talented Students**

1. Toni Morrison is Toni Cade Bambara's editor and personal friend. Have students read one of Morrison's books, such as *The Bluest Eye* or *Sula*, and then ask students to find similarities and differences in the works of these contemporary writers in terms of central characters, themes, and diction. Ask students to share their findings in brief oral reports.

2. Have students read *Gorilla, My Love* or *The Sea Birds Are Still Alive*, collections of short stories by Toni Cade Bambara. Urge them to look for evidence of Bambara's concern about particular social issues in these stories. Have students share their discoveries in a panel discussion. ❧

IdeaBank

▲ **Motivation.** To help students start the Connecting Writing and Reading activity, ask them to brainstorm a complementary list of people who might do the activities that are listed. Students may mention such people as bus passengers, neighbors, teachers, best friends, new bosses, repair persons, family members. Then direct students to mix up their lists, pairing each person with a different action (my French teacher entered my home; my new boss gave me a gift, and so on). Have them consider how different circumstances might change what seems to be an intrusive act. ▲

"The human animal needs a freedom seldom mentioned, freedom from intrusion. He needs a little privacy quite as much as he wants understanding or vitamins, or exercise or praise."

— Phyllis McGinley, *The Province of the Heart,* 1959

IdeaBank

✱ **Limited English Proficient Students**

1. To help students understand the dialect Bambara uses in this story, have a student who is proficient in English read the selection aloud to a small group of LEP students, stopping periodically to allow students to ask questions and discuss the passages they find confusing.

2. To help students understand and appreciate Bambara's inventive use of language, list examples such as the following on the board: "The tall man with a huge camera *lassoed* to his shoulder was *buzzin* our way" (page 120); "And Granny just stared at the twins till their faces swallow up the *eager*. . . ." (page 121); "[Granddaddy Cain] loadin up the truck, with *rocks all in his jaw*, madder than Granny in the first place" (page 121). Discuss the visual images created. ✱

IdeaBank

✤ **Multimodal Activity.** Divide the class into teams, pro and con, to debate the following question: Are today's television news reporters as intrusive as the filmmakers in this story? Ask students to support their opinions with examples from current news coverage of celebrities, political figures, and victims of tragedy. ✤

ResourceBank

For the Student. Walker, Alice. *In Search of Our Mother's Gardens: Womanist Prose*. New York: Harcourt Brace Jovanovich, 1984.

For the Teacher. Bambara, Toni C. and Leah Wise, eds. *Southern Black Utterance Today*. (Southern Exposure Series). Durham, N.C.: Institute for Southern Studies, 1975.

Content Quiz

1. The Cain family moves frequently because people drive Granny crazy.
2. Granny objects to two men who come onto her property carrying a movie camera.
3. Granddaddy Cain nails a chicken hawk to the toolshed door.
4. Granddaddy Cain wrecks the movie camera.
5. With hardly a word to the two men, Granddaddy Cain compels them to leave his place.

Guidelines for Response

Thinking About the Story, pages 124–125

1. Students may find Granny proud, independent, or indignant; Granddaddy, powerful, dignified, or devoted; and the children, alert, observant, curious, and proud.

2. Students may say that Cathy's idea of the hammer's proper use is that it is a powerful instrument that Granddaddy Cain uses well and with restraint. Some may suggest that Cathy tells her story to demonstrate her Granddaddy's dignity, power, and competence in contrast to the futile, almost silly efforts of the filmmakers. Students may note that Granddaddy's behavior shows the filmmakers that he is a strong person who demands respect.

3. Many students will support the Cains' reaction, citing: (a) the rude and familiar use of the word *aunty*, a stereotype generalizing Granny as an old woman without the ability to resist pressure; (b) the trespassing and filming as an invasion of the Cains' privacy; (c) the filmmaker's assumption that the Cain family is an appropriate subject for a film on food stamps; (d) the attitude of the men which reduces the family to the level of "things" and "stuff."

4. Students may suggest that the Cains believe no one has the right to intrude on another person's privacy as the photographers do in the story. The Cains have moved several times due to people's rude and insensitive treatment of the family. Perhaps students will see the formal courtesy the Cains extend to each other as a demonstration of the respect they believe all people owe to one another.

5. Students may imagine that Granny herself might have attempted to force the men from her property, waving her ladle as she told them exactly what she thought of their behavior. Other students may cite the Cains' frequent moves and suggest that Granny's unrelieved aggravation may have led to yet another relocation.

6. Students may note that the narrator's relationship to the family as a granddaughter provides background details to the story. They may also note that the narrator's youthfulness and innocence provides a freshness to the telling of the story. Still, some may criticize the narrator for being too young and inexperienced to understand and convey the full implication of the events in the story.

7. Students, trying to relate a discussion of the blues to their knowledge of mockingbirds, may suggest that blues music expresses serious, strong, and deeply felt emotions that are in no way appropriate subjects for anyone's ridicule or mockery. Students may note that the word *blues* is sometimes used to refer to life itself; in this sense, the title seems to be saying life is not the sweet song of a bird; life, like the blues, is filled with hardship and lamentation.

8. Students who are more concerned about the complexities of family relationships and the importance of living their heritage may cite "Everyday Use" as more important, while students who are more concerned with individual dignity and civil rights may cite "Blues Ain't No Mockin Bird."

Analyzing the Writer's Craft, pages 125–126

Students' diagrams may suggest the following themes:

- **Man on bridge:** No one has the right to intrude on another person's misery; people should not be insensitive.
- **Goldilocks tale:** People should respect each other's property and right to privacy.
- **Hawk incident:** Competence and the proper use of skill demand respect; quiet power and dignified behavior make uncontrolled, purposeless efforts look foolish.
- **Overall theme:** People have the right to maintain their dignity. They need not tolerate rude or insensitive invasions that diminish them as human beings.

Connecting Reading and Writing, page 126

As students prepare to write an evaluation for assignment 3, encourage them to work in small groups to gather details that they feel fulfill each of Bambara's goals.

If the grammar and composition book you use has a lesson on narrative writing, you may want to refer to this lesson.

NAME ______________________ DATE ______________

Blues Ain't No Mockin Bird (page 119)

Test

Part 1 Broad Interpretation

A. Answer the following essay questions based on your understanding of the story. Write your answers on a separate sheet of paper. (*16 points each*)

1. What do you think Cathy has in mind at the end of the story when she talks about "the proper use of the hammer"? Explain your answer.
2. Do you think the reaction of Granny and Granddaddy Cain to the film-makers is reasonable? Explain your answer.
3. Why do you think manners and politeness are so important to Granny? Explain your answer and support it with details from the story.

B. Write **D** if you think Granny would consider the action dignified. Write **R** if you think she would consider the action rude. (*1 point each*)

	4. The men taking pictures without permission.
	5. Goldilocks sleeping in the bears' beds.
	6. Granddaddy saying, "Good day, gentlemen."
	7. Granny calling her husband by his first name in public.
	8. The cameraman calling Granny "aunty."
	9. Granny saying, "Your mama and I are not related."
	10. Mrs. Cooper coming into Granny's kitchen.
	11. Mrs. Cooper commenting on how clean things are.
	12. Granddaddy telling the cameramen to leave.
	13. Granny standing silent when the men speak to her.
	14. Calling Miss Myrtle by her first name alone.

NAME ______________________________ DATE ______________

Part 2 Close Interpretation

A. Think about the ways in which Granny and Granddaddy Cain are similar and the ways in which they are different. Draw lines from their names to the words and phrases that describe them. A term may apply to both characters. *(21 points)*

dignified   slow to anger   intelligent   physically strong   proud

overly sensitive   Granny   Granddaddy   compassionate

easy going   quick-witted   quick to anger   powerful   righteous

B. Think about the two stories told within this story. Then, in the boxes below, note briefly what you think the theme of each of those stories is and how it relates to the theme of the main story. *(10 points each)*

1. The Man on the Bridge

How does it relate to the theme of the main story?

THEME

2. Goldilocks

How does it relate to the theme of the main story?

THEME

November Cotton Flower

Jean Toomer

A Note of Humility

Arna Bontemps

page 128

- **Vocabulary Worksheet,** TG page 121
- **Test,** TG pages 123 and 124

Objectives

1. To respond to two poems that reflect important concerns of the Harlem Renaissance.

2. To practice the reading and thinking skills of an independent reader.

IdeaBank

▲ **Motivation.** Explain to students that the first poem they will read in this lesson deals with an unusual natural phenomenon and the significance people attach to it. Ask students to think of unusual events, experiences, or natural phenomena that people regard as good or bad omens. List students' responses on the board. Have students write in their journals about the last time they did something based on superstition or the last time they interpreted some event or action as an omen of good or bad fortune. Then have students read the poems and think about the speakers' attitudes toward omens. ▲

IdeaBank

❖ **Cooperative Learning.** Divide the class into groups of three students. Ask each group to reread "November Cotton Flower" and "A Note of Humility." Then have students in each group think of three questions to ask about the poems. Ask one student in each group to record the questions, putting the group's favorite question first and least favorite last. When the class reassembles, have a student in one group pose one of its questions to a second group. If the second group answers the question to the first group's satisfaction, then the second group is free to ask a third group, and so on, until all groups have had an opportunity to ask and answer a question. ❖

InformationBank

Historical Note. Several writers of the Harlem Renaissance were close friends who frequently gathered in one another's homes for literary and cultural discussions, much like the writers who belonged to European literary salons during the eighteenth and nineteenth centuries. One group that met at the home of black novelist Wallace Thurman included Langston Hughes, Zora Neale Hurston, Countee Cullen, Arna Bontemps, and Jessie Fauset. Fauset herself hosted regular gatherings of younger black and white writers, editors, social workers, and students. Sometimes, Harlem Renaissance writers met at James Weldon Johnson's home. There, in one evening, the group might have talked with the famous white lawyer Clarence Darrow and listened to the well-known black singer and actor Paul Robeson.

IdeaBank

✾ **Learning Disabled Students.** Students may encounter difficulty with the references to cotton cultivation in the poem "November Cotton Flower." List these terms on the board: *boll weevil, cotton stalk, cotton, cotton flower,* and *branch.* Draw students' attention to the explanation of boll weevil in Approaching the Poems, page 128. Then explain that the white flowers of the cotton plant, which open in the morning and wither the next day, appear until the autumn frost; flowering in November is quite unusual. Explain also that the word *branch* in line 4 refers to a small creek or brook. Then read the poem aloud, stopping frequently to help students picture the barren winter scene so that they can understand the beauty of the unseasonable cotton flower. ✾

InformationBank

Literary Note. Jean Toomer's novel *Cane* (1923) has come to be recognized as an important piece of American literature, employing avant-garde narrative techniques and interior monologue well before such writers as John Dos Passos and William Faulkner. *Cane* is told in three parts. The first part contains stories, sketches, and poems about black laborers in rural Georgia. Part Two uses a similar form to narrate the development of an educated African American in Washington, D.C. Part Three is a one-act play contrasting one uninhibited African-American character with another who has been emotionally and spiritually crippled by the burden of race.

ResourceBank

For the Student. Bontemps, Arna. "The Awakening: A Memoir." *The Harlem Renaissance Remembered*. Edited by Arna Bontemps. New York: Dodd, Mead & Company, 1972.

Jones, Robert B., and Margery Latimer, eds. *The Collected Poems of Jean Toomer*. Raleigh, N.C.: University of North Carolina Press, 1988.

For the Teacher. Bontemps, Arna, ed. *Great Slave Narratives*. Boston: Beacon Press, 1969.

Toomer, Jean. *Cane*. Darwin T. Turner, ed. (Critical Edition Series). New York: W. W. Norton Company, 1987.

❷ Content Quiz

1. In "November Cotton Flower," one thing that threatens the cotton crop is [Students may name any one.] the arrival of the boll weevil; winter's cold; the drought.

2. In "November Cotton Flower," dead birds were discovered in deep wells.

3. The sudden appearance of the cotton flower startles the old folks in "November Cotton Flower."

4. In "A Note of Humility," the speaker believes that his people may triumph for an hour or two.

5. The speaker in "A Note of Humility" compares the situation of his people with the situation of the bee and the ant.

Guidelines for Response

Discussion Questions

1. Explain what the blooming of the cotton flower means to people in "November Cotton Flower."

[Students may point out that the flower's blooming in November is so unusual that "Old folks were startled" (line 10). Students also may observe that the flower blooms during a particularly bad year, a year when boll weevils, cold weather, and drought have ravaged the cotton crop. Students may suggest that the unexpected flower means different things to different people. For many, it is a source of hope, suggesting that beauty can spring out of barrenness. Some students may say that it represents a dramatic upturn in the lives of African Americans: "Brown eyes that loved without a trace of fear" (line 13).]

2. Whom do you think the phrase "men like us" (line 8) refers to in "A Note of Humility"?

[Some students may feel that this phrase refers exclusively to African-American males or perhaps to African Americans as a racial entity. Other students may say that the speaker refers to any people who are oppressed. Still others may feel that the speaker includes all humankind in the phrase. They may contend that everyone must eventually come to the place where "our last songs have lost their sound" (line 3) and that "a note of humility" results from the speaker's awareness of human limitations.]

3. Compare the speakers' views of life in these two poems.

[Students may say that both poems focus on the difficulties of life. They may suggest that "November Cotton Flower" uses images from nature to suggest the blighted life of the black people in the South—for example, the branch, "so pinched and slow, / Failed in its function . . ." (lines 4–5). Some students may feel that the "dead birds" (line 7) represent dead hopes and dreams, victims of the drought of opportunity. Students may mention, however, the speaker's discovery that even out of the most adverse conditions can arise "Beauty so sudden for that time of year" (line 14). They may feel this discovery indicates that the speaker has faith in the possibilities of life. Students may say that "A Note of Humility" also uses images from nature to suggest the difficulties of life. The speaker feels that many hopes "are sown on stony ground" (line 1), producing nothing, and that eventually precious growing things are "choked" by "thorns" (line 5) of racism. Students may observe that the speaker compares humans to insects and birds, perhaps suggesting that like these animals his people will experience some triumph. As in "November Cotton Flower," the speaker in "A Note of Humility" holds out some hope, but students may observe the speaker's conviction that any human triumph will be muted and brief. Some students may assert that "November Cotton Flower" is decidedly more optimistic than "A Note of Humility." Others may feel that the poems are quite similar in their depiction of hardships.]

4. What details in these poems seem most effective to you, and why?

[Some students may find the depiction of the desiccated cotton plants in "November Cotton Flower" striking, citing the rusty cotton stalks (line 2). Others may find the speaker's observation that "dead birds were found / In wells a hundred feet below the ground" (lines 7–8) a compelling detail because of its vividness and force. Some may focus on the miracle of the flower and its effect on the people: "Brown eyes that loved without a trace of fear" (line 13). In "A Note of Humility," students may cite details that suggest the stifling of life and love, such as "When thorns have choked the last green thing we loved" (line 5) and "When love that moved us once leaves us unmoved" (line 7). Some may focus on the speaker's comparison of humans to "the bee" and "The meager ant, the sea-gull and the loon" (lines 9–10), feeling that these images depict the "we" of the poem as humble creatures who may triumph, if only for a moment.]

NAME ______________________________ DATE ______________

November Cotton Flower (page 128)
A Note of Humility (page 128)

Vocabulary Worksheet

Essential Vocabulary

assume *v.* To take on.
meager *adj.* Thin; lean; emaciated.

Useful Word

drought *n.* A prolonged period of dry weather.

Fill in each blank with the correct word from the word list. Each word is used more than once.

1. If you suddenly discovered that you were thirty-fourth in line to the throne of Ruritania and the other thirty-three were missing in a shipwreck, you might ______________ qualities of leadership.

2. If you looked through your car window as you were driving through the countryside and saw land baked by the sun, ______________ cattle trying unsuccessfully to find a few tufts of grass, and dry river beds, you might reasonably conclude that there had been a ______________ or that you were in a state you wouldn't want to live in.

3. Chameleons ______________ protective coloration when they feel threatened; people ______________ an "attitude" in the same situation.

4. There were many causes of poverty during the Great Depression in the U. S. For example, the Dust Bowl was the result of a terrible ______________ that left part of the country so dry it literally blew away.

5. If you're going to serve such a ______________ chicken to a whole family, you'd better have lots of stuffing.

6. Stray cats can be very appealing. Their cries and their often ______________ little bodies go right to your heart. But if you start putting milk and tuna out on your porch, you'd better be ready to ______________ responsibility for a pet, because, pal, you have one.

November Cotton Flower (page 128)
A Note of Humility (page 128)

Open-Book Test

Part 1 Broad Interpretation

A. Answer the following essay questions based on your understanding of the poems. Write your answers on a separate sheet of paper. (*15 points each*)

1. Suppose "November Cotton Flower" were a folk tale passed down from generation to generation. Why do you think it would continue to be told? Explain your answer.
2. What is the situation described in the octave (the first eight lines) of "November Cotton Flower"? What kind of life do you think that situation might represent? What comment does the sestet (the last six lines) make about the people who live such a life? Explain your answers.
3. In your opinion, when does "A Note of Humility" suggest that "men like us" might be allowed to feel a moment's triumph? Explain your answer and support it with details from the poem.

B. In the boxes below, identify several related images in each poem. Write a few words describing the qualities or ideas the images communicate. Then identify the feeling that the imagery helps to convey in each poem. (*14 points*)

"November Cotton Flower"	"A Note of Humility"
Images:	Images:
Qualities or ideas communicated:	Qualities or ideas communicated:
Overall feeling of the poem:	Overall feeling of the poem:

NAME ______________________________ DATE ______________

Part 2 Close Interpretation

A. Reorder the following sentences so that they recount the basic events of "November Cotton Flower." Put an **A** next to the sentence that should go first and so forth. (*3 points each*)

_____ **1.** A natural pest and the onset of winter make the cotton plants look old and brown.

_____ **2.** Amazed, the people see meaning in such a rare occurrence.

_____ **3.** Far from seeing something bad in the unheard-of event, the people respond joyfully to its beauty.

_____ **4.** The cotton flower unexpectedly appears.

_____ **5.** The cotton bolls themselves are almost gone.

_____ **6.** The earth is so dry that it is soaking up all the water, causing birds to die of thirst.

_____ **7.** The stream ("branch") is so dried up that it cannot sweep away the leaves.

B. In "A Note of Humility" the poet uses different kinds of repetition to give the poem unity and texture. In the boxes below, make an **X** next to each kind of repetition you notice in the poem. Then give an example of each kind that you find. (*4 points each*)

Type of repetition	X	Example
8. Rhyme, or repetition of end sounds		
9. Repetition of similar consonant sounds at the beginnings of words		
10. Repetition of phrases		
11. Repetition of similarly structured phrases or sentences		
12. Repetition of images		

The Censors

Luisa Valenzuela
(lo͞o ē′ sä vä len zwe′ lä)

page 130

■ **Test,** TG pages 129 and 130

Objectives

1. To respond to a story about censorship and obsession.
2. To practice the reading and thinking skills of an independent reader.

Plot Summary

Juan lives in a fictitious Latin American dictatorship in which the government censors all mail. Juan writes a letter to Mariana, who has moved to Paris, and then worries that the Censor's Secret Command may pursue her and assassinate her as a result. In order to intercept his letter, Juan takes a job as a post office censor. Despite the dangers and hardships of the job, and despite the fact that he is now part of the brutal government that he once opposed, Juan begins to take the job seriously. He becomes interested, then committed, then zealous. He reports a co-worker for trying to organize a strike. When his letter to Mariana finally does cross his desk, he censors it without regret. He is executed the next morning.

IdeaBank

▲ **Motivation.** Discuss with students the original meaning of the word *obsession*: the act of an evil spirit in possessing a person. Explain that an obsession is a powerful drive, not controlled by reason. Explain, too, that a person can be obsessed by many things: for example, ambition, love, artistic inspiration, jealousy, and revenge. Ask students to brainstorm kinds of obsessions and then make notes in their journals exploring their associations with the idea of obsession. ▲

IdeaBank

✱ **Limited English Proficient Students**
Have pairs of students choose five or ten unfamiliar words from the story and look them up in a dictionary. Then ask students to use a thesaurus to locate synonyms. Next ask students to find or draw pictures that illustrate the words. Finally, ask students to use the words in original sentences about "The Censors." ✱

InformationBank

Literary Notes

1. Valenzuela's story is not strictly within the literary style known as magical realism, which has been developed by such Latin American writers as Gabriel García Márquez and Jorge Luis Borges. However, Valenzuela's style incorporates some aspects of magical realism: in her stories magical, inexplicable, and symbolic events take place alongside the mundane events of daily life. Like the stories of magical realists, Valenzuela's stories resemble parables in their exaggerated, symbolic situations and indirect commentary on political and social realities.

2. Valenzuela's story may be seen as influenced by the Theatre of the Absurd, a term describing a type of literature that flourished after World War II. Absurdists such as Albert Camus, Edward Albee, Jean Genet, Harold Pinter, and Eugène Ionesco wrote plays, novels, and stories showing characters caught in irrational universes, forced to create their own standards, often under the threat of totalitarianism. By celebrating individualism, absurdists questioned the conformity that allowed Nazi atrocities to occur. Often, as in "The Censors," these works use irony, exaggeration, and satire.

IdeaBank

❧ **Gifted and Talented Students.** Censorship can be applied to many forms of expression: speeches, printed materials, plays, films, art, dancing, and even fashion. Ask students to list kinds of modern censorship and prepare short oral reports for a class forum on censorship. Subtopics might include the Film-Rating System; Obscenity Laws; Should Music Be Rated?; Censoring Literature in the Schools; "Bad" Words; Pornography; Laws Governing Public Exposure and Nudity. ❧

Tips from the Classroom

Have students work in small groups to construct a time line of events in Juan's life, noting each conflict and its resolution. Ask each group to present its time line to the class. Then encourage a discussion to compare and contrast students' various interpretatons.

Susan M. Crevcoure
J. A. Craig High School
Janesville, MI

IdeaBank

✤ Multimodal Activities

1. Have small groups of students develop a list of ten do's and don'ts summarizing the contents of an imaginary *Manual for the Post Office's Censorship Division*.

2. Have students develop a logo and a motto for the Censor's Secret Command.

3. Ask students to locate a photograph or to create a collage that will illustrate "The Censors" in an anthology of futuristic stories.

4. Have students interview teachers or administrators regarding censorship in their school. Is there an official policy on censorship in the school library, school newspaper, or the classroom?

5. In general, censorship in the United States today is supposed to be limited by the constitutional guarantees of freedom of the press and freedom of speech. Have students read the Bill of Rights to find the amendments that govern these freedoms and then discuss the way that these freedoms are manifested in the everyday lives of citizens. ✤

IdeaBank

✻ Learning Disabled Students. "The Censors" completely lacks dialogue. Students may need help imagining the dialogue that Valenzuela only suggests or refers to. Have students choose moments in the story in which conversations are mentioned or alluded to and ask them to write or role-play dialogue that might occur during those moments. For example, students might write the actual conversation between Juan and his superiors as he reports the planned strike or the talk between Juan and his worried mother. ✻

ResourceBank

For the Student. Valenzuela, Luisa. *He Who Searches*. trans. Helen Lane. Elmwood Park, Ill.: The Dalkey Archive Press, 1987.

For the Teacher. Bogdan, D. "A Case Study of the Selection/Censorship Problem and the Educational Value of Literature." *Journal of Education* 170 (No. 2, 1988): 39–57.

Tanner, D. E. "The Textbook as a Political Instrument." *The High School Journal* 72 (April/May 1989): 182–87.

InformationBank

Historical/Cultural Note. "The Censors" may be seen as a reaction to the totalitarianism in modern Argentina. Although Valenzuela's native country is a republic, it was ruled by dictators for much of the twentieth century. Beginning in the late 1800's, free elections were held there, but in 1930 a group of army officers and some conservative party leaders seized control of the government. In 1943 a military junta led by Colonel Juan D. Perón overthrew the government. During the next twelve years, Perón seized newspapers and suppressed freedom of speech. He revised the constitution to insure his reelection and began a political quarrel with the Roman Catholic Church. It wasn't until 1958, three years after Perón fled into exile, that free elections took place again in Argentina. Perón returned in 1973 and was elected president. He died ten months later and was succeeded by his wife. A military junta ousted Isabel Martinez de Perón in 1976 on charges of corruption. Not until 1983 did democractic rule return to Argentina. Today, Argentina continues to be a free republic with an elected president.

⌘ Connections

Across Literature. Students may be interested in reading the following books about totalitarian government: *1984* by George Orwell (1949), *Farenheit 451* by Ray Bradbury (1953), *A Clockwork Orange* by Anthony Burgess (1962), *This Perfect Day* by Ira Levin (1970), or *The Dispossessed* by Ursula K. LeGuin (1974).

Across the Humanities. In the United States, foreign intelligence operations are handled by the Central Intelligence Agency (CIA) and domestic intelligence is the responsibility of the Federal Bureau of Investigation (FBI). Have students research these agencies and find out whether censorship of mail or tapping of phone calls is ever legal in the United States.

❓ Content Quiz

1. To whom does Juan write a letter? a woman named Mariana living in Paris

2. What is Juan's new job? He has taken a job as a censor in the Censorship Division of the Post Office.

3. What is one of the tasks Juan performs to check letters? [Students may name any one.] checks for explosives; checks for poison dust; analyzes content; searches for microprint

4. When Juan finally comes across the letter he wrote, what does he do? He censors it.

5. What finally happens to Juan? He is executed.

Guidelines for Response

Discussion Questions

1. What are your thoughts about Juan, the main character?

[Some students may think that Juan is mindless or he would not have caused his own untimely death. These students may explain that stupidity, not fate, has played this "dirty trick." Some students may suggest that Juan deserves his fate since he abandons his values and joins the system. Other students may say that Juan is a victim of an authoritarian control process that suffocates spirit and stifles individual creative thinking. As a result, he has lost the will to think for himself and he perishes.]

2. Why do you think Juan becomes such a perfect censor?

[Answers will vary. Some students may blame fate and say that Juan has no choice: the outcome, for which Valenzuela prepares readers at the start (". . . what he had taken as a stroke of luck was really one of fate's dirty tricks," page 130, will be the same. Other students may feel that a malicious and even evil side of Juan's character leads him to enjoy interfering in other people's lives. Students may also say that because the bureaucracy crushes Juan's will and takes away his control over his own life, he wants control over others.]

3. If you were the writer, how would you have ended this story? Support your answer with specific references to the story.

[Some students may say that the story's ending need not have been so extreme. These students may feel that Juan's being absorbed so totally into an unthinking system is tragedy enough. Other students may explain that the entire story is an exaggeration, that no one who schemes his way into an institution and then climbs its ladder so quickly could be so stupid, and thus a different ending is called for. Other students may find Juan's death inevitable, even essential, to the story's message: the denial of individual freedom eventually leads to the death of a free society. These students of course would stick with the same ending or would modify the ending very little.]

4. In your opinion, what is the story saying about perfection and about working toward goals? Explain your answer.

[Students' responses will vary. Some students may say that Juan's fate bears out the comment, early in the story, that "These things happen the minute you're careless and you let down your guard" (page 130); or "happiness—a feeling you can't trust" (page 130); or ". . . that's why Juan's so down in the dumps . . . because of his letters" (page 130). Students may suggest that Juan works so hard on one phase of his goal that he fails to look at the big picture. Even his mother "couldn't get him back on the right road" (page 131). The perfection Juan strives for becomes his downfall: Juan's narrow view of "any distraction" that "could make him lose his edge" (page 132) actually leads to his death.]

5. Of the social issues addressed in this story, which do you think is most relevant to society today? Explain.

[Students may suggest that the existence of totalitarian regimes remains the most relevant social issue. Some students may cite the corrosive and debilitating effect of bureaucracies or the pressure to conform or the human tendency to be caught up unthinkingly in extreme situations or the acceptance of injustices as inevitable or resistant to individual effort.]

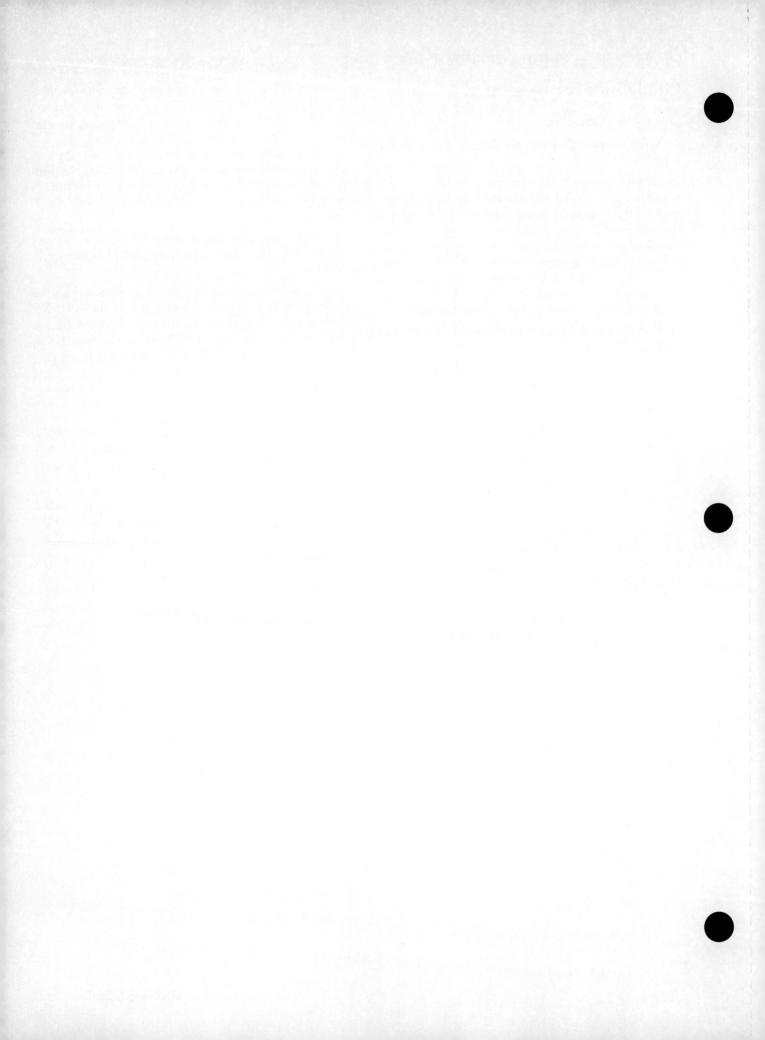

NAME ______________________ DATE ______________

The Censors (page 130)

Test

Part 1 Broad Interpretation

A. Answer the following essay questions based on your understanding of the story. Write your answers on a separate sheet of paper. (*15 points each*)

1. What kind of government is in control of the country where Juan lives? Support your answer with details from the story.
2. What do you think motivates Juan to behave as he does in this story? Explain your answer.
3. How would behavior like Juan's help a government control a country? Explain your answer.

B. Think about how Juan's values change during the course of the story. Then, on the plot line below, note the things that Juan seems to value at the various points in the story. At the right of the line are some words and phrases you may use. Or, if you prefer, you may use your own. (*15 points*)

Juan discovers Mariana's address in Paris.

Juan turns in his fellow employee for trying to start a strike.

Juan begins to fill his censor's basket.

Juan finds his own letter to Mariana.

enjoying life
promotion
Mariana's happiness
achievement
his own life
Mariana's safety
his job
work well done
freedom
his own safety
perfection
security

NAME ______________________ DATE ______________

Part 2 Close Interpretation

A. Write the letter of the best answer. Where noted, there may be more than one answer. (*8 points each*)

____ **1.** Which of the following is a reason Juan is worried at the beginning of the story? (*You may choose more than one answer.*)

a. Mariana may never know he wrote to her.

b. Mariana's safety is endangered by the letter.

c. His safety is endangered by the letter.

d. His letter contains antigovernment statements.

____ **2.** Why does Juan apply for a job at the Censorship Division?

a. He cannot find other work.

b. He wants to get back his letter.

c. He feels he would be a good censor.

d. He wants to fight censorship in his country.

____ **3.** Why does Juan ignore the danger in Section K, even after a fellow worker is injured? (*You may choose more than one answer.*)

a. He is a fearless person.

b. He is being absorbed by his job.

c. He believes the division chief's excuses.

d. He is more concerned about Mariana's danger.

____ **4.** Why does Juan begin to find antigovernment material in the letters in Section E? (*You may choose more than one answer.*)

a. He is becoming a real censor.

b. The innocent letters have been weeded out.

c. Many people are trying to fool the censors.

d. His obsession is making him lose his judgment.

B. Look over the following letter. Try to think the way Juan thinks towards the end of the story. Then, mark out the phrases you think he would censor in the letter. (*8 points*)

Dear Joe,

I'm sorry I haven't written, but you know how hard it is to get anything done these days. Everyone here is fine. Anyway, we can't complain. We hope you like it in your fine new home and, even though we miss you, we know you couldn't pass up an opportunity like that overseas.

There seems to be more rain than usual this year. Weeds are springing up everywhere. You'd hardly recognize the old place, it's changed so much.

Give our love to Maria. Maybe we'll get a chance to come see you.

Sincerely,

David

Literary Protest: Engaging the Reader

Below are suggested answers for the bar graphs assigned on page 133 of the student book. Bar graphs for six other selections are provided. Each bar graph indicates the relative appeal of details used, words chosen, and arguments presented. To a large degree, these graphs are subjective; therefore, accept other answers if students can support them with evidence from the selections.

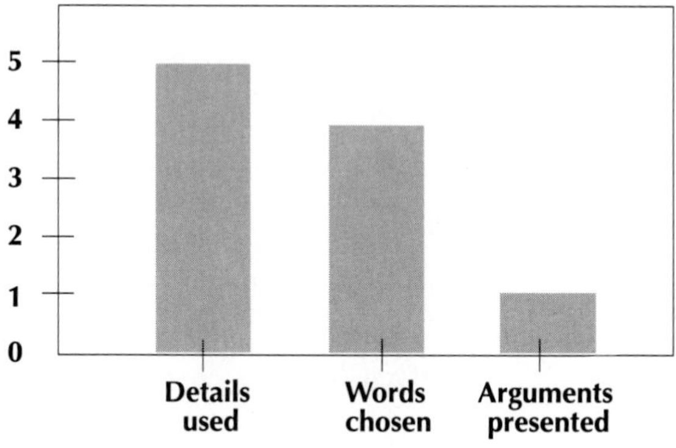

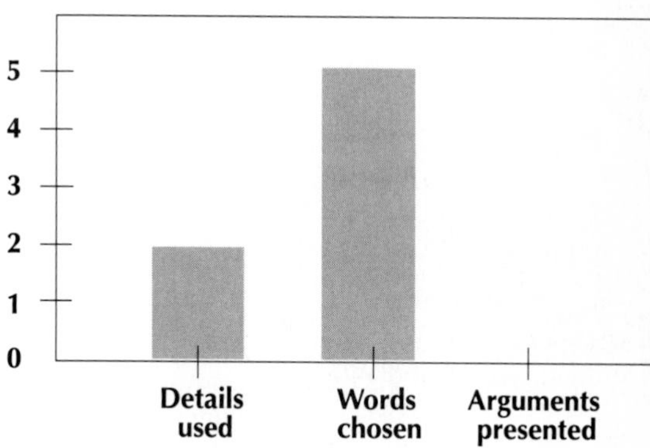

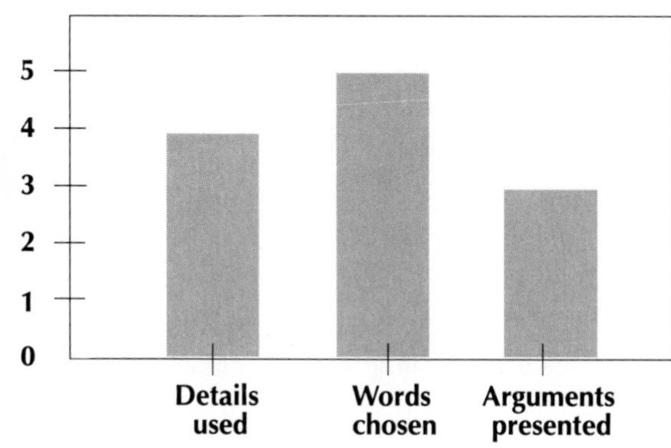

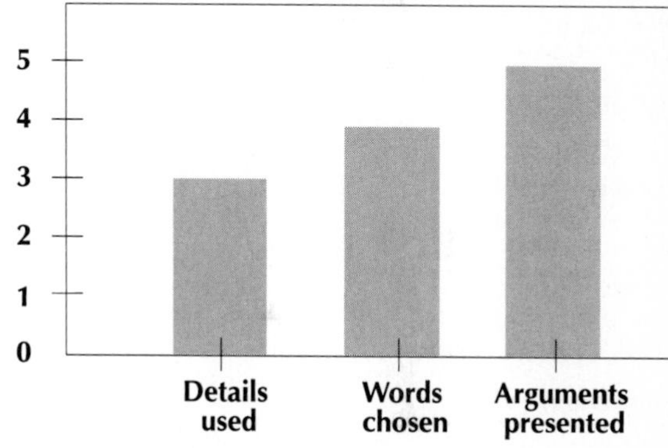

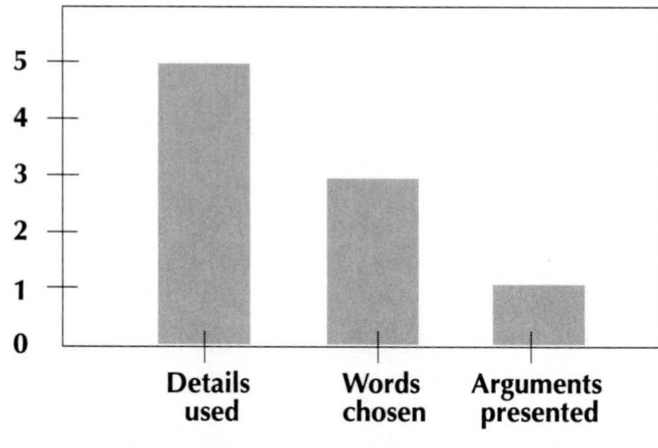

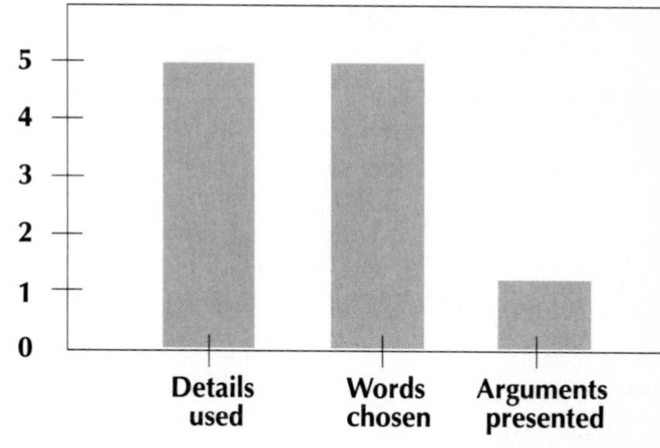

Evaluation Guide for Writing Assignment

The notes for an oral presentation should:

- State at least three generalizations clearly
- Support generalizations with examples from the selections
- Tell whether each selection appeals primarily to the mind or to the emotions
- Reflect a clear sense of audience in the choice of language

UNIT 3 Affirming Identity

Selections	Essential Vocabulary	Literary Skills	Writing Formats	Writing Modes
How It Feels to Be Colored Me				
Student Book page 138 **Teacher's Guide** Lesson, pages 134 and 135 Vocabulary Worksheet, page 136 Test, page 137	extenuating pigmentation veneer	tone diction	journal proposal program notes autobiographical essay article script introduction notes personal response	expressive and personal writing observation and description narrative and imaginative writing informative (expository) writing: synthesis persuasion writing about literature
I Have a Dream				
Student Book page 144 **Teacher's Guide** Lesson, pages 139 and 140 Vocabulary Worksheet, page 141 Test, pages 143 and 144	manacles segregation degenerate discrimination languishing militancy redemptive tribulations discords	persuasion	journal cue cards editorial speech captions instructions review letter petition	expressive and personal writing narrative and imaginative writing informative (expository) writing: classification informative (expository) writing: analysis informative (expository) writing: synthesis persuasion
Getting a Job ***from* I Know Why the Caged Bird Sings**				
Student Book page 151 **Teacher's Guide** Lesson, pages 145 and 146 Vocabulary Worksheet, page 147 Test, pages 149 and 150	supercilious hypocrisy aphorisms	autobiography	journal campaign poster campaign speech character sketch ballad aphorisms storyboards poem biographical sketch	expressive and personal writing observation and description narrative and imaginative writing informative (expository) writing: analysis informative (expository) writing: synthesis persuasion writing about literature
***from* Barrio Boy**				
Student Book page 159 **Teacher's Guide** Lesson, pages 151 and 152 Vocabulary Worksheet, page 153 Test, pages 155 and 156	boisterous formidable alien indignation reverie	tone theme	journal human interest story tribute family tree notes anecdote booklet editorial questions program cookbook	expressive and personal writing observation and description narrative and imaginative writing informative (expository) writing: analysis informative (expository) writing: synthesis persuasion
***from* Hunger of Memory**				
Student Book page 169 **Teacher's Guide** Lesson, pages 157 and 158 Vocabulary Worksheet, page 159 Test, pages 161 and 162	grandiose appraisals epigrams	theme autobiography	journal slogans script report graph autobiographical sketch diary entry	expressive and personal writing informative (expository) writing: analysis informative (expository) writing: synthesis persuasion

Selections	Essential Vocabulary	Literary Skills	Writing Formats	Writing Modes
High Horse's Courting				
Student Book page 175 **Teacher's Guide** Lesson, pages 163 and 164 Test, pages 165 and 166		oral literature	journal story notes speech explanation captions outline	expressive and personal writing narrative and imaginative writing informative (expository) writing: analysis persuasion report (research)
The Secret Lion				
Student Book page 181 **Teacher's Guide** Lesson, pages 167 and 168 Test, pages 169 and 170		style setting	journal handbook speech letter interpretive essay autobiographical sketch dramatic monologue	expressive and personal writing narrative and imaginative writing informative (expository) writing: synthesis writing about literature
My Delicate Heart Condition				
Student Book page 188 **Teacher's Guide** Lesson, pages 171 and 172 Vocabulary Worksheet, page 173 Test, pages 175 and 176	rheumatic	The student book does not contain discussion questions, analysis of literary techniques, or writing assignments for this story. These materials appear in the Teacher's Guide lesson.		
Reviewing Concepts				
Student Book page 193 **Teacher's Guide** page 177				

How It Feels to Be Colored Me

Zora Neale Hurston

page 138

- **Vocabulary Worksheet,** TG page 136
- **Test,** TG page 137

Objectives

1. To respond to an essay that describes the writer's sense of herself as a unique individual.

2. To examine the literary concepts of tone and diction.

3. To express ideas in a variety of writing formats: journal, proposal, program notes, autobiographical essay, article, script, introduction, notes, annotations.

Summary

Zora Neale Hurston describes her first thirteen years in the all-black town of Eatonville, Florida, which gave her no experience of prejudice and racial discrimination. By the time she went to go to high school in Jacksonville, Florida, her sense of herself was too well established to be impaired by racial prejudice. She describes how her awareness of her blackness depends on her circumstances and the people she is with. Above all, she sees herself as an individual filled with hopes, dreams, ambitions, memories, burdens, and fears.

IdeaBank

▲ **Motivation.** As an alternative to the Connecting Writing and Reading activity, ask students to write in their journals answers to these questions: Where did you grow up? Describe that place. What was the best thing about growing up there? What was the worst thing? What is one positive memory you have about that place? What is one negative memory you have? How do you think you might be different if you had grown up somewhere else? Then have students read the essay, noting how Hurston's feelings about herself stem from her growing up in Eatonville, Florida. ▲

IdeaBank

✲ **Collaborative Learning.** Have students work in groups of three and take turns reading segments of the essay aloud. As each student finishes reading, invite the other members of the group to identify effective words and phrases. ✲

⌘ Connections

Across the Language Arts. This essay contains several examples of figurative language, such as the extended metaphor in which Hurston compares herself to a brown bag filled with "a jumble of small things priceless and worthless." Point out that the essay is useful as a model for incorporating figurative language into students' own descriptive and narrative writing.

If the grammar and composition book you use has a lesson on figurative language, you may want to refer to this lesson. The examples and exercises in that lesson can be supplemented with examples drawn from "How It Feels to Be Colored Me."

> *"Zora grew up in a community of black people who had enormous respect for themselves. . . . This community affirmed her right to exist, and loved her as an extension of its self."*
>
> — Alice Walker, *In Search of Our Mother's Gardens,* 1983

IdeaBank

★ **Interactive Assessment.** Ask pairs of students who wrote autobiographical essays or articles for assignment 2 of Connecting Reading and Writing to evaluate each other's essays or articles, looking for the following key elements and offering suggestions:

- specific memories or incidents
- appropriate tone and diction

Have students discuss with their peer editors the changes suggested and then briefly explain on a separate sheet of paper why they did or did not follow a suggestion. Have students attach their peer-editor's suggestions and their own comments to the final copy of their essay. ★

ResourceBank

For the Student. Walker, Alice, ed. *I Love Myself When I Am Laughing and Then When I Am Looking Mean and Impressive: A Zora Neale Hurston Reader*. New York: Feminist Press at the City University of New York, 1979.

For the Teacher. Hurston, Zora Neale. *Dust Tracks on a Road: An Autobiography*. Second edition. Champaign, Ill.: University of Illinois Press, 1984.

❸ Content Quiz

1. What kind of community was Eatonville, Florida, when Zora Neale Hurston was growing up? a black community

2. When did Zora Neale Hurston say she "became colored"? at age thirteen; when she was sent to school in Jacksonville, Florida

3. How does Hurston feel about being black? She feels positive and ready to take on the world.

4. When does Hurston feel her color very strongly? when she is thrown against a sharp white background

5. What comparison does Hurston make to indicate that she thinks people from different races are quite similar inside? She compares people to different colored bags filled with a jumble of priceless and worthless things.

Guidelines for Response

Thinking About the Essay, page 142

1. Some students may say that Hurston seems strong, buoyant, confident, and comfortable with herself. Others may comment that she seems like a keen observer. Some may feel that she is slightly conceited or egotistical.

2. Students may point out that in calling herself a brown bag, Hurston is stressing that she is "a jumble of small things priceless and worthless" (page 141). She sees her kinship with all people who are filled with tokens of past experience. In interpreting Hurston's assertion that if all human "bags" were dumped in a single heap, each bag could be refilled "without altering the content of any greatly" (page 141), students may say that all races share similar impulses, feelings, and experiences. In calling herself a "brown" bag, however, Hurston does suggest her African-American heritage in company "with other bags, white, red, and yellow." Some students may say that without reading this description they would not have grasped the sense of kinship Hurston feels with all other people. Others may say that they would still have the same impression of Hurston as a person who relates well to others.

3. Students may say that when Hurston declares "I am not tragically colored," they think of words such as *positive* or *upbeat* to describe her character. Some students may feel that Hurston shows how strong and realistic she is when she states that slavery is history and that she "must not halt in the stretch to look behind and weep" (page 140). Some students will notice that Hurston feels most aware of her color when she is the lone black person in a situation or when she is with a white person at a gathering of black people. Students may feel that this shows Hurston's sensitivity and understanding of others. They may point out that Hurston often is unaware of her color, such as when she saunters down Seventh Avenue thinking of herself primarily as a woman, "the eternal feminine with its string of beads" (page 141). Students may say that Hurston's overall response to discrimination—"How *can* any deny themselves the pleasure of my company?" (page 141)—shows her self-worth, her confidence, and her determination to succeed by being herself.

4. Students may mention that for the first thirteen years of her life, Hurston had no awareness of herself as "colored" and thus was able to grow and become confident without experiencing discrimination. Some students may feel that if Hurston had felt discrimination at an earlier age, her enthusiasm might have been dampened by such negative experiences. Others may argue that Hurston is such a strong individual that no experience of racial prejudice, even in her formative years, could have held her back.

5. Some students may comment that Hurston does not emphasize her gender except to say that at times she emerges as the "eternal feminine." Even when recalling her experience at Barnard, a women's college, Hurston speaks more of her race rather than her sex as an aspect of her experience. Some students may argue that Hurston is a person who transcends all limitations such as race and sex, seeing herself as "merely a fragment of the Great Soul" (page 141).

6. Students may feel that Hurston's view of her heritage is more positive than Hughes's and Cullen's. Hughes writes of "the wall" that darkens his life and hides the light of his dreams. Cullen sees humans as linked, but his primary emphasis is on sharing sorrows: "My sorrow must be laid / On your head like a crown." Hurston refuses to let discrimination diminish her pride: "Sometimes, I feel discriminated against, but it does not make me angry. It merely astonishes me" (page 141).

Analyzing the Writer's Craft, page 143

Key words and phrases students may identify include *plunges, constricts the thorax, splits the heart, narcotic harmonies, rambunctious, rears on its hind legs, primitive fury, clawing it, exultingly, dance wildly, yell within, whoop, shake my assegai, living in the jungle way, throbbing like a war drum,* and *the veneer we call civilization.*

Connecting Reading and Writing, page 143

For assignment 1, bring in program notes for several different kinds of assemblies to serve as models.

For assignment 3, have students read their completed scripts, taking the parts of the host and the featured writers.

For assignment 4, provide samples of annotated poems for students to examine.

NAME ______________________________ DATE ______________

How It Feels to Be Colored Me (page 138)

Vocabulary Worksheet

Essential Vocabulary

extenuating *adj*. Lessening or seeming to lessen the seriousness of by giving excuses.

pigmentation *n*. Coloration due to the presence of pigment in the tissue.

veneer *n*. A thin surface layer of fine wood or costly material laid over a base of common material; any attractive but superficial appearance.

Useful Words

constrict *v*. To make smaller or narrower by binding or squeezing.

deplore *v*. To be regretful or sorry about; regard as unfortunate.

exultingly *adv*. In a way that shows great rejoicing; triumphantly.

raiment *n*. Clothing.

thorax *n*. In humans, the part of the body between the neck and the abdomen; chest.

Fill in each set of blanks with the correct word from the word list. (Clue: The boxed letters will spell the personal aspect that Hurston explores in this essay.)

1. If you're literally too big for your britches, your pants do this to you. _ _ _ _ _ _ [ ] _ _
2. We do this regarding serious subjects, such as homelessness, and less serious ones, such as a friend's bad taste. [ ] _ _ _ _ _ _
3. This is something of great use to furniture makers and phonies. _ _ _ [ ] _ _
4. You hope that this describes the circumstances you tell the judge in an effort to justify your speeding. _ _ _ _ [ ] _ _ _ _ _ _
5. People who work on their tans are trying to increase this in themselves. _ _ _ _ _ _ [ ] _ _ _ _ _
6. This is what people put on, whether it's blue jeans, blazers, berets, or bobby socks. _ _ [ ] _ _ _ _
7. This is where a bear hug puts the squeeze on you. [ ] _ _ _ _ _
8. This is how people usually react to winning a big game, a major battle, or a hard-fought campaign. _ _ _ _ _ _ _ _ _ [ ]

NAME ______________________ DATE ______________

How It Feels to Be Colored Me (page 138)

Test

Part 1 Broad Interpretation

Answer the following essay questions based on your understanding of the essay. Write your answers on a separate sheet of paper. *(30 points each)*

1. What do you think Hurston means when she says you could empty the different-colored bags into one pile and then refill them without significantly changing the nature of their contents? Do you agree with her? Explain your answers.
2. In your opinion, would a group of black people be more likely to appreciate Hurston's views on life than a group of white people would? Explain your answer.

Part 2 Close Interpretation

Hurston's diction, or choice of words, in her essay is important in conveying her tone, or attitude. For each quotation below, underline the key word or phrase that helps to convey Hurston's attitude. In the boxes on the right, briefly identify her attitude. (*10 points each*)

Key word or phrase	Tone
1. "I have seen that the world is to the strong regardless of a little pigmentation more or less."	
2. "The game of keeping what one has is never so exciting as the game of getting."	
3. "Among the thousand white persons, I am a dark rock surged upon, and overswept, but through it all, I remain myself. When covered by the waters, I am; and the ebb but reveals me again."	
4. "Perhaps that is how the Great Stuffer of Bags filled them in the first place—who knows?"	

I Have a Dream

Martin Luther King, Jr.

page 144

- **Vocabulary Worksheet,** TG page 141
- **Test,** TG pages 143 and 144

Objectives

1. To respond to a speech about an important national problem.
2. To analyze the literary technique of persuasion.
3. To express ideas in a variety of formats: journal, cue cards, editorial, speech, captions, instructions, review, letter, petition.

Summary

Martin Luther King, Jr., delivered this speech at a rally for civil rights in Washington, D.C., on August 28, 1963. He recalls that the Emancipation Proclamation freed the slaves; however, he believes that African Americans are still experiencing the effects of segregation laws and discrimination. King calls for the immediate granting of equal rights for all Americans, regardless of race. King reminds his people that their protest must be nonviolent. He cites many examples of injustices suffered by African Americans in the United States and encourages his listeners to continue with their struggle in the South and in northern cities. The stirring phrase "I have a dream" dramatically highlights King's faith in a future in which he envisions brotherhood and equality between all Americans.

IdeaBank

▲ **Motivation.** Have students rate the following national problems from 1 to 9, numbering the most important problem as 1 and the least important problem as 9.

__ pollution	__ acid rain
__ homelessness	__ budget deficit
__ poverty	__ crime
__ drug abuse	__ illiteracy
__ racism	

Students can add any additional national problems that they feel are important to the list. Ask them to conduct a class survey to discover which problem facing the nation is most important to the class as a whole. ▲

InformationBank

Historical Note. The idea of holding a March on Washington for jobs and freedom resulted from a conference attended by many civil rights leaders. The participants marched from the Washington Monument to the Lincoln Memorial, where they heard freedom songs and speeches by civil rights, labor, and religious leaders. A newspaper columnist from *The New York Times*, Russell Baker, said of the event: "The sweetness and patience of the crowd may have set some sort of national high-water mark in mass decency."

"I Have a Dream" was the last speech delivered in the five-hour program. The famous speech was largely extemporaneous; moved by the significance of the event, King discarded the text he had prepared and spoke from his heart. Many march participants were moved to tears. Many Northern newspapers praised the speech and quoted it extensively. The speech was heard or read by millions of people in Europe, Africa, and Asia as well as the United States.

> *"A nation or civilization that continues to produce soft-minded men purchases its own spiritual death on the installment plan."*
>
> — Martin Luther King, Jr., from *Quotations in Black,* Anita King, ed., 1981

IdeaBank

✤ **Multimodal Activity.** Students might be interested in watching a videocassette recording of the PBS series *Eyes on the Prize,* which is about the civil rights movement—particularly the episode that deals with the 1963 march on Washington. ✤

⌘ Connections

Across the Language Arts. Examples drawn from "I Have a Dream" may be used to illustrate sentence variety and figurative language. Point out how these examples enrich King's speech. Encourage students to use them as models for their own writing.

Across the Humanities. Have students research the Civil Rights movement in the United States during the 1950's and 1960's. Encourage them to find out about Rosa Parks, John Lewis, the Freedom Riders, and other Civil Rights leaders.

ResourceBank

For the Student. *Doctor Martin Luther King, Jr. . . An Amazing Grace*. 62 min., 3/4" and 1/2" videocassette. CRM/McGraw-Hill Films, 1978.

King, Dr. Martin Luther, Jr. *I Have a Dream: Original Address from the March on Washington, August 1963*. 20th Century Fox Records, 1968. Sound disk.

For the Teacher. Mills, Micolaus. "Heard and Unheard Speeches: What Really Happened at the March on Washington?" *Dissent* 35 (Summer 1988): 285–292.

Thornton, Jeannye. "King's Dream: How It Stands 20 Years Later." *U.S. News and World Report* 95 (August 29, 1983): 47.

Guidelines for Response

Thinking About the Speech, page 149

1. Responses may vary. Some students may be impressed by the repetition of the famous "I have a dream" section of the speech. Others may choose from the many metaphorical passages in the piece.

2. Students may suggest that the root of the problems King outlines is the difference in status of whites and blacks in this country; the examples of discrimination that he mentions include police brutality, lack of voting rights, lack of access to public accommodations, and discrimination in housing (page 147). The solution therefore lies in demanding that blacks have the same rights and privileges as whites. They may cite King's dream that "the sons of former slaves and the sons of former slave owners will be able to sit down together at the table of brotherhood" (page 148) and his hope that his children will be judged not by their color but by their character (page 148).

3. Students may suppose that quotations from the Declaration of Independence, the Constitution, and the national anthem remind King's listeners that the United States historically represents individual freedom, equality, and justice; these documents also add credence and respectability to King's arguments. Others may note that these are important documents for all races. Students may suggest that the spiritual adds a religious tone or that it emphasizes a unique part of African-American culture.

4. The concrete examples in King's "I have a dream" passage, students may suggest, are examples of what King means by freedom and justice. To King, justice means an end to segregation and police brutality. Freedom means equal opportunity for jobs and a chance to escape from poverty, a nation where sons of slaves and slave owners will sit down together, or a nation where children are judged not by their color but by their character. Others may note that King insists that freedom and justice come with "dignity and discipline."

5. Responses will vary. Some students may believe that King would still address the general issues of freedom and justice for African Americans. Others may think that he might include specific problems that have become more serious since 1963, such as drug use, gang violence, homelessness, and the breakdown of the family; he might also mention the need for more role models in the African-American community.

6. Students may suggest that the issue of freedom and justice is an issue that transcends a particular time and place. They may cite some of the specific issues that King uses, such as segregated motels and drinking fountains, as more directly tied to the problems in 1963.

7. Students may find many elements that make this a great speech: its poetic, lyrical tone; the use of metaphor and repetition; the way it builds power to convey its message. Other students may find that some of these same techniques, especially repetition, detract from the message.

Analyzing the Writer's Craft, pages 149–150

Students should note that King uses many techniques to accomplish his purposes. He cites well-known authorities and uses arguments that appeal both to logic and emotion.

Connecting Reading and Writing, page 150

Students who do assignment 1 may need help in locating media accounts of the march on Washington in 1963.

Before beginning item 3, the assignment on metaphor, small groups of students may wish to discuss some of the metaphorical language in King's speech.

If the grammar and composition book you use has a lesson on persuasive writing, you may want to refer to this lesson.

❷ Content Quiz

1. Martin Luther King, Jr., gave this speech during a huge demonstration that called for civil rights for African Americans.

2. The demonstration took place in Washington, D.C.

3. In his speech King cautions the marchers against the use of physical violence in the struggle for civil rights.

4./5. King dreamed that one day his children would be judged by the content of their character, rather than the color of their skin.

NAME ______________________________ DATE ______________

I Have a Dream (page 144)

Vocabulary Worksheet

Essential Vocabulary

degenerate *v.* To become less moral, cultured, and so on.
discords *n.* Tones sounded together that lack harmony.
discrimination *n.* A showing of favoritism or prejudice in treatment.
languish *v.* To live under distressing conditions or in a state of suffering.
manacles *n.* Handcuffs.
militancy *n.* The state of being ready and willing to fight, especially, aggressively active in support of a cause.
redemptive *adj.* Having the power to restore one by making up for wrongdoing.
segregation *n.* The policy of forcing racial groups to live apart from each other, go to separate schools, etc.
tribulation *n.* A cause of great misery and distress; a deep sorrow.

In each blank below, fill in the word from the list above that fits the description. If more than one word seems to fit, decide which fits best.

__________ **1.** This is unfair treatment. When a person or group is treated differently because of race, sex, or belief, this is what is going on.

__________ **2.** This is the opposite of "to become better" or "to rise above." A neighborhood can do this by becoming a slum. Some illegal drugs cause a person to do this.

__________ **3.** This comes from a Latin word that means "to be faint." When people do this, they lose their strength. It is often said that people do this in poverty or in prison.

__________ **4.** This comes from a Latin word that means "to cause suffering." It is something that is hard to bear. It is the opposite of a blessing.

__________ **5.** This comes from a Latin word that means "apart." It was once legal in many parts of our country and was symbolized by drinking fountain and washroom signs that said Whites Only.

__________ **6.** This comes from the Latin word for soldier. We encourage this when we tell people not to let others walk all over them. We try to discourage this in someone who seems to be just itching for a fight.

__________ **7.** This comes from a Latin word that means "to get or buy back." If you felt guilty for wronging someone and then felt better after doing a good deed for that person, your good deed would have been this.

__________ **8.** These are sounds that are disagreeable to hear because they don't blend. They may be the sounds of disagreement itself. You would hear them while listening to clashing swords or bad piano playing.

__________ **9.** This comes from the Latin word for hand and means "objects used to restrain the hands."

NAME ______________________ DATE ______________

I Have a Dream (page 144)

Test

Part 1 Broad Interpretation

A. Think about King's dream. Then, write the letters of the things that are a part of his dream in the space at the right. *(12 points)*

a.	freedom	**m.**	despair
b.	justice	**n.**	faith
c.	equality	**o.**	violence
d.	racism	**p.**	gloom
e.	fear	**q.**	poverty
f.	peace	**r.**	segregation
g.	pride	**s.**	bitterness
h.	joy	**t.**	cooperation
i.	hatred	**u.**	patriotism
j.	hope	**v.**	spirituality
k.	guilt	**w.**	forgiveness
l.	charity	**x.**	self-respect

B. Answer the following essay questions based on your understanding of the speech. Write your answers on a separate sheet of paper. *(12 points each)*

1. Imagine that you were part of the crowd assembled around the Lincoln Memorial in 1963 to protest racism and listen to King deliver his speech. Years later, your grandchildren ask you, "What was it like to be part of that day?" How would you answer them? Explain.
2. How do you think King expected his dream to be realized? Use examples from the speech to support your answer.
3. After reading the speech, how would you describe King's view of human nature and human potential?
4. To what extent do you think King's dream has come true? Do you think the parts of the dream as yet unfulfilled will still come true? Explain your answer.

Part 2 Close Interpretation

A. Write the letter of the best answer. Where noted, there may be more than one answer. *(7 points each)*

____ **1.** King thinks that a promissory note was written by America's forefathers to

a. white Americans only.

b. black Americans only.

c. all Americans, regardless of race.

____ **2.** Which of the following does King believe is true of the Constitution?

a. It must be replaced before his dream can be realized.

b. It has served black Americans as well as it has served white Americans.

c. It promises black Americans the same rights that it promises white Americans.

____ **3.** Who does King think will benefit from the realization of his dream?

a. White Americans only.

b. Black Americans only.

c. All Americans, regardless of race.

____ **4.** Which of the following does King believe *cannot* coexist with freedom? *(You may choose more than one answer.)*

a. Peace.

b. Poverty.

c. Discrimination.

____ **5.** Which of the following is part of an extended metaphor employed by King in the speech? *(You may choose more than one answer.)*

a. A dream.

b. A promissory note.

c. A cotton plantation.

B. King's speech had a persuasive impact on many people. Fill in the bar graph to show how important you think his appeal to reason and his appeal to emotion were. *(5 points)*

	Not important ... Very important
Appeal to reason	
Appeal to emotion	

Getting a Job

from I Know Why the Caged Bird Sings

Maya Angelou

page 151

- **Vocabulary Worksheet,** TG page 147
- **Test,** TG pages 149 and 150

Objectives

1. To respond to an autobiographical excerpt about a fifteen-year-old's determination to get a job.

2. To understand autobiography.

3. To express ideas in a variety of writing formats: journal, campaign poster, campaign speech, character sketch, ballad, aphorisms, storyboards, poem, and biographical sketch.

Summary

Fifteen-year-old Marguerite Johnson decides to get a job. Through the process of elimination, she settles on the idea of becoming a conductorette on the San Francisco streetcars. Her mother tells her that blacks do not work on streetcars, but Marguerite is determined. Predictably, the receptionist at the streetcar office turns Marguerite away, telling her that they are only taking applicants from agencies. Marguerite demands to talk to the personnel manager but is told that he is out for the day. Traveling home on the streetcar, Marguerite becomes even more determined to get the job. After many efforts to gain support, Marguerite is finally given an application. Soon thereafter, she is hired as a conductorette, becoming the first black to work on the streetcars. Marguerite resumes classes in the spring, thinking that now, with her own bank account and new clothes, she will be more like her classmates. Instead, she realizes that through her experiences she has grown away from them.

IdeaBank

▲ **Motivation.** After students complete the job applications for the Connecting Writing and Reading activity, have them work in pairs to role-play interviews for a job they would like to have, taking turns as applicant and interviewer. Allow five minutes for each interview. Encourage students to discuss any jobs or volunteer positions they may have actually applied for, and have them compare their experiences with those of Marguerite. ▲

IdeaBank

✱ Limited English Proficient Students
Divide the selection into sections of about one page each. Pair LEP students with native speakers. Have the native speaker read each page aloud, a paragraph at a time, while the LEP student formulates questions based on the reading. After all the pairs have finished, have each pair present its questions for response by the class. ✱

IdeaBank

✤ Multimodal Activities

1. Have students present a one-minute television or radio announcement to advertise the motorette and conductorette jobs mentioned in this excerpt from *I Know Why the Caged Bird Sings*.

2. Have students compose a blues song, either comical or serious, about the difficulties of looking for a job. Invite a student who plays bass guitar to accompany students who perform their songs for the class. ✤

InformationBank

Historical Note. That Maya Angelou succeeded in becoming the first black to work on the San Francisco streetcars is all the more remarkable in light of the fact that the civil rights movement was at least a decade away. It was not until 1954, for example, that the Supreme Court's decision in *Brown v. Board of Education of Topeka* reversed the 1896 "separate but equal" ruling on compulsory segregation in public schools.

ResourceBank

For the Student. Allman, Joanna *et al. The Black Female Experience in America.* Welfare Women's Educational Equity Act Program. Knoxville, Tenn.: University of Tennessee, 1979; distributed by Education Development Center, Inc., Newton, Mass.

For the Teacher. Feistritzer, P. "Maya Angelou: Confronting Life with Wonder." *Momentum* 16 (December 1985): 11.

Mayer, J. E. "Neighborhoods: Maya Angelou's 'Harlem Hopscotch'." *English Journal* 77 (September 1988): 86–87.

IdeaBank

★ **Interactive Assessment.** Have students who prepared campaign posters or speeches for the first Connecting Reading and Writing activity try to elicit responses from their classmates. Have students who made posters display them in the classroom, attaching a sheet of notebook paper for comments and suggestions. ★

Guidelines for Response

Thinking About the Selection, page 156

1. Some students may see Marguerite as determined, assured, tireless, strong, and confident. Others may feel that she is stubborn, inflexible, and uncompromising.

2. Some students may believe that Marguerite has romanticized the job to the point that she is determined to make this dream a reality. Other students may say that Marguerite is responding to the challenge of becoming the first black conductorette and overcoming the prejudice that she encounters. Some students may attribute Marguerite's determination to adolescent stubbornness, whereas others may point out that Marguerite wants to prove her self-sufficiency and maturity to herself and her mother.

3. Students may suggest that Marguerite's persistence and determination wear down the personnel manager. Others may suggest that some of the black organizations that Marguerite appealed to for help eventually pressured the company to hire her. Some students may note that the company had advertised for conductorettes and that the labor pool was probably reduced because of the war.

4. Students may react positively to all the aphorisms that her mother uses to encourage Marguerite to pursue her dream, seeing them as the essence of her philosophy of life. They may feel that she is most concerned with preparing Marguerite for the real world and that she will support her daughter in whatever she wants to do. Some may say that Marguerite's mother seems negligent since she is not upset when Marguerite chooses to work for a semester instead of going to school. They may also feel that she does not give Marguerite realistic advice.

5. Some students may predict a successful life for Marguerite because she is so determined to reach her goals. Others may feel that she might become disillusioned if she finds she continually has to fight the same battles against prejudice. Since Marguerite's experiences are so different from those of her classmates, some may say that she will have a difficult time fitting in at school.

6. Many students will recognize similarities between this selection and a short story. They may note that it has a basic plot structure that is built around a conflict—the conflict between Marguerite and the personnel department of the streetcar company. Students may also note that this selection has believable, motivated characters and an inspiring message about personal determination.

7. Students may suggest that the title refers to the joy that can be found in even the most difficult situations. They may note that although Marguerite battles prejudice to get her job and works long, hard hours to keep it, she enjoys having fulfilled her dream. Students may suggest that the caged bird represents Marguerite's potential trapped behind the bars of prejudice and complacency. Students may say that the bird can still sing because of its inner need for self-expression and self-fulfillment.

8. Students may mention that prejudice is still an obstacle in certain situations today and that such situations would require the determination exhibited by Angelou. Less complex situations might also be mentioned: making an athletic team, finding a summer job, saving money for a purchase, or working hard to make the honor roll.

Analyzing the Writer's Craft, page 157

Some poems by students may focus on Marguerite's determination. Other poems may include expressions of the joy Marguerite feels when riding the streetcars or the isolation she feels on returning to school at the beginning of the new semester.

Connecting Reading and Writing, page 157

Students who do the option to assignment 1 might enjoy reading their campaign speeches to their classmates.

To help students with assignment 3, model the activity by writing your own aphorism on the board and discussing its significance with the class.

❷ Content Quiz

1. What job does Marguerite decide she wants? street-car conductorette

2. Why does Marguerite's mother try to discourage her at first? She thinks the attempt will be futile because there are no black conductorettes.

3. How does the receptionist at the Market Street Railway Company respond to Marguerite? She turns her away, telling her that the company is only accepting applicants from agencies and that the personnel manager is out.

4. From whom does Marguerite receive advice? her mother; black organizations

5. What is one thing Marguerite must do before she is given a job? [Students may name any one.] fill out a job application form; have an interview; take a blood test; take an aptitude test; take a physical coordination test

NAME ______________________ DATE ____________

Getting a Job

Vocabulary Worksheet

from I Know Why the Caged Bird Sings (page 151)

Essential Vocabulary

aphorism *n.* A short sentence expressing a wise observation or a general truth.

hypocrisy *n.* A pretending to be what one is not or to believe what one does not.

supercilious *adj.* Looking down on others; characterized by pride or scorn.

Useful Words

alien *adj.* Strange; not natural.

ancestor *n.* Any person from whom one is descended.

aperture *n.* An opening; hole.

charade *n.* An action or show of feeling that is easily seen as misleading or insincere.

conveyance *n.* A vehicle; a way to transport things.

gumption *n.* Courage and boldness.

terse *adj.* Using no more words than are needed.

Fill in each set of blanks with the correct word from the word list. (Clue: The boxed letters will spell one kind of job.)

1. The most sincere sounding apology will be taken to be this if a grin is tugging at the sides of your mouth while you speak. _ _ _ _ _ [ ] _
2. Pool hustlers and spies have to be good at this to be successful. _ _ _ [ ] _ _ _ _ _
3. It takes this to be a pioneer or an explorer or to make fun of bullies to their faces. [ ] _ _ _ _ _ _ _
4. Whether this describes basketball players depends more on their attitudes than on their notable physical characteristics. _ _ _ _ _ [ ] _ _ _ _ _ _
5. In an unfamiliar situation, you might use this word to describe how you feel. [ ] _ _ _ _
6. A parent is always one and so is a father, but a brother or sister may or may not be. _ _ _ _ _ [ ] _ _
7. This may be a truck, a horse, a unicycle, or a person wearing a backpack. _ _ _ _ _ _ _ _ [ ] _
8. "Two's company, three's a crowd" is an example of this. _ _ [ ] _ _ _ _ _
9. One who says "Please accept my greatest, most grateful gratitude, and how can I ever repay you?" instead of "Thanks" is not this. _ [ ] _ _ _
10. A doughnut has one; a doughnut hole doesn't. _ _ _ _ _ _ [ ] _

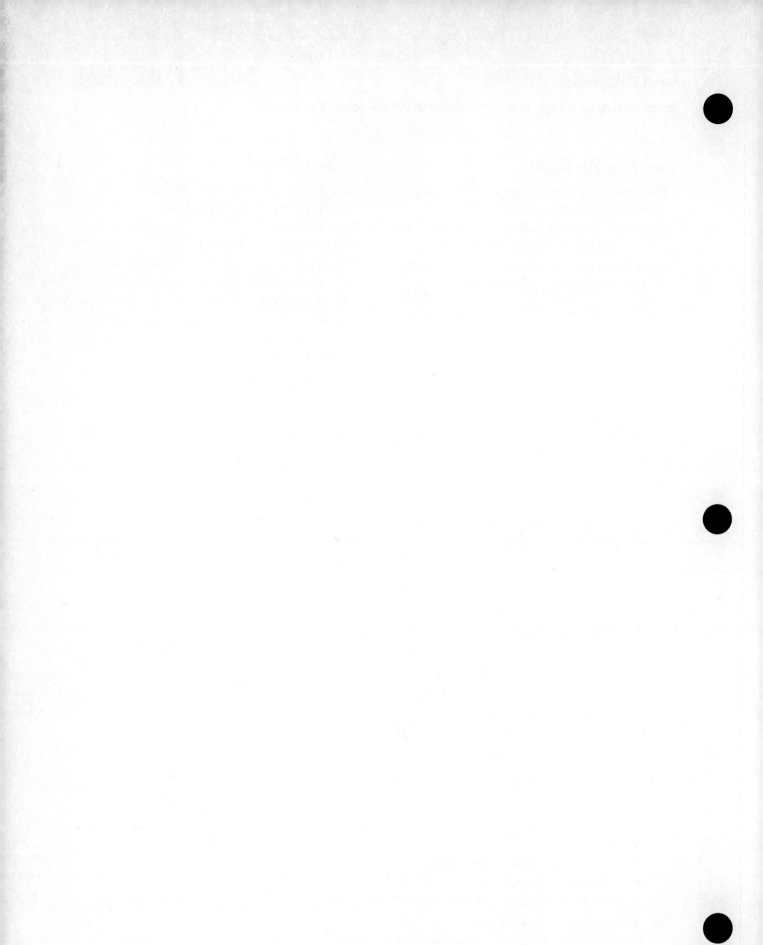

NAME ____________________ DATE ____________

Getting a Job

from I Know Why the Caged Bird Sings (page 151)

Test

Part 1 Broad Interpretation

Answer the following essay questions based on your understanding of the selection. Write your answers on a separate sheet of paper. (*20 points each*)

1. What do you think Marguerite learns from the experience of getting and doing a job? Explain your answer.
2. What do you think motivates Marguerite to go after this particular job with such determination? Support your answer with details from the selection.
3. How would you describe Marguerite's mother? Support your answer with details from the selection.

Part 2 Close Interpretation

A. Think about how Marguerite views the encounter with the receptionist and how her view changes after her exchange with the conductorette. Then, in the boxes below, write brief notes reflecting your thoughts. (*20 points*)

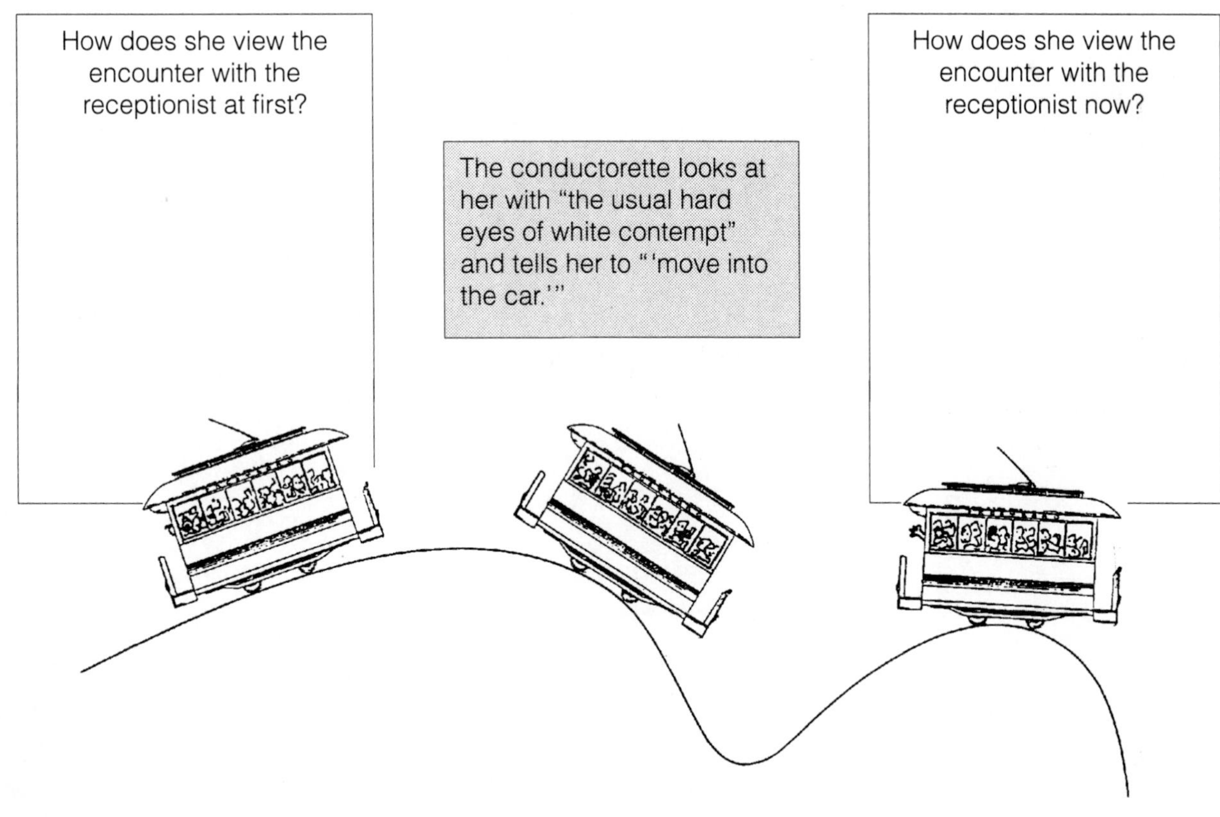

How does she view the encounter with the receptionist at first?
The conductorette looks at her with "the usual hard eyes of white contempt" and tells her to "'move into the car.'"
How does she view the encounter with the receptionist now?

NAME ______________________ DATE ______________

B. In this autobiographical excerpt the writer reveals a great deal about what kind of person she is. In each of the boxes on the left, identify a characteristic of Marguerite's. In each box on the right, note a detail from the selection that reveals that characteristic. (*20 points*)

Characteristic	Detail that reveals it

from Barrio Boy

Ernesto Galarza

page 159

- **Vocabulary Worksheet,** TG page 153
- **Test,** TG pages 155 and 156

Objectives

1. To respond to an autobiographical excerpt that recounts a young boy's adjustment to a new country.

2. To understand the theme of a selection.

3. To express ideas in a variety of writing formats: journal, human interest story, tribute, family tree, notes, anecdote, booklet, editorial, questions, program, and cookbook.

Summary

Ernesto Galarza, who has moved to the United States from Mexico, encounters many unfamiliar customs in Sacramento, California, where his family has settled. His mother accompanies him to the Lincoln School, where Miss Hopley, the principal, greets them warmly. Miss Hopley brings Ernesto to his first-grade teacher, Miss Ryan, whose patience, attention, and enthusiasm enable Ernesto to learn quickly. He meets students from different nations and compares the school to a "griddle" because it roasts racial hatreds out of them. Ernesto learns to be proud of his Mexican heritage while becoming a proud American. In the third grade, he runs for class president, but loses to fellow student Homer; he begins to learn the meaning of democracy. One morning, Ernesto witnesses Miss Hopley's "sizzling Americanism" when she orders the Superintendent of Schools and a guest to take off their hats during the flag salute. To Galarza, these early memories of life in America still have poignancy.

IdeaBank

▲ Motivation. As an extension of the Connecting Writing and Reading activity, have students rank the following activities according to how difficult they believe each would be for them if they were living in a new country. Remind them that they do not understand the language, the customs, or the social norms of this country. Have them rank the activities from 1 to 4, with 1 being the easiest and 4 the most difficult.

_____ asking directions
_____ ordering food in a restaurant
_____ playing sports or games
_____ making friends ▲

IdeaBank

✱ Limited English Proficient Students
This excerpt from *Barrio Boy* provides an excellent opportunity for Spanish-speaking students to explain the Spanish terms in the text (e.g., *mercados, barrio, vecindades*) and for all LEP students to share their experiences of adjusting to a new culture. Have students discuss how their responses to a new culture compare with Ernesto's. ✱

InformationBank

Literary Note. Several paragraphs have been omitted from this excerpt to avoid any confusion that might result from references to characters and events not fully described in this part of the book.

⌘ Connections

Across the Humanities. Have students research the accomplishments of Mexican Americans and their contributions to American culture. Suggest that they research such areas as education, medicine, music, art, food, theater, and government. Ask them to supply pictures of notable Mexican Americans.

InformationBank

Historical Note. The description of the rapid acculturation of the Galarza family in the early twentieth century parallels the experience of the more than 22 million immigrants who arrived in the United States between 1890 and 1930. Europeans and Asians sailed across the seas, Mexicans entered from the south, and Canadians came from the north. As increasing numbers of people arrived, the clamor to halt immigration grew.

The first federal law to control immigration was the 1882 Chinese Exclusion Act, which was followed by the Gentleman's Agreement of 1907–1908, aimed at limiting the number of Japanese emigrating to America. The most sweeping attempt at exclusions, however, came with the Immigration Act of 1924 and the National Origins Act of 1929, which limited the total number of people allowed to enter the country each year.

ResourceBank

For the Student. Rodriguez, Richard. *Hunger of Memory: The Education of Richard Rodriguez.* Boston: David Godine, 1982.

InformationBank

Biographical Note. According to Galarza, *Barrio Boy* began as a series of anecdotes he related to his family. "Quite by accident," he recalls, "I told one of these vignettes at a meeting of scholars and other people. It was recorded on tape, printed in a magazine, and circulated . . . here and there." He was persuaded to write his recollections of his childhood after numerous people requested reprints of the article.

Guidelines for Response

Thinking About the Selection, pages 166–167

1. Some students, especially any who did not speak English when they entered American schools, may identify closely with Ernesto's experiences, whereas others may feel that the experiences of immigrant students today are quite different from Ernesto's. Many students will have found the selection upbeat and optimistic.

2. Some students may feel that Ernesto's adjustment is remarkably smooth. They may note that he seems to learn English easily and eventually becomes one of the translators for the principal; that he has positive experiences with teachers; and that he appears to enjoy school. They may also note that with the exception of a few playground fights, Ernesto seems to get along with other students. Students may feel that the most difficult adjustments for Ernesto are those he makes outside of school. They may point out that Ernesto notes many baffling differences between Mexican and American shopping customs and that he has trouble understanding the organization of American towns and neighborhoods.

3. Students may believe Galarza was motivated to relate these experiences because education in general and Lincoln School in particular were major influences in his life. They may cite the closing passage to show just how significant this school was for the author and his family (page 166). Other students may suggest that Galarza feels that the public schools serve the important function of "Americanizing" immigrants.

4. Students may say that Miss Hopley is strong-willed and opinionated, as evidenced by the way she stands up to the superintendent and his guest, but that she is also open, warm, and welcoming in the way she greets Ernesto and his mother. Students may observe that Miss Hopley is patriotic. She sets out to make her students good Americans while still respecting their differences.

5. Some students may feel that in the 1990's the school would play a smaller role in helping a young immigrant adjust to life in America. They may cite the deterioration of some city schools, a loss of respect for education, and the added problems caused by drugs and crime as reasons for this change. Others may say that with increased technology, increased competition for jobs, and more focus on academics, school would be more important to a young immigrant today. Some may speculate that the transition would be even easier in this decade because of the influence of television, which saturates children with words and images, enabling them to learn English and to learn about American culture more easily.

6. Students may describe the tone as cheerful, loving, and sentimental. To support this view, students might refer to the writer's obvious regard for education and for past events that helped shape his success story.

7. Students may say that an educator might learn the importance of respecting cultural differences; that a person new to this country might learn that a good education can help one succeed; and that a person born in this country might learn the value of tolerance.

Analyzing the Writer's Craft, page 167

Students may infer the following themes:

First quotation—Do not be hasty in passing judgment; *strangeness* is a relative term.

Second quotation—One should relish the uniqueness of each individual; no one benefits from assimilation.

Third quotation—Caring people can make a difference.

Fourth quotation—Positive experiences can have a lifelong impact; education can be a powerful instrument.

Connecting Reading and Writing, page 168

For assignment 2, provide students with models of family trees.

Encourage students working on the option to assignment 4 to work in groups to brainstorm questions.

Content Quiz

1. Where does Ernesto come from? Mazatlán, Mexico

2. What is the name of the school Ernesto attends? Lincoln School

3. What is one American custom that Ernesto finds strange? [Students may name any one.] People shop in grocery stores; they put groceries in paper bags; they have different holidays; they live in separate houses; they enjoy different kinds of entertainment.

4. What is one important lesson that Ernesto learns at the Lincoln School? [Students may name any one.] to be proud of his heritage; to become a good American; to speak and read English; to get along with students of different nationalities; how democracy works

from Barrio Boy (page 159)

Vocabulary Worksheet

Essential Vocabulary

alien *adj*. Belonging to another country or people; foreign.
boisterous *adj*. Noisy and unruly.
formidable *adj*. Causing fear; awe-inspiring; strikingly impressive.
indignation *n*. Anger at something that seems unjust.
reverie *n*. The condition of being lost in thought; daydreaming.

Useful Words

anchorage *n*. A secure place to hold on to.
menace *n*. A threat; that which threatens.
promenade *n*. A leisurely walk; a parade.

Fill in each blank with the word from the word list that best completes the sentence.

1. The crowd moved casually down the street, everybody sipping the tall, cool drinks they bought from vendors along the way. It was a ________________ with lemonade.

2. Back when he worked out, he was one scary-looking guy. Laziness and jelly doughnuts have taken their toll, for he's lost his former ________________ form.

3. Our aunt from Idaho was apparently delighted with what she considered to be her sons' angelic behavior. But to us they seemed to be somewhat ________________ Boise boys.

4. The lecturer was a respected authority on dinosaur fossils and had traveled thousands of miles to present his notes. He was an ________________ paleontologist.

5. The woman at the Star Trek convention kept coming back to the huge poster, always totally absorbed in another time and place. It was apparent that Captain James T. Kirk filled her every ________________.

6. Motorists thought the new traffic law was unfair, and the police, who agreed, didn't want to enforce it. There was resentment on the road and ________________ at the station.

7. Dr. Fry always thought of himself as a pleasant, gentle, and sensitive health care professional who would never intentionally harm anyone. He didn't know that people found him terrifying or that, behind his back, they called him "Dentist the ________________."

8. The seasick sailor had never felt safe or comfortable scrambling across the decks of ships on the high seas. So, after he finally got out of the navy, he moved to Alaska because someone told him he could find ________________ there.

NAME ______________________________ DATE ______________

from Barrio Boy (page 159)

Test

Part 1 Broad Interpretation

A. Answer the following essay questions based on your understanding of the selection. Write your answers on a separate sheet of paper. (*12 points each*)

1. Do you think that as a child, the writer was glad that his family immigrated to America? Do you think that he feels the same now that he is an adult? Use details from the selection to support your answer.
2. Think of Miss Hopley and the writer's teachers. What lessons in life do they try to instill in all of the children at the Lincoln School? How do they go about instilling these lessons? Use details from the selection to explain your answer.
3. Do you think that immigrant children today might have an easier time dealing with their new home in America than the writer did? Explain your answer.
4. What theme concerning the immigrant experience in America do you think is suggested by the following quotation from the selection? "Like the city, the Sacramento *barrio* did not have a place which was the middle of things for everyone." In what ways does the selection support this theme?

B. The writer says, "The Americanization of Mexican me was no smooth matter." Fill in the bar graph below to show how difficult you think each thing was for the writer in his process of becoming an American. (*10 points*)

	Fairly easy — Very difficult
Learning English	
Learning new customs	
Letting go of old customs	
Winning acceptance by his peers	
Accepting his new self-image	

Part 2 Close Interpretation

A. Write the letter of the best answer. (*6 points each*)

____ 1. According to the writer, which of the following is an American characteristic?

a. Being short-tempered.
b. Being narrow-minded.
c. Showing emotions quietly.
d. Showing emotions openly and loudly.

NAME ______________________________ DATE ______________

_____ 2. According to the writer, which of the following is a Mexican characteristic?

a. Being short-tempered.

b. Having trouble with words.

c. Showing emotions quietly.

d. Showing emotions openly and loudly.

_____ 3. In the election for the president of the third grade, the writer is taught a lesson concerning

a. grammar.

b. cheating.

c. discrimination.

d. freedom of choice.

B. Think about the differences that the writer mentions between Mazatlán and Sacramento. What do these differences between the towns suggest about the differences between the cultures? In the boxes below, briefly note what you think the quotations suggest about each culture. (*24 points*)

Quotation	MAZATLÁN	SACRAMENTO
"The grocers [in Sacramento] did not give children a *pilón;* they did not stand at the door and coax you to come in and buy, as they did in Mazatlán. The fruits and vegetables were displayed on counters instead of being piled up on the floor. The stores smelled of fly spray and oiled floors, not of fresh pineapple and limes."		
"It was just as puzzling that the Americans did not live in *vecindades*, like our block on Leandro Valle. Even in the alleys, where people knew one another better, the houses were fenced apart, without central courts to wash clothes, talk, and play with the other children."		

from Hunger of Memory

Richard Rodriguez

page 169

- **Vocabulary Worksheet,** TG page 159
- **Test,** TG pages 161 and 162

Objectives

1. To respond to an autobiographical excerpt in which the writer recalls a personal reading program.
2. To analyze autobiography.
3. To express ideas in a variety of writing formats: journal, slogans, script, report, graph, autobiographical sketch, diary entry.

Summary

In this autobiographical excerpt, Richard Rodriguez describes his ambitious childhood reading program. Beginning in the fourth grade, he decides to read all the "important books" that his teachers recommend—partly because he enjoys reading but mostly to advance his education. For a long time, he assumes that a book's value lies solely in its theme or moral message; he undervalues the books he really enjoys. As an adult looking back, Rodriguez realizes that his appetite for knowledge made some students envious and separated him culturally from his parents. Nonetheless, education has given him the key to a rich life.

IdeaBank

▲ **Motivation.** To help students think of book titles for the Connecting Writing and Reading activity, have them review their journals, reading logs, class notebooks, reading lists, and the table of contents of this textbook. Hold an informal round-table discussion to encourage students to share their memories of reading books. ▲

IdeaBank

✱ **Limited English Proficient Students**
Give students an opportunity to share ideas about learning English. Have them discuss Richard Rodriguez's reading program and debate whether it would work for them. Encourage students to list favorite books, television or radio programs, videos, films, and other resources that they find helpful in working toward becoming more proficient in English. ✱

InformationBank

Literary Note. This excerpt is taken from the middle of the second chapter of Rodriguez's book. One sentence containing the phrase "kiss ass" was deleted. A sentence near the end of the chapter was added as a summary.

IdeaBank

❃ **Learning Disabled Students.** Students who have difficulties with the written word may feel threatened by Rodriguez's emphasis on reading. Before they read, point out that Rodriguez will describe both positive and negative results from his reading. List the following questions on the board: What is the most important thing to be gained from reading? What other skills besides reading help a person to get along in school? What do you think happens when a person spends all his or her spare time reading? After students have expressed their opinions about these questions, have them read the excerpt to see if Rodriguez shares their opinions. ❃

IdeaBank

✲ **Collaborative Learning.** Have groups of three or four students write and present skits dramatizing a scene in which Rodriguez learns the reaction of either his parents, fellow students, or teachers to his reading program. ✲

InformationBank

Biographical Note. In a *Contemporary Authors* interview, Richard Rodriguez describes his attitudes toward writing. "I see myself straddling two worlds of writing: journalism and literature. There is Richard Rodriguez, the journalist—every day I spend more time reading newspapers and magazines than I do reading novels and poetry. I wander away from my desk for hours, for weeks. I want to ask questions of the stranger on the bus. I want to consider the political and social issues of the day. Then there is Richard Rodriguez, the writer. It takes me a very long time to write. What I try to do when I write is break down the line separating the prosaic world from the poetic world. I try to write about everyday concerns—an educational issue, say, or the problems of the unemployed—but to write about them as powerfully, as richly, as well as I can."

ResourceBank

For the Student. Rodriguez, Richard. *Hunger of Memory: The Education of Richard Rodriguez: An Autobiography*. Boston: D. R. Godine, 1981.

For the Teacher. Kanellos, Nicolas, ed. *A Decade of Hispanic Literature: An Anniversary Anthology*. Arte Publico, 1982.

Guidelines for Response

Thinking About the Selection, pages 172–173

1. Students may find Rodriguez's reading program ambitious, intimidating, silly, or impressive, depending on their own interests. Students may find it sad that he seems to have read exclusively what other people recommended.

2. Some students may think that reading has primarily negative effects on Rodriguez because he is unhappy with his academic life and his reading isolates him from others. Other students may feel that Rodriguez's discipline pays off, noting that he completes his education and becomes proficient in English. Students may also note that reading sustains his inner life.

3. Some students will identify most closely with Rodriguez's feeling of being "at home in a fictional world" (page 171). Others may share Rodriguez's belief that books are crucial to academic success. Some students may possess one or both of the preconceptions that the value of a book is contained in its theme and that enjoyable books are not important, but becoming aware of Rodriguez's changed attitudes about these two points may lead these students to question their preconceptions. Other students, referring to Rodriguez's statement that he "lacked a point of view" when he read, may state their own belief in the necessity of questioning what they read.

4. Students may answer that Rodriguez might begin by reading a book he enjoys and then continue by reading other works by the same author. Other students may answer that he might ask for the names of books that friends had read and enjoyed, or he might ask for books about a particular subject or on a particular theme. Others might believe that he would read less and try to remain closer to his family and fellow students.

5. Responses will vary. Some students may state that Richard Rodriguez seems more committed than most students in their school to reading and to academic success, as shown by the list of the "hundred most important books of Western Civilization" that he clips from a newspaper (page 171), diligently crossing off each title after finishing the book. These students may add that Rodriguez craves excessive attention from teachers (page 172). Other students may state that Rodriguez is similar to many students in his desire to succeed and be noticed. Like them, he wants to do something well and pushes himself to succeed.

6. Some students may answer that they would consult Ernesto Galarza for advice because he vividly recalls what it was like to be a non-native speaker in a first-grade classroom. These students may add that Galarza experienced how a caring, patient teacher can help a frightened student over the hurdle of learning English by providing private lessons and public praise (page 163). Other students may assert that Rodriguez would be their first choice as a consultant. These students may mention that Rodriguez has given careful thought to the effect that education can have on the relationship between non-native speakers and their parents (page 172).

Analyzing the Writer's Craft, pages 173–174

Examples students may list include the following: "In the sixth grade I simply concluded that what gave a book its value was some major idea or theme it contained" (page 170) shows his youthful earnestness and naiveté; "Merely bookish, I lacked a point of view when I read" (page 171) reveals the insight he has gained as an adult on his limited expectations in childhood; "My mother wonder[ed], 'What do you see in your books?' " (page 170) reveals his alienation from his family. Many students will believe that Rodriguez's most effective and interesting technique is interpreting his experience from an adult perspective.

Connecting Reading and Writing, page 174

To help students in doing a report or a graph, suggest that they list the book titles reported by their respondents in descending order (least to most) according to how many people have named each title.

If the grammar and composition book you use has a lesson on autobiography, you may want to refer to this lesson.

❓ Content Quiz

1. What one type of book does Rodriguez *not* want his teachers to recommend to him? children's books

2. Name one place Rodriguez enjoys reading books. [Students may name any one.] in bed; in the library; in the park; on front porches; in backyards

3. When Rodriguez is in the sixth grade, what does he decide to record in a notebook? the themes of the books he has read

4. What is one list that Rodriguez completes in high school? [Students may name either one.] a list of all the books he had ever read; an English professor's list of the hundred most important books in Western civilization

5. According to Rodriguez, at what point in their school careers are scholarship students appreciated most? when they are young

NAME ______________________________ DATE ______________

from Hunger of Memory (page 169)

Vocabulary Worksheet

Essential Vocabulary

appraisal *n.* A judgment of quality or worth.
epigram *n.* A short, witty, pointed statement.
grandiose *adj.* Impressive; on a large scale.

Useful Word

disheartened *adj.* Discouraged; deprived of enthusiasm.

Put an **X** next to the piece of dialogue that goes with the underlined word.

1. What someone who is **disheartened** might say:

____ **a.** "You can go on and do a cheer if you want, but now that we need eleven touchdowns to tie, I would stay away from 'We are the Warriors, the mighty, mighty, Warriors.'"

____ **b.** "Look, there's a chance! There's always a chance if we make a real effort and do our best. Fear of failure only encourages failure. So let's get out there and fight!"

2. What someone giving an **appraisal** might say:

____ **a.** "Your paper is due a week from Wednesday, and I expect you to work hard on it. One-third of your grade will be based on your work on this assignment. Papers turned in after the due date will not be accepted."

____ **b.** "Your use of language is very good, quite clear and accurate. But the idea you present —that Tennessee Tuxedo and Tennessee Williams were actually the same person— well, you just do not offer adequate support."

3. What someone planning a **grandiose** dinner might say:

____ **a.** "It will be a cozy, romantic dinner for the two of us. I'll get candles, you get a single red rose, and we'll shop for our favorite food. Oh, would you change your shirt?"

____ **b.** "You won't have to do much; we'll get it catered. Feed the Masses, Inc., can easily handle dinner for two hundred. All you have to do is wash and iron the linen tablecloths, polish the silver, and make an ice sculpture of the first Thanksgiving."

4. What someone who often speaks in **epigrams** might say:

____ **a.** "The way people drive today arouses the suspicion that much of the horse sense of the good old days was possessed by the horse."

____ **b.** "If drivers could only hold in their minds the realization that behind every other steering wheel there also sits a human being with hopes and dreams and loved ones, we would all be safer on the road."

NAME ______________________________ DATE ______________

from Hunger of Memory (page 169)

Test

Part 1 Broad Interpretation

A. Answer the following essay questions based on your understanding of the selection. Write your answers on a separate sheet of paper. (*20 points each*)

1. If Rodriguez were to start his "reading program" over again, what do you think he would do differently? Use details from the selection to explain your answer.
2. Why do you think that lists are so important to Rodriguez while he is growing up? What do you think they represent to him? Explain your answer.
3. Rodriguez says, "I lacked a point of view when I read. Rather, I read in order to acquire a point of view." What is the distinction between reading with a point of view and reading to acquire a point of view? Do you think that wide reading should be attempted before one has established a point of view? Explain your answers.

B. Think about how this autobiographical selection reveals, from Rodriguez's perspective as an adult, thoughts that he had as a child. Then write **C** if the statement is one that Rodriguez would have been likely to make as a child. Write **A** if it is one that he would be likely to make as an adult. Write **B** if he would be likely to have made the statement as both a child and an adult. (*18 points*)

Reading is a pleasure.	
A reader must bring something to the reading process.	
Extensive reading leads to skill in speaking and writing.	
The harder a book is, the more important it is to read it.	
The real meaning of a book can be stated in one sentence.	
Finishing a book is sometimes more important than understanding it.	
Experiencing a story with the characters is an important part of reading.	
Little value can be gained from a book that is much too complex for the reader.	
It is possible to overestimate the value of books that other people find important.	

NAME ______________________________ DATE ______________

Part 2 Close Interpretation

Read the following quotation from the selection. Think about various autobiographical techniques Rodriguez uses, such as quoting directly from himself and others, revealing his thoughts as a child, interpreting from an adult perspective, and reporting how others viewed him. In the box on the left, identify the technique that you think is used most effectively in the passage. In the box on the right, briefly describe what is conveyed about the young Rodriguez. (*22 points*)

> "What *did* I see in my books? I had the idea that they were crucial for my academic success, though I couldn't have said exactly how or why. In the sixth grade I simply concluded that what gave a book its value was some major idea or theme it contained. If that core essence could be mined and memorized, I would become learned like my teachers. I decided to record in a notebook the themes of the books that I read. After reading *Robinson Crusoe,* I wrote that its theme was 'the value of learning to live by oneself.' When I completed *Wuthering Heights,* I noted the danger of 'letting emotions get out of control.' Rereading these brief moralistic appraisals usually left me disheartened. I couldn't believe that they were really the source of reading's value. But for many more years, they constituted the only means I had of describing to myself the educational value of books."

Technique used most effectively	Qualities of young Rodriguez conveyed

High Horse's Courting

Black Elk

As told through John G. Neihardt (Flaming Rainbow)

page 175

■ **Test,** TG pages 165 and 166

Objectives

1. To respond to a story about a traditional Sioux courtship.
2. To understand the purposes and qualities of oral literature.
3. To express ideas in a variety of writing formats: journal, story, notes, speech, explanation, captions, outline.

Plot Summary

Black Elk begins by discussing the problems of love and courtship among members of his tribe. He then tells the story of High Horse, a young man who is lovesick over a beautiful girl. High Horse offers the girl's father two horses, then four horses in exchange for his daughter, but the father refuses. High Horse then makes two attempts to steal the girl from her tepee at night, but both attempts fail. Finally, High Horse and his friend go on the warpath together and steal an entire herd of horses from a Crow camp. With this herd of horses as proof of his manhood, High Horse wins the girl for his wife.

IdeaBank

▲ **Motivation.** As an alternative to the Connecting Writing and Reading activity, ask students to think about courtship. What would compel them to pursue a relationship with someone who played hard-to-get? Ask them to consider the qualities they value in another person that would make pursuit worthwhile. Have them jot their reflections in their journals and keep in mind their reasons for courtship as they read about High Horse. ▲

IdeaBank

❖ **Cooperative Learning.** Have groups of three students find some Native American tales and choose one tale to share with the class. Have one student read it aloud, another comment on its meaning, and the third compare its humor and message to "High Horse's Courting." ❖

IdeaBank

✤ **Multimodal Activities**

1. Invite a historian to the classroom to discuss the everyday life of the Sioux during the period in which Black Elk lived. Have students prepare questions to ask the historian.
2. Ask students to imagine that this story is being produced as part of a TV series on Native American tales. Have them create sketches of the costumes and set designs for the production.
3. Show students the illustrations by Standing Bear in the 1961 University of Nebraska Press edition of *Black Elk Speaks* or other examples of Sioux art. Then have them find their own examples from the library. ✤

InformationBank

Historical Note. Until he met John Neihardt, Black Elk had refused to grant interviews despite his fame as a holy man. When Neihardt first visited him in August 1930, Black Elk felt that through Neihardt he could speak to future generations. Black Elk presented Neihardt with a sacred ornament—a leather star tinged with blue from which hung a strip of buffalo hide and an eagle's feather—which he called the Morning Star. Neihardt returned to Black Elk the following spring and found that a tepee had been erected for him to live in. For days, Black Elk would talk to him from after breakfast until late at night. Black Elk's son, Ben, acted as interpreter and Neihardt's daughter, Enid, transcribed the conversations.

"What I know was given to me for men and it is true and it is beautiful. Soon I shall be under the grass and it will be lost. You were sent to save it."

— Black Elk to John Neihardt, *Black Elk Speaks,* 1972

IdeaBank

❧ **Gifted and Talented Students.** Have students brainstorm together to think of other tactics High Horse might have tried. Ask individual students to write a version of the scene in the style of "High Horse's Courting." Have them mimic the voice, diction, and style of Black Elk as they have High Horse try one more courtship tactic. ❧

ResourceBank

For the Student. *Music of the Pawnee*. Sung by Mark Evarts. New York: Folkways Records, 1965.

Grinnell, George Bird. *Blackfoot Lodge Tails* (1892). Lincoln: University of Nebraska Press, 1962.

———. *By Cheyenne Campfires* (1926). Lincoln: University of Nebraska Press, 1971.

For the Teacher. Nichols, Roger I. *American Indian: Past and Present*. 3rd edition. New York: McGraw Hill, 1985.

Guidelines for Response

Thinking About the Story, page 179

1. Many students may feel glad and relieved. Some students may feel disappointed that High Horse had to steal to win his bride and prove his manhood. Some may wonder if the girl was worth the effort.

2. Students may point out that High Horse is motivated by lovesickness; this is why he keeps trying different ways to win the girl. Some students may speculate that he also desires to prove his manhood by winning her; she makes him feel "as brave as a bison bull." Students may see the girl motivated both by her feelings and by social constraints: she "liked him maybe a little," but she has her pride and her tribal customs. Some students will note that because she "thought a great deal of herself," she "wanted to be bought like a fine woman" (page 177). Students may find the father motivated by pride or by love for his daughter and concern for her honor. He wants "a son who is a real man and good for something," so he waves High Horse off until he proves himself. Students may find Red Deer motivated by friendship to help High Horse and perhaps also by love of mischief and adventure.

3. Students may suggest that High Horse has become a man because he has satisfied the tribal requirements for manhood and marriage: he has acquired the price for his bride and paid it. Some students may further observe that he has matured also by learning to achieve a difficult goal through perseverance, cleverness, and daring.

4. Some students may believe that his relationship with the tribe might have changed little. Girl-stealing is apparently sometimes practiced, since the idea comes readily to Red Deer who tells High Horse that he can come back safely after a while (page 177). Other students might point out that by stealing the girl, High Horse wouldn't earn the same respect as he did by capturing the horses.

5. Students may infer that adherence to tribal values is quite important to these Sioux. Values that students may propose include a high regard for persistence (High Horse must show that he will keep trying in order to win the girl); an emphasis on marriage as the accepted channel for male-female love (the parents tie the girl down so she will not be stolen and cannot run away); the belief that young men must prove their manhood and worthiness as providers in order to marry (High Horse is accepted by the girl's father only after stealing the horses); the importance of friendship (Red Deer helps High Horse); a respect for the spirit world (the people fear High Horse when he looks like an evil spirit but will not shoot him); and a love for oral literature (the telling of the story itself). Students may mention values that seem negative: a low regard for life or property in other tribes (the two men kill the horse guard and steal the horses with no apparent guilt) and the regarding of women as property.

6. Many students may respond that High Horse's feelings of youthful lovesickness are universal and timeless and that they can easily identify with them. Some may say they also identify with parental opposition to one's love, with the strong bonds of friendship that the young men show, with the young person's struggle against the authority of his elders, or with the daring of youth.

Analyzing the Writer's Craft, page 180

Students may need to focus on ways to convey significant narrated ideas, descriptions, implications, and observations through dialogue and action.

Connecting Reading and Writing, page 180

Students' writings in assignment 2 may be presented orally as the class sits around an imagined campfire at a tribal meeting. Other tribe members (students) may comment on the speeches and explanations.

If the grammar and composition book you use has a lesson on narrative writing, you may want to refer to this lesson.

❓ Content Quiz

1. What causes High Horse's sickness at the beginning of the story? He is in love with a young girl and wants her for his wife.

2. What gift does High Horse offer to the girl's father in exchange for his daughter? horses—first two, then four, and finally one hundred

3. What do the girl's parents do to prevent anyone from stealing her in the night? They tie her to her bed with rawhide thongs.

4. How does Red Deer disguise High Horse the second time they try to steal the girl? He makes High Horse strip naked and paints him black and white.

5. What do the two cousins steal from the Crow camp? one hundred horses

NAME ______________________ DATE ______________

High Horse's Courting (page 175)

Test

Part 1 Broad Interpretation

A. Answer the following essay questions based on your understanding of the story. Write your answers on a separate sheet of paper. (*16 points each*)

1. How would you describe the character of High Horse? What elements in High Horse's character do you think contribute to the humor of the story? Support your answer with details from the story.
2. What do you think was the main purpose of this story when it was first told? Support your answer with details from the story.
3. What values are revealed in the story as important in the Sioux culture? Support your answer with details from the story.

B. Each of the characters in the story wants something and is determined to get it or to accomplish it. Fill in the boxes below with what each character wants. If you feel it is appropriate, you may note more than one thing. (*16 points*)

High Horse

The girl

The girl's father

Red Deer

NAME ______________________ DATE ______________

Part 2 Close Interpretation

The storyteller of "High Horse's Courting" creates humor in a number of different ways. These include exaggerated language, verbal irony, and descriptions of comic behavior. In the boxes, note which humorous techniques you see used in each quotation. (6 *points each*)

1. "Then High Horse went back to the old man and said he would give four horses for the girl—two of them young and the other two not hardly old at all."	
2. "That made High Horse feel so very sick that he could not eat a bite, and he went around with his head hanging down as though he might just fall down and die any time."	
3. "When High Horse had crawled inside, he felt so nervous that he could hear his heart drumming, and it seemed so loud he felt sure it would 'waken the old folks."	
4. "But he was getting along all right and all the thongs were cut down as far as the girl's thigh, when he became so nervous that his knife slipped and stuck the girl. She gave a big, loud yell."	
5. "Now when it was getting light in the tepee, the girl awoke and the first thing she saw was a terrible animal, all white with black stripes on it, lying asleep beside her bed. So she screamed, and then the old woman screamed and the old man yelled. High Horse jumped up, scared almost to death, and he nearly knocked the tepee down getting out of there."	
6. "Then they drove the whole herd right into the village and up in front of the girl's tepee. The old man was there, and High Horse called out to him and asked if he thought maybe that would be enough horses for his girl."	

The Secret Lion

Alberto Alvaro Ríos

page 181

■ **Test,** TG pages 169 and 170

Objectives

1. To respond to a story about the changes experienced by a boy growing up in southern Arizona.
2. To appreciate the significance of setting in a story.
3. To express ideas in a variety of writing formats: journal, handbook, speech, letter, interpretive essay, autobiographical sketch, and dramatic monologue.

Plot Summary

When he is twelve years old and just beginning junior high school, the narrator and his friend Sergio spend most of their after-school hours exploring the nearby southwestern wilderness that they are forbidden to roam. As they embark on an adventure one day, the two boys discover a grinding ball—a tool used in mining—in the arroyo near the narrator's home. The boys regard the ball as their special perfect object, and they bury it in the arroyo rather than let adults see it and ruin its perfection for them. A week later, however, they cannot find it. The missing ball reminds the narrator that life, or nature, continues to teach him lessons everywhere he turns. As the narrator continues his reminiscences, he recalls an earlier adventure when he was about five years old. While exploring the hills beyond the narrator's home, the two boys discover a lush grassy area that seems like heaven. Soon, men carrying bags appear and yell at them, and the boys learn about golf courses. In the narrator's mind, these two experiences bring an awareness of reality and change and are linked with the experience of moving into the new world of junior high school and the mysterious period of growth and change that it brings.

IdeaBank

✲ **Collaborative Learning.** Question 3 in Thinking About the Story (page 186) asks students to explain what "the lion" in the story represents and why it is "secret." When students have completed their answers, ask volunteers to share their ideas. On the board create a cluster diagram around the phrase "secret lion," using words and phrases representing students' ideas. Students may then revise their original answers by incorporating new ideas from the cluster diagram. ✲

IdeaBank

▲ **Motivation.** To extend the Connecting Writing and Reading activity, ask students to categorize the school transition experiences they noted in their journals. Copy the following chart on the board as an example for students, but suggest that they may wish to add additional categories to their charts. Now have students read the story and compare their experiences with those of the two boys.

Surprising	Pleasant	Unpleasant	Confusing

ResourceBank

For the Student. Line, Francis R. *Sheep, Stars, and Solitude: Adventure Saga of a Wilderness Trail.* Irvine, CA: Wide Horizons Press, 1986.

Ríos, Alberto. *The Iguana Killer: Twelve Studies of the Heart.* Lewiston, ID: Blue Moon Press, 1984.

For the Teacher. Ríos, Alberto. *Whispering Fool to the Wind.* New York: The Sheep Meadow Press, 1982.

IdeaBank

✱ **Learning Disabled Students.** Before students begin to read the story, tell them that the events in the first part of the story happened *after* the events in the second part. Direct them to watch for clues that give the correct chronology of the events, such as the age of the narrator in each story part. ✱

⌘ Connections

Across Literature. Students may wish to compare the theme of transition in this story with the themes found in the poem "As I Grew Older" (page 96), the excerpt from *I Know Why the Caged Bird Sings* (page 151), the excerpt from *Barrio Boy* (page 159), and the short story "Marigolds" (page 399) in the student book.

Across the Humanities. Have students research the geography and climate of southern Arizona, especially the native vegetation and the land features formed by water and wind erosion.

❓ Content Quiz

1. In the first recollection, the narrator's age is twelve.

2. In the first recollection, every day after school, the narrator and Sergio go to the arroyo, a place they have been forbidden to visit.

3. The boys discover a grinding ball in the arroyo.

4. In order to protect their newfound perfect treasure, the boys bury it in the arroyo.

5. In the second recollection, the "heaven" the boys find is actually a golf course.

Guidelines for Response

Thinking About the Story, pages 185–186

1. Students' impressions will vary. Some students may note the fun, independence, and sense of adventure the boys experience. Other students will perhaps note the disappointments and sense of loss the narrator describes. Other students may identify with the boys' experiences and see such confusion as a natural consequence of being in junior high or middle school.

2. Students may feel that the boys' experience at the golf course prepares them for the later episode with the grinding ball. They may note that the earlier discovery that their beautiful green heaven is actually a golf course teaches them that they can neither keep their innocent ideas nor trust their first impressions. Some may say that the grinding ball symbolizes the nameless magic of their own relationship at the arroyo during junior high school. Knowing that adults would not understand and that the perfection could not last, the boys bury the ball. When they cannot find the ball, knowing from their earlier experience at the golf course that "things get taken away" (page 185), they do not "look so hard for it" (page 185).

3. The lion may represent the fierce force that brings about the changes young people experience during junior high or middle school. Throughout the story, the boys learn to value their shared experiences, the ones they achieve before adults or time take them away. In these experiences, students may see the roaring lion as representing the boys' newfound vitality, sense of adventurous independence, and excitement during times of discovery. Students may suggest that when the excitement and emotion of these experiences seem beyond control, mysterious, and beyond the realm of adult understanding, a secret lion becomes an apt symbol for this time in their lives.

4. Students may suggest that at a time when the boys feel abandoned and awkward, they go to the arroyo—"the one place we were not supposed to go" (page 182). Students may point out that the boys feel personally abandoned in junior high: "When a person had all these teachers now, he didn't get taken care of the same way . . ." (page 182). Unable to communicate with girls they have known for years, or even to ask questions, the boys go to the arroyo and shout the comments and questions they cannot speak in school. Students may understand that by doing what they choose to do in a place they are forbidden to go, the boys regain some measure of power in their lives.

5. Students' responses will depend on their own experiences. Some students may draw parallels between their feelings and those expressed by the narrator. Others may remember a special place shared with a friend at that time.

6. Students may imagine that in an urban environment, the boys would seek their adventures in an empty lot, an alley, or on a rooftop. They might find their "heaven" in a private garden or a park or playground. Even a cemetery might be mentioned as a place of beauty and serenity in a "concrete city." Some may suggest that in a city, the boys would be less likely to remain a twosome and would probably become part of a larger group of boys. Students may say that living in a city might make the boys less naive and perhaps more sociable at this age.

7. Students may cite these following elements of style: the use of comparisons, such as junior high school to the tablecloth trick or the "lion," nature's changes to a tough gang, the golf-course "heaven" to *The Wizard of Oz*, and the grinding ball to the "lion"; the use of words that capture a young person's world, such as *teach-erz, backwardlike, geeGuythis*, or *what'zin*; the use of paragraph-length sentences that present stream-of-consciousness perceptions immediately followed by a two- or three-word sentence recreating the young person's perception of the experience.

8. Responses will vary. Some students may say that in the excerpt from *Barrio Boy* the adults seem most sensitive to the needs of young people. These students may mention that the principal of Lincoln School appreciates the different cultures of her students and that the first-grade teacher takes personal interest in the children in her class, making them feel that she is on their side. Other students may mention that in the excerpt from *Hunger of Memory* Richard Rodriguez's teachers praise him highly for his reading, partly because his success reflects well on them. Some students may say that in "The Secret Lion" the adults seem unresponsive to the needs of young people. The narrator feels isolated from his teachers, unwilling to trust them or to seek answers from them.

Analyzing the Writer's Craft, page 187

After drawing the maps, students may conclude that visualizing the story's setting helps them to share the boys' experiences. Differences in the maps may lead to a discussion of why variant perceptions develop during reading.

Connecting Reading and Writing, page 187

Suggest that students work together to compile their handbooks. As necessary, give guidance in the actual preparation and distribution of the handbooks.

To prepare students for the option to assignment 3, you might play recordings of dramatic monologues.

NAME ______________________________ DATE ______________

The Secret Lion (page 181)

Test

Part 1 Broad Interpretation

A. Answer the following essay questions based on your understanding of the story. Write your answers on a separate sheet of paper. (*15 points each*)

1. The boy says "things get taken away." What are the things he is talking about? Who or what takes them away? Explain your answer.
2. Why is the grinding ball special to the boy and his friend, but not special to the boy's mother? What do you think accounts for this difference of opinion?
3. What makes junior high school different from what the boy thinks school should be? What has changed? Explain your answers.

B. The story has a lot to say about adolescence and growing up. Read each of the statements in the chart below. If the statement agrees with the message of the story, check the box marked *Yes*. If it disagrees, check the box marked *No*. (*3 points each*)

Yes		No
	4. Rebellion is an important part of growing up.	
	5. Disappointment is an important part of growing up.	
	6. Adolescents find it easy to understand themselves and their actions.	
	7. Even if it is difficult, it is important that adolescents be honest with adults.	
	8. Growing up is something that happens whether people wish it to or not.	

Part 2 Close Interpretation

A. Write the letter of the best answer. (*5 points each*)

____ **1.** Which of the following helps make the grinding ball special to the boys? (*There is more than one answer.*)

a. No one else knows about it.

b. It seems to be perfect.

c. It is something adults can appreciate.

d. It is something that can't be taken away.

NAME ______________________ DATE ____________

____ 2. Which of the following is how the boys attempt to solve junior high school?

a. By talking to girls.

b. By asking their teachers questions.

c. By going to the arroyo after school.

d. By getting their parents to explain things to them.

B. In the story, the narrator describes the settings mainly as he saw them as he was growing up. His perception of these places affects him greatly. Each box on the left names a setting in the story. In each box in the middle, give a brief description of the setting. Then, in each box on the right, briefly explain the effect the setting has on the boy. *(30 points)*

SETTING	DESCRIPTION	EFFECT ON THE BOY
The arroyo		

SETTING	DESCRIPTION	EFFECT ON THE BOY
The junior high school		

SETTING	DESCRIPTION	EFFECT ON THE BOY
Heaven / the golf course		

My Delicate Heart Condition

Toni Cade Bambara
(bam bər′ ə)

page 188

- **Vocabulary Worksheet,** TG page 173
- **Test,** TG pages 175 and 176

Objectives

1. To respond to a short story that explores children's fears and misconceptions.

2. To practice the reading and thinking techniques of an independent reader.

Plot Summary

Harriet Watkins prides herself on being able to scare her friends with her spooky stories. She claims that she has become hardened to terror by watching a family of acrobats who perform death-defying stunts. Then at summer camp Harriet meets Willie, who has a "romantic" heart, her misunderstanding of *rheumatic*. A counselor, George, tries to scare Willie with stories. Instead of participating, Harriet tries to protect Willie.

She overhears two camp counselors refer to all the "underprivileged kids" who attend the camp. Harriet then concludes that she, like Willie, has an "underprivileged heart." This realization changes her attitude. Fearful of anything that might be harmful to her heart, she no longer enjoys activities that are scary.

IdeaBank

▲ **Motivation.** In their journals, students can list three or four reasons why people enjoy being frightened by horror movies and ghost stories. Tell students that, as they read the story, they might think about why Harriet enjoys telling ghost stories. ▲

IdeaBank

✤ Multimodal Activities

1. Using narrators to set the scene and give necessary information, have groups of students act out various scenes from the story, such as watching the circus, the first night at camp, or the big campfire party including the conversation between the counselors.

2. Have students create a sociogram illustrating the relationships among the characters in the story.

3. Have students identify several qualities that Harriet exhibits, such as loyalty and compassion. Then have students create bar graphs for two of these qualities that show how each of these aspects of her character changes by the end of the story.

4. Ask students to create—or possibly videotape—a commercial for a TV movie that is based on the story "My Delicate Heart Condition." ✤

InformationBank

Historical Note. Many circus acts, such as that of the fictional Fly family in Bambara's story, are extremely dangerous. Lillian Leitzel, known for her breathtaking aerial act in which she hung spinning from a rope, fell to her death during a performance in 1931 when part of her equipment snapped. Most famous and tragic, however, were the Great Wallendas, a circus family from Germany. Seven of them stood on each others' shoulders in a three-tiered pyramid and then walked across a high wire. In 1962 the pyramid collapsed. Two members of the family were killed and a third was paralyzed. Another member of the Wallenda family was killed in a 1963 accident and still another in 1972. Karl, the founder and father of the family, died in a fall from a wind-whipped wire in 1978.

⌘ Connections

Across the Language Arts. Some of the narrator's confusion results from her misunderstanding of *rheumatic*, *romantic*, and *underprivileged*. Although the dictionary offers short definitions of these words, each is complex in its meaning and connotation. Have students research the origins and usages of these three words. Suggest the use of a good collegiate dictionary.

You may want to refer to the lesson on reference works in the grammar and composition book you use.

ResourceBank

For the Student. Bambara, Toni Cade. *The Sea Birds Are Still Alive: Collected Stories*. New York: Random House, 1977.

Bambara, Toni Cade. *Gorilla, My Love*. New York: Random House, 1972.

For the Teacher. *Toni Cade Bambara, An Interview*. Audiotape cassette. American Audio Prose Library, n.d.

Washington, Mary Helen. "Black Women Image Makers." *Black World* 23: 10–18.

Guidelines for Response

Discussion Questions

1. What are your final impressions of Harriet? Jot them down in your journal.

[Students will differ in their responses to Harriet. Most will find her sharp and interesting, and some may be moved by the misunderstanding that tames her behavior at the end.]

2. Why do you think Harriet is so fascinated with the Fly family and "spooky" things?

[Harriet likes to see herself as tough and fearless, superior in strength to her friends and relatives. Knowledge of frightening things gives Harriet power. Scaring other children, such as her cousin Joanne, makes her feel better about herself and in control.]

3. Why is summer camp such an important experience for Harriet?

[Students will probably suggest that camp takes Harriet away from home and exposes her to kinds of people she might not meet otherwise, such as George. Harriet sees George's cruelty, especially to Willie, and this makes Harriet want to use her strength to help and protect others, instead of to scare them. She does not want to be like George, who is an insensitive bully. Camp also causes Harriet to understand for the first time that she and the other children there are somehow different. They are "underprivileged," and while she misinterprets this word, it subdues her behavior, making her feel less strong than she felt before.]

4. How is Harriet changed by hearing the counselors mention the fact that all the kids at the camp are underprivileged? Do you think this change will be permanent?

[Since the counselors' conversation (page 192) is specifically about Willie, who has a defective heart, by association Harriet mistakenly concludes that *underprivileged* means "having a delicate heart." She thinks that since she is underprivileged, she cannot strain her heart; therefore she no longer does such things as going to scary movies or holding her breath. Some students may believe that this change will be permanent, but others will think that once Harriet learns what underprivileged really means, she will revert to her old ways.]

5. How would you describe Harriet's relationships with other people?

[Some students may emphasize the aspect of Harriet's character that likes to exert power over others, such as her cousin Joanne, by scaring them with spooky stories. Other students will notice that she changes her behavior when she realizes that Willie, because of his heart condition, could be harmed by her stories. Many students will also point out that Harriet's attitude toward George also shows that she is compassionate: She gets angry at him when he bullies kids.]

6. Choose a paragraph or two from the story and analyze the effectiveness of Harriet's language.

[Students' choices will differ. Help students see that Harriet's use of slang and otherwise colorful diction is a major force in making this story interesting. So are her sentences, which at times are breathless run-ons, at other times decisive and effective fragments. Have students talk about how different this story would be if it were not in Harriet's own voice.]

Content Quiz

1. For fun, Harriet likes to scare other children with her spooky stories.

2. Every summer, Harriet tries to train herself not to be afraid by watching the Fly family.

3. Mary accuses George of picking on Willie.

4. Her mother thinks Harriet's change in behavior occurs because Harriet is growing up.

5. Harriet changes her behavior because she thinks there is something wrong with her heart.

NAME ______________________________ DATE ______________

My Delicate Heart Condition (page 188)

Vocabulary Worksheet

Essential Vocabulary

rheumatic

Useful Words

infirmary **revival**
phantom **underprivileged**

Read the following poems and use the context clues to figure out the meanings of the underlined words. Then use these meanings to help you work the exercise below. If you like, you may use a dictionary to check the meaning of a word.

I

My legs feel so **rheumatic.**
I know that sounds dramatic,
But they're swollen and they're painful
And they're reddish. Yes, I know,
My test's at nine tomorrow,
And I am full of sorrow
That, although I have my brain full
Of the answers, I can't go.
So I'll just stay in bed, and then
I think that I'll be cured by ten.

II

When I was growing up,
We all wore sneakers every day.
The more you had, the cooler you could be.
Paul had a dozen pair,
From pink to royal blue.
And I felt **underprivileged** with three.

III

Keep yourself quiet and murmur-y
While visiting in an **infirmary.**
Try never to screech or to yell,
For the patients are not feeling well.

IV

Oh! **Phantom** sounds of demons groaning!
More now! Are the spirits moaning?
Oh, grow up. Show some matureness.
Can't you tell it's just the furnace?

V

In all kinds of weather,
Folks still get together
To sing and to pray and to meet.
For nothing can rival
An old-time **revival**
For bringing a crowd to its feet.

Match each underlined word in the poems with the correct definition below.

______________________ 1. Poor; not having the normal or expected benefits of a society.

______________________ 2. A place for the care of the sick or injured.

______________________ 3. A series of meetings held to stir up religious feelings.

______________________ 4. Painfully inflamed.

______________________ 5. Ghostly.

NAME ______________________ DATE ______________

My Delicate Heart Condition (page 188) Test

Part 1 Broad Interpretation

A. Answer the following essay questions based on your understanding of the story. Write your answers on a separate sheet of paper. *(15 points each)*

1. What do you think Harriet means when she says that she lost the battle with the Fly family? Explain your answer.
2. How do you think Harriet feels when she overhears the camp counselors and learns that she is "an underprivileged kid"? Why do you think she feels this way?
3. Harriet's experience at camp changes both the way she sees herself and the way she behaves. Which Harriet do you like better, the old one or the new one? Why?

B. In the box on the left, write the letters of the things that you think are important to Harriet before her camp experience. In the box on the right, write the letters of the things that you think are important to Harriet after her camp experience. Not all things will be used. *(15 points)*

a. being ladylike
b. being the bravest
c. going to the circus
d. stirring up excitement
e. behaving in a grown-up way
f. making fun of other people
g. terrifying the crybabies at camp
h. taking care of her heart condition
i. creating nicknames for children at camp
j. being sensitive to other people's feelings
k. protecting children who are being picked on
l. scaring children by telling them ghost stories

IMPORTANT BEFORE	IMPORTANT AFTER

NAME ______________________________ DATE ______________

Part 2 Close Interpretation

Write the letter of the best answer. Where noted, there may be more than one answer. *(8 points each)*

_____ **1.** Why does Harriet train herself for the Fly family performances? *(You may choose more than one answer.)*

a. She wants to be cool.

b. She wants to test herself.

c. She wants to perform with them.

d. She wants to learn about circus acrobatics.

_____ **2.** Why does Harriet tell scary stories? *(You may choose more than one answer.)*

a. She wants to entertain the children.

b. She likes being the center of attention.

c. She believes the children like being frightened.

d. She thinks it's fun to see others frightened when she isn't afraid.

_____ **3.** According to Harriet, how has her attitude towards George, the camp counselor, changed as she has grown older?

a. She has decided that he's fun.

b. She has become indifferent to him.

c. She has begun to see him as a bully.

d. Her admiration for him has grown.

_____ **4.** What does Harriet show about herself when she stops George from putting spiders in Joanne's soup? *(You may choose more than one answer.)*

a. She's mean.

b. She's afraid of spiders.

c. She's loyal to her family.

d. She cares about Joanne's feelings.

_____ **5.** Who is ultimately *most* responsible for Harriet's learning that it is cruel to have fun at the expense of others?

a. Aunt Hazel

b. the Fly family

c. Harriet's mother

d. Willie, the new kid at camp

Minority Voices: Conveying Attitudes

Below are suggested answers for the chart assigned on page 193 of the student book. Listed are the titles of seven other selections in Unit 3, words that describe the tone of each selection, and examples of diction, or word choice, that suggest that tone. Accept other descriptions of tone and examples of diction if students can support them with evidence from the selections.

Title	Tone	Diction
I Have a Dream	urgent, prophetic, passionate, triumphant	"the fierce urgency of now"; "the bright day of justice"; " 'Free at last' "
"Getting a Job" from *I Know Why the Caged Bird Sings*	determined, indomitable, bold, assured	"the mind is locked like the jaws of an enraged bulldog"; "my veins stand out and my mouth tighten into a prune"; "to exhaust every possibility before giving in"
from *Barrio Boy*	upbeat, cheerful, loving, appreciative	"did not mean feeling ashamed of being a Mexican"; "La Leen-Con . . . became a benchmark in our lives"; "we sensed . . . she was with us"
from *Hunger of Memory*	serious, thoughtful, analytical	"The scholarship boy pleases most when he is young"; "education to remake himself"; "culturally separated from my parents"
High Horse's Courting	light, humorous, warm	"so nervous that he could hear his heart drumming"; "waiting for the old woman to snore"; "he nearly knocked the tepee down getting out of there"
The Secret Lion	frustrated, uncertain, bewildered	"like the tablecloth those magicians pull"; "we felt personally abandoned somehow"; "Things get taken away"
My Delicate Heart Condition	lively, spirited, energetic	"I get spookier on purpose"; "my stomach was like steel"; "I would rather marry the wolfman than grow up and be his wife"

Evaluation Guide for Writing Assignment

The complete student instructions for the oral presentations should do the following:

- Describe two contrasting tones conveyed by the writers
- Include examples of words and phrases that convey these tones
- Provide specific suggestions about pace, volume, and pitch that students might follow in preparing oral interpretations

UNIT 4 Exploring Cultural Conflicts

Selections	Essential Vocabulary	Literary Skills	Writing Formats	Writing Modes
Two Kinds				
Student Book page 198 **Teacher's Guide** Lesson, pages 180 and 181 Vocabulary Worksheet, page 182 Test, pages 183 and 184	prodigy preludes discordant devastated fiasco	conflict simile	journal dialogue letter dramatic skit story guidelines summary	expressive and personal writing narrative and imaginative writing informative (expository) writing: synthesis writing about literature report (research)
Seventeen Syllables				
Student Book page 210 **Teacher's Guide** Lesson, pages 185–187 Vocabulary Worksheet, page 188 Test, pages 189 and 190	vernaculars anaesthetic garrulous infinitesimal repartee rapt vacillating indiscretion glib	plot theme	journal haiku annotations diary entry note scene journal notes oral presentation dramatic scene	expressive and personal writing narrative and imaginative writing writing about literature report (research)
***from* Kaffir Boy**				
Student Book page 222 **Teacher's Guide** Lesson, pages 191–193 Vocabulary Worksheet, page 194 Test, pages 195 and 196	coteries austere inscrutable mores	dialogue	journal monologue script expository essay notes letter poem	expressive and personal writing narrative and imaginative writing informative (expository) writing: classification persuasion writing about literature report (research)
Hiccups				
Student Book page 234 **Teacher's Guide** Lesson, pages 197–199 Test, page 200			journal question/answer column letter essay dialogue memo annotations	expressive and personal writing narrative and imaginative writing informative (expository) writing: classification informative (expository) writing: synthesis writing about literature
***from* Arctic Dreams**				
Student Book page 239 **Teacher's Guide** Lesson, pages 201–203 Vocabulary Worksheet, page 204 Test, pages 205 and 206	fecundity benign gargantuan implacable austerity pervasive adumbration	metaphor description	journal catalog grant proposal persuasive speech publicity slogans annotation poster descriptive essay captions	expressive and personal writing observation and description informative (expository) writing: analysis informative (expository) writing: synthesis persuasion

Selections	Essential Vocabulary	Literary Skills	Writing Formats	Writing Modes
***from* Notes of a Native Son**				
Student Book page 249 **Teacher's Guide** Lesson, pages 207 and 208 Vocabulary Worksheet, page 209 Test, pages 211 and 212	conundrum rhetoric bravura interloper	paradox conflict	journal sermon editorial autobiographical sketch outline letter report card introduction personality profile	expressive and personal writing observation and description informative (expository) writing: classification informative (expository) writing: analysis persuasion writing about literature
***from* American Hunger**				
Student Book page 257 **Teacher's Guide** Lesson, pages 213 and 214 Vocabulary Worksheet, page 215 Test, pages 217 and 218	cynical reprisal	The student book does not contain discussion questions, analysis of literary techniques, or writing assignments for this selection. These materials appear in the Teacher's Guide lesson.		
Reviewing Concepts				
Student Book page 261 **Teacher's Guide** page 219				

Two Kinds

Amy Tan

page 198

- **Vocabulary Worksheet,** TG page 182
- **Test,** TG pages 183 and 184

Objectives

1. To respond to a short story that explores the issue of parental expectations.

2. To understand the author's use of simile.

3. To express ideas in a variety of writing formats: journal, dialogue, letter, dramatic skit, story, guidelines, summary.

Plot Summary

The narrator's mother had emigrated from China to the United States in 1949 after she lost everything—mother, father, home, first husband, and baby twin daughters. Now, she has high hopes that her nine-year-old daughter can be a prodigy who accomplishes anything she sets her mind to do. Eventually, the mother sets her hopes and dreams on the narrator becoming a great pianist. Despite the narrator's protests, her mother forces her to take piano lessons from their downstairs neighbor, Mr. Chong, a retired piano teacher who is now deaf. Knowing that Mr. Chong cannot hear her playing, the narrator tricks him into believing that she is trying her best when, in fact, she is determined not to try at all. At a piano recital, she plays miserably, humiliating her mother. Afterwards they have a bitter argument, one that leaves the narrator with a terrible burden of guilt. Her mother never asks her to play piano again, and the narrator never does—until years later, after her mother's death.

• Tips from the Classroom •

Many students will identify with the situation in which the narrator finds herself—subject to the unrealistic expectations of her mother and feeling unworthy. Divide students into groups to discuss whether they feel that the confrontation could have been handled differently and what they would recommend to a friend who has the same problem. Have a recorder from each group report to the class.

Sharon Wilson
Bowie High School
Bowie, MD

IdeaBank

▲ **Motivation.** To help students get started, ask them the following questions: What feelings would you have if your mother insisted that you practice violin for hours? What feelings would you express directly to your mother? What feelings would be difficult to express? You might also ask students to suggest reasons why people sometimes expect more from individuals than they are willing or able to do. ▲

InformationBank

Literary Note. This story has been presented intact except for the deletion of the word *breasted,* a modifier describing a girl who sings in the talent show.

IdeaBank

✤ **Multimodal Activity.** Many of the narrator's mother's ideas about the United States came from television and popular magazines. Have students use pictures from magazines to create a collage showing the impression of life in the United States that an immigrant might derive from these publications. Then discuss why this impression might be misleading. ✤

InformationBank

Biographical Note. Amy Tan dedicated her first book, *The Joy Luck Club,* to her mother. In the dedication she wrote: "You asked me once what I would remember. This and much more." Much of this book, which tells the story of four Chinese women immigrants and their Chinese-American daughters, is autobiographical.

IdeaBank

❧ **Gifted and Talented Students.** Ask students to think about why the author chose to write the story from the daughter's point of view. Then have students rewrite or retell the story, or a scene from the story, using a different point of view: the father's, the mother's, Mr. Chong's, or a friend's. Suggest that they think about the character's voice, feelings, and beliefs and about the character's self-concept and his or her feelings about the other characters in the story. ❧

⌘ Connections

Across the Humanities. During the 1930's and 1940's, political upheaval in China caused many Chinese people to emigrate to the United States. Have students explore the history of this period. Students could also learn about the history of Chinese communities in various cities in the United States, such as San Francisco, New York, and Boston.

ResourceBank

For the Student. Yep, Laurence. *Sea Glass.* New York: Harper & Row, 1979.

For the Teacher. Lipson, Eden Ross. "The Wicked English-speaking Daughter (Chinese-American Writer Amy Tan)." *The New York Times Book Review* (March 19, 1989): 3.

Guidelines for Response

Thinking About the Story, pages 206–207

1. Students' responses will vary. Some may feel compassion and empathy for the daughter and understand the rebellion she stages. Others may feel that the mother is well-intentioned and the daughter need not be so cruel.

2. Students may speculate that these songs characterize the relationship between the mother and daughter. As a child, the daughter seems to plead that her mother let her be herself. As an adult, she has established a better relationship with her mother and come to terms with her mother's earlier ambitions, as is evidenced by her playing the piano after her mother's death (page 205). Students may suggest that if the daughter had not asserted herself in her relationship with her mother, she might not have been able to find the contentment she feels at the end of the story.

3. Students may suggest that the idea of being a prodigy at first appeals to the narrator, but as she realizes that she is not and cannot be a genius in the areas her mother chooses, she begins her revolt. Students may feel that the narrator is beginning to understand who and what she wants to be. Some may suggest that she begins to dislike her mother's ideas just because they are not her own.

4. Those who feel that the mother is right may emphasize that it is important to try hard and that through learning discipline the daughter could have learned a lot about succeeding in life. Students who sympathize with the daughter may argue that it is her life and that she ought to be able to decide some things on her own.

5. Responses will vary. Students may suggest that the great loss the mother suffered could have caused her to attach more importance to her one remaining daughter and thus put more pressure on her to succeed.

6. Some students may feel that the conflict is not resolved fully because there is not much interaction between the mother and the daughter after the piano incident. Others may feel that the mother's offer of the piano, the daughter's pleasure in the offer, and finally the daughter's realization about the two songs indicate a resolution of the conflict.

7. Responses will vary. Some students may say that the title is appropriate because it reflects important contrasts in the story: for example, the titles of the two pieces, "Perfectly Contented" and "Pleading Child," played by the narrator; the mother's lofty expectations and the daughter's need to frustrate them; the underlying tension between American and Chinese values. Other students may say that a title such as "Clash of Wills" would have been more appropriate for a story featuring such an intense mother-daughter conflict.

8. Students may suggest that the descriptive language in the piece helps them visualize the events and characters.

Analyzing the Writer's Craft, pages 207–208

The diagram below is an additional sample, which illustrates this simile: "It seemed as if everybody were coming up, like gawkers at the scene of an accident, to see what parts were actually missing."

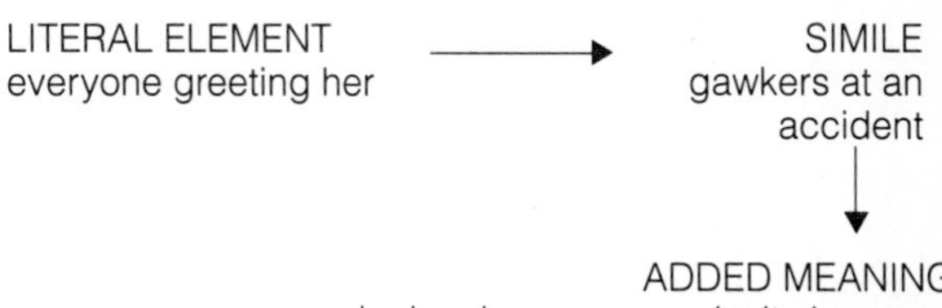

Connecting Reading and Writing, page 208

Students may need to discuss the type of advice given by school counselors in order to write from this viewpoint.

❓ Content Quiz

1. The narrator's mother wants her to be a child star like Shirley Temple.

2. Because Mr. Chong is deaf, he does not realize that the narrator is cheating at her lessons.

3. After the talent show, the narrator feels embarrassed, ashamed because of her performance.

4. The narrator deeply hurts her mother by reminding her of her twin babies who died in China.

5. On the narrator's thirtieth birthday, her mother wants to give her the piano.

NAME ______________________________ DATE ______________

Two Kinds (page 198)

Vocabulary Worksheet

Essential Vocabulary

devastate
discordant
fiasco
prelude
prodigy

Useful Words

envision
lament

Read the following poem and use the context clues to figure out the meanings of the underlined words. Then, use these meanings to work the exercise below. If you like, you may use a dictionary to check the meaning of a word.

A very young lady from Glasgow
Gave a concert that was a **fiasco.**
T'was not a success,
We were filled with distress,
For she sang like she'd swallowed Tabasco.

Now a **prodigy's** rather a treasure
A child with skill beyond measure,
And the sounds from this youth
Left us gasping, in truth,
But from agony rather than pleasure.

The **prelude** she sang to get started
Was not something for the faint-hearted.
We **lamented** in pain.
(We had cause to complain!)
And half of us up and departed.

I'd thought only a tormented cat
Could **devastate** music like that.
She ruined each note
Coming forth from her throat,
And the few that survived were all flat.

It's hard to believe there could be
As **discordant** a singer as she.
First one note, then another,
At war with each other
As if they would never agree.

I realize it is unfair
To ask you to picture us there.
No one could **envision**
With any precision
That scene of dismay and despair.

Match each underlined word in the poem with the correct definition below.

______________________ **1.** Moaned, complained.

______________________ **2.** Not in harmony, clashing.

______________________ **3.** To imagine.

______________________ **4.** A complete or ridiculous failure.

______________________ **5.** An introductory musical work.

______________________ **6.** To destroy completely.

______________________ **7.** A child who is amazingly talented or intelligent.

NAME ______________________ DATE ______________

Two Kinds (page 198)

Test

Part 1 Broad Interpretation

A. Answer the following essay questions based on your understanding of the story. Write your answers on a separate sheet of paper. *(12 points each)*

1. Why do you think that "Pleading Child" and "Perfectly Contented" seem to be two halves of the same song to the narrator?
2. Why do you think the narrator feels both strong and frightened when she fights with her mother over the piano lessons?
3. Why do you think the mother wants her daughter to be a prodigy? What does she hope this will achieve for her daughter? What do you think she hopes it will achieve for herself?
4. The mother thinks that her daughter can learn to be a prodigy. Do you think there is anything wrong with her reasoning? In other words, do you think it is possible to learn to be a prodigy? Why or why not?

B. Think about what the piano means to the mother and what it means to the daughter. Then, in the boxes below, write what you think the piano means to each of them at the beginning of the piano lessons and, years later, when the mother gives the piano to her daughter. *(12 points)*

MOTHER	DAUGHTER
At the beginning of the piano lessons	At the beginning of the piano lessons
When the mother gives the piano to the daughter	When the mother gives the piano to the daughter

NAME ______________________________ DATE ______________

Part 2 Close Interpretation

A. Write **R** if the event shows that the daughter is rebelling against her mother. Write **N** if it does not. *(4 points each)*

_____ **1.** The daughter watches Shirley Temple movies on television.

_____ **2.** The daughter tries to predict daily temperatures in Los Angeles, New York, and London.

_____ **3.** The daughter counts the foghorn bellows during her mother's tests.

_____ **4.** The daughter practices her curtsy for the talent show.

_____ **5.** The daughter refuses to practice the piano anymore.

B. Write the letter of the best answer. Where noted, there may be more than one answer. *(6 points each)*

_____ **6.** What does the narrator fear in her relationship with her mother? *(You may choose more than one answer.)*

- **a.** That her mother will leave her.
- **b.** That her mother loves her too much.
- **c.** That her mother will be disappointed in her.
- **d.** That her mother doesn't love her for who she is.

_____ **7.** After which of the following events does the narrator finally decide to stop trying to be a prodigy?

- **a.** The talent show.
- **b.** The mother's death.
- **c.** The first piano lesson.
- **d.** Seeing Shirley Temple on television.

C. One sentence in the following quotation from the story contains a simile. Circle that sentence, and then, in the boxes below, tell what two things are compared in the simile. *(8 points)*

"I was a dainty ballerina girl standing by the curtains, waiting to hear the right music that would send me floating on my tiptoes. I was like the Christ child lifted out of the straw manger, crying with holy indignity. I was Cinderella stepping from her pumpkin carriage with sparkly cartoon music filling the air."

[ ] is compared to 

Seventeen Syllables

Hisaye Yamamoto
(hē sä′ ye yä mä mô′ tô)

page 210

■ **Vocabulary Worksheet,** TG page 188

■ **Test,** TG pages 189 and 190

Objectives

1. To respond to a story that explores a girl's feelings about the conflict in her family.

2. To understand the literary elements of plot and theme.

3. To express ideas in a variety of writing formats: journal, haiku, annotations, diary entry, note, scene, journal notes, oral presentation, dramatic scene.

Plot Summary

Rosie is the teenage daughter of Japanese-American parents who have a farm in California. As the story opens, Rosie's mother has a newfound passion for writing haiku, which is how she spends her evenings when the farm work is done. Rosie's father resents this interest. He shows this resentment when he curtails a visit with another family because his wife is conversing with the other husband about haiku. Meanwhile, Rosie has discovered that she has romantic feelings for a boy, Jesus, who is two years older than she is and who helps the family on their farm. One day a publisher comes to present Rosie's mother with a prize she has won in a haiku contest. The father angrily takes the prize, a painting, outside and destroys it. Inside the house, Rosie's mother tells her for the first time that she married Rosie's father solely out of desperation—she wanted to escape Japan, where she was stigmatized by a failed love affair that had resulted in a stillborn illegitimate son. The mother demands that Rosie promise never to marry, while the memory of her encounters with Jesus lingers in Rosie's mind.

IdeaBank

▲ **Motivation.** As an alternative to the Connecting Writing and Reading activity, ask students to speculate about how they might handle a conflict with a parent, sibling, boyfriend, girlfriend, or teacher. Have students write down in their journals the most effective methods of conflict resolution they know. Then ask students to compare their ideas about resolving conflict with the nature of conflict resolution in the story. ▲

IdeaBank

❖ **Cooperative Learning.** Students should form groups of three or four and retell "Seventeen Syllables" in the form of a series of haiku linked together. Students in each group should work together to identify several incidents or images that lend themselves to being developed as haiku. Then individual students should choose one or more of these images and compose a rough-draft haiku for each. When these drafts have been completed, the group should reassemble and evaluate the individual haiku; students should help each other revise if necessary. Finally, one student in each group should read the completed haiku to the rest of the class. ❖

IdeaBank

✤ **Multimodal Activities**

1. Have students find recorded music that would be appropriate as background music for "Seventeen Syllables"—preferably in a Japanese musical style. One student can play the recording as another student reads from the story.

2. In groups of three, have students role-play the mother, father, and daughter in the story. Have each student in a group take the role of one of the characters and express that character's feelings. Then have volunteers from each group summarize the insights that they have gained into the feelings and motivations of the characters in the story as a result of their role-playing. ✤

IdeaBank

✾ **Learning Disabled Students.** Although the haiku form is explained in the story, students with certain perceptual problems may not understand the explanation. Some students, for example, might not have enough facility with the concept of syllables to understand the definition given in the story. To clarify the concept, show the students some haiku that follow the classic 5-7-5 syllable pattern. Alternatively, give students a simplified definition of haiku, going so far as to say, if necessary, that it is a three-line poem and that the mother in the story loves to write this kind of poetry. Later, as students develop an understanding of the story, you can elaborate on the special characteristics of haiku. ✾

InformationBank

Historical Note. Rosie's secret friendship with Jesus, whose name is a common one among Spanish-speaking males, reflects the coexistence of Hispanic and Japanese cultures, both of which remain strong in California. California once was a colony of Spain, and descendants of the early Spanish settlers still live in California. Through the years, immigrants from Mexico have added to the Hispanic population. Thousands of people immigrated to California from Japan between 1850 and 1900, first to work on the transcontinental railroad, then seeking employment in other industries.

IdeaBank

❧ **Gifted and Talented Students.** In "Seventeen Syllables," Hisaye Yamamoto writes of the relationship between an immigrant mother and her American-born daughter. Students might read other works that explore this situation, such as the fictional *The Joy Luck Club* by Amy Tan and the nonfiction works *The Woman Warrior* by Maxine Hong Kingston and *In My Mother's House* by Kim Chernin. To guide their interpretation of the mother-daughter relationship, students might try to answer the following questions:

- How do the mother's experiences in her native country affect her attitude toward her daughter?
- What problems do cultural differences create in the relationship between mother and daughter?
- What special wisdom or insights does the daughter gain from her mother?

Have small groups compare their responses. ❧

IdeaBank

✏ **Self-Assessment.** Before students make the oral presentation for assignment 4 in Connecting Reading and Writing, they might ask someone to videotape them as they give a preliminary version. They can then look at this "first draft" to see whether they have explained their ideas clearly and whether their delivery could be improved. ✏

⌘ Connections

Across the Humanities

1. Have interested students find books in the library on marital problems and their effects on children. Then have the students write an essay analyzing the family situation in this story. Alternatively, have students write dialogue involving Rosie and her parents. The dialogue should reveal the family conflicts and show how the characters respond to each other.

2. Have students find reproductions of prints by Hiroshige in books in the library. Students can share the prints with the rest of the class, perhaps by using an opaque projector. Then all the students might write about whether or not they would be excited to receive an original Hiroshige print as a prize for winning a poetry contest.

Across Literature. Suggest that students read the excerpt from *Kaffir Boy* (page 222), in which a child is forced to take sides in a conflict between his parents.

ResourceBank

For the Student. Yamamoto, Hisaye. *Seventeen Syllables and Other Stories*. Latham, N.Y.: Kitchen Table/Women of Color Press, 1988.

For the Teacher. Mori, Toshio. *The Chauvinist and Other Stories*. Los Angeles: University of California Press, 1979.

Yamada, Mitsuye. *Camp Notes*. San Lorenzo, Calif.: Shameless Hussy, 1979.

❓ Content Quiz

1. Where do Rosie and her parents live? on a farm in California
2. What new interest has Rosie's mother recently discovered? writing haiku
3. In what circumstances did Rosie and Jesus become friends? while picking tomatoes
4. What did Rosie's mother receive as a prize for her haiku? a print by a Japanese artist
5. What promise did Rosie's mother attempt to elicit from Rosie at the end of the story? not to marry

Guidelines for Response

Thinking About the Story, pages 219 and 220

1. Some students will indicate that they were thinking of Rosie as they finished reading, whereas others may have been thinking of Rosie's mother or father.

2. Students who feel Mrs. Hayashi is justified may point out that her marriage to Rosie's father obviously has problems that she would like Rosie to avoid. Those students may say that Mrs. Hayashi is not moved by Rosie's tears because she is more concerned with the larger context of Rosie's future than with her momentary distress.

Students who feel that Mrs. Hayashi is not justified may suggest that no one has the right to make that kind of demand on another person and that Rosie may not repeat her mother's mistakes. Those students may recognize that Rosie's American upbringing may help her assert her individuality and personal rights if she does marry.

3. Students may answer that Rosie's father resents Mrs. Hayashi's writing partly because it gives other men access to her and he feels jealous: she sits talking with Mr. Hayano about haiku all evening, and she receives the attentions of the editor who speaks in an "elegant Japanese" (page 217). Students also may suggest that what she expresses in her haiku she withholds from her husband and that her writing, which she does almost every evening, leaves no time for them to spend together. Students may recognize that Mr. Hayashi's reaction is based on a feeling of rejection and not on anything that Mrs. Hayashi is doing wrong, since she "kept house, cooked, washed, and . . . did her ample share of picking tomatoes" (page 211). Students may point out that as a man of "simple mind" and "kindly heart," Mr. Hayashi simply does not understand the artistic side of his wife's temperament and wants an ordinary wife—one similar to Mrs. Hayano—whose sole concern is to care for him.

4. Students may speculate that Mrs. Hayashi could be honest with her husband about her needs. Other students may say that she might agree to spend one or more evenings with him each week and to spend some time with him when they have company rather than talking exclusively about haiku. Some students may suggest that Mrs. Hayashi should ask her husband how he feels about her writing and then discuss with him his concerns. Some students may suggest that no matter what Mrs. Hayashi might try to do to resolve the conflict, her traditional husband may not be satisfied unless she simply quits writing.

5. Incidents students may cite include the following: she feels a "rush of hate" and wishes for the car to crash as they drive home from the Hayanos (page 213); "she suddenly felt like doing a lot of yelling" when her father brusquely refuses to wash her back (page 215); she stands "frightened and vacillating" as she watches her father going to the house to destroy the picture (page 218).

6. Students may respond that Rosie seems to have a strong, independent personality that will probably keep her from being defeated by life. Students may suggest that Rosie has grown up in the American culture and that she has more options open to her than her mother had. Some students may argue, however, that Rosie's observations of her parents' marriage may cause her to decide against marriage for herself.

7. Students may point out that Mr. and Mrs. Hayashi obviously knew little about each other when they married and that perhaps they would not have married if they had learned more about each other first. They may suggest that Mr. Hayashi, who holds traditional expectations for a wife, may have recognized Mrs. Hayashi's artistic nature and that he may have decided that she would not meet his needs. Similarly, students may indicate that Mrs. Hayashi married Mr. Hayashi apparently unaware of his "simple mind" and his need for a completely traditional wife.

8. Students who agree with this critical interpretation may note the irony in the mother's adopting a pose associated with marriage proposals while begging her daughter never to marry. Students who disagree with this interpretation may point out that kneeling is also a pose of supplication and is associated with religious ritual and that Mrs. Hayashi's kneeling in supplication to her daughter reveals the intensity and urgency of her demand.

Analyzing the Writer's Craft, page 221

Students' time lines may be similar to the following:

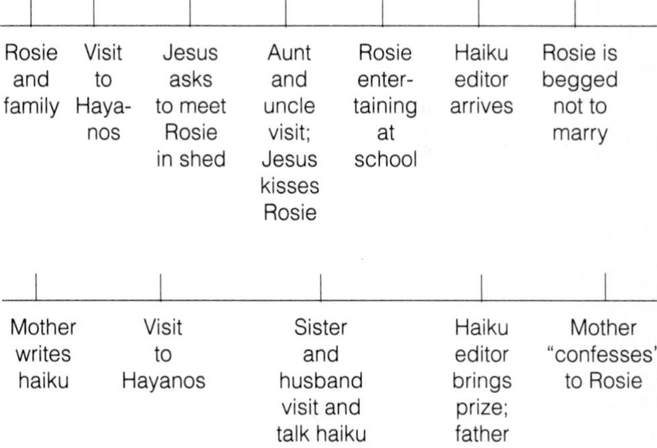

Students may say that the intersections of plot reinforce the theme of coming of age by associating Rosie's awakening romantic feelings with the fact that she must come to terms with who her parents really are and with the realities of their relationship. Students may suggest that as Rosie's feelings for Jesus offer escape from her parents' conflicts, her mother's experiences temper the possibility of Rosie's experiencing unbridled romanticism.

Connecting Reading and Writing, page 221

For assignment 1, bring in several examples of haiku to show students.

Suggest that students who have trouble getting started with their diary entries for assignment 2 begin by using the form "When my mother ________________, I felt ___________ because it meant to me that __________."

If the grammar and composition book you use has a lesson on writing dialogue or dramatic scenes, you may want to refer to this lesson.

NAME ______________________________ DATE ______________

Seventeen Syllables (page 210)

Vocabulary Worksheet

Essential Vocabulary

anaesthetic **glib** **indiscretion** **repartee** **vernacular**
garrulous **infinitesimal** **rapt** **vacillate**

Read the following poem and use context clues to figure out the meanings of the underlined words. Then use these meanings to help you work the exercise below. If you like, you may use a dictionary to check the meaning of a word.

"I thought that I could last it out," said Freda to her guy,
"Though you were just so **garrulous** I thought that I would die.
You've chattered 'til my ear fell off and then gone on some more,
And what you said was **anaesthetic**, thoroughly a bore.
If we had only shared some **repartee**, some clever chat,
A joke or two to make the evenings somewhat less than flat,
Or if your thoughts had been of some magnificence and size
And not **infinitesimal**, like ants or gnats or flies,
Or even if you'd gossiped, told a tale or two with spice
About a neighbor's **indiscretion**, weakness, fault, or vice,
I know I'd have been **rapt**! You could have hypnotized me then!
Instead you made me yawn and then you made me yawn again.
But now you've piled the final straw upon this camel's back
By reading from **vernaculars** for those who speak Dyak—
Although I like a newspaper as well as anyone.
(That statement is not **glib**. I read the *Tribune* and the *Sun*.)
You're handsome as a movie star. At dancing, you're a whiz.
So I've gone back and forth and wobbled, mentally that is.
But I'll **vacillate** no more. Goodbye. I'd rather be alone
Than have to go on smiling while I listen to you drone.

Match each underlined word in the poem with the correct definition below.

__________________ **1.** Newspapers printed in a native language.
__________________ **2.** Waver in opinion.
__________________ **3.** Numbing; making one fall asleep; dull.
__________________ **4.** An act showing lack of good judgment.
__________________ **5.** Spoken in a smooth, careless manner, often in a way that is not convincing.
__________________ **6.** Quick, witty conversation.
__________________ **7.** Talkative.
__________________ **8.** Completely absorbed; paying close attention.
__________________ **9.** Too small to be measured; infinitely small.

NAME ________________________ DATE ____________

Seventeen Syllables (page 210)

Test

Part 1 Broad Interpretation

Answer the following essay questions based on your understanding of the story. Write your answers on a separate sheet of paper. (*15 points each*)

1. Why does Rosie's mother ask her to promise that she will never marry? Why does Rosie give her mother this promise?
2. Do you think Mr. Hayashi's destruction of the painting can be justified in any way? Explain your answer.
3. Why does Rosie think "Don't tell me now . . . don't tell me today" when her mother asks if Rosie knows why she married Rosie's father?
4. How do you think the story of Rosie's mother would be different if the plot line about Jesus were not in the story? How would the story of Rosie and Jesus be different if it were told alone? Explain your answers.

Part 2 Close Interpretation

A. Write the letter of the best answer. (*4 points each*)

_____ 1. Which of the following is lacking in Rosie's attitude toward her mother throughout most of the story?

- a. Love.
- b. Respect.
- c. Sympathy.
- d. Understanding.

_____ 2. What in Rosie's life at home causes the greatest problem for her?

- a. Strictness.
- b. Parental disapproval.
- c. Friction between her parents.
- d. The hard work she is expected to do.

_____ 3. What is Rosie's strongest emotion as she goes to meet Jesus?

- a. Love.
- b. Guilt.
- c. Worry.
- d. Excitement.

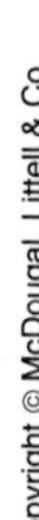

____ **4.** Why does Rosie hide when Jesus comes to the packing shed the day after their meeting?

a. She never wants to see him again.

b. She doesn't know quite how to react to him.

c. She is afraid that he doesn't like her anymore.

d. She wants to increase his interest in her by playing hard to get.

____ **5.** What is the most accurate parallel that can be drawn between the form of poetry that Mrs. Hayashi writes and her career as a poet?

a. They are both well known.

b. They are both difficult to understand.

c. They are both complete and satisfying.

d. They are both very short and condensed.

B. Think about the parallels that might be drawn between the Hayashi couple and the Hayano couple. In the boxes below, mark the characters described by each statement. Then, in the final box, briefly describe another similarity you noticed between any two of these people. (*20 points*)

	Mrs. Hayashi	Mr. Hayashi	Mrs. Hayano	Mr. Hayano
They are crippled, emotionally or physically.				
They have difficulty interacting with people outside their families.				
Their interactions with their families are limited to practical matters.				
They were physically or emotionally changed by the birth of their first child.				
Another similarity between any two of these four characters				

from Kaffir Boy

Mark Mathabane
(mä tä bä′ ne)

page 222

- **Vocabulary Worksheet,** TG page 194
- **Test,** TG pages 195 and 196

Objectives

1. To respond to an excerpt from an autobiography that deals with the value of education in an oppressive political system.

2. To interpret dialogue in a selection.

3. To express ideas in a variety of writing formats: journal, monologue, script, expository essay, notes, letter, poem.

Summary

Mark Mathabane describes what it was like growing up black under the system of apartheid in Johannesburg, South Africa, in the 1960's. Mark enjoys the adventurous life of a gang member and vows never to attend school. One morning, however, his mother takes him to a tribal school in Alexandra to register him as a student. Later that evening, Mark's parents argue about his education. Mark learns that his mother wants him to attend school to avoid the difficulties that she and his father have faced. He begins to appreciate her struggle to give him a better future, and he commits himself to knowledge rather than ignorance.

IdeaBank

▲ Motivation. To prepare students for the Connecting Writing and Reading activity, ask them to think about how their current interests might evolve into a rewarding career. Suggest that students create charts like the following in order to identify their career goals before they think about the education necessary to achieve those goals.

Category	Activity	Possible job or career
favorite school subjects		
extracurricular activities		
hobbies		
part-time jobs		

IdeaBank

✤ Multimodal Activities

1. Have students listen to the recording of Howard Rollins reading *Kaffir Boy*. Then have them discuss their favorite passages.

2. Ask students to present this excerpt from *Kaffir Boy* as Readers Theater, portraying the narrator, his mother and father, Granny, Aunt Bushy, the strange woman, the school principal, and the nosy neighbors. ✤

InformationBank

Literary Note. On page 228, offensive language used by the father has been deleted.

IdeaBank

✱ Limited English Proficient Students

1. To help LEP students understand the cultural context of the excerpt, write these terms on the board and help students define them: *township, veld, pass raids, tribal school.* Help students develop an overview of South-African apartheid. Then have students compare any discriminatory experiences they may have had or heard about with those of Mark Mathabane.

2. Help students create a flow chart on poster-sized paper or on the board to show in chronological order the steps Mrs. Mathabane takes to register Mark in the tribal school. ✱

IdeaBank

❧ Gifted and Talented Students

1. Have students read all of *Kaffir Boy* and/or its sequel *Kaffir Boy in America.* Ask students to write a book review analyzing the books' strengths and weaknesses. You may want to provide students with samples of critical reviews.

2. Have students read Richard Wright's *Black Boy*, Claude Brown's *Manchild in the Promised Land*, Maya Angelou's *I Know Why the Caged Bird Sings*, or a similar autobiography dealing with racial prejudice. Ask them to write an essay, a poem, or a short story or to find a visual way to make connections between the work they read and this excerpt from *Kaffir Boy.* ❧

InformationBank

Historical/Cultural Note. The word *apartheid* means "separateness" in Afrikaans, the language developed by South Africa's Dutch settlers. A government policy since 1948, apartheid separates South Africa's four racial groups—whites, blacks, "coloreds" (people of mixed race), and Asians. Public schools, transportation, housing, and recreation areas in South Africa were completely segregated by law until the late 1980's.

IdeaBank

❖ **Cooperative Learning.** Divide the class into seven groups, and assign each group one of the following characters: Mark Mathabane, Mrs. Mathabane, Mr. Mathabane, the principal, the gang of boys, the strange woman, Granny. Have the groups prepare for a debate on the best way to achieve racial equality in either South Africa or the United States, each group taking its character's point of view. Have group members take turns representing their character as the debate moves from group to group. ❖

InformationBank

Biographical Note. At age eighteen, Mark Mathabane left South Africa for the United States. He attended Limestone College in South Carolina, St. Louis University in Missouri, Quincy College in Illinois, and Dowling College in New York, from which he graduated in 1983. Mathabane attended Columbia University's School of Journalism but quit to work full time on *Kaffir Boy*. In 1987, Mark's brother George came to the United States to attend private school, and his sisters Linah and Dianah came to attend middle school.

IdeaBank

✏ **Assessment.** Have students assess their understanding of dialogue by answering these questions:

1. What is dialogue?
2. How is dialogue different from narration and description?
3. What is an example of effective dialogue in the excerpt from *Kaffir Boy*? Who is speaking? What makes the dialogue effective?

If students have trouble with any question, have them ask each other for help. ✏

ResourceBank

For the Student. First, Ruth. *One Hundred Seventeen Days*. (Voices of Resistance Service). New York: Monthly Review Press, 1989.

Griffiths, I. *Crisis in South Africa*. (Flashpoints Service). Vero Beach, Fla.: Rourke Corporation.

Mathabane, Mark. *Kaffir Boy in America*. New York: Charles Scribner's Sons, 1989.

———. *Kaffir Boy*. Read by Howard Rollins. Two sound cassettes. Studio City, Calif: Dove Books on Tape, 1988.

For the Teacher. Bunn, David, and June Taylor, eds. *From South Africa: New Writing, Photographs, and Art*. Chicago: University of Chicago Press, 1988.

⌘ Connections

Across the Humanities

1. Have students research the policy of apartheid in South Africa. Encourage them to find out about the African National Congress, the Group Areas Act, the Nationalist Party, Afrikaners, Nelson Mandela, Stephen Biko, the Pan-African Congress, and the Anglo-Boer Wars. Ask students to present their findings in written or oral reports.

2. Have students investigate the kinds of education— public, private, vocational, and technical—available in your community and any laws related to guaranteeing an education, outlawing discrimination in education, or providing financial support for those who cannot afford an education.

Across Literature. Other works of literature that deal with the value of education include the following:

I Know Why the Caged Bird Sings, Maya Angelou

The Mill on the Floss, George Eliot

Freedom Road, Howard Fast

❓ Content Quiz

1. At the beginning of the excerpt, Mark Mathabane is a member of a street gang of young boys.

2. Mark's mother takes him to be registered at a tribal school.

3. The principal is worried when he finds that Mark's father comes from another tribe.

4. After Mark is registered for school, his parents have an argument.

5. Mark's father believes that an education is a way for whites to take things away; his mother believes that education is the key to a new world and a new way of life.

Guidelines for Response

Thinking About the Selection, page 232

1. Responses will depend on what aspect of the account is most striking to individual students. Many students will express sympathy for the hard lives of the township people and anger at the racial discrimination they face. Many students will also feel admiration for the mother's struggles and anger at her husband's violent behavior.

2. Individual students will probably choose different aspects of the mother's struggle. Some may decide that the mother's greatest problem is getting her son to realize the importance of education; they may note how the gang influences the son to resist school and point out that it is usually very difficult for parents to overcome such peer pressure. Others may focus on the fact that the boy's father opposes the mother on this issue and even beats her because of it; they may note that it takes enormous courage and conviction to go against such brutal behavior. The mother's determination to defy her husband is especially remarkable considering the tribal regulations and customs that regard a married woman as the property of her husband. Other students may feel that most people would be defeated by the bureaucratic impediments that blacks face in trying to register their children for school—obtaining birth certificates, proving tribal affiliation, and so forth.

3. Most students will probably agree with the narrator's mother. They may cite the fact that the selection is an excerpt from an autobiography and infer that the narrator's early education was a first step in enabling him to become a successful writer. Many students may have written in their journals about the economic necessity of an education, and they may note that the narrator's mother points out that she herself cannot find a job because "white people mainly want to register people who can read and write" (page 230). Some students may also have written in their journals about the less tangible benefits of learning, and they may agree with the mother that education helps one "embrace what's good and shun what's bad and evil" (page 230). However, some students may note that education is not a panacea, particularly in a society that is so obviously prejudiced against people of color.

4. Some students may respond that if the father wanted his son to have an education, the narrator might be more willing to go to school and that the excerpt would reflect this attitude. Students may point out that any parent's wishes are more likely to prevail when he or she has the support of the other parent; in addition, students may note that boys often tend to identify with their fathers' values. Other students may realize, however, that the father's violent opposition inspires the boy to come to his mother's defense—"I chose to fight on my mother's side" (page 231). They may feel that, ironically, if the father behaves differently, the narrator may never change his own negative attitude toward school.

5. Answers may vary. Some students may think that the primary message involves the importance of education, since most of the selection deals with the mother's struggle for her son's education. They may note the violent and desperate behavior of the boys in the junkyard gangs, who "come to hate school and forget about the future" (page 226). Others may think that the education message is subordinate to the broader theme of anger at the conditions that must be endured by the black people in the township—and admiration for those people who struggle to improve their lot despite these factors. Students may point out the pervasive references to poverty, unemployment, and violence. They may think that while the mother ascribes the father's brutality to his lack of education (page 230), the hopelessness of his life is at least partly responsible for his desperate behavior.

6. Many students may think that an anti-apartheid crusader would value the cause-and-effect relationship brought out between apartheid regulations and socioeconomic hardships. At several points in the excerpt, violence and other forms of antisocial behavior are linked specifically with unemployment—for example, when the gang boys cannot find work caddying, they "steal beer and soda bottles" (page 223), and unemployed men and women indulge in "intense beer drinking" (page 225). Unemployment, in turn, is repeatedly ascribed to lack of education, as when the mother says that the father "didn't learn to read and write; therefore, he can't find a decent job" (page 230). Yet the apartheid system makes it almost impossible for blacks to enroll their children in school, as evidenced by the paperwork and regulations mentioned in the mother's conversation with the principal (pages 226–227).

Analyzing the Writer's Craft, page 233

Students might tape-record or videotape their dramatic readings and then play the recordings for the class. Ask listeners to identify the characters' attributes as shown by the qualities of the dialogue.

Connecting Reading and Writing, page 233

Suggest that students note the characteristics of public service announcements on television before they begin the assignment 1 option.

If the grammar and composition book you use has a lesson on research reports, you may want to refer to this lesson.

NAME ______________________________ DATE ______________

from Kaffir Boy (page 222)

Vocabulary Worksheet

Essential Vocabulary

austere **inscrutable**
coterie **mores**

Useful Word

admonish

Read the following poems and use the context clues to figure out the meanings of the underlined words. Then use these meanings to help you work the exercise below. If you like, you may use a dictionary to check the meaning of a word.

I

The principles by which we live
Make sense, though that is relative.
The customs that we follow here
Seem obvious and plain and clear.
But strangers to our shores may find
Our **mores** the confusing kind.
For what makes sense to us may be
Inscrutable to them, you see.
While ways of life that they defend
We cannot always comprehend.

II

The billies and the nannies and their kiddies frisk and play.
They graze upon the hillside as a herd the livelong day.
And scientists have studied them. They've taken many notes
Describing social patterns in this **coterie** of goats.

III

They say he never smiles, but frowns
At all life's little ups and downs,
Admonishing his students when
They cough or laugh or drop a pen
Or yawn or tell a joke. I hear
This teacher's manner is **austere**.

Match each underlined word in the poems with the correct definition below.

______________ 1. A close circle of friends with common interests or backgrounds; clique.

______________ 2. Severe or stern.

______________ 3. That cannot be easily understood; completely mysterious.

______________ 4. Criticizing; warning of a fault.

______________ 5. Folkways that seem favorable to the welfare of a society and are often incorporated into law.

NAME ______________________ DATE ____________

from Kaffir Boy (page 222)

Test

Part 1 Broad Interpretation

A. Answer the following essay questions based on your understanding of the selection. Write your answers on a separate sheet of paper. *(12 points each)*

1. What do you think is the most important factor that compels Mathabane to take his first step out of the "dark, yawning void" toward the "beacon of light"? Explain your answer.
2. Why, under the system of apartheid, might it be sensible for a black child to get an education? Why might it seem better not to get an education? Use examples from the selection to support your answers.
3. In what ways does the government of South Africa hamper Mathabane's ability to get an education? In acting this way, whose interests does the government attempt to serve, and why?
4. Did reading the selection affect the way that you think about your education? Explain your answer.

B. Think about what causes Mathabane to feel "torn between two worlds." Then, in the boxes on the top, complete the sentences by listing all the ways that you can think of that the person expresses support or opposition to the boy's going to school. In the boxes on the bottom, briefly tell what motivates the person's actions. (*8 points each*)

5. HIS MOTHER SUPPORTS his going to school by:
Motivations:

6. HIS FATHER OPPOSES his going to school by:
Motivations:

7. THE STRANGE WOMAN SUPPORTS his going to school by:
Motivations:

NAME ______________________ DATE ____________

8. THE PRINCIPAL SUPPORTS his going to school by:
Motivations:

C. Think about the things that complicate the issue of Mathabane's attending school. Then fill in the bar graph below. (*8 points*)

	Doesn't complicate at all … Complicates a great deal
Family ties	
Peer pressure	
Religious beliefs	
Racial discrimination	
Tribal ties and customs	
Financial considerations	
Concern for physical safety	
Mathabane's ability to learn	

Part 2 Close Interpretation

Read the dialogue below. Then, in the boxes, note at least three qualities of Mathabane's mother and three of his grandmother that you think are implied or suggested by the dialogue. (*12 points*)

> "Don't talk like that about your father, child," Granny said. "Despite all, he's still your father, you know. Anyway, he asked for *lobola* only because he had to get back what he spent raising you. And you know it would have been taboo for him to let you or any of your sisters go without asking for *lobola*."
>
> "You and Papa seemed to forget that my sisters and I have minds of our own," my mother said. "We didn't need you to tell us whom to marry, and why, and how. If it hadn't been for your interference, I could have married that schoolteacher."

Mother	Grandmother

Hiccups

Léon Damas
(le ô*n*′ dà mà′)

page 234

■ **Test,** TG page 200

Objectives

1. To respond to a poem about a parent-child relationship.

2. To express ideas in a variety of writing formats: journal, question/answer column, letter, essay, dialogue, memo, annotations.

IdeaBank

▲ **Motivation.** As an alternative to the Connecting Writing and Reading activity, present the following list and ask students to check what they think are the three most important parental qualities. Invite students to list additional qualities that they think are important.

_____ wisdom	_____ strictness
_____ patience	_____ affection
_____ unselfishness	_____ tolerance
_____ kindness	_____ energy
_____ humor	

After they have read "Hiccups," ask students to review their lists and revise them, if necessary. Have students discuss any changes they make and the reasons for those changes. ▲

IdeaBank

✣ **Multimodal Activity.** Have students rehearse and then present a dramatic reading of "Hiccups." Encourage students to use different tones for mother and son as they read. ✣

IdeaBank

❧ **Gifted and Talented Students.** Have students read the prose poem "Girl" that appears in *At the Bottom of the River* by the Caribbean writer Jamaica Kincaid. Ask students to compare and contrast this poem with "Hiccups" in an essay, a poem of their own, or in a series of drawings. ❧

InformationBank

Historical/Cultural Notes

1. The mother in "Hiccups" forbids her son to play the banjo or guitar. The banjo probably originated in Asia and Africa and was later brought to the Western Hemisphere by West-African slaves. The guitar probably originated in ancient Egypt and was brought to Europe in A. D. 711 by the Moors of northern Africa. The mother prefers to have her son play the violin, an instrument native to Europe, and to practice the European diatonic scale (*do re mi fa sol la ti do*); in other words, she pressures him to embrace his European heritage.

2. The word *Creole* comes from the Spanish word *criollo*, which means "native to the place." The term has different meanings in different cultures. In the United States, Creoles are descendants of the early French and Spanish settlers in the Gulf States, primarily Louisiana. In the West Indies, Creoles are people who are native-born but whose ancestors are European. In French Guiana, the term refers to those who have adopted a European way of life, regardless of their skin color or their ancestry. Nearly ninety percent of the population of French Guiana is considered Creole.

3. French is the official language of French Guiana, and most people practice Roman Catholicism. Spanish explorers first claimed the area in 1500, but the French settled in the region in 1604. The Dutch West India Company then brought African slaves to the area to work on the coffee and cotton plantations. After French Guiana abolished slavery in 1848, indentured workers were brought in from India, China, and Southeast Asia. French Guiana, today a French *département*, has become a mixture of African, European, and Asian cultures.

IdeaBank

✱ **Limited English Proficient Students**
To help students understand the cultural context of "Hiccups," review with them the clues that indicate the speaker's religion, social class, and Creole heritage ("in the name of the Father," "well-bred stomach," "French French," and so on.) Explain that the son is rebelling both against his mother and against the dominance of European values. You may wish to have students compare their own experiences of rebellion against adult and cultural norms with those being described in the poem. ✱

IdeaBank

✲ **Collaborative Learning**

1. Ask students to reread "Hiccups" and then work together in small groups to write a newspaper column about etiquette from the mother's point of view. Refer students to the column "Ask Miss Manners" or to similar features on acceptable social behavior in magazines or newspapers. Then have each group write a letter to the editor, responding to the group's column from the son's point of view.

2. To help students understand the conflict of values in "Hiccups," draw a two-columned chart on the board. Ask students to identify the mother's and the son's contrasting values, goals, and desires and then add their ideas to the diagram or chart. Then encourage students to discuss why the two are in conflict and how the conflict might be resolved. ✲

⌘ Connections

Across the Language Arts. Write a stanza or two from "Hiccups" on the board, and point out the absence of standard punctuation. Have students paraphrase the lines from the poem, adding appropriate standard punctuation. Then ask students which, if any, of the following were reasons for Damas's using few punctuation marks in his poem:

- to emphasize the son's rebellion against rules and conventions
- to produce the effect of hiccups
- to create a certain kind of rhythm
- to imitate the relentless nature of the mother's nagging

You may want to refer students to pages covering the standard use of end marks, commas, semicolons, colons, apostrophes, quotation marks, and other punctuation in the grammar and composition book you use.

Across the Humanities. Have students research one aspect of Creole culture such as history, customs, traditions, food, language, or music. Ask students to present their findings by creating a classroom mural or map, by writing an article for a travel guide, or by giving an oral report assisted by music, visual aids, and short skits or interpretive readings.

ResourceBank

For the Teacher. Merryfield, Mary, and Adams Timbo. *Teaching About Francophone Africa.* Bloomington, Ind.: Indiana University Press, 1983.

InformationBank

Literary Note. Léon Damas, one of the most original poets of the Négritude movement, was influenced both by traditional African dance and song and by the French surrealist poetry of Jacques Prévert and Robert Desnos. Damas's poems are characterized by puns, staccato rhythms, informal language, and the repetition of key images and phrases.

IdeaBank

✏ **Self-Assessment.** Have students complete the following tasks to determine whether they completely understand the poem "Hiccups":

- Write one sentence stating the theme of the poem.
- Describe how the form the author chose for the poem fits its subject.

Encourage students to ask each other for help if they have difficulty with either of these tasks. ✏

IdeaBank

★ **Interactive Assessment.** Ask pairs of students to exchange their Connecting Reading and Writing assignments and use the following questions to evaluate each other's work: (1) Does the writing fulfill the purpose of the assignment? (2) Does the writer present ideas clearly and logically? (3) Are any parts of the writing confusing? Why? (4) What do you think are the most effective parts of the writing? (5) What do you think are the least effective parts? ★

❓ Content Quiz

1. What terms does the speaker in "Hiccups" repeatedly use to describe his childhood? [Students may name either one.] a calamity; a disaster

2. What is one of the good manners the mother tells her son to practice at the table? [Students may name any one.] keep hands on the table; break bread rather than cut it; eat carefully and neatly; never burp; don't use a fork as a toothpick; don't pick your nose; sit up straight

3. What language does the mother want the son to speak? French French

4. Where is the son not supposed to play? in the street or on the grass or in the park

5. What instrument does the mother want her son to play? the violin

Guidelines for Response

Thinking About the Poem, pages 237–238

1. Most students will have negative feelings about the speaker's mother, seeing her as rigid, demanding, intimidating, and insensitive. However, some students may sympathize with the insecurity that accounts for much of her behavior, an insecurity that is perhaps caused by racial prejudice. Individual students may react differently to the mother's desire that her son have "the very best marks" (line 38); some students may feel that she puts too much pressure on him, but others may think that she is showing legitimate parental concern and ambition.

2. Some students will view the relationship between parent and child as one of alienation and repressiveness. In their journal entries, students may have indicated in one way or another that parents should generally use a positive approach toward their children—that is, be supportive, encouraging, and accepting, rather than restrictive, belittling, and unreasonably demanding. Students may contrast their own ideas with the mother's destructive and guilt-inducing behavior toward her son, as typified by her insistence that the speaker be a "mama's boy" (line 54) and her comment that "This child will disgrace our family name" (line 43). Students may mention that the mother is insensitive to her son's needs and is unwilling to allow him to develop his own interests, as shown by her demand that he learn to play the violin rather than the banjo, since she thinks that the violin is more acceptable socially. Most students will infer that the mother and the son have very different values, a fact that contributes to their alienation from each other. The mother attaches great importance to outward appearances, religious conformity, and social status, emphasizing such things as table manners and socially acceptable dialect—"the French of France" (line 48). The speaker, in contrast, rejects these values, treating them ironically in lines such as "don't let me catch you . . . / playing . . . / . . . with what's-his-name / . . . who isn't even baptized" (lines 57–62). Some students may see some positive aspects in the mother-son relationship, saying that even though the mother's behavior is misguided, she must care deeply about her son; otherwise, she would not want so much for him or be so concerned about all aspects of his life.

3. Many students will feel that the words *calamity* and *disasters* are justified since the impression of the speaker's childhood is overwhelmingly negative. They may note that the mother's reprimands are harsh, sarcastic, and belittling; as an example of the mother's tone, students may cite her abrupt reprimand about her son's speech—"be quiet / have I or have I not / told you to speak French" (lines 45–47)—or her sarcastic repetition of the word *banjo* in lines 78–87. Students may also point out that the speaker's childhood experiences were so unpleasant that they continue to have a powerful emotional impact on him; when he thinks about his childhood, he has a fit of hiccups, and his recollected feelings of guilt are so powerful that he uses the simile "like the criminal to the crime" to characterize the experience of remembering. His desire to distance himself from those memories is so strong that he refers to his childhood self as "her son" rather than "me," possibly implying that as a child he was compelled to be the product of his mother's ideas rather than develop his own personality. Some students may also think that the speaker uses the words *calamity* and *disasters* ironically, since his supposed failings were hardly so terrible as his mother made him believe.

4. Responses may vary. Many students may think that if the speaker had grown up to be what his mother wanted, he would have gained her approval but lost his individuality and self-respect. Some students may also point out that if he had followed her dictates, he might have achieved the social status that was so important to her. However, by suppressing his impulses to do such things as play the banjo, he would have denied both his creativity and his identity as a black man.

5. Since humor and strong emotion are both present in the poem, students may agree that the poem is "charged with an emotion concealed by humor." However, others may feel that the reverse is true. The speaker's emotions—primarily bitterness and anger—are so strong that the humor does not conceal or lighten them at all; rather, the strong emotion overwhelms the humor. Those students who do feel the humor, however, might note lines such as "a stomach has to have good manners too" (line 19) and "a well-bred nose / doesn't sweep the plate" (lines 26–27); students may also mention the breaking of the word *violin* into three syllables for humorous emphasis (line 77).

Connecting Reading and Writing, page 238

For assignment 1, show students examples of advice columns that have the question/answer format; students can use these columns as models. Many magazines include such columns.

For the option to assignment 2, you might have students work in pairs to create the dialogue and then perform it for the class.

For the option to assignment 3, you might provide students with samples of annotations.

NAME ______________________ DATE ______________

Hiccups (page 234)

Open-Book Test

Part 1 Broad Interpretation

Answer the following essay questions based on your understanding of the poem. Write your answers on a separate sheet of paper. (*15 points each*)

1. How do you think the speaker in this poem feels about his mother? Support your answer with reference to the thoughts and language of the poem.
2. Do you think the mother's attitudes would be harmful to a child? Explain your answer.
3. How might the son have benefited from the mother's lessons? Explain your answer.
4. Would your reaction to the poem be different if the last two lines were removed? Why or why not?

Part 2 Close Interpretation

Think about the kind of person the speaker's mother wanted her son to be. Think about how that image is communicated in the poem. Then, in each box at the top of the chart below, write a word or phrase that names a quality that kind of person has. In the box below each word or phrase, note lines or sections of the poem that communicate that quality. (*40 points*)

from Arctic Dreams

Barry Lopez

page 239

- **Vocabulary Worksheet,** TG page 204
- **Test,** TG pages 205 and 206

Objectives

1. To respond to a nonfiction account that describes the arctic wilderness and the factors that threaten the region.
2. To understand description in a literary work.
3. To express ideas in a variety of writing formats: journal, catalog, grant proposal, persuasive speech, publicity slogans, annotation, poster, descriptive essay, captions.

Summary

Lopez begins by describing two moments that inspired him: In the first, during one long Alaskan summer night, he observes the ground nests of tundra birds, marvels at the birds' vulnerability and resilience, and bows to them out of respect. In the second, while seeing the grave of an astronomer who died on an arctic expedition in 1884, he wonders why people are drawn to explore the Arctic. He then moves on to a lush description of the arctic landscape. He notes the range and variety of the landscape's geologic features, from waterfalls to huge glaciers to flower-filled meadows. He notes the "wealth of biological detail" that belies the impression that the tundra is largely empty and barren. Then Lopez describes the recent rapid changes in the region because of the incoming technology and industry and asks questions about the relationship of human beings to the Arctic. He believes that humans must strive to live wisely on the land.

IdeaBank

▲ **Motivation.** As an alternative to the Connecting Writing and Reading activity, have students make cluster diagrams with the word *Arctic* as the central idea. You might guide their associations with questions such as these:

- What physical features do you picture when you think of the Arctic? What is the land like? What animals live there? what plants?
- What kind of people live in the Arctic? Where do they live?
- What impressions have films, books, stories, or television programs given you of the Arctic?

As students read, have them compare their impressions with those described by Lopez. ▲

IdeaBank

❃ **Learning Disabled Students.** Lopez relies heavily on figurative language to enrich his descriptions and to emphasize his philosophical points. Students may have some difficulty understanding some of his dense similes and metaphors at first reading. Spend some time discussing several examples. For example, he writes that "caribou drift like smoke through the valley." Help students explore the simile by trying to visualize how a herd of caribou could appear to move across the land in the same way that smoke softly floats in drifts and wisps. Also encourage students to list ways in which the caribou and the smoke are alike—for example:

- Both are brown or gray in color.
- Both wander in curving patterns.
- Both are driven by natural forces.
- Both are a bit mysterious.

Point out how many of Lopez's metaphors and similes compare an element from the natural world to an element from the world of human activity. ❃

"Only to the white man was nature a 'wilderness' and only to him was it infested with 'wild' animals and 'savage' people. To us, it was tame."

— Luther Standing Bear, *Land of the Spotted Eagle*, 1933

IdeaBank

✲ **Collaborative Learning.** Inspired by Lopez's belief that "it is possible to live wisely on the land, and to live well," students can create their own "how to" books about preserving the land, its animals, and its plants. Before they begin, designate roles such as the following: editor in chief, production editor, editors, reporters, proofreaders, typists, illustrators, business manager. Have reporters collect ideas and write them as 100–200 word "tips." Have editors choose which ones will appear in the publication and offer suggestions for revisions. Have the editor in chief write an introduction to the publication that all students critique. The whole group should also conduct a discussion about a title for the booklet and reach a consensus. Have the production manager oversee the typing, illustrating, and final layout and have proofreaders check the final copy. The business manager should oversee the budget and distribute the booklet among other students in the school, possibly as part of an Earth Day celebration. ✲

IdeaBank

✤ Multimodal Activities

1. Provide students with a detailed map of the Arctic (Alaska and Northern Canada), complete with an index, and ask them to locate places referred to in this selection. Ask them to use the legend to measure distances between several places.

2. Have students create a large collage on a bulletin board with illustrations and/or photos of the various animals and images described by Lopez.

3. Show a narrative film that uses the Arctic as its setting, such as Walt Disney's *Never Cry Wolf*.

4. Have students make posters that encourage people to respect the wilderness, using short quotations from this selection. ✤

IdeaBank

✏ **Self-Assessment.** If students choose to write descriptive essays, encourage them to assess their work by applying the following questions:

- Have I appealed to as many of the five senses as possible?
- Have I included an effective simile or metaphor to strengthen my description?
- Do my details combine to convey one distinct emotional impression?
- Have I used specific nouns and active verbs throughout my description? ✏

ResourceBank

For the Student. Alaska Magazine Staff, ed. *Alaska: A Pictorial Geography*. Edmonds, Wash.: Alaska Northwest Publishing Co., 1982.

Galapagos. Photos by Nathan Farb, Introduction by Barry Lopez, Text by Michael Jackson. New York: Rizzoli, 1989.

Swan, Brian, and Arnold Krupat, eds. *I Tell You Now: Autobiographic Essays by Native American Writers* (American Indian Lives Series). Lincoln, Neb.: University of Nebraska, 1987.

Never Cry Wolf. Burbank, Calif.: Walt Disney Home Video, 1984. VHS videocassette.

For the Teacher. Hobson, Geary, ed. *The Remembered Earth: An Anthology of Contemporary Native American Literature*. Albuquerque: University of New Mexico Press, 1981.

⌘ Connections

Across the Language Arts. Use this selection from *Arctic Dreams* to emphasize that present participles do double duty in good description. On the one hand, they function as adjectives to enhance the meanings of nouns. In addition, since they are verbals, they give a sense of action and movement to any description. Ask students to cite examples of both single-word participles and participial phrases such as these:

- "*scintillating* stars" (page 245)
- "Israel's grave in the *falling* light" (page 241)
- "the boreal owl *clutching its frozen prey to its chest feathers to thaw it*" (page 245)

As students write their own descriptions, such as those for Connecting Reading and Writing, assignment 4, encourage them to make good use of present participles.

You may want to refer to the lesson on verbals and verbal phrases in the grammar and composition book you use. The examples and exercises in that lesson can be supplemented with examples drawn from *Arctic Dreams*.

Across the Humanities. Have students choose research topics from the many references Lopez makes to explorers (for example, Robert Peary, Edward Greely), to geographic points (for example, the Hood River, the Humboldt Glacier), or to examples of industry (for example, the trans-Alaska pipeline, walrus hunting). Encourage students to organize and combine their reports into an anthology or symposium titled "The Arctic: Past and Present."

Across the Curriculum. Have students research and share illustrations of and information about the various fauna referred to in this selection, such as caribou, musk ox, narwhals, and polar bears.

> *"We are the children of our landscape; it dictates our behavior and even thought, in the measure to which we are responsive to it."*
>
> — Lawrence Durrell, *Justine*, 1957

❓ Content Quiz

1. Lopez writes that this selection was inspired by two specific moments. What type of animals did he observe in detail during the first of these moments? arctic birds

2. Who was Edward Israel? a nineteenth-century arctic explorer who died on an expedition

3. What is the "recent change" that Lopez writes of in detail? the coming of new industries to the Arctic

4. What discovery in 1968 led to these vast changes in Alaska? the discovery of oil at Prudhoe Bay

5. What did the military men on the DEW line feed to the sled dogs? steaks

Guidelines for Response

Thinking About the Selection, pages 246–247

1. Students may describe impressions of extreme beauty, vastness, mystery, richness, bounteous diversity, desert landscape, cataclysmic change, disruption, human misunderstanding of the natural world, and mystical communion.

2. Students' answers will vary and may include encounters with birds; descriptions of the mystery that drew explorers to the Arctic; descriptions of landforms, geographical features, and physical forces; descriptions of the biosphere; and descriptions of interactions and interrelationships between humans and nature.

3. Students may say that Lopez's hope for the future of the wilderness is justified because the "astronomical" costs of development and the "marginal and in some instances artificial" successes (page 244) might limit further development. Others may cite Lopez's beliefs in the strength of the "individual's dreams" that the wilderness is worth preserving (page 245) and in the way the "wisdom of our past bears down on our future" (page 245). Some may also say the Arctic will survive, at least in part, because of its vast size. Students who disagree may point out that the future of the wilderness lies "in the hands of people with enormous economic resources but a poorly developed geographic sense of the region" (page 244) and point to the military men and oil drillers as examples. Some may say the wilderness, with its vulnerable life forms, is too fragile to survive. Others may state that sacrifice of the wilderness to make its tangible resources available to the rest of the world is necessary.

4. Students may respond that Lopez seems to have a deep knowledge of and reverence for nature that distinguish his perspective from that of the miners, oil drillers, and others seeking profit. In contrast to explorers such as Israel, who found the climate harsh and unwelcoming, Lopez is aided by modern conveniences and is thus able to appreciate arctic beauty. Students may note that Lopez's attitude toward the Arctic seems most similar to that of local residents who have traditionally lived in harmony with the land and are only recently adopting modern ways.

5. Students may answer that the oil spill may have damaged Lopez's belief that "it is possible to live wisely on the land" and made him more fearful for the fragile ecosystems of the Arctic. Students may point out that Lopez described "radical changes" and a "rippling effect" (page 244) but did not discuss irreversible catastrophes, either their possibility or their effects; the spill may have made him more aware of permanent loss. Other students may say that Lopez might be hopeful that the publicity surrounding the spill would lead to more safeguards for the Arctic.

6. Metaphors students may identify as most powerful include "the unfoldings of their obscure lives" (page 240); "a bloom of spray" (page 240); "an ocean that is the tundra" (page 242); the calving of icebergs into the sea (page 242); "the land . . . is rung with a harmonious authority" (page 243); "dreams, projections of hope" (page 245). Students may say that the metaphors help convey a mystical sense of the land. Others may say that the most powerful metaphors convey the size of the Arctic or the unexpectedness of life in the vast region.

7. Students may say that Lopez effectively conveys the need to protect the Arctic from human intrusion by presenting an appealing view of the area while knowledgeably discussing environmental issues. They may note that his poetic style convincingly portrays the beauty of the wilderness. Students also may point out that Lopez gives practical reasons against commercial explorations that disrupt the environment: such explorations are costly and result only in "marginal" success. Other students may argue that the essay is not organized as a point-by-point explanation of why we should protect the wilderness and that its presentation of environmental issues may be overshadowed by its lyrical qualities.

Analyzing the Writer's Craft, page 248

Examples of descriptions students may find interesting or moving follow: "the late-night sun, small as a kite in the northern sky, poured forth an energy that burned against my cheekbones" (page 240); "their eggs glowed with a soft, pure light, like the window light in a Vermeer painting" (page 240); "bituminous shale fires that have been burning underground for hundreds of years make those coastal hills seem like a vast, smoldering heap of industrial slag" (page 242); "the boreal owl clutching its frozen prey to its chest feathers to thaw it" (page 245). Students may say that these descriptions bring the scene to life. They may add that the descriptions give them the desire either to see or to save the Arctic.

Connecting Reading and Writing, page 248

For assignment 1, after students have listed all the artifacts, suggest that they organize these artifacts into categories, such as prehistoric animals, animals that exist now, human artifacts from twenty or more years ago, and recent human artifacts.

Students writing grant proposals should give reasons why these artifacts warrant further study.

Suggest that students writing a persuasive speech begin by expressing in their own words some of Lopez's reasons for preserving the wilderness and then, using those statements, think of other reasons for protecting the wilderness.

If the grammar and composition book you use has a lesson on persuasive writing, you may want to refer to this lesson.

NAME ____ DATE _______________

from Arctic Dreams (page 239)

Vocabulary Worksheet

Essential Vocabulary

adumbration *n*. A vague foreshadowing or sketchy suggestion of things to come.
austerity *n*. The quality or condition of being forbidding or very plain and severe.
benign *adj*. Favorable; beneficial; kindly.
fecundity *n*. Fertility; productivity.
gargantuan *adj*. Huge; monumental.
implacable *adj*. Relentless.
pervasive *adj*. Tending to spread throughout.

Useful Words

awry *adv*. Wrong; amiss.
estrangement *n*. A state of being kept apart or separate.
fixation *n*. Exaggerated interest; obsession.

Fill in each set of boxes with the correct word from the word list. (Clue: The double-boxed letters will spell what one sees a lot of in the Arctic.)

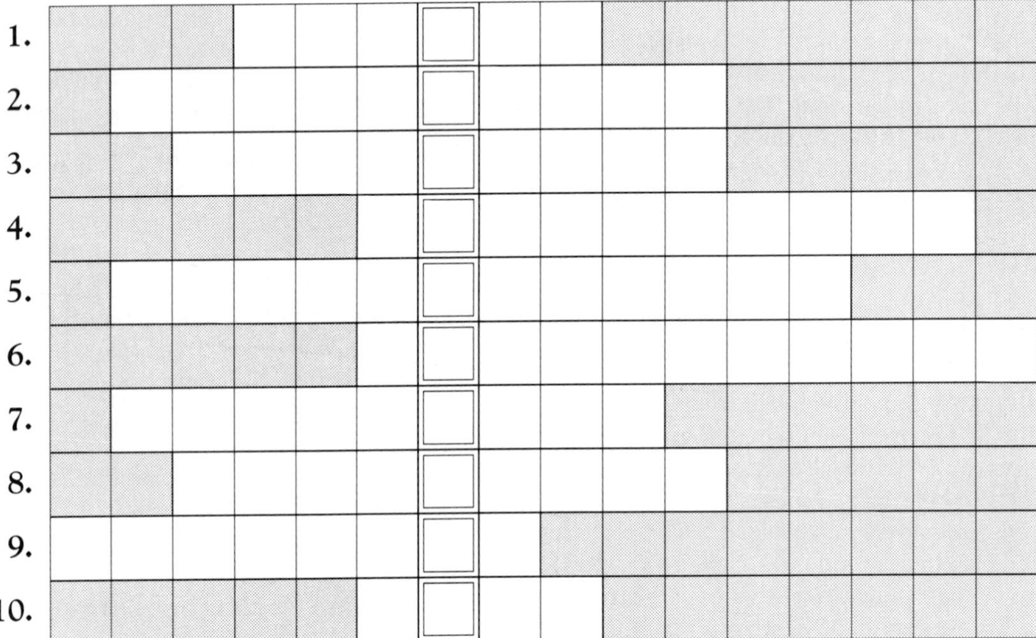

1. This is the perfect word to describe Santa Claus.
2. This describes the pursuit of evil by superheroes of the past and present.
3. This quality is often associated with a monk's cell.
4. This describes most office buildings now being built in big cities—at least, downtown.
5. This is what usually comes before, and legally comes after, a divorce.
6. This filled the air as Scrooge followed the ghost of Christmas Future.
7. This describes joy in the stands—on the winning side—after a close game.
8. Rabbits are known for this.
9. This word could be used in association with a person who owns five hundred pairs of shoes.
10. This is how the best laid plans of mice and men often go.

NAME ______________________ DATE ______________

from Arctic Dreams (page 239)

Test

Part 1 Broad Interpretation

Answer the following essay questions based on your understanding of the selection. Write your answers on a separate sheet of paper. (*25 points each*)

1. How would you describe the dream that Lopez presents for the future of the Arctic? How does it relate to the individual dream that "one's own life will not have been lived for nothing"? Explain your answers.
2. Why do you think Lopez feels that "behaving respectfully toward all that the land contains" is essential to a successful future for humans in the Arctic? Use details from the selection to support your answer.

Part 2 Close Interpretation

A. Read the following quotations from the selection. In the boxes below, note the sense or senses that the imagery appeals to and then note examples of figurative language in the quotation. (*10 points each*)

1. "It was breezy there on Ilingnorak Ridge, and cold; but the late-night sun, small as a kite in the northern sky, poured forth an energy that burned against my cheekbones."

Sense or senses imagery appeals to	Example of figurative language

2. "As I approached, golden plovers abandoned their nests in hysterical ploys, artfully feigning a broken wing to distract me from the woven grass cups that couched their pale, darkly speckled eggs. Their eggs glowed with a soft, pure light, like the window light in a Vermeer painting."

Sense or senses imagery appeals to	Example of figurative language

NAME ______________________________ DATE ______________

B. After reading the passage below, underline words and phrases that demonstrate Lopez's precise and careful use of language. In the box at the bottom, write brief notes about how the description makes you feel about the subject. (*10 points*)

"Like other landscapes that initially appear barren, arctic tundra can open suddenly, like the corolla of a flower, when any intimacy with it is sought. One begins to notice spots of brilliant red, orange, and green, for example, among the monotonic browns of a tundra tussock. A wolf spider lunges at a glistening beetle. A shred of musk-ox wool lies inert in the lavender blooms of a saxifrage. . . . [I] catch [the] sudden and unexpected sight of the silken cocoon of an arctic caterpillar."
How the description makes you feel about the subject

C. After reading the passage below, briefly explain what each character or object might represent in what is happening in the Arctic at large. (*20 points*)

"A man from Tuktoyaktuk, a village near the mouth of the Mackenzie River, told me a pointed story. In the 1950's he traveled regularly up and down the coast by dogsled. When a distant early warning (DEW) line radar station went up along his accustomed route, he decided to stop to see what it was. The military men welcomed him not as a resident of the region but as a figure of arctic fable. They enthusiastically fed his dogs a stack of raw steaks. Each time the man came, they pounded him on the back and fed his dogs piles of steaks. Their largess seemed so odd and his rapport with them so unrealistic he stopped coming. For months afterward, however, he had tremendous difficulty controlling the dogs anytime they passed near the place."

The dogsledder	The steaks	The military men

The dogsledder's reaction	The dogs' reaction

from Notes of a Native Son

James Baldwin

page 249

- **Vocabulary Worksheet,** TG page 209
- **Test,** TG pages 211 and 212

Objectives

1. To respond to an essay about what is important in becoming a writer.
2. To understand the literary element of conflict.
3. To express ideas in a variety of writing formats: journal, sermon, editorial, autobiographical sketch, outline, letter, report card, introduction, personality profile.

Summary

In this essay from *Notes of a Native Son*, James Baldwin describes his life of reading and his early attempts to write short stories, plays, songs, and poems despite his stepfather's desire that he be a preacher. Baldwin mentions some influences on his work—the Bible, the storefront church, and Charles Dickens—and then explains why he feels that being black has had the greatest impact on his writing. Ultimately, Baldwin believes that his greatest responsibility is to be honest and to be a good writer.

IdeaBank

▲ **Motivation.** As an alternative to the Connecting Writing and Reading activity, have students review their previous writing assignments or writing portfolio work. Have them answer these questions in their journal: (1) What do you like best about writing? What do you like least? (2) What are your strengths? your weaknesses? As they read the essay, students should consider how Baldwin might answer these questions. ▲

IdeaBank

❖ **Cooperative Learning.** Divide the class into groups of three students. Have each group create a chart with the headings "Influences," "Difficulties," "Concerns." Ask each student in the group to supply details from the essay for one of the three categories. The group as a whole should then discuss the chart, revising details if necessary. Have students turn in their revised charts for evaluation. ❖

InformationBank

Biographical Note. In *Notes of a Native Son*, James Baldwin recalls a significant talk with his stepfather: "We were walking, just the two of us, in our usual silence, to or from church. I was in high school and had been doing a lot of writing and I was, about this time, the editor of the high school magazine. But I had also been a Young Minister and had been preaching from the pulpit. Lately, I had been taking fewer engagements and preached as rarely as possible. It was said in the Church, quite truthfully, that I was 'cooling off.' My father asked me abruptly, 'You'd rather write than preach, wouldn't you?' I was astonished at his question—because it was a real question. I answered, 'Yes.' That was all we said. It was awful to remember that that was all we had *ever* said."

⌘ Connections

Across the Humanities. Have students report on discrimination against African Americans in the United States prior to the civil rights movement in the 1950's and 1960's. Ask students to focus on how African Americans were affected by discrimination in voting, employment, education, and housing.

ResourceBank

For the Student. *Black American Odyssey*. Los Angeles: Handel Film Corporation, 1987. 16mm film reel.

James Baldwin: The Price of the Ticket. New York: Maysles, 1989. 16mm film reel.

For the Teacher. "James Baldwin Encourages High-Schoolers at No-Holds-Barred Seminar." *American Libraries* 18 (January 1987): 80.

❷ Content Quiz

1. What does James Baldwin do at the same time that he cares for his sisters and brothers? reads books

2. What does Baldwin's stepfather want him to be? a preacher

3. What is the greatest influence on Baldwin's writing? being born an African American

4. According to Baldwin, what is the source of everything that a writer writes about? his or her own experience

5. What is one interest other than writing that Baldwin mentions? [Students may name any one.] making experimental films; eating; drinking; arguing; laughing

Guidelines for Response

Thinking About the Essay, page 254–255

1. Students' responses may include the following: a writer is largely on his or her own in the world; writers are people who love to read; a writer's task is to probe a subject; writing must come from one's own experience; writing is work that requires diligence and perseverance.

2. Students may report that they find Baldwin logical, philosophical, critical, intellectual, interested in questions of right and wrong, and honest with himself. Students may say that he seems highly intelligent, serious, in possession of a very dry sense of humor, and committed to writing.

3. Students who see writing as part of the process of discovering or revealing truth probably will agree with Baldwin that a writer should conduct a "genuinely penetrating search" (page 253), such as that which Baldwin sees in the work of Faulkner, Warren, and Ellison. Students who see writing as a tool to address social or political issues may not agree with Baldwin's belief that social affairs are not the writer's concern. Some may believe that fiction writers and poets write from experience; others may say that these writers rely more on imagination. Some students may say that Baldwin's belief that writers "go beneath the surface" is a good description of the writer's duty. Others may say that, as Baldwin is a minority writer, his statements do not apply to everyone.

4. Students may say that if Baldwin had lived in a predominantly African-American society, he would have had a more direct connection with his heritage and would not have felt like an "interloper" (page 253). He might have addressed more directly what he saw and experienced instead of analyzing the effects of being African American. If Baldwin had been part of the majority, he might have felt less alienated.

5. Students may answer that one of the things that hurt Baldwin was the expectation that he would write about the "Negro problem," because it placed limitations on his subject matter. Others may point out that it was the necessity of examining the "Negro problem" that forced Baldwin to probe his experiences and heritage. Students may feel that Baldwin, as a young man, was hurt by religion. Others may say that he cites both the Bible and the rhetoric of the storefront church as positive influences and that he later used his church experiences as the subject of a book. Some may feel that the opposition of his stepfather, while hindering Baldwin temporarily, strengthened his resolve to write. Students may note that although Baldwin felt like an interloper who had no claim to a European heritage, he chose to appropriate that heritage and used his outsider status to help him criticize flaws in Western society.

6. Students may say that Baldwin expresses general concern when he explains that a writer's business is "to examine attitudes, to go beneath the surface, to tap the source" (page 251). These students may add that Baldwin's purposes in writing, namely to write from his own experience and to create order out of disorder, express concerns shared by many writers. Some students may suggest that Baldwin's need to explore his identity as an African American and his attitude toward European culture reflects concerns particular to minority writers.

Analyzing the Writer's Craft, page 255

External conflicts students may identify are the censoring of a story Baldwin wrote about the Spanish revolution, his struggle with the "world of commerce and industry" (page 250), his inability to sell to publishers the books he wrote on fellowships, and his unwillingness to continue reviewing books about the "Negro problem." As examples of inner conflicts, students may list Baldwin's feelings of hatred and fear toward white people, black people, and the world (page 253), which put him in a "self-destroying limbo"; his conflict about drawing relentlessly on his own experience and feeling "prohibited" (page 253) from doing so because of being "a Negro writer"; and his feeling that by writing about his experience as a Negro, he would be covering a subject that had already been written about thoroughly.

Connecting Reading and Writing, page 256

To help students in writing a sermon, suggest that they read sermons by Martin Luther King, Jr., or the Pope, whose Christmas and Easter sermons appear in *The New York Times*.

For the option to assignment 1, provide students with samples of editorials from *The New York Times* or from other metropolitan newspapers.

NAME ______________________ DATE ______________

from Notes of a Native Son (page 249)

Vocabulary Worksheet

Essential Vocabulary

bravura
conundrum
interloper
rhetoric

Useful Words

advent
ambiguity
articulate
relentlessly

Read the following story and use context clues to figure out the meanings of the underlined words. Then use these meanings to help you work the exercise below. If you like, you may use a dictionary to check the meaning of a word.

"The goal," said Frank, "is to use the **rhetoric** of salesmanship—the special techniques of language developed by salespeople over the centuries—without letting anyone notice you're doing it. You have to be **articulate**: plain and easy to understand. There's no room for **ambiguity**."

"Until you get to the contract, right?" asked Della. "Then it's all right to leave room for more than one interpretation, right?"

"Wrong!" thundered Frank. "We use fair, honest methods. And no half-brained attempts at **bravura** either. That means no sneaking in the patio door, no threatening to blow yourself up, and no pretending, Della, to be an Internal Revenue Service agent. Now, once you do get into the customer's house, remember that you're a kind of **interloper**. You don't really belong there."

"But I'm going to stay there until they buy, right?"

"Wrong again! You're going to present the product and then leave, even if there's no sale."

"And come back the next day, right?"

"Wrong, wrong, wrong. Nobody in this company is going to keep after a customer **relentlessly**, never letting up. If the customer doesn't want us there, we just leave."

"Frank, old buddy, this is a **conundrum**," said Della. "It's a complete mystery to me why you would want us to use such gutless, watered-down sales methods. I'm going to have to quit."

"Wait a minute," said Frank. "Don't give up yet. We're about to announce the **advent** of a spectacular new product that will practically sell itself. Its introduction might just change your mind. It's a sort of do-it-yourself recycler, see? Whatever you put into it comes out again as *shoelaces*! Plastic shoelaces, steel shoelaces, paper shoelaces, ham shoelaces . . . "

Frank went on, but Della had stopped listening. She was wondering whether the brush company up the street needed any new sales staff.

Match each underlined word in the story with the correct definition below.

______________ **1.** Puzzling question or problem.
______________ **2.** The art of using words effectively in speaking or writing.
______________ **3.** Intruder.
______________ **4.** Expressing oneself clearly and easily.
______________ **5.** A coming or arrival.
______________ **6.** Uncertainty.
______________ **7.** Bold attempts or displays of daring.
______________ **8.** Without slackening or giving up.

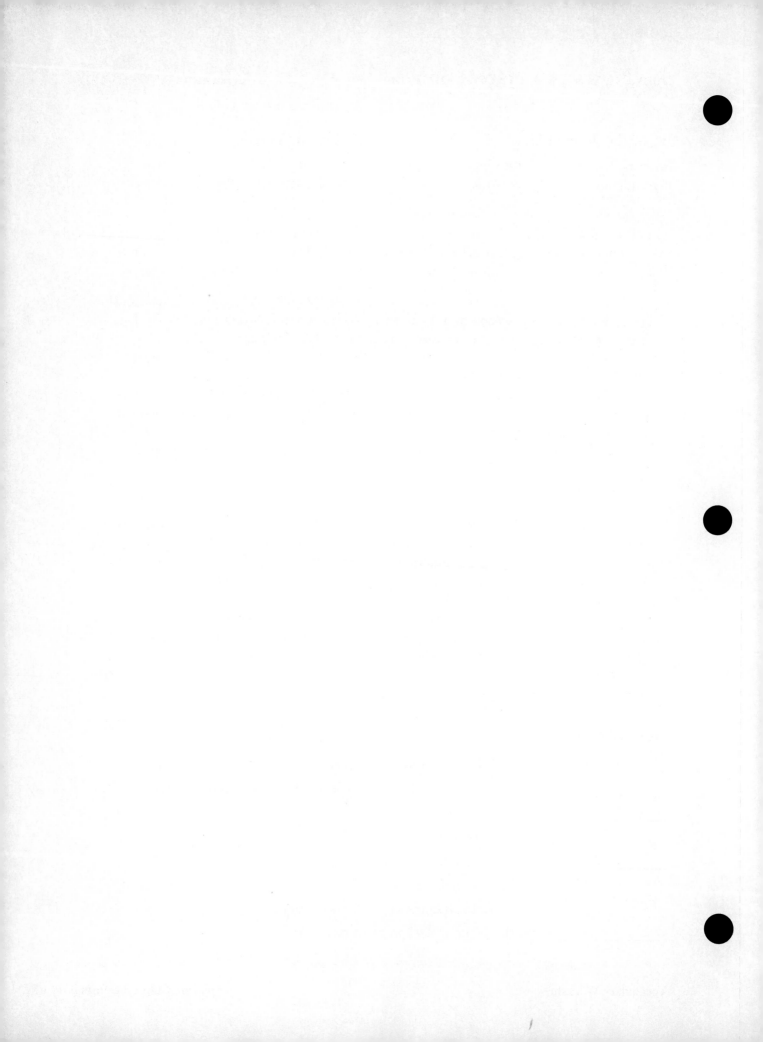

NAME ______________________ DATE ____________

from Notes of a Native Son (page 249)

Test

Part 1 Broad Interpretation

A. Answer the following essay questions based on your understanding of the essay. Write your answers on a separate sheet of paper. (*15 points each*)

1. What kind of person does Baldwin say that he would like to be? Do you think he became that kind of person? Explain your answer.
2. What do you think Baldwin looked for and failed to find in the European cultural tradition? Explain your answer.
3. Do you agree with Baldwin that each American has a responsibility for the social conditions that minorities face in this country? Why or why not?

B. Baldwin states a number of ideas and insights clearly and concisely in this essay. Many of them would be ideal to post on a bulletin board or hang above a desk. Put a check mark next to the one you like best. Then, in the box on the right, explain what you think Baldwin means in that quotation, and tell why you think it would make a good inspirational sign. (*15 points*)

	Quotation
☐	"Any writer . . . finds that the things which hurt him and the things which helped him cannot be divorced from each other."
☐	"The past is all that makes the present coherent."
☐	"This is the only real concern of the artist, to re-create out of the disorder of life that order which is art."
☐	"One must find . . . one's own moral center and move through the world hoping that this center will guide one aright."

NAME ______________________ DATE ______________

Part 2 Close Interpretation

A. Write the letter of the best answer. Where noted, there may be more than one answer. (*6 points each*)

____ **1.** According to Baldwin, what makes people think that he is "automatically an expert" on the Negro question?

a. His race.
b. His education.
c. His profession.
d. His individuality.

____ **2.** According to Baldwin, what is the most difficult problem of the African-American writer?

a. Getting an education.
b. Writing books that sell.
c. Gaining confidence in one's abilities.
d. Analyzing the African-American experience.

____ **3.** At the end of the essay, Baldwin mentions several kinds of people he dislikes. Which of the following is among those kinds of people? (*You may choose more than one answer.*)

a. People who argue.
b. People who are introspective.
c. People who are earnest.
d. People whose main goal is pleasure.

B. Baldwin states, "I was forced to admit . . . that I hated and feared white people. This did not mean that I loved black people; on the contrary, I despised them." In the boxes below, briefly describe the reasons for his feelings toward white Americans and toward African Americans. Then, in the box at the bottom, briefly explain how these feelings complicated his writing. (*22 points*)

Reasons for feelings toward white Americans	Reasons for feelings toward African Americans

How these feelings complicated his writing

from American Hunger

Richard Wright

page 257

- **Vocabulary Worksheet,** TG page 215
- **Test,** TG pages 217 and 218

Objectives

1. To respond to an autobiographical excerpt about physical, intellectual, and emotional hunger.

2. To practice the reading and thinking techniques of an independent reader.

Summary

Richard Wright describes his life in 1927 just after he has moved to Chicago. After working as a dishwasher in a café, he takes a job as a temporary clerk at the post office, which affords him more time to write. He hopes to achieve a permanent appointment as clerk, but he fears he will not meet the minimum weight requirement. Despite his efforts to eat abundantly in order to overcome years of malnutrition, he cannot gain weight. Wright also experiences emotional and social hunger. He longs for meaningful companionship and positive human relationships; his past has deprived him of both. He writes in an effort to capture the intensity of his hunger. He fails his physical examination for postal clerk and returns to his menial café job. Looking back, Wright sees within the hungers he felt as a young man the seeds of the person he was to become.

IdeaBank

▲ Motivation. Before you have students read this selection, ask them to think about their experiences with hunger, both literal and metaphorical, and then write in their journals about those experiences. Offer students the following questions to guide their journal writing:

- When in your life have you felt physically hungry?
- What other kinds of hunger have you experienced?
- What do these different kinds of hunger have in common?

Ask students to read the selection and compare their experiences with hunger to Wright's. ▲

"To the hungry soul every bitter thing is sweet."
— Proverbs 27:7

InformationBank

Biographical Note. In *Black Boy*, Wright describes the physical hunger of his childhood: "Hunger had always been more or less at my elbow when I played, but now I began to wake up at night to find hunger standing at my bedside, staring at me gauntly. . . . This new hunger baffled me, scared me, made me angry and insistent. Whenever I begged for food now my mother would pour me a cup of tea which would still the clamor in my stomach for a moment or two; but a little later I would feel hunger nudging my ribs, twisting my empty guts until they ached. I would grow dizzy and my vision would dim. I became less active in my play, and for the first time in my life I had to pause and think of what was happening to me."

Copyright © Philippe Weisbecker.

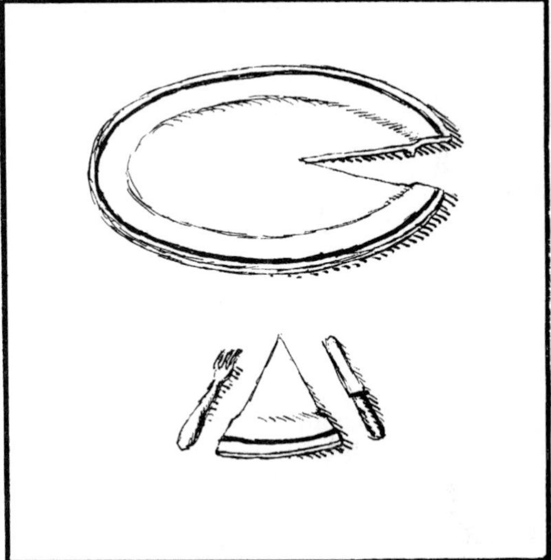

IdeaBank

✾ Learning Disabled Students. Wright's vocabulary and syntax may be difficult for students. Read the selection aloud to students and have them focus on words and parts of sentences they understand. Stop to paraphrase and discuss what is happening and what it means. ✾

IdeaBank

✲ Collaborative Learning. Have students form small groups to prepare lists of books that have shaped their lives. Through discussion and consensus, have the class generate a "Top Ten" list of books to recommend to young readers, books that will, in Wright's words, "open up new avenues of feeling and seeing." ✲

⌘ Connections

Across Literature. Have students compare and contrast Wright's concerns as a writer with Baldwin's, as expressed in the excerpt from *Notes of a Native Son* (page 249).

Across the Humanities. Wright refers to the fact that he was paid seventy cents an hour as a temporary postal clerk, a fact that will surprise most teenagers. What did seventy cents buy in 1927? Have students research the history of hourly wages in this country since 1900 and answer the following questions: When was the first minimum wage law passed? What was that minimum wage? What forces or institutions have been responsible for changing wages?

Across the Curriculum. Have students research malnutrition and poor nutrition in the United States today. What is malnutrition? What causes it (other than merely not having enough to eat)? Who suffers from it? What steps does the government take to protect its citizens from this condition? What are some of the effects of malnutrition on the individual, the family, and the community?

ResourceBank

For the Student. *Almos' a Man*. Library Video Classics Project. Learning in Focus, 1978. 39 min. VHS videocassette.

For the Teacher. Wright, Richard. *American Hunger*. New York: Harper & Row, 1983.

❓ Content Quiz

1. In what city does Wright live during the part of his life covered in this selection? Chicago
2. What temporary job does Wright have that he hopes will turn into a permanent job? postal clerk
3. What job requirement is Wright unable to meet? a minimum weight of 125 pounds
4. To what kind of job does Wright return after he fails his physical examination? a job as dishwasher in a café
5. What two activities does Wright say will "dull his sense of loss" and also express the intensity of his own emotions? reading and writing

Guidelines for Response

Discussion Questions

1. Why do you think Wright describes his way of life in Chicago as "a dangerous way to live"?

[Students may suggest that Wright sees danger in his isolation and alienation from other people. Students may point out that Wright himself says his self-sufficiency kept him "distant from others, emotionally and psychologically." Others may note that Wright's retreat into his own thoughts and feelings could have led him to get lost "in the fogbound regions of compelling fantasy." Wright says that "my attitude of watchful wonder had usurped all other feelings, had become the meaning of my life" (page 260). Students may see this usurpation as having the potential to lead Wright into antisocial behavior or mental illness.]

2. Based on what you have read, do you think *American Hunger* is an appropriate title for Wright's autobiography? Why or why not?

[Students may indicate that the title is very appropriate, noting that Wright writes a great deal about the physical hunger he has experienced. He says at one point, "Hunger had long been my daily companion." Students might also suggest that Wright focuses on other kinds of hunger as well, such as emotional, intellectual, and spiritual hunger. They may say that he hungers for work, for acceptance as a writer, and for "a life in which there was a feeling of closeness with others." Students may observe that in the final paragraph, Wright says he is "hungry for insight into my own life and the lives about me." Some students might recognize the irony that in America, a land known for its prosperity, a man such as Wright could grow up experiencing such hunger.]

3. What do you think made it possible for Richard Wright to triumph over his early harsh experiences to become a respected writer?

[Students may refer to Wright's obvious intelligence and determination as key avenues to his success. Students might mention his perseverence, even against great odds. Students may point out that Wright is a perceptive person, acutely aware of his own problems and motives as well as those of others. Others may add that Wright knows how to compensate for losses; when he felt self-doubts and deprivation, he says, "I dulled the sense of loss through reading, reading, writing, and more writing" (page 260).]

4. What advice do you think Richard Wright might offer aspiring young writers today?

[Answers will vary. Some students may suggest that Wright might caution aspiring writers to avoid the kinds of problems he faced. Such students may indicate that Wright would tell potential writers to make sure their physical needs are met so that they have the energy to write. He might also warn them not to isolate themselves from other people as he did. Some students may indicate that Wright probably would not tell aspiring writers to do things differently than he did, because he recognizes each person's need to find his or her own voice through personal experience.]

NAME ______________________________ DATE ______________

from American Hunger (page 257)

Vocabulary Worksheet

Essential Vocabulary

cynical *adj*. Doubting the sincerity of people's motives and actions.

reprisal *n*. The doing of injury in return for injury received; retaliation.

Useful Words

disconsolate *adj*. So unhappy that nothing will comfort.

libation *n*. A ritual offering of drink.

lucid *adj*. Clear; readily understood.

obsession *n*. The state of being preoccupied with a persistent idea, desire, or feeling.

subjective *adj*. Relying upon one's personal thinking or feeling; not objective.

translucently *adv*. In a way that lets light pass through but spreads it so that objects on the other side cannot be clearly seen.

usurp *v*. To take and hold by force or without right.

Write on each line the word from the word list that relates most clearly to each type of writing or that you are most likely to find in each type of writing.

______________ **1.** A book in which an astronomer abandons the scientific method to give personal ideas about the origin of the universe.

______________ **2.** A review of a biography in which the author questions the intentions and deeds of a well-known doctor.

______________ **3.** An article in a journal of anthropology that describes a tribe's ceremonial attempt to quiet an angry god.

______________ **4.** A poem that describes the pain and grief caused by the loss of a favorite grandparent.

______________ **5.** A catalog description of the qualities of different types of stained, frosted, and pebbled glass.

______________ **6.** A doctor's notes on a patient who has made a complete return to consciousness.

______________ **7.** A news report about military action in a part of the world where two countries are at war.

______________ **8.** A psychologist's confidential notes about a patient who feels a constant need to wash and rewash his hands.

______________ **9.** A chapter in a history text about an attempt to take over a throne from the rightful king.

NAME ______________________ DATE ____________

from American Hunger (page 257)

Test

Part 1 Broad Interpretation

A. Answer the following essay questions based on your understanding of the selection. Write your answers on a separate sheet of paper. (*15 points each*)

1. At the end of the selection, Wright says that the mold of his life was set when he was twenty. What do you think is the most important thing that Wright discovers about himself? about his goals in life? Use details from the selection to explain your answers.
2. In what ways do you think the circumstances of Wright's life hampered his becoming a writer? In what ways do you think they might have helped him become a better writer? Use details from the selection to explain your answers.
3. Do you think that the people who knew Wright during this period of his life would have realized that he was destined for greatness? Why or why not?

B. Think about the various "hungers" that haunt Wright at this period in his life. Then, in the boxes below, briefly identify examples of each kind of hunger that Wright experiences. (*15 points*)

PHYSICAL HUNGER	MENTAL HUNGER	EMOTIONAL HUNGER

NAME ______________________ DATE ____________

Part 2 Close Interpretation

Think about Wright's growth as a writer. In the boxes below, write brief notes about what each quotation suggests to you about Wright's qualities as a writer and his feelings about writing. (*10 points each*)

	Qualities and feelings suggested
1. "Repeatedly I took stabs at writing, but the results were so poor that I would tear up the sheets."	
2. "Under the influence of Stein's *Three Lives*, I spent hours and days pounding out disconnected sentences for the sheer love of words."	
3. "I strove to master words, to make them disappear, to make them important by making them new, to make them melt into a rising spiral of emotional stimuli, each greater than the other, each feeding and reinforcing the other, and all ending in an emotional climax that would drench the reader with a sense of a new world."	
4. "I read Proust's *A Remembrance of Things Past*. . . . But it crushed me with hopelessness, for I wanted to write of the people in my environment with an equal thoroughness, and the burning example before my eyes made me feel that I never could."	

The Clash of Cultures: Confronting Opposing Values

Below are suggested answers for the chart assigned on page 261 of the student book. For six other selections, the name of a character in conflict, an identification of opposing values, and a description of the handling of the conflict are listed. Accept other answers if students can support them with evidence from the selections.

Characters in conflict	Opposing values	Handling of conflict
narrator in "Two Kinds"	mother's expectations that her daughter be a prodigy and narrator's desire to be herself	Narrator chooses to disappoint her mother.
Mrs Hayashi in "Seventeen Syllables"	husband's expectation that Mrs. Hayashi be a traditional wife and her desire for artistic expression	Mrs. Hayashi writes haiku after her evening chores while still keeping house and helping her husband pick tomatoes.
speaker in "Hiccups"	mother's expectation that her son be perfect according to her views of a French gentleman and the speaker's desire to assert independence	Speaker rebels against mother's attempts to mold him and bitterly resents her insensitivity.
Barry Lopez in the excerpt from *Arctic Dreams*	progress and inevitable environmental change and the appeal of the unspoiled wilderness and native culture	Lopez holds out the hope that humans will learn to live wisely in the wilderness.
James Baldwin in the excerpt from *Notes of a Native Son*	the importance of writing from experience and the need for a minority writer to find a place in European culture	Baldwin chooses to write about the problems of African Americans and to appropriate European culture from a minority perspective.
Richard Wright in the excerpt from *American Hunger*	the need for a writer to find his or her own voice and the value of emulating techniques used by great prose artists	Wright chooses to write in his own voice about people in his own environment with the artistry shown by great writers.

Evaluation Guide for Writing Assignment

The well-developed student essay will meet the following criteria:

- Names two characters from the selections, one admired most and the other admired least
- Gives reasons for choosing the two characters
- Supports these reasons with examples from the selections

UNIT 5 Engaging the Imagination

Selections	Essential Vocabulary	Literary Skills	Writing Formats	Writing Modes
A Very Old Man with Enormous Wings				
Student Book page 266 **Teacher's Guide** Lesson, pages 222 and 223 Vocabulary Worksheet, page 224 Test, pages 225 and 226	terrestrial hermetic cataclysm repose providential tribulations	point of view tone style: magical realism	journal eyewitness account headlines notes human interest story letter review sequel dramatic scene	expressive and personal writing observation and description narrative and imaginative writing writing about literature
The Youngest Doll				
Student Book page 274 **Teacher's Guide** Lesson, pages 227–229 Vocabulary Worksheet, page 230 Test, pages 231 and 232	furtively ostentatious exorbitant	mood	journal informal note story catalog copy TV commercial essay pamphlet list of questions profile	expressive and personal writing observation and description narrative and imaginative writing informative (expository) writing: analysis informative (expository) writing: synthesis informative (expository) writing: classification persuasion writing about literature
What I Have Been Doing Lately				
Student Book page 281 **Teacher's Guide** Lesson, pages 233–235 Test, page 236		style: diction mood plot	journal episode monologue graphic representation expository essay	expressive and personal writing narrative and imaginative writing informative (expository) writing: analysis
Tenement Room: Chicago **Loo-Wit**				
Student Book page 287 **Teacher's Guide** Lesson, pages 237 and 238 Vocabulary Worksheet, page 239 Tests, pages 241 and 242	destitution gaudy buttes	personification	journal	expressive and personal writing
Rhythms **Prayer to the Pacific**				
Student Book page 293 **Teacher's Guide** Lesson, pages 243 and 244 Test, page 245			journal free verse poem sonnet instructions introduction notes proposal review chart	expressive and personal writing observation and description informative (expository) writing: classification informative (expository) writing: analysis writing about literature

Selections	Essential Vocabulary	Literary Skills	Writing Formats	Writing Modes
The Form of the Sword				
Student Book page 298 **Teacher's Guide** Lesson, pages 247–249 Vocabulary Worksheet, page 250 Test, pages 251 and 252	interlocutor opprobrium utopian apodictic aplomb vertigo infamy	The student book does not contain discussion questions, analysis of literary techniques, or writing assignments for this story. These materials appear in the Teacher's Guide lesson.		
Ode to the Watermelon				
Student Book page 302 **Teacher's Guide** Lesson, pages 253 and 254 Vocabulary Worksheet, page 255 Test, page 256	phlegmatic profundity	The student book does not contain discussion questions, analysis of literary techniques, or writing assignments for this poem. These materials appear in the Teacher's Guide lesson.		
Reviewing Concepts				
Student Book page 305 **Teacher's Guide** page 257				

A Very Old Man with Enormous Wings

Gabriel García Márquez

(gä′ vrē el′ gär sē′ ä mär′ kes)

page 266

- **Vocabulary Worksheet,** TG page 224
- **Test,** TG pages 225 and 226

Objectives

1. To respond to a short story about people who are confronted with something beyond their understanding.

2. To appreciate the style called magical realism.

3. To express ideas in a variety of writing formats: journal, eyewitness account, headlines, notes, human interest story, letter, review, transparencies, and poster.

Plot Summary

One day Pelayo discovers a very old man with enormous wings lying in his courtyard. He tells his wife, Elisenda, about his discovery. A neighbor identifies the creature as an angel, and Pelayo and Elisenda lock him in the chicken coop. The local priest determines that the creature is not an angel and corresponds with the church in Rome for verification. Ignoring the priest's verdict, however, the villagers spread word of a captured angel and the entire neighborhood comes to look at it. Elisenda capitalizes on the angel's fame by charging admission to see it; the excitement quickly dies down, however, when the carnival arrives with other strange creatures. With the admission money they have earned, Pelayo and Elisenda build a mansion for themselves and buy fancy clothes. The angel lives with them for many years until a day in December. New-grown feathers enable him to try to fly again and he flies away as suddenly as he appeared.

IdeaBank

▲ **Motivation.** As an alternative to the Connecting Writing and Reading activity, have students imagine the arrival of some creature or object that would puzzle or confuse people. Encourage students to draw on their own imaginations as well as on stories, films, or television shows. Have students describe their imaginings in their journals, including how they think people will react to such a puzzling entity. Then have students read the story and compare it with their own writings. ▲

InformationBank

Historical/Cultural Note. *Angel* comes from a Greek word for "messenger." Religious tradition has angels acting as messengers between God and humans. In the Christian religion practiced by the characters in this story, there are nine orders of angels, seraphim ranking highest, followed by cherubim, thrones, dominations, virtues, powers, principalities, archangels, and angels.

InformationBank

Literary Note. The term *magical realism* was first used in 1925 by art critic Franz Roh to describe the work of certain German artists. Roh described their work as a mingling of the fantasy and reality found in real life. The term was then used to describe the writings of Latin American writers such as Gabriel García Márquez, Jorge Luis Borges, and Alejo Carpentier. Their writing style can be traced in part to the myths and legends of Hispanics, Creoles, native peoples of Latin America, and African slaves, and to traditional books of chivalry (*Libros de caballerías*) about incredible adventures of heroes. Some critics connect magical realism with the absurd and unpredictable events of life under a dictatorship.

IdeaBank

❃ **Learning Disabled Students.** To help students appreciate the style of magical realism, create a chart with the headings *Realistic* and *Magical.* Have students supply details from the story for each column of the chart. ❃

⌘ Connections

Across Literature. Other works in this text that deal with people who confront events beyond their understanding include "The Censors," Luisa Valenzuela (page 130); "The Youngest Doll," Rosario Ferré (page 274); "What I Have Been Doing Lately," Jamaica Kincaid (page 281).

ResourceBank

For the Student. Márquez, Gabriel García. "The General's Departure." Edith Grossman, trans. *The New Yorker* 66 (July 16, 1990): 30–42.

For the Teacher. Wolin, M. L. "Hollywood Goes Havana." *The New Republic* 202 (April 16, 1990): 17–20.

❓ Content Quiz

1. What does Pelayo discover in the rear of the courtyard? a very old man with enormous wings; an angel

2. Where does Pelayo keep his discovery? in a chicken coop

3. What does Elisenda do to deal with the curious crowds? She fences in the yard and charges admission to see the angel.

4. What event causes the curious townspeople to abandon their visits to the creature in the courtyard? the arrival of the spider woman

5. What finally happens to the creature? One day, after a period of ill health, he flies away.

Guidelines for Response

Thinking About the Story, pages 271–272

1. Student responses will vary. Some may wish to question García Márquez about the meaning of the old man. Others may express admiration or confusion.

2. Some may agree with the neighbor that the old man is an angel; others may agree with Father Gonzaga that the old man is a devil. Those who see him as an angel may believe that he has been sent to help the family and may cite his miracles: the boy is cured soon after the old man arrives and Pelayo and Elisenda are much better off financially. Students may also feel that although the old man does not fit the common view of angels, there may be different types of angels. They may suggest that the old man is an angel who has been sent to remind humans of their failings. Students who see the old man as a devil may believe that he has been sent to cause dissension in the village. Some may believe that the old man is a mutant mortal or even an alien from another planet.

3. Students may be struck by the cruelty and indifference shown the old man. Some may suggest that humans approach the unfamiliar as they would approach a sideshow attraction. Others may feel that humans approach the unknown with a lack of imagination, trying to fit the unfamiliar into preconceived ideas; according to Father Gonzaga, if the old man cannot understand Latin, he cannot be an angel because Latin is the language of God.

4. Many students may feel that this story accurately describes the behavior of people who are faced with the unfamiliar. As proof they may cite sideshows or zoos where people often make cruel comments, taunt the animals, or throw unhealthful foods. Others may cite times when they themselves have been insensitive to the customs of a different culture. Some may suggest that fear and suspicion are normal human reactions to the unknown.

5. Some students may believe that the old man is returning to heaven, hell, or his home planet, while others may feel that he leaves to find a more congenial refuge.

6. Students may suggest that the third-person omniscient point of view gives a better picture of the old man by allowing the reader to see him through the eyes of several characters. If the story were written from the point of view of a single character, the reader's understanding of the old man would be much more narrow, since most characters would have a limited perception of who he is.

7. Students may use words such as *ironic*, *detached*, *objective*, *ambiguous*, and *humorous* to describe Márquez's tone in this story. Some students may add that irony is part of the dark humor in the story. They may cite as examples the Church's interest in finding out if the old man has a navel, because an angel would not be born as a human (page 269), or the incongruity between the appearance of this dirty, foul-smelling, lice-infested being and his ascribed function as a heavenly messenger (page 268).

8. Responses will vary. Some students may note that the society depicted in Márquez's story has an unpleasant, darker side, similar to the less pleasant side of contemporary American society. These students may draw parallels between the insensitive ways that the townspeople in the story treat the old man, supposedly a heavenly emissary, and the insensitive ways that some Americans treat people from different cultures. Other students may mention the craving for the sensational, evident in the attraction of the townspeople first toward the old man and later toward the woman transformed into a spider, and suggest a parallel between this craving and that of some Americans drawn to bizarre, sensationalized accounts in supermarket tabloids. Still other students may point out a similarity between the way the people in this story lose interest in the old man and the way many people in American society lose interest in last month's celebrity.

Analyzing the Writer's Craft, page 273

Additional realistic details include the old man's "strong sailor's voice" (page 267), his "unbearable smell of the outdoors" (page 268), and his ranting "with tears in his eyes" when the crowd burns him (page 269).

Connecting Reading and Writing, page 273

Bring in and post examples of sensational headlines from tabloids such as *Star* or the *National Enquirer*.

NAME ______________________________ DATE ______________

A Very Old Man with Enormous Wings

Vocabulary Worksheet

(page 266)

Essential Vocabulary

cataclysm *n.* Any great upheaval that causes sudden and violent changes.

hermetic *adj.* Hard to understand; obscure.

providential *adj.* As if decreed by God.

repose *n.* Rest.

terrestrial *adj.* Of this world; earthly.

tribulation *n.* A thing that causes suffering or distress.

Useful Words

conjecture *n.* A guess, judgment, or prediction based on incomplete evidence.

decrepit *adj.* Broken-down or worn out by old age.

Fill in each set of blanks with the correct word from the word list. (Clue: The boxed letters will spell the native country of the author of this story.)

1. Work horses are traditionally put out to pasture when they reach the point that this word describes them. _ _ [ ] _ _ _ _ _
2. You may be in this state in any state in the Union, but wherever you are, you're taking it easy. _ _ _ [ ] _ _
3. A tidal wave or volcanic eruption is surely this; a revolution may be. _ _ _ _ _ [ ] _ _ _
4. This is what Sergeant Friday used to discourage when he'd ask for "just the facts, ma'am. Just the facts." _ [ ] _ _ _ _ _ _ _ _
5. This describes quantum physics, tax laws, and the views of fourteenth-century philosophers—at least for most of us. _ _ _ [ ] _ _ _ _
6. The quality that makes a person a whiner is the belief that almost any inconvenience qualifies as this. _ _ _ [ ] _ _ _ _ _ _ _
7. E.T. is not described with this word, because he's a guy with something extra. _ _ _ _ _ _ _ _ [ ] _ _
8. If you feel that the good events in your life are blessings from God, this is how you would describe them. _ _ _ _ _ _ _ _ _ _ [ ] _

NAME ______________________ DATE ______________

A Very Old Man with Enormous Wings (page 266)

Test

Part 1 Broad Interpretation

Answer the following essay questions based on your understanding of the story. Write your answers on a separate sheet of paper. (*15 points each*)

1. Do you think the winged man is an angel? Explain your answer.
2. How do you think the people you know would react if the winged man were to appear in their town? Compare the behavior you would expect from them with that of the people in the story.
3. What idea or quality might the winged man represent in this story? Explain your answer.
4. Poet Marianne Moore wrote that poems should be "imaginary gardens with real toads." Do you think this description could be applied to García Márquez's style of writing in this story? Support your answer with details from the story.

Part 2 Close Interpretation

A. Fill in the bar graph below, indicating how much you think the elements of the story would be changed if the story had been told from the point of view of one of the characters in it. (*16 points*)

	Affected very little	Affected greatly
Plot		
Setting		
Characterization		
Tone		

NAME ______________________ DATE ______________

B. Mark the elements of style that you think are most significant in the quotations on the left. You may mark more than one element for a quotation. *(4 points each)*

	Realistic detail	Ironic tone	Bizarre events	Unusual humor
1. "He was dressed like a ragpicker. There were only a few faded hairs left on his bald skull and very few teeth in his mouth, and his pitiful condition of a drenched great-grandfather had taken away any sense of grandeur he might have had."				
2. "That was how they skipped over the inconvenience of the wings and quite intelligently concluded that he was a lonely castaway from some foreign ship wrecked by the storm."				
3. "Besides, the few miracles attributed to the angel showed a certain mental disorder, like the blind man who didn't recover his sight but grew three new teeth, or the paralytic who didn't get to walk but almost won the lottery."				
4. "The parish priest had his first suspicion of an imposter when he saw that he did not understand the language of God [Latin] or know how to greet His ministers."				
5. "The most unfortunate invalids on earth came in search of health: a poor woman who since childhood had been counting her heartbeats and had run out of numbers; a Portuguese man who couldn't sleep because the noise of the stars disturbed him; a sleepwalker who got up at night to undo the things he had done while awake; and many others with less serious ailments."				
6. "His only supernatural virtue seemed to be patience, especially during the first days when the hens pecked at him, searching for the stellar parasites that proliferated in his wings."				

The Youngest Doll

Rosario Ferré

(rô sä′ rē ô fer rā′)

page 274

- **Vocabulary Worksheet,** TG page 230
- **Test,** TG pages 231 and 232

Objectives

1. To respond to a short story about a "living doll."
2. To define mood in a short story.
3. To express ideas in a variety of writing formats: journal, informal note, story, catalog copy, TV commercial, essay, pamphlet, list of questions, profile.

Plot Summary

When she was young, a maiden aunt was bitten in the leg by a prawn. Despite treatment, her wound continued to fester, and her doctor explained that the prawn was alive inside her leg. Now, because of her condition, the aunt stays at home making dolls for her nine nieces. The dolls, which began as plain toys, gradually become more elaborate and lifelike. Each year, each niece receives a life-size doll—the aunt has made so many dolls that they are stored in a special room. When the girls marry, the aunt gives them each a special wedding doll filled with honey. When only the youngest niece is left at home, the aunt's doctor pays his monthly visit, bringing his son along. The young man, himself a doctor, discovers that the ulcerous leg could have been cured long ago. The old doctor reveals that he exploited the aunt's condition to pay for the young man's education. The young doctor courts and marries the youngest niece, but the marriage turns sour. The husband becomes more and more greedy, even trying to sell parts of his wife's wedding doll. Years later, the millionaire doctor uncovers a startling fact: his wife is the doll, filled with living prawns.

IdeaBank

▲ **Motivation.** As an alternative to the Connecting Writing and Reading activity in their books, have students draw their favorite childhood toys in their journals. Have them briefly describe each toy's features—size, shape, color, unique characteristics. Encourage students to explain why they had a special attachment to the toys. As students read the selection, have them compare the characteristics of their favorite toys with those of the dolls in the story. ▲

IdeaBank

✤ **Multimodal Activity.** Encourage students to make their own dolls, using readily available materials. For ideas have students reread the passages describing the maiden aunt's techniques and materials. Suggest that they look at pictures in an encyclopedia article on dolls to get an overview of the kinds of dolls that have been created throughout history. If possible, ask students to create a doll that resembles themselves in some way. Arrange the dolls that students have fashioned in a display case. ✤

"Life is a dream; when we sleep we are awake, and when awake we sleep."

— Michel de Montaigne, *Essays*

InformationBank

Biographical Note. In an essay titled "The Writer's Kitchen," Rosario Ferré describes how she was inspired to write her first story. "Sitting at the head of the table, dropping a slow spoonful of honey into her tea, my aunt began to tell a story while I listened. It had taken place at a sugar cane plantation some distance away, at the beginning of the century, she said, and its heroine was a distant cousin of hers who made dolls filled with honey. The strange woman had been the victim of her husband, a ne'er-do-well and a drunkard who had wasted away her fortune, kicked her out of the house, and taken up with another woman. . . . Soon after her arrival at the plantation, my aunt's cousin, who was still young and beautiful, had developed a strange ailment: her right leg began to swell with no apparent cause, and her relatives sent for the doctor from the nearby town so he could examine her. The doctor, an unscrupulous young man recently graduated from a university in the United States, made the young woman fall in love with him, then falsely diagnosed her ailment as incurable. Applying plasters like a quack, he condemned her to live like an invalid in an armchair while he dispassionately relieved her of the little money the unfortunate woman had managed to save from her marriage." The strangeness of this account reinforces Ferré's statement that "reality in Puerto Rico is so complex that it always overflows the receptacle of fiction."

"Illusions are art for the feeling person, and it is by art that we live, if we do."

— Elizabeth Bowen, *The Death of the Heart,* 1938

Tips from the Classroom

I ask students to map all the details the story gives about the young doctor, beginning with "the prawn that [paid] for [his] education" and including the bouquet like "a sea urchin turned inside out." Then I ask students to come to some conclusions about what this man represents.

Barbara A. Knopp
Guilford High School
Rockford, IL

IdeaBank

✲ **Collaborative Learning.** Have students research the topic of dolls to gain additional insight into this selection. Suggest that they focus on the kinds of dolls, the history of dolls, the art of dollmaking, the uses of dolls, the care and repair of dolls, and so on. Encourage students to work in groups to develop an oral report on some aspect of their findings. Make certain that students connect their research in some way to "The Youngest Doll." ✲

InformationBank

Literary Note. The cotranslator (along with Ferré), Diana Vélez, says that she faced a difficult decision in translating the word *guanabana*. Should she use the English dictionary equivalent, *sweetsop*, which might have negative associations for a North American audience? Should she leave the word in its original language and hope that its sound would compensate for the loss of literal meaning? Should she use the name of a more familiar, nontropical fruit? Or should she add adjectives to *sweetsop*, which might weaken the effect?

IdeaBank

★ **Interactive Assessment.** If students wrote stories, called for in the option for Connecting Reading and Writing, assignment 1, have pairs act as peer reviewers for each other's writing. Reviewers might use the following questions to guide their assessment: Is the identity of the narrator clear? Do the details in the story reflect that narrator's viewpoint? What parts of the story are especially original or appealing? Is the mood appropriate? How satisfying is the resolution, or end, of the story? ★

IdeaBank

❧ **Gifted and Talented Students.** Have students read more stories by Rosario Ferré in the collection titled *The Youngest Doll*. (See Resource Bank.) Then have students identify motifs that recur in Ferré's writing and suggest generalizations about Ferré's style, subjects, and themes. ❧

⌘ Connections

Across the Humanities. Have students find out more about Puerto Rico, particularly the circumstances of its changing economy at the beginning of the twentieth century. Direct students to locate information about the aristocracy, making connections with the lifestyle of the family described in "The Youngest Doll." Ask them to write a brief report based on their findings.

ResourceBank

For the Student. Ferré, Rosario. *The Youngest Doll*. Lincoln, Neb.: University of Nebraska Press, 1991.

Rodriguez, Orlando. *They Have to Be Puerto Ricans*. Chicago: Puerto Rican Parade Committee, 1988.

For the Teacher. Ferré, Rosario. *Sweet Diamond Dust*. New York: Ballantine Books, 1988.

Rodriguez de la Laguna, Asela, ed. *Images and Identities: The Puerto Rican in a Two World Context*. New Brunswick, N.J.: Transaction Books, 1987.

The Puerto Ricans: A Resource Unit for Teachers (Pamphlet). New York: Anti-Defamation League of B'nai B'rith.

❷ Content Quiz

1. How does the doctor explain the ulcer on the maiden aunt's leg? He says a prawn is living inside it.
2. For whom does the aunt make dolls? for her nine nieces
3. What are the only items not made by her that the aunt uses in the dolls? glass eyeballs
4. Whom does the youngest niece marry? the doctor's son
5. What does the millionaire doctor discover about his wife at the end of the story? that she is a living doll full of prawns

Guidelines for Response

Thinking About the Story, pages 278–279

1. Students' questions may include the following: Why does the doll end up being filled with prawns? What happened to the youngest niece? Were there really prawns in the aunt's leg all those years?

2. Students may say that the young woman has achieved freedom; she has had "her Easter Sunday" (page 276). Students may note that inside the doll, in the prawns and the seawater, the doctor sees the natural life that has been repressed in women. Students may say that the doctor finds in the bedroom the doll that he has been looking for. Some students may answer that the young doctor is looking at what society has become: a mask of pretense hiding corruption. Other students may say that the young doctor observes his own creation: a doll-wife.

3. If students had the conception of a "living doll" as a beautiful woman, they may now say that a "living doll" is a woman who is treated as an object. Students who thought that "living doll" was an expression of praise now may say that it describes someone whose life has been stifled. Still other students may answer that a "living doll" in the context of this story is an artistic creation that is alive.

4. Students may answer that the aunt is attempting to preserve the lives of her nieces, citing some of the following passages as evidence: when the aunt is not making dolls she is gazing out across the sugar cane fields, observing nature (page 276); she uses her nieces as models for the dolls; she observes the completion of a doll as if it were a birth (page 275); she puts into the dolls natural materials, such as the dried pulp and honey (page 276); in submerging the dolls' eyes in water (page 276), she sensitizes the dolls to the living world; in presenting the dolls to her nieces with the words "Here is your Easter Sunday," she gives her nieces the promise of resurrection from the living death of marriage.

5. Some students may answer that the young doctor is most evil and the youngest niece the most victimized. Other students may argue that the older doctor is most evil because his deception of the aunt ruined her life and possibly her niece's life as well. Similarly, students may argue that the most victimized character is the aunt, who is forced to live with a curable infection.

6. Students may answer that the prawn bite would not have affected the aunt in the same way, for a doctor might not have deliberately failed to treat her for his own gain; she might have died or been cured by a traditional herbal remedy; she would not have had the time to spend making dolls or the money to buy the materials.

7. Students may answer that the writer views Puerto Rican society as being highly stratified, with superficial values and no moral or spiritual depth. Students may note that the old doctor is a cheat, the younger one an egocentric opportunist, the younger doctor's patients fat and "self-satisfied" (page 278), and young women repressed. Students may say that the sugar cane aristocracy is in decay, as represented by the image of the honey inside the doll being eaten away by ants. Students may say that women in this society seem to have no other purpose than to marry and serve as display pieces for social-climbing husbands. Students may say that the prawn symbolizes life and vitality, that the hidden ulcer represents the persistence of natural forces, that the scent of oozing sweetsop symbolizes the tendency of that vitality to emerge in spite of attempts to keep it hidden.

8. Students may say that both stories contain examples of exaggeration, magical elements, and striking contrasts. Examples of exaggeration include the dolls being filled with seawater and prawns in "The Youngest Doll" and the old man's wings being dirty, half-plucked, and lice-infested in "A Very Old Man with Enormous Wings." Examples of magical elements include the sensitivity of the dolls' eyes to the movements of the prawns' antennae (page 276) and Pelayo's discovery of a winged man in the courtyard. Examples of striking contrasts include the contrast between the living niece and the doll-wife filled with seawater and prawns and the contrast between the miracles expected from the old man and those attributed to him, such as the sprouting of sunflowers from a leper's sores.

Analyzing the Writer's Craft, page 280

Students' images, with the associated moods, may include the prawn lodged under the aunt's skin (repulsion, fascination), the crumbling of the chandelier (uneasiness), the room full of life-sized dolls (eeriness), the dolls' eyes responding to the movements of the prawns' antennae (puzzlement, fascination), the dolphin flesh (sensuality), the young doctor's "paper silhouette" (anger, interest), the doll infested by ants (repulsion), the doll filled with seawater and prawns (repulsion, horror, confusion).

Connecting Reading and Writing, page 280

Suggest that students working on assignment 3 consider the plight of young women in today's society before trying to make connections between the story and high school students today.

For assignment 4, have students work together to brainstorm questions to ask the writer.

NAME ____________________ DATE __________

The Youngest Doll (page 274)

Vocabulary Worksheet

Essential Vocabulary

exorbitant *adj.* Going beyond what is usual; excessive.
furtively *adv.* Sneakily; not openly.
ostentatious *adj.* Showy; flashy.

Useful Words

fixedly *adv.* Without wavering; with intense concentration.
frenzied *adj.* Marked by extreme, usually excited, activity.
impassive *adj.* Showing no emotion.
stupor *n.* A daze; state of reduced awareness.

Fill in each set of blanks with the correct word from the word list. (Clue: The boxed letters will spell the first name of the author of "The Youngest Doll.")

1. This might describe the behavior of a diehard fan whose team is down by one in the last game of the World Series. _ [ ] _ _ _ _ _ _
2. This might describe the parents who arrive in furs and a limousine at the PTA meeting. _ _ _ _ _ _ _ _ _ [ ] _ _
3. This might describe someone sitting next to the fan in number one, who doesn't give a hoot about baseball. _ _ _ _ _ [ ] _ _ _
4. This often describes the cost of the refreshments at movie theaters and stadiums. _ _ _ _ _ _ _ [ ] _ _
5. This describes how you might try to leave an intensely boring party given by your best friend. _ _ [ ] _ _ _ _ _ _
6. This is the way the fan in number one might stare at the television screen as the pitcher winds up for the crucial pitch. _ [ ] _ _ _ _ _
7. This is the state you might be in if that party in number five went on until dawn, and you hadn't managed to leave. _ _ _ _ [ ] _

NAME ______________________ DATE ____________

The Youngest Doll (page 274)

Test

Part 1 Broad Interpretation

Answer the following essay questions based on your understanding of the story. Write your answers on a separate sheet of paper. (*15 points each*)

1. Think of the bizarre or strange occurrences in this story and how they affected you. What picture did you form of the world in which this story takes place?
2. For which of the characters do you feel the most sympathy: the aunt, the young doctor, or the youngest niece? Use details from the story to support your answer.
3. If this story were a fable, what do you think would be its moral? Support your answer with details from the story.
4. Based on the relationship between the youngest niece and her husband and on the apparent transformation the niece undergoes once she is married, what do you think the story is saying about marriage?

Part 2 Close Interpretation

A. Think about how the story works as social criticism. What are the weaknesses of the rising middle class, as represented by the young doctor? What are the weaknesses of the declining aristocracy, as represented by the aunt and the youngest niece? In the boxes below, name or describe as many of these weaknesses as you can think of. (*15 points*)

MIDDLE CLASS	ARISTOCRACY

NAME ______________________________ DATE ______________

B. Write the letter of the best answer. Where noted, there may be more than one answer. (*5 points each*)

____ **1.** The doctor doesn't cure the aunt because he

a. doesn't know how to.

b. wants his son to have the honor of discovering a cure.

c. wants the money that a long period of treatment will bring him.

____ **2.** The doctor's son marries the niece *mainly* because he

a. is hopelessly in love with her.

b. wants to raise his social standing by marrying into the aristocracy.

c. pities her and wants her to have a better life.

____ **3.** Which of the following quotations is a clue to the surprise ending? (*You may choose more than one answer.*)

a. "As the girls grew up, the aunt devoted herself to making dolls for them to play with."

b. "A few months later, the doctor noticed the doll was missing from her usual place and asked the youngest what she'd done with it."

c. "His [the young doctor's] interest in the youngest was evident from the start, so the aunt was able to begin her last doll in plenty of time."

C. Think about how the writer creates different moods in the story. Read each quotation below and underline words and phrases that help create a mood. Then, in the box below each quotation, tell what you think the mood of the quotation is. (*5 points each*)

"As a young woman, she had often bathed in the river, but one day when the heavy rains had fed the dragontail current, she had a soft feeling of melting snow in the marrow of her bones. With her head nestled among the black rocks' reverberations, she could hear the slamming of salty foam on the beach rolled up with the sound of waves, and she suddenly thought that her hair had poured out to sea at last. At that very moment, she felt a sharp bite in her calf. Screaming, she was pulled out of the water and, writhing in pain, was taken home on a stretcher."

"The young doctor took her off to live in town, in a square house that made one think of a cement block. Each day he made her sit out on the balcony, so that passersby would be sure to see that he had married into high society. Motionless inside her cubicle of heat, the youngest began to suspect that it wasn't only her husband's silhouette that was made of paper, but his soul as well."

What I Have Been Doing Lately

Jamaica Kincaid

page 281

■ **Test,** TG page 236

Objectives

1. To respond to a short story that contains bizarre and surprising elements.
2. To understand diction as a component of style.
3. To express ideas in a variety of writing formats: journal, episode, monologue, graphic representation, expository essay.

Plot Summary

As the story begins, the narrator is lying in bed when the doorbell rings. There is no one at the door, but after stepping outside, the narrator inexplicably begins a sort of dream journey in which time is circular and events do not follow realistic cause-and-effect sequences. The narrator encounters a monkey in a tree, a body of water, a dog, a boy playing with a ball, a deep hole, and a woman who asks her what she has been doing lately. In reply, the narrator recounts the same dream journey she has just experienced, with some variations. Suddenly, the narrator decides that she does not like her dream journey and she returns to the moment when she is lying in bed, just before the doorbell rings.

IdeaBank

▲ **Motivation.** As an alternative to the Connecting Writing and Reading activity, ask students to describe in their journals a dream they may have experienced. Have them list details from their dreams that seem bizarre or unreal. Which details seem frightening? Which details seem puzzling? What exotic settings or people appear in the dream? As students read "What I Have Been Doing Lately," have them think about the qualities of the story that match the characteristics of the dreams they described. ▲

"I write about myself completely. I try not to write about anybody else but my mother and my family. I don't really know anybody else very well and I'm not interested in them."

— Jamaica Kincaid, 1990

IdeaBank

❧ **Gifted and Talented Students.** Other examples of circular works are *Finnegans Wake* by James Joyce and *The Third Policeman* by Flan O'Brien. *Finnegans Wake* begins in the middle of the same sentence in which the book ends. Have interested students locate and read this sentence noting its diction and commenting on its effect. You might also have students read *The Third Policeman*, comparing its dreamlike characteristics with those found in "What I Have Been Doing Lately" in a two-column chart. ❧

InformationBank

Historical Note. The philosopher Friedrich Nietzsche constructed a theory of eternal recurrence. He said that if time is infinite, then perhaps existence is infinite as well. He believed that the patterns of a person's life might repeat themselves again and again, in different places and in different times. Because these recurring patterns would be separated by trillions of years, the person whose life experiences were repeated would be unaware of their repetition. The unfolding of the story in "What I Have Been Doing Lately" recalls Nietzsche's theory in that the narrator's experiences seem to recur without a discernible end.

IdeaBank

✣ **Multimodal Activity.** Have pairs of students stage side-by-side oral readings of "What I Have Been Doing Lately" and comparable passages they select from Lewis Carroll's *Alice's Adventures in Wonderland* and *Through the Looking Glass* or another work in which the limitations of time and space have been stretched. ✣

IdeaBank

✱ **Limited English Proficient Students**
The nonlinear elements of this selection may be difficult for LEP students. To help them understand this story, help them make a chart listing different images that are repeated throughout the story. Discuss whether each image seems real or fantastic. You might ask students to listen as you read the story aloud, having them think about how the pattern of the story is similar to random thought patterns that occur when a person is relaxed or dreaming. ✱

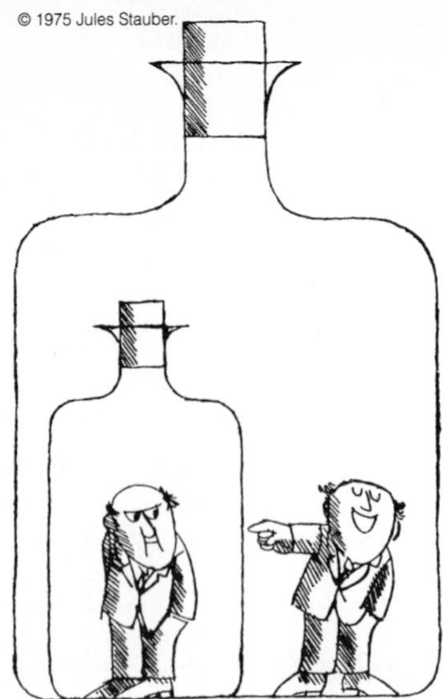

IdeaBank

✽ **Learning Disabled Students.** To help students grasp the dream-logic style of "What I Have Been Doing Lately," ask them to find pictures in travel magazines that contain images of monkeys, a night sky, water, a bridge, a dog on a veranda, and so on. Have students cut up these pictures and rearrange the elements to create a mural that represents the abstract nature of this story. ✽

⌘ Connections

Across the Language Arts. Many of the sentences in "What I Have Been Doing Lately" are compound sentences connected by the conjunctions *and, so*, and *but*: for example, "I wanted to get across it but I couldn't swim" (page 282). Others are sentences with adverb phrases or clauses indicating time: for example, "When this woman got closer to me, she looked at me hard . . ." (page 282). Have students write a narrative of a sequence of events using only these two kinds of sentences. Ask students to try departing from reality only slightly within any one sentence or any pair of sentences.

If the grammar and composition book you use has a lesson on phrases and clauses, you may want to refer to this lesson.

Across the Humanities. In many African, North American, and South American myths, the concept of time is nonlinear rather than linear. Time is often multidimensional. Have students locate a myth in which time is nonlinear. In particular, students might look up the myths of the Arawak and the Carib, who inhabited northern South America and the West Indies at the time of Columbus. Ask students to make recordings as they read one myth that they chose, or have them write their own myth in which time is not fixed and linear.

IdeaBank

✲ **Collaborative Learning.** Encourage students to work together to explore one of these psychological phenomena: dreams, delusions, hallucinations, psychoses, the subconscious. Have students collect data and then try to assess whether the narrator's experiences in "What I Have Been Doing Lately" might be explained scientifically. ✲

IdeaBank

★ **Interactive Assessment.** Have pairs of students exchange the episodes they completed for Connecting Reading and Writing, assignment 1. Guide them to make bar graphs to show their evaluations of the work, as shown below. They should indicate whether the work is excellent (5), poor (1), or in between (2, 3, 4) in each category. Require students to support their evaluations with specific examples and for grammar and usage to note applicable pages of the composition and grammar text used in your classroom.

	1	2	3	4	5
Style					
Content					
Structure					
Grammar and usage					

ResourceBank

For the Student and the Teacher. Kincaid, Jamaica. *A Small Place*. New York: Farrar, Straus & Giroux, Inc., 1988.

———. *At the Bottom of the River*. New York: Random House, Inc., 1985.

———. *Lucy*. New York: Farrar, Straus & Giroux, Inc., 1990.

❓ Content Quiz

1. Why does the narrator get up out of bed? The doorbell rings.
2. Whom does the narrator encounter as she walks? [Students may name any one.] a boy; a woman
3. How does the narrator reply to the woman's question? She tells her story again.
4. What is one animal the narrator sees while walking? [Students may name any one.] a monkey; a dog
5. What does the narrator do at the end? goes back to bed

Guidelines for Response

Thinking About the Story, pages 284–285

1. Some students may wonder about the point of this story. They may wonder why the version the narrator tells the woman she meets is different from what happens before she meets the woman. Students may write that they are left wondering whether the doorbell is going to ring again and whether the story will repeat itself. They may wonder whether the narrator is dreaming.

2. Some students may say that the ending reveals that the narrator can control events and that her adventures are entirely her own creation. Students may say that the narrator is like a child who becomes so wrapped up in an imaginary world that she becomes exhausted by imaginary adventures. Students may say that the person ringing the doorbell could be anyone—it does not matter who rings it; the important thing is that the doorbell seems to be a summons to repeat the narrator's adventure.

3. Students may say that the narrator is childlike; the world in which she journeys is a condensed version of the strangeness a child experiences as she learns about the real world. Students may mention that the narrator has a sense of humor. Students may suggest that the narrator sees the woman who looks like her mother, and by extension her mother, as a comfort and refuge. The narrator wishes to return to her own home, bed, kitchen, and mother when she is tired at the end of the story.

4. Students may say that the first account is directed to the reader and the narrator wants to sound grown-up and confident; the second account is directed to a mother figure, and the narrator wants to express to this mother figure her fear and her need for comfort. Some students may say that the accounts are of two different journeys, citing that the initial incident of falling down the hole (page 282) occurs only in the first account and the account of the mud people on the beach only in the second (page 283). Students may note that the account of events to the woman who looks like her mother ends with the narrator lying in bed, instead of meeting the mother figure. These students may argue that the narrator could not have told the mother figure everything that happened up to the time she encountered her.

5. Students may imagine that the story could continue with the doorbell ringing again, sending the narrator on a journey that is similar in some ways but different in other ways to the two recounted in this story. Students may suggest that the story could continue with repetitions of similar journeys or with other equally bizarre adventures.

6. Students may answer that the overall mood is surreal, dreamlike, but that the mood changes from the first account to the second. Students may point out that the first telling is matter-of-fact and self-assertive, but that the second is disturbed and fearful: for example, in the first account she simply observes the monkey and walks on, but in the second she throws stones at the monkey, which throws a stone back at her, gashing her forehead. The second account is full of expressions of emotions and desires (page 283: "If only I could get out of this"; "I felt very sad so I sat down").

7. Students may define plot as any sequence of events that holds the reader's interest, regardless of how the events are related, or whether the story is resolved.

8. Students may say that a new immigrant might have to deal with issues of language. They may note that on page 282 nothing is familiar to the narrator as she looks behind her; this incident may reflect the experience of an immigrant, who might feel disoriented and unfamiliar with a new city. Students might suggest that a walk down the streets of a new city parallels the narrator's experiences: she observes a monkey, crosses a river, passes a house with a dog on the veranda, and sees a boy with a ball. On turning around, she recognizes nothing behind her.

9. Students may find this story highly inventive: a person's experiences represented as immediate images or as a subconscious struggle. Students may find this story less inventive if they compare it with stories in which details are crafted and carefully put together to induce readers to examine their assumptions, as in "A Very Old Man with Enormous Wings," or with stories that provide richly symbolic descriptions of the world, as in "The Youngest Doll."

Analyzing the Writer's Craft, page 285

To help students imitate the narrator's diction in "What I Have Been Doing Lately," direct students' attention to the frequency with which the narrator uses the conjunctions *and*, *but*, and *so* to form compound sentences. The narrator also uses participial phrases from time to time; otherwise there is very little variation in sentence structure. Another important element in the narrator's diction is her reporting of what she thought and what she said to herself at various times. Point out to students that she sometimes presents her thoughts out of sequence and in a disjointed manner that conveys meaning but does not do so in a particular order.

Connecting Reading and Writing, page 285

To help students represent the story graphically in assignment 2, ask them to consider whether they can do so using a simple geometric figure, such as a rhombus or parallel time lines. For other examples of diagrams that may be adapted to literary works, students may refer to structural chemical formulas, graphs of mathematical equations, and kinship diagrams in anthropology.

NAME ______________________________ DATE ______________

What I Have Been Doing Lately (page 281)

Test

Part 1 Broad Interpretation

Answer the following essay questions based on your understanding of the story. Write your answers on a separate sheet of paper. (*35 points each*)

1. In what ways is this story like a dream? Explain your answer and support it with details from the story.
2. Why do you think someone might give this kind of answer to the question "What have you been doing lately?"

Part 2 Close Interpretation

Think about what you would expect to find written under the title "What I Have Been Doing Lately." Then, in the boxes below, answer the questions. (*30 points*)

	USUALLY	IN THIS STORY
What kinds of events are described?		
What kind of diction is used?		
What is communicated?		

Tenement Room: Chicago

Frank Marshall Davis

Loo-Wit

Wendy Rose

page 287

- **Vocabulary Worksheet,** TG page 239
- **Tests,** TG pages 241 and 242

Objectives

1. To respond to two poems that attribute human qualities to nonhuman things.
2. To understand the use of personification in poetry.

IdeaBank

▲ Motivation. To help students think of objects, animals, or ideas for Connecting Writing and Reading, copy this pie chart on the board:

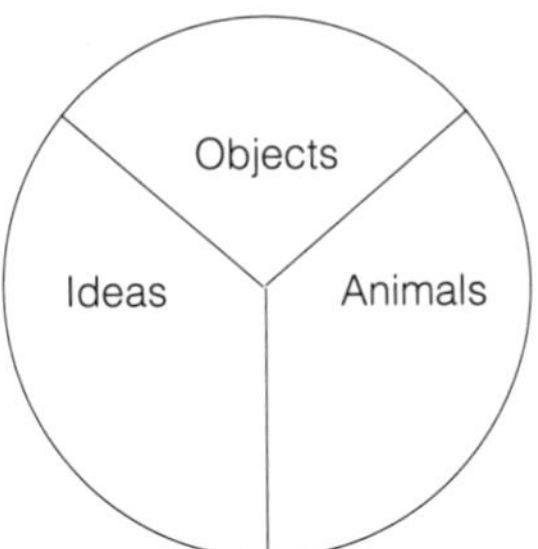

Have the class brainstorm items from nature, the classroom, a city scene, or other areas. Write their suggestions in the appropriate portions of the pie chart. Direct students to select from the pie chart at least five different items with which they associate human qualities. Have them list these items in their journals. ▲

IdeaBank

✣ Multimodal Activity. Have students locate a photograph that could be used to illustrate the tenement room described in Davis's poem. Direct them to find a photograph that evokes either actual details from the poem or the overall impression conveyed. Suggest that students look at photographs by Jacob Riis, Lewis W. Hine, Robert Capa, Walker Evans, or Margaret Bourke-White. ✣

IdeaBank

✲ Collaborative Learning. Have students work in pairs to write a poem that personifies a familiar natural object, such as a mountain, a tree, the sun, or the moon. Encourage them to use "Loo-Wit" as a model. ✲

IdeaBank

❧ Gifted and Talented Students. Challenge students to locate Native-American myths, stories, or songs in which a natural object is personified. Have them compare the work they find with the poem "Loo-Wit." ❧

IdeaBank

✱ Limited English Proficient Students
To help students understand the personification of a volcano in "Loo-Wit," provide photographs of an erupting volcano or newspaper and magazine accounts of the eruption of Mount Saint Helens in 1980. Have students identify details in the photographs that might correspond to such images as "black tobacco," "ashes on the snow," and "huckleberry ropes," and then have them discuss the meaning of these images. ✱

InformationBank

Historical Note. The 1980 eruption of Mount Saint Helens was so powerful that it blew off the entire summit, leaving a vast gaping caldera, or crater. The eruption was the first to occur in the contiguous forty-eight states since 1921. It caused forest fires, melted snow, and deposited one foot of ash in surrounding areas of the state of Washington. The melting snow created floods and mud slides that washed away roads, buildings, and bridges. The blast itself knocked down millions of trees; vegetation and animals in the blast zone were obliterated. However, within weeks of the eruption, small plants and insects began to reappear.

⌘ Connections

Across the Curriculum. Have students research volcanoes around the world. Students can give brief lectures, illustrating their presentations with slides, photographs, and diagrams of volcanoes and the devastation that they cause when they erupt.

ResourceBank

For the Student. Davis, Frank Marshall. *I Am the American Negro*. Reprint of 1937 edition. Freeport, N. Y.: Books for Libraries Press, 1971.

Poetry of the American Indian Series: Wendy Rose. Video series. American Visual Communications Bank, 1978.

For the Teacher. Carney, J. D. "Interpreting Poetry." *Journal of Aesthetic Education* 17 (Fall 1983): 53–60.

Content Quiz

1. What condition of life is personified in "Tenement Room: Chicago"? poverty

2. What is one object in the room that is personified in "Tenement Room: Chicago"? [Students may name any one.] table; chair; bed; stove; trunk; gas jet

3. To what is Loo-wit compared? an old woman

4. What is one action performed by Loo-wit in the poem? [Students may name any one.] She spits black tobacco; she stretches; she sprinkles ashes on the snow; she crouches; she raises her weapons; she sings.

5. What happens when Loo-wit sings? the sky shakes (the volcano erupts)

Guidelines for Response

Thinking About the Poem, page 289

1. Feelings students may describe include sadness, depression, anger, or dejection.

2. Students may envision the room as a person exhausted by an overwhelmingly difficult life. This impression is conveyed by the use of words such as "drooping" and "spiritless" to describe the room's furnishings and by actions such as crying and sleeping.

3. Answers will vary but should be similar to a sentence such as "The victim of crushing poverty, a bruised and battered room seeks relief from the exposure of daylight in the soothing camouflage of night."

4. Students may suggest that the room's occupant would be a single person, perhaps elderly, who is very poor. Students may see the person as someone who shares the room's destitution, poorly clothed and physically unable to cope with life.

5. Some students may suggest that the details describing the room's physical condition could be as depressing without the personification, because the room is in such bad shape. Other students may feel that they would have been less responsive to the room if the suffering had not been presented in human terms, because they can identify with the feelings associated with the room.

6. Some students may feel that such details as the "flabby stove," "the solitary gas jet," and the "chromium light" make the poem seem dated. Other students may feel that the poem is not dated because the devastating poverty it describes still exists today, particularly in inner cities.

Thinking About the Poem, page 291–292

1. Responses will vary. Some students may feel a sense of satisfation at Loo-wit's triumph; others may regard her with foreboding and awe. Other students may regret the human actions that seem to force her to react.

2. Students may cite human activities such as spitting, stretching, sleeping, giving warnings, hearing, using weapons, clearing a throat, and singing. They may also identify body parts as well as human qualities such as indifference.

3. Details that would point to the identity of Loo-wit include the mention of ashes (line 10) and slopes (line 34), in addition to phrases such as "centuries of cedar / have bound her / to earth" (lines 16–18).

4. Students may indicate that the poem suggests the volcanic eruption occurs in response to human beings using machinery to strip the surfaces of the mountain. The poem pictures an elderly sleeping woman whose power is unleashed when she becomes aware that people and machines are disturbing her rest.

5. Students may suggest that if Loo-wit were screaming, she would seem a fearsome or wicked creature, whereas the portrayal of Loo-wit singing shows her as a majestic, powerful creature whom humans have underestimated. Others may say that more sympathy would have been aroused for Loo-wit if she had been screaming in pain or anguish.

6. Students may think that the poet judges the actions of humans who alter and exploit nature. Students may cite details such as "machinery . . . ploughs great patches of her skin" (lines 23–26) as evidence that Rose views humans as guilty of abusing Loo-wit.

7. Students may feel that the personification of Loo-wit, her indifference, the light that appears with her shuddering, her warnings, and finally her singing all support the idea that she is a natural object with a soul.

Analyzing the Writer's Craft, page 292

Following the presentations, students may suggest that "Tenement Room: Chicago" presents the message that poverty can be overwhelmingly destructive and sad and that "Loo-Wit" suggests that natural forces may at any time triumph over human endeavors. Students may note that words or gestures that are particularly expressive of human qualities help to convey ideas clearly.

NAME ______________________________ DATE ______________

Tenement Room: Chicago (page 287)

Loo-Wit (page 287)

Vocabulary Worksheet

Essential Vocabulary

butte
gaudy
destitution

Useful Word

tenement

Read the following story and use context clues to figure out the meanings of the underlined words. Then use these meanings to help you work the exercise below. If you like, you may use a dictionary to check the meaning of a word.

"Ladies and gentlemen," said Ray Zeno, the famous comedian, "we are here tonight to raise money to help those who are living in **destitution** in our own country and around the world. Their starvation, their lack of medical care, their need for the basics of human survival are not funny. But all of us on this stage are comics. And what we do best is make people laugh. So tonight, we're going to joke the money right out of your pockets.

"And I know, personally, about poverty. My family was so poor, I was the family pet. We couldn't afford a dog. The Chinese restaurant in our neighborhood didn't have fortune cookies. It had *misfortune* cookies. Of course, we lived in a **tenement.** Sixteen apartments and every one with a view—of the tenement next door. The walls were so thin, every time our phone rang, our neighbors answered theirs. Every time my mother peeled an onion, the guy next door cried. My dad went to the landlord. He said, 'The roof is leaking, the rain is coming in the broken windows, and the floors are flooded. How long do we have to put up with this?' The landlord says, 'How do I know? Am I a weatherman?'

"But I'll tell you. Our building was pretty colorful in the summertime. A lot of the neighbors hung their laundry out the window. Not my mother. She thought it was **gaudy.** Wouldn't hang anything in the window but sausage. Of course, my mother was always very proper. Every time she opened a can, she knocked first.

"I can tell you, it was a real shock when I left the neighborhood. I went to work on a dude ranch out in Arizona. I got off the train and asked a guy when the next horse left for Flagstaff. That night on the ranch, I looked out my window. There was nothing for miles around but this one tall **butte,** off in the distance. On top of it, there was a coyote, howling. I figured somebody would call the cops and get him arrested for disturbing the peace. Nobody did, so I figured the coyote's brother-in-law must be a police dog.

"But seriously, folks. Dig into your pockets for the cause. Give what you can afford and then give more. And remember. There's only one advantage to being poor. It's inexpensive."

Match each underlined word in the story with the correct definition below.

_______________ **1.** A steep, isolated hill.

_______________ **2.** An apartment building, specifically a run-down, overcrowded one.

_______________ **3.** Bright and showy but lacking in good taste.

_______________ **4.** Miserable poverty.

NAME ______________________ DATE ______________

Tenement Room: Chicago (page 287)

Open-Book Test

Part 1 Broad Interpretation

Answer the following essay questions based on your understanding of the poem. Write your answers on a separate sheet of paper. *(30 points each)*

1. How do you think the speaker feels about the room and the people who may live in it? Explain your answer.
2. There is a proverb that says "It is the weariness of the poor that keeps the rich in power." Do you think this poem communicates the weariness of poverty? Use specific words and images from the poem to support your answer.

Part 2 Close Interpretation

In the following excerpt from "Tenement Room: Chicago" underline words and phrases that personify the room and its contents. Then answer the questions in the bottom boxes. *(40 points)*

"A crippled table, gray from greasy water;
Two drooping chairs, spiritless as wounded soldiers shoved into a
prison hole;
A cringing bed, age-weary;
Corseted with wire, squats a flabby stove;
In this corner slumps a punished trunk;
Through the lone window, broken-paned, light and weather spill on
the dust-defeated and splintered floor."

What kind of life might have brought about these qualities in a person?	What kind of "life" might have brought about these qualities in a room?

NAME ______________________________ DATE ______________

Loo-Wit (page 287)

Open-Book Test

Part 1 Broad Interpretation

Answer the following essay questions based on your understanding of the poem. Write your answers on a separate sheet of paper. *(29 points each)*

1. Why do you think Loo-wit decides to erupt? Support your answer with details from the poem.
2. What evidences do you find in "Loo-Wit" of Native American culture? Support your answer with details from the poem.

Part 2 Close Interpretation

Think about the personification of the volcano in "Loo-Wit." In the boxes on the right, briefly describe the event or circumstance depicted by each example of personification. *(7 points each)*

Personification	Event or circumstance described
1. "spits her black tobacco / any which way"	
2. "huckleberry ropes / lay prickly / on her neck"	
3. "machinery growls, / snarls and ploughs / great patches / of her skin"	
4. "She was sleeping"	
5. "the pull of the blanket / from her thin shoulder"	
6. "Loo-wit sings and sings and sings"	

Rhythms

Diana Chang

Prayer to the Pacific

Leslie Marmon Silko

page 293

■ **Test,** TG page 245

Objectives

1. To respond to two poems that explore the rhythms of nature.

2. To express ideas in a variety of writing formats: journal, free-verse poem, sonnet, instructions, introduction, notes, proposal, review, chart.

IdeaBank

▲ **Motivation.** As an alternative to Connecting Writing and Reading, ask students to consider a specific place in nature that they feel strongly about, such as a forest, a mountain peak, or a prairie. Have them identify this place in their journals, and then ask them to describe its outstanding features or characteristics. When they read the poems, they should note how different places in nature affect the poets. ▲

IdeaBank

✾ **Learning Disabled Students.** To help students with the lack of punctuation in "Rhythms," write the poem on the board. Ask volunteers to suggest places where punctuation might be added. For example, they might suggest punctuating lines 3–5 in the following manner: "A horse / detaches himself / from a fence." Read the punctuated version aloud. ✾

IdeaBank

❧ **Gifted and Talented Students.** Have students locate traditional Native American myths or legends about the ocean alluded to in "Prayer to the Pacific." Challenge them to retell a myth or legend in their own words, either to their own class or to a class of younger students. ❧

"The land and seas, the animals, fishes and birds, the sky of heaven and the orbs, the forests mountains and rivers, are not small themes."

— Walt Whitman, Introduction to *Leaves of Grass,* 1855

InformationBank

Historical Note. In "Prayer to the Pacific," the speaker describes a myth about Indians crossing the Pacific Ocean thirty thousand years ago. Europeans did not know of the existence of the Pacific until the sixteenth century. The Spanish explorer Vasco Núñez de Balboa discovered the Pacific Ocean; he claimed it for Spain in 1513. In 1768 English explorer Captain James Cook was the first European to explore and chart the South Pacific.

IdeaBank

✤ **Multimodal Activity.** Plan a classroom celebration of nature. Ask students to create a visual representation of a rhythm of nature that is particularly appealing to them. Encourage them to use a variety of materials and to consider a range of forms: sculpture, collage, silk screen, photo display, original video, and so on. Have students organize and set up a display of their work to share with other classes. ✤

⌘ Connections

Across Literature. Other selections in this text that concern the natural world include the following:

from *Arctic Dreams*, Barry Lopez

"Loo-Wit," Wendy Rose

"November Cotton Flower," Jean Toomer

"The Tropics in New York," Claude McKay

Across the Curriculum. Invite a science teacher, a marine biologist, or an oceanographer to talk to students about the Pacific Ocean. Have students ask questions about unusual features, sea life, storms, and environmental problems that are associated with the Pacific Ocean today.

ResourceBank

For the Student. Silko, Leslie Marmon. *Storyteller*. New York: Seaver Books, 1981.

IdeaBank

★ **Interactive Assessment.** Ask students to read to the class their free-verse poems or sonnets (assignment 1 in Connecting Reading and Writing). Remind students to listen for the effective use of imagery, rhythm, and sound devices (alliteration, consonance, and assonance) in the poems. Have volunteers suggest changes that they think will improve the impact of the poems. ★

❓ Content Quiz

1. In "Rhythms," what drops out of a tree? a child
2. In "Rhythms," what things collect in heaps? crows
3. Where does the speaker in "Prayer to the Pacific" travel from in order to get to the ocean? the southwest
4. What is one thing the speaker in "Prayer to the Pacific" returns to the ocean? [Students may name either one.] turquoise; red coral
5. According to "Prayer to the Pacific," how did Indians come across the ocean? They rode giant sea turtles.

Guidelines for Response

Thinking About the Poems, pages 296–297

1. Students who select "Rhythms" may mention the rhythmic movement and fluidity of things breaking apart and coming together as having created a strong impression on them. Those who choose "Prayer to the Pacific" may note that the images of sea turtles and the Pacific Ocean made a strong impression on them.

2. Students may suggest that the speaker travels to the Pacific Ocean for the following reasons: the speaker is aware, from the Indian origin myth, of the debt her people owe to the ocean as the source of much-needed rain and has traveled to the ocean to pay homage and give thanks; the speaker may have traveled to the ocean to feel connected to her ancestors and to return to the ocean the turquoise and coral it had provided; or the speaker may have traveled to the ocean to ensure that her native region will receive necessary rainfall.

3. Students may suggest that the rhythms illustrate that life is a constant ebb and flow of things breaking apart (landscape changing, horse running, "criminal of love" leaving, child falling, ship departing, cars driving) and coming together (crows collecting, stone and sky growing). Students may point out that some of these rhythms are part of nature and that all are part of daily life. The last ten lines convey the sense that things in nature continually build and rebuild.

4. Students' responses will vary. Students who choose "Rhythms" may say that the poem reflects their own sense of the constant cyclical change occurring around them and that it captures the element of mystery or inscrutability that they find in the rhythms of nature. Students who choose "Prayer to the Pacific" may indicate that the poem expresses their own feeling of an intimate connection with nature, much as the speaker recognizes an ancient, elemental connection to the ocean. Those students may suggest that the poem reveals a reverence for nature and for the connections between nature and humans. Students should support their opinions by drawing logical connections between their choice of poem, their cluster diagram, and specific lines in the poem.

5. Some students may feel that traditional rhyme and meter would detract from the effect of natural rhythms in the poems and make them seem too forced. Other students may feel that rhyme and meter would create a definite, regular pattern to stress the rhythms of nature. Still others may note that traditional rhyme and meter would perhaps make the poems easier to understand. Some students may feel that their responses would not change.

6. Students may respond that Silko is telling how her ancestors crossed the Pacific, where rain and the ocean come from, why the Pacific is important to her, why Native Americans celebrate nature, or how humans can appreciate the ocean and its gifts.

7. Students who agree with the opinion may point out that "Rhythms" relies on Chang's use of sound devices for a lyrical effect. Students may say that the poem is so condensed as to be considered cryptic and that its condensed nature makes it difficult to understand. Students who disagree may point out that the arrangement of images in the poem tells a story about nature; they may think that the poem is concise and direct, not condensed or abstract.

Connecting Reading and Writing, page 297

For the option to assignment 1, provide samples of both Petrarchan and Shakespearean sonnets for students to examine.

To help students with their reviews for assignment 4, provide a copy of *Storyteller* by Leslie Marmon Silko and back issues of the *New York Times Book Review*, *American Poetry Review*, or another literary magazine.

For the option to assignment 4, you may want to refer to the lesson on comparison and contrast in the grammar and composition book you use.

NAME ______________________ DATE ______________

Rhythms (page 293)

Prayer to the Pacific (page 293)

Open-Book Test

Part 1 Broad Interpretation

Answer the following essay questions based on your understanding of the poems. Write your answers on a separate sheet of paper. (*20 points each*)

1. In your opinion, where does the most significant change in rhythm occur in "Rhythms"? Why do you think it occurs there? Explain your answers.
2. If the images in "Rhythms" were the opening scenes of a film, what do you think the film would be about? In answering, use your imagination and specific images from the poem.
3. What do you think the speaker of "Prayer to the Pacific" seeks and finds at the ocean? Explain your answer.

Part 2 Close Interpretation

Choose three images from "Prayer to the Pacific" that communicate most strongly to you. In the boxes on the left, identify the images. Then, in the boxes on the right, note the feeling or feelings that are communicated to you by the images. (*40 points*)

Image		Feelings
	communicates	
	communicates	
	communicates	

Rhythms

The landscape comes apart
in birds

A horse
detaches himself

from a fence
A criminal of love

breaks away
The child drops out of a tree

A ship uncouples
from the street

The canal, unhinged,
proceeds

Cars are pieces of the world
tearing away

But the crows
collect

in heaps
And stone

and sky
poised with being

grow steep
before

they faint
into the wind

and things
fly

again

The Form of the Sword

Jorge Luis Borges
(hôr′ hə lo͞o es′ bôr′ hes)

page 298

- **Vocabulary Worksheet,** TG page 250
- **Test,** TG pages 251 and 252

Objectives

1. To respond to a short story about an incident that occurred in Ireland during the civil war.

2. To practice the reading and thinking skills of an independent reader.

Plot Summary

During a trip through the northern provinces of Brazil, the narrator encounters the "Englishman of La Colorada" and asks him about a noticeable scar across his face. The Englishman, who is actually Irish, relates the following story. In 1922 he joined in the Irish struggle for independence. One evening he met John Vincent Moon, a communist, with whom he argued. The two men were fired upon by soldiers, and the Englishman rescued Moon and took him to a vacant country house. Although he had a superficial wound, Moon refused to fight and remained in the house for nine days. On the tenth day, the Englishman overheard Moon talking on the telephone; he pursued the traitorous informant and cut him across the face with a cutlass. At the end of the story, the Englishman explains that Moon fled to Brazil. Then, with a sob, the Englishman points to his scar and reveals that he himself was the informant—he is John Vincent Moon.

IdeaBank

▲ Motivation. Before students read "The Form of the Sword," have them create tree diagrams for *Ireland*. Have students include words and phrases they associate with Irish history, culture, customs, geography, government, and contributions. ▲

InformationBank

Biographical Note. In his "Autobiographical Essay," Borges writes about his love of short stories. "In the course of a lifetime devoted chiefly to books, I have read but few novels, and, in most cases, only a sense of duty has enabled me to find my way to their last page. At the same time, I have always been a reader and rereader of short stories. Stevenson, Kipling, James, Conrad, Poe, Chesterton, the tales of Lane's *Arabian Nights*, and certain stories by Hawthorne have been habits of mine since I can remember. The feeling that great novels like *Don Quixote* and *Huckleberry Finn* are virtually shapeless served to reinforce my taste for the short story form, whose indispensable elements are economy and a clearly stated beginning, middle, and end. As a writer, however, I thought for years that the short story was beyond my powers, and it was only after a long and roundabout series of timid experiments in narration that I sat down to write real stories."

IdeaBank

✱ Limited English Proficient Students
If possible, show a film (*Ireland*, 22 min., Journal; *Ireland: An Introduction*, 20 min., Centre), a videotape, or slides to help students grasp the context of the story. Refer to the Historical/Cultural Notes for further details about the Irish struggle for independence. ✱

IdeaBank

✤ Multimodal Activity. Divide the class into groups of four students to role-play events in "The Form of the Sword." Direct students to portray the narrator of the frame story, the Englishman, and John Vincent Moon, and have one student tape-record or videotape each presentation. To aid in classroom management, have groups work at staggered times or allow some groups to go to a quiet, supervised area. Present the tapes to the class and ask students to compare the different versions. ✤

InformationBank

Historical/Cultural Notes

1. In 1801 Ireland became an official part of Great Britain; however, in the late 1800's many Irish began to demand home rule. In the early 1900's secret organizations were formed, including the Irish Republican Brotherhood, whose goal was an independent Irish republic. On Easter Sunday in 1916, a bloody rebellion in Dublin led to the execution of fifteen Republican leaders. In 1919 Irish rebels and British soldiers again clashed after Republicans declared Ireland an independent republic. In 1920 the Government of Ireland Act divided Northern Ireland from the rest of Ireland. Each area had its own parliament and government, but both remained part of Great Britain. The Irish Republican Army, to which men in "The Form of the Sword" belonged, fought the Black and Tans (British special police who wore black-and-tan uniforms) until the Anglo-Irish Treaty made southern Ireland a British dominion in 1921. Civil war broke out in 1922 between treaty supporters and those who favored total independence from British rule. In 1949, southern Ireland became an independent republic, but Northern Ireland remained part of the United Kingdom. Civil war continues in Northern Ireland to this day.

2. John Vincent Moon believes in dialectical materialism, a nineteenth-century view that historical and social change is caused by material forces. According to Karl Marx and Friedrich Engels, economic factors in particular effect change. Communism is based on the philosophy of dialectical materialism.

IdeaBank

❧ Gifted and Talented Students

1. Ask students to think about why a writer might choose to create a frame story. Then challenge students to write their own frame stories about real or imagined events.

2. You might also have students read the poem "Easter 1916" by W. B. Yeats or another work about the Irish independence movement by an Irish writer. Have students summarize the events and emotions portrayed in the work they read and present their summaries to the class.

3. If possible, suggest that students investigate and summarize the British point of view at the time of the Irish struggle for independence. ❧

⌘ Connections

Across the Humanities

1. Have students do additional research on the history of the Irish struggle for independence, prior to and after the civil war described in this selection. Have students devise simple time lines or more complex cause-and-effect charts to indicate important events in the struggle. You might have students create a *Who's Who in Irish History* to explain some of the allusions in "The Form of the Sword."

2. Encourage students to locate current newspaper and magazine articles about the Republic of Ireland and Northern Ireland today. They might look for articles about contemporary Irish politics, art, customs, music, and literature. Have students work together to create and organize an annotated bibliography for use by other classes.

Across the Curriculum. Ask students who are proficient in Spanish to read the story in its original language. Have them write a critical review in Spanish for the fictitious magazine *Literature Latinoamérica* and then share their reviews with other Spanish-speaking students.

ResourceBank

For the Student. Borges, Jorge Luis. *Labyrinths: Selected Short Stories and Other Writings*. Donald Yates and James E. Irby, eds. New York: Random House, Inc., 1984.

Inner World of Jorge Luis Borges. Films for the Humanities, 1972. 16mm, 28 min. film reel.

Profile of a Writer: Jorge Luis Borges. Volume 7, BBC Production in Association with RM Arts, 1983. 76 min. VHS videocassette.

For the Teacher. Borges, Jorge Luis. *Dreamtigers*. (Texas Pan American Series). trans. Mildred Boyer and Harold Morland. Austin, Tex.: University of Texas Press, 1964.

———. *Twenty-four Conversations with Borges*. New York: Grove Press, 1984.

❷ Content Quiz

1. To whom does the Englishman tell his story? the narrator

2. Why was the Englishman fighting in 1922? He fought in the civil war for Irish independence.

3. Whom did the Englishman rescue? John Vincent Moon

4. How did the Englishman respond to being betrayed? He cut Moon across the face with a cutlass.

5. What is the Englishman's real identity? He is actually the informant John Vincent Moon.

Guidelines for Response

Discussion Questions

1. How do you feel about John Vincent Moon at the end of the story?

[Students may express admiration for his courage in telling his story. They may express pity or sympathy for the burden of his past that he carries with him and of which he obviously is ashamed. Students also may express embarrassment at Moon's past cowardice and at his tears as he finishes his story. Some students may express negative feelings about Moon, saying that his traitorous act is unforgivable.]

2. What was your reaction to Moon's command at the end of the story to "Despise me"?

[Students may say that Moon's command evokes pity and sympathy, partly because in his comparison of himself to Judas and in his referring to his "mark of infamy" (page 301), he indicates that he himself despises what he has done. Students may point out that Moon's command comes after such a damning self-portrayal that by the time the reader learns Moon's identity further condemnation is unlikely.]

3. Do you think that Moon is being too hard on himself?

[Some students might look upon Moon's betrayal as a youthful indiscretion for which Moon should have been forgiven long before. Other students might believe that Moon is appropriately hard on himself, given the serious nature of his act. These students might look upon Moon as deserving of derision, especially since he fled to Brazil, escaping the consequences of his act.]

4. What does the "frame" contribute to this story?

[Students may answer that the frame sets a mood. It enables the narrator to characterize Moon as a solitary man, given to idiosyncratic behavior, and reluctant to tell his story. Students may suggest that the tension between Moon and the narrator contributes to the suspense in the story and that without the frame the reader would not learn what happened to Moon in later life.]

5. What does the setting in La Colorada add to the story?

[Students may say that the remoteness of the setting helps the reader believe that Moon is partly compelled to tell his story out of loneliness. The setting of Argentina is "neutral ground," far removed from the passions of the Irish and therefore a more suitable setting for the recollection of events from the distant past for a non-judgmental listener. Students also may conclude that the setting is part of Moon's self-punishment. He has condemned himself to a lifetime of hard work in undesirable conditions: he works alongside his peasants to restore overgrown fields and to "remedy" the bitterness of the well water.]

6. What might Moon mean when he says "I am all others, any man is all men"?

[Students may suggest that the statement implicates the narrator in Moon's treachery: if that statement is true, then the narrator is Vincent Moon and Vincent Moon is the narrator. Other students may point out that the statement is ironic, as Moon assumes a particular identity. Students also may note that the statement creates another puzzle that a reader may try to sort out: the connections among this idea, the crucifixion of Christ referred to on page 300, and Moon's comparison of himself to Judas on page 301.]

7. In "The Form of the Sword" a narrator presents Vincent Moon as someone distinct from himself. How would you explain why this technique is effective in the story?

[Students may say that using this technique enables the narrator to share impressions as an apparently trustworthy observer of Vincent Moon, the subject of the tale. The technique also leads to a surprise and to a sudden, significant revelation about the narrator. Some students may note that the revelation provides a context for cryptic details previously mentioned in the story. For example, the revelation suggests why the Englishman of La Colorada remains so alone and possibly why he is cruel "but scrupulously fair"(page 298).]

NAME ______________________ DATE ______________

The Form of the Sword (page 298)

Vocabulary Worksheet

Essential Vocabulary

aplomb *n.* Poise; composure.

apodictic *adj.* Involving or expressing necessary truth; absolutely certain.

infamy *n.* Disgrace, especially when it is widely known and involves well-deserved and extreme contempt; notoriety.

interlocutor *n.* One who takes part in a conversation; talker; interpreter.

opprobrium *n.* Scorn or contempt, especially involving condemnation.

utopian *adj.* Based on ideas of perfection in social and political organization.

vertigo *n.* A condition in which one has the feeling of whirling, causing imbalance; a dizzy, confused state of mind.

A word from the word list is the "I" in each of the following riddles. Fill in each blank with the correct answer.

1. It wasn't 'til Bell had invented the phone
   That I could be found in a room all alone.
   What am I? ______________________

2. I'm at war with admiration. You might feel me for a fool.
   I'm a kind of disapproval that is worse than ridicule.
   What am I? ______________________

3. I am a weird and an odd woozy feeling.
   I can make you fall down or at least send you reeling.
   What am I? ______________________

4. I mean idealistic, so I may describe a thought.
   My kind of life has been pursued but never yet been caught.
   What am I? ______________________

5. I am the substance of many a story.
   I'm fame without honor, renown without glory.
   What am I? ______________________

6. From those who lose their dignity, you'll find that I have fled.
   I'm only kept and held by you if you can keep your head.
   What am I? ______________________

7. When tossing balls into the air, you probably have found
   That I describe the saying "What goes up will soon come down."
   What am I? ______________________

NAME ______________________________ DATE ______________

The Form of the Sword (page 298)

Test

Part 1 Broad Interpretation

A. Answer the following essay questions based on your understanding of the story. Write your answers on a separate sheet of paper. (*14 points each*)

1. Why does the Englishman despise himself? Do you agree that he is despicable? …ot?

…punishes Cain for killing his brother by making Cain live … murderer. Do you think that Moon's scar is the same …t? Do you think that it is a fit punishment for his crime? …r.

…ys, "I told you the story the way I did so that you would … What are some reasons that the writer might have told … did? Did anything in the story foreshadow the ending? …s using details from the story.

…m of a frame story and how it works in this story. Then, …he main characters and setting of the "frame." In the … characters and setting of the central part of the story. … of the story the Englishman's secret is revealed.

____

____

Characters

____

____

Setting

____

Is the secret revealed? _______

Setting ______________________

Is the secret revealed? _______

Correction Notice

The poem "Rhythms" on page 294 of the student edition has type missing from the ends of four lines. You will find a correct copymaster of this poem for your use on page 246 of this *Teacher's Guide*.

NAME ______________________ DATE ____________

Part 2 Close Interpretation

A. Write the letter of the best answer. Where noted, there may be more than one answer. (*10 points each*)

____ **1.** The Englishman agrees to tell his story only with the understanding that his listener will respond with complete

a. pity.

b. scorn.

c. respect.

d. forgiveness.

____ **2.** Which of the following is described in this quotation from near the end of the story? "And that afternoon, he watched some drunks in an impromptu firing squad in the town square shoot down a manikin." (*You may choose more than one answer.*)

a. The superficial wounding of Moon.

b. The final result of Moon's betrayal.

c. Soldiers practicing their marksmanship.

d. The execution of a Republican freedom fighter.

B. Think about the elements that make this story entertaining. Then fill in the bar graph below to show how important you think each element is in making the story entertaining. (*10 points*)

	Not important — Very important
Setting	
Suspense	
Surprise ending	
Characterization	
Insights about life	

Ode to the Watermelon

Pablo Neruda

(pä′ blō nə rōō′ də)

page 302

- **Vocabulary Worksheet,** TG page 255
- **Test,** TG page 256

Objectives

1. To respond to an ode that explores the idea of longing and gratification.
2. To practice the reading and thinking techniques of an independent reader.

IdeaBank

▲ **Motivation.** Have students complete the following chart in their journals. For each longing or condition listed, ask them to write a specific thing that would satisfy that condition.

Condition	Satisfaction
Hunger	
Thirst	
Loneliness	
Hot and dry	
Cold and wet	

As students read the poem, have them notice what the speaker is longing for and what specific thing gratifies the longing. ▲

IdeaBank

✤ **Multimodal Activity.** Remind students that Neruda's poem is about longing and gratification, which he conveys in a variety of seemingly unrelated images: heat is "a sword"; watermelon is "a green whale," "a jewel box," and so on. Then have students convey their own themes of longing and gratification through collages, using diverse visual images the way Neruda uses diverse figures of speech. Students may draw their own images, cut them from magazines, or a mixture of both. If possible, provide students with feathers, beads, sequins, and similar objects. ✤

IdeaBank

❧ **Gifted and Talented Students.** Have students find other examples of Neruda's poetry and organize a poetry reading. Students may dramatize their readings in various ways. For example, one student might read a poem while others contribute gestures or movements that "act out" the poem's meaning. ❧

InformationBank

Literary Note. Neruda's ode comes from a long literary tradition that began with the ancient Greeks. The original Greek poetic structure of the ode was rigidly defined as having three parts—strophe, antistrophe, and epode. Greek odes were sung by a chorus, which dramatized each part differently. Although he did not maintain all of the original characteristics of an ode, Neruda did use the three-part structure.

IdeaBank

✱ **Limited English Proficient Students**
To help convey the richness of other cultures, have an "international poetry day" in which ESL students choose or write poems in their native languages to read to the class. Have them prepare a short statement in English about their poem and/or poet. Native English speakers could write or contribute their favorite poems in English.

As an additional exercise, ESL students could write English translations of their own or each other's poems. The originals and translations could be posted on the bulletin board with a title such as "Many Languages, Many Cultures." ✱

"I have never thought of my life as divided between poetry and politics. I am a Chilean who for decades has known the misfortunes and difficulties of our national existence and who has taken part in each sorrow and joy of the people. I am not a stranger to them. I come from them, I am part of the people."

— Pablo Neruda, from *Writers at Work*, George Plimpton, ed., 1981

IdeaBank

❖ **Cooperative Learning.** Have students form groups of three. Explain that each student in the group is responsible for one of the three "sections" of Neruda's ode (lines 1–37; lines 38–52; and lines 53–93). Each student should reread the assigned section and complete the following tasks: (1) Explain what the section is mainly about; (2) write down all of the color and sensory words from that section. Have each group member be responsible for teaching the others about his or her section. Then the group should choose three images from the poem and explain how those images support what is being said in the poem. Call on one member in each group to explain one of those images to the class. ❖

ResourceBank

For the Student. Neruda, Pablo. *Late and Posthumous Poems, 1968–1974*. Edited and translated by Ben Belitt. New York: Grove Press, 1988.

For the Teacher. Vogel, Mark. "A Geography of the Self: Pablo Neruda's 'We are Many.' " *English Journal* 76 (September 1987): 97–100.

InformationBank

Biographical Note. Neruda once spoke to his translator, poet Robert Bly, about the importance of Temuco, Chile, and its surroundings to his poetry. He said: "Poetry in South America is a different matter altogether. You see, there are in our countries rivers which have no names, trees nobody knows, and birds which nobody has described. . . . Our duty, then, as we understand it, is to express what is unheard of. Everything has been painted in Europe. But not in America. In that sense, Whitman was a great teacher. . . . He had tremendous eyes to see everything—he taught us to see things. He was our poet."

❓ Content Quiz

1. What colors are used to describe the "tree of intense summer"? blue (sky); yellow (sun)

2. What part of the body suffers from the heat more than all the toes? the mouth (the throat, the teeth, the lips, the tongue)

3. What animal is the watermelon compared to? a whale

4. What color is the flag of the watermelon? green, white, red

5. In the poem, what does the watermelon change into? cool light; water; wild rivers

Guidelines for Response

Discussion Questions

1. Why do you think the poet has chosen to commemorate the watermelon in this rather formal poem?

[Some students may suggest that the poet wishes to exalt the fruit and its power to quench the thirst. Others may surmise that the poet wishes to share memories of eating a watermelon on a hot day and wishes to emphasize the importance of the fruit and of other such physical pleasures in this formal poem.]

2. Why do you suppose the poet concentrates on describing summer before beginning to describe the watermelon?

[Some students may suggest that the poet is interested in re-creating a hot, torrid scene to contrast with the coolness of eating watermelon. They may cite specific contrasts in the sections, such as "the brightness and the world/weigh us down" and "you don't weight us down/in the siesta hour." Others may suggest that the poet is trying to re-create the sensory experience of eating watermelon on a hot day.]

3. How do the images of taste, sight, smell, and touch create the experience of eating a watermelon?

[Some students may cite images that use sight and feeling to create the scene of blazing dry heat, such as "fatigue in drops" and "a scorched shoe." They may contrast these with the "firmament of coolness" of the watermelon and the "flag/green, white, red,/that dissolves into/wild rivers." Students may cite passages that contrast the effects of the heat—"the throat/becomes thirsty"—to the taste of watermelon that "dissolves into/wild rivers, sugar, delight!"]

4. How effective would this poem be for a reader who has never seen or tasted a watermelon?

[Some students may suppose that the images such as "cool light/that slips in turn into/spring water" could create the experience of eating a watermelon for someone unfamiliar with the fruit. Others may feel the poem would only re-create the experience of eating watermelon for someone who had already tasted it.]

NAME ______________________ DATE ______________

Ode to the Watermelon (page 302)

Vocabulary Worksheet

Essential Vocabulary

phlegmatic **profundity**

Useful Words

ember **hemisphere**
firmament **intense**

Read the following poems and use the context clues to figure out the meanings of the underlined words. Then, use these meanings to help you work the exercise below. If you like, you may use a dictionary to check the meaning of a word.

I
Stars fell on Alabama's hills
One evening last September,
While I was camped out near Mobile,
At ten, as I remember.
It seemed the heavens fell to bits
And landed on my tent.
Afraid, I wished I'd camped beneath
A firmer **firmament.**

II
The fire's old, its flaming logs
Have sunk to **embers,** glowing,
And now its light is less **intense**
Than when it first was growing.

III
The umpire stood and scratched his head.
He couldn't make the call.
The problem that he faced was not
An easy one, nor small.
The fierceness of the batter's blow
Had cleanly split the ball.
The fielder caught one **hemisphere;**
The other cleared the wall.

IV
"Why did you drop a rock into
The well?" I asked. Said she,
"I counted slowly 'til I heard
It splash and, thus, you see,
I have a way to estimate
The well's **profundity.**"

V
He won't arouse himself to bark
At strange sounds in the night.
He's not the kind of dog that gives
A stranger any fright.
He never gets upset by things;
He's undisturbed and cool.
To think that he's a watchdog, you
Would have to be a fool.
The names that I have called him
Are much better left unsaid.
This canine's so **phlegmatic**
People think that he is dead.
Some burglars came one night and took
The silverware and more,
Just stepping over Rover, stretched
Serenely on the floor..

Match each underlined word in the poems with the correct definition below.

______________________ **1.** Extreme.
______________________ **2.** Glowing fragments from a fire.
______________________ **3.** Half of a sphere, globe, or ball.
______________________ **4.** Depth, especially great depth.
______________________ **5.** The vault or arch of the sky; the heavens.
______________________ **6.** Calm and composed.

NAME ______________________________ DATE ______________

Ode to the Watermelon (page 302)

Open-Book Test

Part 1 Broad Interpretation

Answer the following essay questions based on your understanding of the poem. Write your answers on a separate sheet of paper. *(20 points each)*

1. What are the two main ways that a watermelon is wonderful, according to the poem? What other wonderful things about the watermelon are mentioned in the poem?
2. What are some of the ways the people spoken of in the poem suffer from the heat?
3. Do you think the speaker wants you to take all the magnificent descriptions of the watermelon with absolute seriousness? Why or why not?

Part 2 Close Interpretation

A. In the chart below, write two images from the poem and identify the sense or senses each appeals to. *(20 points)*

IMAGE	SENSE OR SENSES

B. Write **S** if the image is used in the poem to describe the hot summer. Write **W** if it is used to describe the watermelon. *(4 points each)*

_____ **1.** a sword

_____ **2.** a scorched shoe

_____ **3.** a whale

_____ **4.** a planet

_____ **5.** a tree

The Power of Imagination: Creating Unusual Perspectives

Below are suggested answers for the chart assigned on page 305 of the student book. Listed here for each of seven selections in the unit is the perspective conveyed by the writer. Accept other answers if students can support them with evidence from the selections.

Selection	Perspective Conveyed
The Youngest Doll	A work of art actually embodies the spirit of its creator.
What I Have Been Doing Lately	Events may happen in a random sequence without any causal connection.
Tenement Room: Chicago	A tenement room actually experiences misery and spirit-killing poverty.
Rhythms	The rhythm of the world consists of divergence and convergence.
Prayer to the Pacific	Myth can explain the intimate relationship between humans and the Pacific Ocean.
The Form of the Sword	All human beings share the guilt for the despicable acts committed by any person.
Ode to the Watermelon	The taste of a watermelon can yield mystical fulfillment.

Evaluation Guide for Writing Assignment

The well-developed student essay will meet the following criteria:

- Discusses three selections
- Explains the perspectives offered by the writers by citing examples from the selections
- Tells whether these perspectives did or did not change the student's understanding
- Provides reasons supporting the student's position

UNIT 6 Examining Life Experiences

Selections	Essential Vocabulary	Literary Skills	Writing Formats	Writing Modes
Kitchenette Building **One wants a Teller in a time like this** **Speech to the Young/Speech to the Progress-Toward** **Horses Graze**				
Student Book page 310 **Teacher's Guide** Lesson, pages 260 and 261 Vocabulary Worksheet, page 262 Tests, pages 263–266	aria majestic oblivion affirmation	theme speaker alliteration repetition tone	journal poem aphorisms report card memo letter introductory speech	expressive and personal writing narrative and imaginative writing informative (expository) writing: classification informative (expository) writing: synthesis persuasion writing about literature
A Raisin in the Sun				
Student Book page 319 **Teacher's Guide** Act One Lesson, pages 267 and 268 Vocabulary Worksheet, page 269 Test, pages 271 and 272 Act Two Lesson, pages 273 and 274 Test, pages 275 and 276 Act Three Lesson, pages 277 and 278 Test, pages 279 and 280	indictment vindicated assimilationism resignation retrogression	conflict stage directions character mood drama symbolism	journal playbill director's notes diagram note dramatic scene monologue letter review	expressive and personal writing observation and description narrative and imaginative writing informative (expository) writing: analysis informative (expository) writing: synthesis persuasion writing about literature
A Visit to Grandmother				
Student Book page 386 **Teacher's Guide** Lesson, pages 281 and 282 Vocabulary Worksheet, page 283 Test, pages 285 and 286	indulgence engaging	setting dialogue	journal dialogue newspaper advice column personality profiles pamphlet newspaper column research report	expressive and personal writing observation and description narrative and imaginative writing informative (expository) writing: synthesis report (research)
Choices **Oranges**				
Student Book page 395 **Teacher's Guide** Lesson, pages 287 and 288 Test, page 289		style	journal	expressive and personal writing

Selections	Essential Vocabulary	Literary Skills	Writing Formats	Writing Modes
Marigolds				
Student Book page 399 **Teacher's Guide** Lesson, pages 291 and 292 Vocabulary Worksheet, pages 293 and 294 Test, pages 295 and 296	futile impoverished poignantly stoicism perverse degradation contrition	flashback symbol	journal cluster diagram proposal word search puzzle script sermon editorial note dialogue	expressive and personal writing observation and description narrative and imaginative writing informative (expository) writing: synthesis persuasion writing about literature
My City **The Tropics in New York**				
Student Book page 408 **Teacher's Guide** Lesson, pages 297 and 298 Vocabulary Worksheet, page 299 Test, page 300	laden mystical benediction	imagery	journal	expressive and personal writing
Mississippi Solo				
Student Book page 411 **Teacher's Guide** Lesson, pages 301 and 302 Vocabulary Worksheet, page 303 Test, pages 305 and 306	intuition ethereal zealot skeptics comradery	The student book does not contain discussion questions, analysis of literary techniques, or writing assignments for this selection. These materials appear in the Teacher's Guide lesson.		
Reviewing Concepts				
Student Book page 417 **Teacher's Guide** page 307				

Kitchenette Building

One wants a Teller in a time like this

Speech to the Young/ Speech to the Progress-Toward

Horses Graze

Gwendolyn Brooks

page 310

- **Vocabulary Worksheet,** TG page 262
- **Tests,** TG pages 263–266

Objectives

1. To respond to four poems that describe the ways in which different speakers react to life.
2. To analyze the speaker in a poem.
3. To express ideas in a variety of writing formats: journal, poem, aphorisms, report card, memo, letter, and introductory speech.

IdeaBank

▲ **Motivation.** To help students get started with the Connecting Writing and Reading activity, have them brainstorm a list of problems that they have faced, such as being fired from a job, facing prejudice, or having a serious argument with a family member. Have them record these problems in their journals, along with their reactions to the problems. Then ask them to circle their most frequent reaction. ▲

InformationBank

Biographical Note. Gwendolyn Brooks has always been interested in encouraging young writers. According to her daughter, Nora Brooks Blakely, "Our house became a regular meeting place and thinktank." Each year, Brooks travels to schools around the country to talk to young people about writing and literature. She has sponsored poetry competitions and offered grants to promising students, paying for the awards out of her own pocket. Blakely describes her mother as a person who gives "'til it hurts."

"Your poem does not need to tell your reader everything. A little mystery is fascinating."

— Gwendolyn Brooks, *Young Poets Primer,* 1980

ResourceBank

For the Student. Gwendolyn Brooks. *Reading Selected Poems.* New York: Caedmon, 1973. Cassette. 52 mins.

Brooks, Gwendolyn. *Annie Allen.* New York: Harper & Row, 1949.

———. *The Bean Eaters.* New York: Harper & Row, 1960.

For the Teacher. Kent, George E. *The Life of Gwendolyn Brooks.* Lexington, Ky.: The University Press of Kentucky, 1990.

Madhubuti, Haki R. *Say That the River Turns: The Impact of Gwendolyn Brooks.* Chicago: Third World Press, 1987.

Content Quiz

1. In "Kitchenette Building," what does the speaker doubt can survive in this setting? a dream
2. What is one smell described in "Kitchenette Building"? [Students may name any one.] onion fumes; fried potatoes; yesterday's garbage
3. In "One wants a Teller in a time like this," what does the speaker want the Teller to say about God? that God is actual
4. In "Speech to the Young / Speech to the Progress-Toward," what sport does the speaker allude to? baseball (a "home-run")
5. What animal besides the horse does the speaker mention in "Horses Graze"? the cow

Guidelines for Response

Thinking About the Poem, page 312

1. Students may describe their state of mind as pensive, sad, or perhaps angry.
2. Words and phrases students may suggest include *mundane, workaday, drab, dominated, rushed, overwhelming, weary,* or *short on hopes and dreams.*
3. Students may say that the dream gets swallowed up as people fall into dreary patterns of survival.
4. Students may say that the tenants dream of warmth,

food, pleasant surroundings, privacy, and security and perhaps about education, recreation, and entertainment.

5. Some may say that the message of the poem applies most directly to the poor. Others may say that anyone who feels trapped by his or her surroundings or circumstances, for whatever reason, could identify with the message.

6. Some students may suggest that the first three stanzas of the poem sound more like formal poetry and that the final stanza sounds more like natural speech. Other students may say that the entire poem sounds like natural speech because of the poet's choice of words.

Thinking About the Poem, pages 313–314

1. Students may wonder what the winding street is that one cannot walk, what a Teller is, and why one would need such a Teller.

2. Students may suggest that when people feel insecure or lost, they want order, direction, and reassurance.

3. Some students may speculate that the "time" represents adolescence. Others may propose that the phrase refers to a period in history when certain cultural or societal norms might spell trouble for the individual.

4. Students may say that if Brooks had used *I* or *you,* the poem would have been a more personal telling of a story or giving of advice, whereas using *one* enables Brooks to make universal points about life.

5. Students may seek qualities such as compassion, inner strength, stability, foresight, and honesty.

6. Students may say that the poem depicts essential details about a person's life, the basic elements of life's condition, and the desire to resolve life's dilemmas, thus demonstrating Brooks's point. Others may say that the development of characters and plot in a novel enables the writer to broach a range of subjects in greater depth.

Analyzing the Writer's Craft, page 314

Students may infer that the speaker has experienced numerous difficulties; has experienced a more secure time, when the path through life seemed clearer; and was once told simple rules to follow and now yearns for more.

Thinking About the Poem, page 316

1. Students may be left with a sense of inner strength and resolve. They may feel encouraged by and grateful for the speaker's support.

2. Students may suggest that the speaker is addressing young people—or people of any age who are in the process of bettering themselves—who may be discouraged by experiences they cannot understand or control. In line 12 the speaker is telling the "young" and the "progress-toward" to enjoy every day of life rather than be discouraged and distracted by difficult or distant goals.

3. Some students may suggest that the message would be the same, since a wealthy person certainly can experience negative situations. Others may feel that if the speaker were wealthy, he or she would not see life as an uphill struggle; such a speaker might stress the probability of winning the battle and focus on the rewards to be reaped.

4. Students may speculate that Brooks uses alliteration to place negative emphasis on those she refers to. Students may also speculate that the use of repetition gives the speaker a demeanor of assurance and strength, thereby encouraging the reader to stick firmly to principles.

5. Some may theorize that the "young" and the "progress-toward" may find it hard to follow the speaker's advice because, as the poem implies, they will have some difficult times ahead. Others may feel that Brooks's poem will empower the "young" and the "progress-toward."

Thinking About the Poem, page 318

1. Some students may welcome the message that the creatures nobly enjoy life by living with as few complications as possible. Other students may feel that animal lives are narrow and thus offer little appeal as models.

2. Students may say that compared with humans, who are frantic in their attempts to better themselves, horses have the ability to see what is important in life, an ability that gives them dignity and a sense of contentment.

3. Some may agree that people are too wrapped up in the "follies" of life to be satisfied. Others may believe that the intricacies of life are to be applauded because they testify to the advanced intelligence humans possess.

4. Students may speculate that an essay would have been drier and less imaginative than the poem. Students may suggest that the poetic form allows Brooks to imply ideas rather than state them directly and that such a technique actively engages the reader's mind.

5. Students may propose that the poem's message could be applied to any situation in life where people become so involved in planning for or worrying about the future that they forget to live in the present.

6. Students may note that Brooks demonstrates an awareness of human frustration and the need for reassurance and that she seems to believe firmly that such reassurance is possible.

Connecting Reading and Writing, page 318

Post several aphorisms on a bulletin board as models for students completing the assignment 1 option.

For assignment 3 provide students with background information about the Nobel Prize, listing the names of poets who have received the honor.

NAME ______________________ DATE ____________

Kitchenette Building (page 310)

Vocabulary Worksheet

One wants a Teller in a time like this (page 310)

Speech to the Young / Speech to the Progress-Toward (page 310)

Horses Graze (page 310)

Essential Vocabulary

affirmation *n.* Positive declaration.
aria *n.* A song or melody for a solo voice in an opera.
majestic *adj.* Very grand or dignified.
oblivion *n.* Lack of awareness; disregard.

Useful Words

folly *n.* Foolishness; lack of good sense.
giddy *adj.* Frivolous; flighty; heedless.
involuntary *adj.* Unintentional; accidental.
tranquil *adj.* Calm; peaceful.

Draw a line from each phrase in the first column to the phrase in the second column that is closest to being *opposite* in meaning.

1. awful aria	solemn snatcher
2. oodles of oblivion	purposeful plunge
3. forceful folly	a little alertness
4. admirable affirmation	weak wisdom
5. giddy giver	distressed deliverer
6. majestic mountain	plain plain
7. involuntary increase	nasty no
8. tranquil trapper	delightful ditty

The word **oblivion** comes from a Latin word meaning "to smooth over or wipe out." If you are in a state of oblivion, every single thought or sensation is wiped out of your brain.

NAME ____________________ DATE ____________

Kitchenette Building (page 310)

Open-Book Test

Part 1 Broad Interpretation

Answer the following essay questions based on your understanding of the poem. Write your answers on a separate sheet of paper. *(15 points each)*

1. Who is the "we" in the poem? What is life like for them? Use details from the poem to support your answers.
2. Why do you think that the people in the poem aren't willing to embrace dreams wholeheartedly? Use details from the poem to explain your answer.
3. What do you think might make the people in the poem willing to dream? Explain your answer.

Part 2 Close Interpretation

Think about how the poet contrasts the lives and concerns of the people in the poem with the idea of a dream. Also consider how the poet uses sensory imagery to develop this contrast. Then fill in the boxes below. You may use ideas that are directly stated in the poem or that you think are implied. *(55 points)*

	The people's lives	The idea of a dream
HEARING Sounds associated with:		
SMELL Smells associated with:		
SIGHT Sights associated with:		
TASTE Tastes associated with:		
TOUCH Physical feelings associated with:		

NAME ______________________ DATE ____________

One wants a Teller in a time like this (page 310) Open-Book Test

Part 1 Broad Interpretation

Answer the following essay questions based on your understanding of the poem. Write your answers on a separate sheet of paper. *(15 points each)*

1. What kinds of things does the speaker probably find comforting, and why? Use details from the poem to explain your answer.
2. What do you think is the "time" that the speaker has in mind? In your answer, consider why the speaker says "*in* a time like this" instead of "*at* a time like this."
3. What kind of person do you think would relate best to the ideas expressed in this poem? Explain your answer.
4. Who comes closest to functioning as a Teller in your life? Support your choice with details from the poem.

Part 2 Close Interpretation

What kind of person do you think the speaker in the poem is? Write words describing your impression of the speaker in the boxes below. *(40 points)*

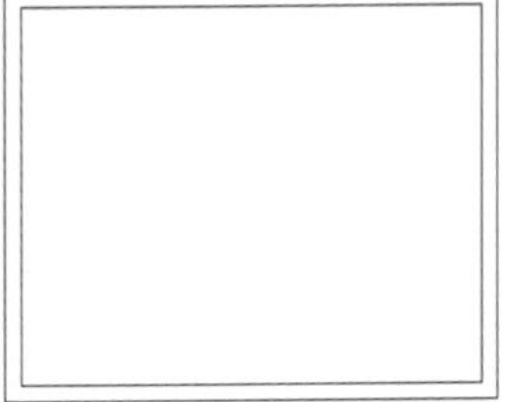

NAME ______________________ DATE ____________

Speech to the Young / Speech to the Progress-Toward (page 310)

Open-Book Test

Part 1 Broad Interpretation

A. Answer the following essay questions based on your understanding of the poem. Write your answers on a separate sheet of paper. *(18 points each)*

1. What do you think it means to "live in the along"? Explain your answer.
2. What do you think the speaker asks of the young? Explain your answer.
3. Under what circumstances do you think it might be easy to follow the speaker's advice? Under what circumstances might it be difficult? Explain your answers.

B. Circle the letter of the best answer. *(6 points)*

Of the following popular sayings, which one would the speaker be *least* likely to agree with?

- **a.** "One day at a time."
- **b.** "If life gives you lemons, make lemonade."
- **c.** "Winning isn't everything, it's the only thing."
- **d.** "Today is the first day of the rest of your life."

Part 2 Close Interpretation

In the boxes below, briefly answer the questions about the people in the poem. *(40 points)*

What words would you use to describe down-keepers, sun-slappers, self-soilers, and harmony-hushers?	
When you imagine a down-keeper, whom do you think of, and why?	When you imagine a sun-slapper, whom do you think of, and why?
When you imagine a self-soiler, whom do you think of, and why?	When you imagine a harmony-husher, whom do you think of, and why?

NAME ______________________ DATE ______________

Horses Graze (page 310)

Open-Book Test

Part 1 Broad Interpretation

Answer the following essay questions based on your understanding of the poem. Write your answers on a separate sheet of paper. *(20 points each)*

1. According to the speaker, what knowledge makes horses sane? Explain your answer.
2. What do you think this poem says about human nature? Explain your answer.
3. How might life be different if people were more like the horses described in this poem? Explain your answer.

Part 2 Close Interpretation

Think about the contrast that is developed in this poem between horses and people. In each of the double-ruled boxes on the left, identify an aspect of horses that the speaker admires. In the double-ruled boxes on the right, identify aspects of people that are contrasted with those aspects of horses. In the boxes at the bottom, write notes about how the aspects are described or how they are implied in the poem. *(40 points)*

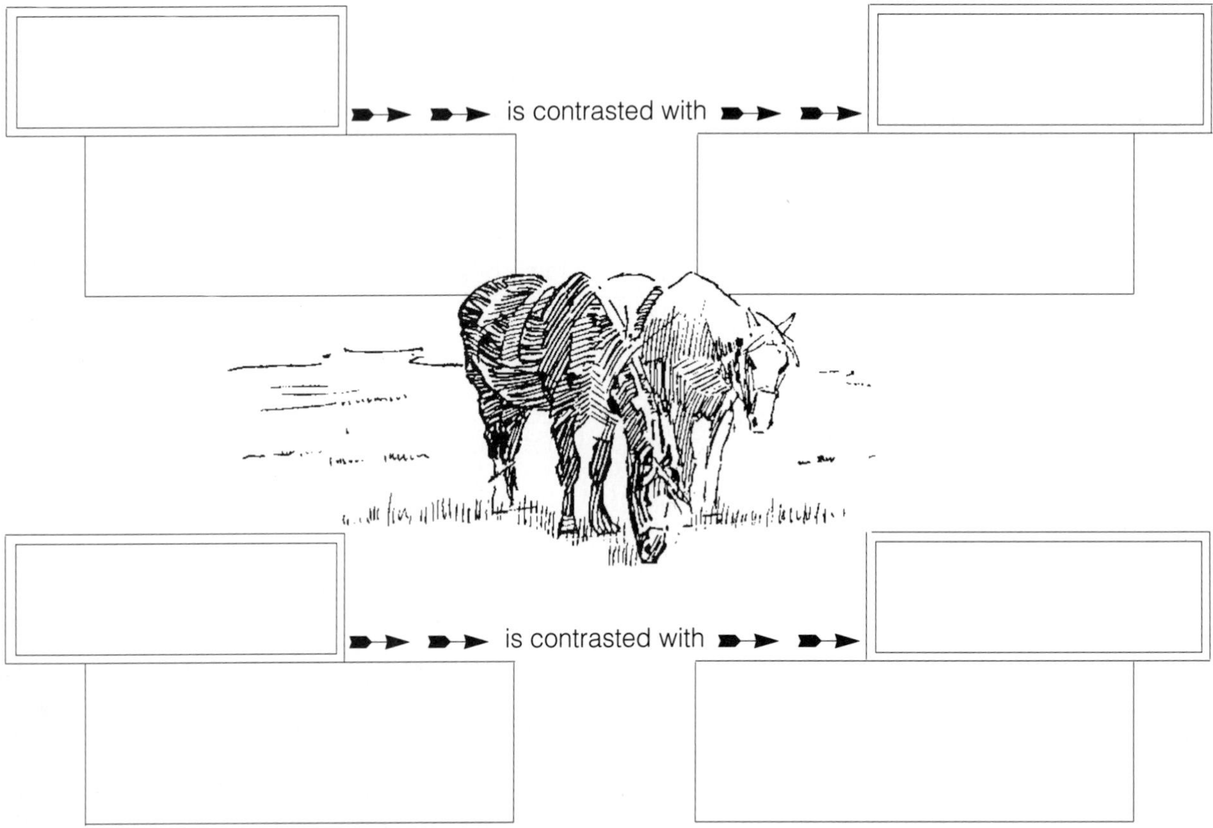

A Raisin in the Sun, Act One

Lorraine Hansberry

page 319

- **Vocabulary Worksheet,** TG page 269
- **Test,** TG pages 271 and 272

Objective

To respond to a play that explores an African-American family's dreams for the future.

Plot Summary

In Act One the Youngers are awaiting the arrival of a check for ten thousand dollars—the late Big Walter's life insurance. All the adult members of the family have dreams they would like to pursue; this money could help them achieve their dreams. The money belongs to Mama, Big Walter's widow, but her son, Walter Lee, wants to use the money to buy a liquor store. His dream is to own a business so that he can quit his job as a chauffeur and provide a better life for his wife, Ruth, and their son, Travis. Walter Lee's sister, Beneatha, wants to become a doctor. Her dream is to use the money to finance her medical school education. Mama has not quite decided what to do with the money but would like to use some of it for Beneatha's education and some of it to buy a small house for the family. Ruth shares Mama's dream of moving from their overcrowded, dingy, cockroach-infested apartment. Tension is created by the family members' conflicting dreams and by other factors. Walter, Ruth, and Beneatha resent Mama's control over their lives. Mama is disturbed by new values her children have adopted. Ruth is pregnant and must decide whether to have the baby. Beneatha, searching for her identity, confronts the expectations of her family and of two very dissimilar boyfriends.

IdeaBank

▲ **Motivation.** To help students visualize one of their dreams for the future, prompt them to imagine the career they hope to have, the family they hope to create, the home they hope to live in, honors they hope to attain, skills they hope to perfect, or thoughts they hope others will have about them. Ask students to indicate how they imagine their lives in the future either by drawing cartoons or by writing biographical notes about themselves. As students read Act One, they should compare their dreams to the dreams of Walter, Ruth, Beneatha, and Mama. ▲

InformationBank

Literary Note. The following portion of dialogue from the original play has been deleted in Act One, Scene 1, in the student text:

Beneatha (*shrugging*). How much cleaning can a house need, for Christ's sakes.

Mama (*not liking the Lord's name used thus*). Bennie!

InformationBank

Historical Note. *A Raisin in the Sun* was first performed in 1959 at the Ethel Barrymore Theater in New York City. It ran for 530 performances. The original cast included Ruby Dee as Ruth, Sidney Poitier as Walter Lee, Claudia McNeil as Mama, Diana Sands as Beneatha, and Glynn Turman as Travis. The play was both a critical and a financial success. The film version of the play was produced by Columbia Pictures in 1961 and featured the original Broadway cast. In 1973 the play was adapted as a musical, *Raisin*, which ran on Broadway for three years. The play experienced a revival in the 1980's, around the time of its twenty-fifth anniversary. New productions restored scenes and lines that had been cut from the original production, notably, one scene in which Beneatha unveils an Afro hairstyle and another in which a neighbor, Mrs. Johnson, warns the family about attacks on blacks in white neighborhoods. One such anniversary production, starring Esther Rolle and Danny Glover, was televised as an *American Playhouse* special in 1989.

ResourceBank

For the Student. *A Raisin in the Sun*. New York: RCA/Columbia Pictures Home Video, 1981. VHS videocassette. Original cast.

A Raisin in the Sun. Hollywood: Fries Home Video, 1990. VHS videocassette. Twenty-fifth anniversary production.

A Raisin in the Sun. New York: Caedmon/Harper Audio, 1991. Two cassettes; 141 mins.

⌘ Connections

Across Literature. Other works by African Americans in this text that explore life in the United States include the following: "Blues Ain't No Mockin Bird," Toni Cade Bambara; from *I Know Why the Caged Bird Sings*, Maya Angelou; "Tenement Room: Chicago," Frank Marshall Davis; "Kitchenette Building," Gwendolyn Brooks.

❷ Content Quiz

1. Where does the Younger family live? in a small apartment on the South Side of Chicago

2. What is the whole Younger family waiting for in Act One? the arrival of a ten-thousand-dollar insurance check

3. What does Walter want to invest in? a liquor store

4. What does Beneatha want to become? a doctor

5. What does Mama dream of buying? a house

Guidelines for Response

Thinking About Act One, pages 346–347

1. Some students may find the family's situation depressing. Some students may think that Mama means well but needs to give her children more independence. Some students may find Walter self-centered, while others may sympathize with his frustrations. Some students may see Beneatha as selfish, while others may view her aspiration for a career as the only bright hope in the family. Some may think that Ruth is noble and loyal, while others may think she fails to satisfy herself or Walter.

2. Students may note that having a dream deferred can make a person bitter and violent, as shown by Walter's lashing out at Ruth and at the mundane existence represented by the eggs she urges him to eat. Students may also suggest that Mama's reminiscences about the plans she and Big Walter shared years ago illustrate that dreams that are deferred too long can simply dissolve. Students may note a sharp contrast between Beneatha's determination and Mama's and Walter's passiveness in pursuing their dreams. Students may indicate that Walter's and George's sexist reactions to Beneatha's dreams seem to annoy Beneatha but do not deter her from her goals.

3. Students who feel that Walter's dream is most worthwhile may note that as an independent businessman, he would no longer have to serve a white employer and would be better able to provide for his family. Some students may suggest that Mama and Ruth, who share the dream of having a home of their own, possess the most worthwhile dream, since a better living environment could improve each family member's life. Other students may argue that Beneatha's dream is the most worthwhile, since it would help the larger community.

4. Some students may suggest that money, or the lack of it, is the main source of conflict within the family. Other students may recognize that most of the conflict develops from the fact that no family member feels completely understood and supported by the others. Walter, who believes that men need women to build them up, feels that Ruth is indifferent to his dreams. Walter fails to appreciate Beneatha's goal of becoming a doctor, and she, in turn, has contempt for his goals. Mama, the head of the family, tramples Ruth's independence by criticizing the way she cares for Travis; she tramples Beneatha's independence by forbidding her to express a lack of faith in God. Mama feels that her children do not appreciate anything she has done for them. She is shaken by Beneatha's atheism and Walter's materialism, values that are very different from those she has taught them.

5. Responses will vary. Some students may predict that Mama will save part of the money for Beneatha's education and use part of it to buy a house, as she said she would. These students may guess that Walter will become bitter if Mama does this. Other students may predict that Mama will allow Walter to make some decisions regarding the money.

6. Some students may suggest that if Big Walter were still alive, the family might be functioning better. Students may point out that Big Walter would bring in additional income; his enthusiasm for children would enhance Ruth, Walter, and Travis's life as a family; he might be able to offer Walter more support and understanding than Walter currently gets; and he would be a source of strength for Mama. Other students may note that although the family might be more stable if Big Walter were still alive, the family would never have received the large insurance check.

7. Students may propose that without Hansberry's elaborate stage directions their understanding of both the characters and their actions would be diminished. They may note that the physical descriptions of Ruth on page 321 and Mama on page 328 also reveal how these characters have been shaped by past experiences. Students may also indicate that stage directions alert them to Ruth's true desires for a home and make them aware of her weakened physical state even before it is recognized by Mama. Students may also suggest that the stage directions amplify their understanding of the emotions expressed during Beneatha and Walter's argument.

8. Students who find the characters true to life may mention that they know people who are similarly frustrated by a dead-end job, dominated by their parents, or disappointed in their surroundings. Students may also note that the characters, like real people, are multidimensional. They are neither completely good nor completely bad, and they express a range of feelings. Many students may argue that the characters are not stereotypical, but some may feel that Mama resembles the stereotype of the domineering matriarch often seen in portrayals of African-American families.

9. Students may propose that the poems do capture some frustrating physical aspects of the Youngers' environment—worn, tired furnishings and a shared bathroom—but fail to capture the Youngers' dedication to their dreams. Both poems imply that the occupants are without dreams.

NAME ____________________ DATE ____________

A Raisin in the Sun (page 319)

Vocabulary Worksheet

Essential Vocabulary

assimilationism *n.* The policy of completely absorbing groups into the main culture.
indictment *n.* An accusation; blame.
resignation *n.* A passive acceptance.
retrogression *n.* A moving backward, especially into a worse condition.
vindicated adj. Cleared from criticism or guilt.

Useful Words

beseechingly *adv.* In a begging way; pleadingly.
defer *v.* To put off; postpone; delay.
disheveled *adj.* Untidy and rumpled; disordered.
graphically *adv.* In realistic detail; vividly.

Fill in each set of blanks with the correct word from the word list. (Clue: The boxed letters will spell something that is the opposite of a raisin in the sun.)

1. This is supported by those who think that the United States should function as a melting pot.
_ _ _ _ _ _ _ [ ] _ _ _ _ _ _ _

2. This is the opposite of headway, advancement, and development.
_ _ _ _ _ [ ] [ ] _ _ _ _ _ _

3. This is *not* how one usually wants an illness or operation described.
_ _ [ ] [ ] _ _ _ _ _ _ _

4. This is almost always found in statements that begin with "How dare you . . . !"
_ _ _ _ _ _ _ [ ] _ _

5. When you have to do something and you can't do it with enthusiasm, you may do it with this.
_ _ _ [ ] _ [ ] _ [ ] _ _ _

6. This describes you after you've been pulled backwards through a hedge.
_ _ _ [ ] _ _ [ ] _ _ _

7. This is how children ask for something they really, *really*, REALLY want.
_ _ [ ] _ _ _ [ ] _ _ _ _ _

8. This is how you would feel if it were proven that the dog really *did* eat your homework.
_ _ _ _ _ _ [ ] _ _ [ ]

9. Rain at the beginning of a ballgame can do this to the start of play.
_ [ ] _ _ _

NAME ______________________ DATE ______________

A Raisin in the Sun, Act One (page 319)

Test

Part 1 Broad Interpretation

A. Think about the poem that opens the play and its connection to the deferred dreams of the Younger family. In the boxes at the top, identify the dream of each of the characters. In the middle boxes, briefly tell why each dream is important to the person. Then, in the bottom boxes, circle the word or phrase from the poem that you think best describes how the person might react if the insurance check doesn't make his or her dream come true. *(40 points)*

Mama	Walter	Ruth	Beneatha
Her dream	His dream	Her dream	Her dream
Why is this dream so important to her?	Why is this dream so important to him?	Why is this dream so important to her?	Why is this dream so important to her?
She will: sag "like a heavy load" or "explode."	He will: sag "like a heavy load" or "explode."	She will: sag "like a heavy load" or "explode."	She will: sag "like a heavy load" or "explode."

B. Answer the following essay questions based on your understanding of the first act of the play. Write your answers on a separate sheet of paper. *(10 points each)*

1. Whose dream seems most worthwhile to you, and why?
2. Why have the dreams of the Younger family been deferred? Use details from the play to explain your answer.
3. What do you think Beneatha means when she says, "We've all got acute ghetto-itus"?

NAME ______________________ DATE ____________

Part 2 Close Interpretation

Think about the conflicts that exist between the members of the Younger family. Then, in the boxes below, write brief notes describing and explaining the conflicts between each pair of characters. *(30 points)*

Ruth and Walter
Ruth and Mama
Ruth and Beneatha
Walter and Mama
Walter and Beneatha
Mama and Beneatha

A Raisin in the Sun, Act Two

Lorraine Hansberry

page 348

■ **Test,** TG pages 275 and 276

Objective

To analyze patterns of mood in a drama.

Plot Summary

In Act Two Beneatha, in her Nigerian costume, and a drunken Walter dance to the beat of African drums. George Murchison, Beneatha's wealthy date, arrives to take her to the theater. He and Beneatha argue about African heritage, and then a bitter Walter attacks George for his pretentious airs. Mama finally returns home and reveals that she has made a down payment on a house in a white neighborhood after learning that similar houses in black neighborhoods cost twice as much. Although Ruth, Travis, and Beneatha are excited, Walter is deeply disappointed. Mama decides to give Walter the remainder of the insurance money, asking only that he put a portion of it in the bank for Beneatha's education. As the members of the family begin packing to move, they are interrupted by a visit from Karl Lindner, a representative of the Clybourne Park Improvement Association, who tries to convince the Youngers not to move into the white neighborhood. He offers to buy the house from them so that they will make a profit. Walter, Ruth, and Beneatha angrily refuse his offer. While the family continues with preparations to leave, Walter learns that his friend Willy has absconded with the rest of the insurance money, including Beneatha's share, instead of using it to buy the liquor store.

InformationBank

Literary Note. The following portions of the original play were deleted in Act Two in the student text:

George. . . . your heritage is nothing but a bunch of raggedy-assed spirituals and some grass huts! (Scene 1, page 350)

Walter. You happy?—you contented son-of-a-bitch—you happy? (Scene 1, page 352)

Ruth. . . .To these Goddamned cracking walls! (Scene 1, page 356)

Walter. THEN TELL ME, GODDAMNIT . . . WHAT'S THE MATTER WITH YOU? (Scene 3, page 369)

IdeaBank

✲ **Collaborative Learning.** Have students research any of these aspects of African or African-American culture alluded to in Act Two: Jomo Kenyatta; Chaka; Ashanti; Songhay; Bénin; Bantu; Nigerian clothes, dance, and music; the NAACP; blues; civil rights; Negro spirituals. Ask them to share the results of their research in oral reports with illustrative pictures or recordings. ✲

⌘ Connections

Across the Humanities. Ask students to read or reread Martin Luther King, Jr.'s "I Have a Dream" speech (page 144), delivered in August 1963 during the civil rights march in Washington, D.C. Have them compare King's dream with the dreams of Ruth, Walter, Beneatha, or Mama. Encourage students to write and present to the class an "I Have a Dream" speech that one of the play's characters might deliver.

Across the Curriculum. Ask students to find out the rate of inflation between 1950 and the present year and to multiply ten thousand by this rate in order to determine the approximate value of the insurance money today. Ask students to discuss whether the Youngers' plans would be feasible today, given the cost of housing, medical school, or owning a small business.

InformationBank

Biographical Note. In 1938 Lorraine Hansberry's father, Carl, challenged Chicago's "restrictive covenants," or housing discrimination laws, by purchasing a house in an all-white neighborhood. The Hansberrys had barely moved in when incensed neighbors gathered in front of the house and began to throw bricks. A friend was able to disperse the mob by brandishing a loaded gun, but not before a brick narrowly missed hitting eight-year-old Lorraine in the head. Despite this violent incident and others like it, the Hansberry family continued to live in the house until a court order forced them to leave. With the help of an attorney from the National Association for the Advancement of Colored People (NAACP), the family fought the case all the way to the Supreme Court. The Court's decision in 1940 in *Hansberry* v. *Lee* abolished housing discrimination. Unfortunately, Carl Hansberry died soon after the decision was handed down. Lorraine believed that the stress of the court battle cost him his life; she said that he died "of a cerebral hemorrhage, supposedly, but American racism helped kill him."

❷ Content Quiz

1. Where does Mama buy a house with part of her insurance money? in Clybourne Park, a white neighborhood

2. What does Mama tell Walter to do with the rest of the insurance money? She wants him to put three thousand dollars into a savings account for Beneatha's education and the rest in his own checking account.

3. Why does Karl Lindner visit the Youngers? to convince them not to move into his white community

4. What do Walter, Ruth, and Beneatha give Mama for the new house? a set of gardening tools

5. What does Bobo tell Walter at the end of Act Two? that Willy has run off with all of their money

Guidelines for Response

Thinking About Act Two, page 371

1. Students may describe feelings of shock, disgust, or hopelessness.

2. Responses will vary. Students may see Walter as the person hurt most by Willy's theft, because he sees his dreams of respectability and a comfortable life for his family shattered and because he recognizes that the money represented years of his father's labor. Some students may see Mama as the person most hurt by the theft, noting that she begins to beat Walter as memories of her husband's apparently wasted struggles haunt her. Other students may feel that Ruth is most hurt by Willy's action, since Ruth's hopes for Walter, her marriage, and her family were tied to Walter's emerging self-esteem. Some students may feel that Beneatha is the most devastated by the financial loss, since her dream—having a medical career—will be either impossible or indefinitely deferred without some significant financial support from her family. Other students may suggest that Travis suffers the most, since the money was meant to improve his future.

3. Students may disagree about the wisdom of the decisions Mama makes to keep the family together. Some students may support her decisions to buy the house, noting that Ruth's outlook improves as a consequence. Other students may criticize this decision, pointing out that Walter is devastated and that the whole family may face danger from hostile neighbors. Some students may suggest that Mama does the right thing in trusting her son with the remaining money; they may note the improvements in the family's relationships once Mama has given Walter the financial responsibility. Other students, pointing to the tragedy that occurs, may feel that Mama makes a mistake in giving the money to the untrustworthy Walter.

4. Some students may suggest that the increased respect between Beneatha and her mother results from Mama's sensitivity to Beneatha's needs. Students may indicate that when Mama shows that she trusts Walter's judgment by giving him the rest of the money, she changes their relationship to one of mutual respect. Students may note that once Walter feels in control of his life, he is able to forge a better relationship with Ruth.

5. Some students may predict that all the family members will abandon their dreams of a better life and that tensions between them will become intolerable. Other students may predict that the family members will manage to endure their troubles or that they will find other ways to achieve their dreams.

6. Some students may believe that had Mama not given Walter the money, he would eventually have recognized the value of home ownership and reconciled himself to the idea. Other students may feel that Walter would never have forgiven his mother for denying him respect and the opportunity to develop his business venture, that he would have stopped functioning as a family member, and that ultimately his bitterness and lack of self-respect would have destroyed him.

7. Some students may report that the references to Africa strengthen the play and heighten their interest in it. These students may recognize that the African references are linked to the play's theme of forging a positive identity in a hostile society. Africa is one place in which Walter and Beneatha look for their identity; they see in Africa a glorious past, an appreciation of blackness, and a commitment to ending white dominance. Asagai values his African identity; George, on the other hand, rejects Africa and prefers to find his identity in his social and economic position. Students may also suggest that the Younger family's struggle for dignity and independence takes on a universal dimension when placed alongside similar struggles in African nations. Other students may feel that the African references weaken the play because they are allusions to events and people with which the audience may be unfamiliar.

8. Some students may believe that Mr. Linder's segregationist attitude is still widespread, citing incidents of racial prejudice and harassment that have occurred nationwide in recent years. Other students may believe that attitudes such as Linder's are less common today; these students may point to increased integration in housing, schools, and workplaces.

Analyzing the Writer's Craft, page 372

Students' diagrams should reflect the many drastic shifts of mood in Act Two and show that the mood is at its darkest at the end of the act. Students may suggest that Hansberry structures Act Two as she does in order to build dramatic tension and to emphasize the family's potential for growth as well as for destruction.

NAME ______________________________ DATE ______________

A Raisin in the Sun, Act Two (page 348)

Test

Part 1 Broad Interpretation

Answer the following essay questions based on your understanding of the first two acts of the play. Write your answers on a separate sheet of paper. *(13 points each)*

1. How do you judge Walter at this point in the play? Is the loss of the money his fault? Is Mama justified in attacking him? Explain your answers.
2. Who do you think will be most affected by the loss of the money? Explain your answer.
3. After Mama tells the family about buying the house, she asks Walter to say that he approves of what she has done. He replies, "What you need me to say you done right for?" Why do you think she needs him to say it? Use details from the play to explain your answer.
4. In the first act, Walter says that money "is life." Why, then, do you think he refuses Mr. Lindner's offer to buy the new house? Explain your answer.

Part 2 Close Interpretation

A. Write the letter of the best answer. *(6 points each)*

_____ 1. Which of the following groupings of characters *best* describes the sides taken in the Ocomogosiay episode?

a. Ruth, Walter, and Beneatha versus George.
b. Ruth and Walter versus Beneatha and George.
c. Walter and George versus Beneatha and Ruth.
d. Walter and Beneatha versus George and Ruth.

_____ 2. When Mama decides to use the rest of the money for what her children want, she reveals that she

a. has given up her dreams.
b. is sensitive to her children's needs.
c. no longer cares what happens to her children.
d. no longer cares what happens to the money.

_____ 3. Mr. Lindner's chief purpose in visiting the Youngers is to

a. swindle them out of their money.
b. keep them out of his neighborhood.
c. protect them from making a tragic mistake.
d. help them make a hefty profit on the home.

NAME ______________________________ DATE ______________

B. Think about how the mood changes throughout the second act of the play. Then, for each of the episodes listed in chronological order below, make a mark to indicate whether the overall mood of the episode is dark or light. *(2 points each)*

	Light	Dark
4. The Ocomogosiay episode occurs.		
5. Walter and George talk.		
6. Ruth offers Walter food.		
7. Mama reveals that she has bought a new house.		
8. Mama reveals the location of the new house.		
9. Mama asks Walter to say that he approves of the new house.		
10. After the play, Beneatha asks George to leave.		
11. Walter tells about his driving trips.		
12. Mama gives Walter the rest of the money.		
13. Walter talks with Travis about the future.		
14. Ruth explains to Beneatha that Walter has changed.		
15. Walter teases Beneatha about her views on race.		
16. Lindner enters and offers to buy back the new house.		
17. The family gives Mama her gardening tools and hat.		
18. Bobo enters with the news that Willy has taken the money.		

A Raisin in the Sun, Act Three

Lorraine Hansberry

page 373

■ **Test,** TG pages 279 and 280

Objectives

To express ideas in a variety of writing formats: journal, playbill, director's notes, diagram, note, dramatic scene, monologue, letter, review.

Plot Summary

In Act Three a mood of sorrow and disappointment hangs over the Younger family. Joseph Asagai arrives to help with the moving and discusses idealism with Beneatha. Asagai then proposes that Beneatha return with him to Nigeria. Walter searches for a scrap of paper and dashes out the door. He has decided to call Karl Lindner and accept the offer to buy them out. In the meantime, Mama has also reached the decision not to move, despite Ruth's pleas to the contrary. Walter returns and explains his decision to the stunned family. Although Walter thinks he is beating "The Man" at his own game, Mama believes that accepting the money offered by the whites to keep them from moving into the house is a fatal loss of dignity. The moving men arrive at the same time that Karl Lindner arrives, thus forcing the family to make a crucial decision. Mama relinquishes to her son her position as head of the family; Walter finally comes into his manhood by refusing Lindner's offer. The family moves as planned: one dream for the future is realized.

IdeaBank

❖ **Cooperative Learning.** Divide the class into six groups. Assign each group one of the following sections of the play to perform in a dramatic reading: one of the two scenes in Act One, one of the three scenes in Act Two, or all of Act Three. Ask students to select roles and rehearse their assigned section of the play, encouraging them to help each other with dialogue. (It might be necessary for some students in a group to take more than one role.) Have each group present its section of the play to the rest of the class. ❖

InformationBank

Literary Note. This line of dialogue from the original play—spoken by Walter— was changed in Act Three in the student text: "I'm going to look that son-of-a-bitch in the eyes and say—. . ."

IdeaBank

▲ **Motivation.** Before students read Act Three, have them create tree diagrams for the concept of manhood. Ask them to draw these diagrams, which show branching associations, in their journals. A partial tree diagram follows.

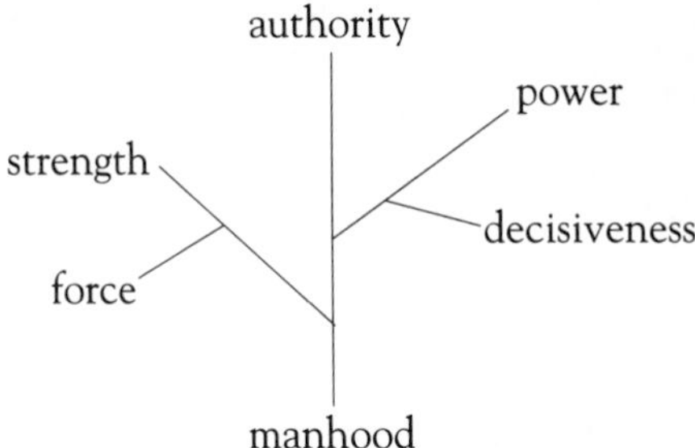

As they read the conclusion of *A Raisin in the Sun*, students should add details to their tree diagrams. ▲

IdeaBank

★ **Interactive Assessment.** Have students perform the dramatic scenes or deliver the monologues they prepared for assignment 3 of Connecting Reading and Writing. Direct the class to listen carefully, and ask volunteers to evaluate the performers' predictions about the future of the Younger family based on what they already know about each character. Ask them to point out the strengths and weaknesses of each dramatic scene or monologue, offering suggestions for improvement. You might suggest that students also rate the performances on a scale of 1 to 5, with 1 being the most effective presentation. ★

❷ Content Quiz

1. What does Asagai suggest that Beneatha do when the family crisis is over? He suggests that she come with him to Nigeria.

2. Whom does Walter go to call in Act Three? Karl Lindner

3. What does Walter tell the rest of the family he is going to do? He is going to accept the money that the Clybourne Park Improvement Association offered for the house.

4. What does Walter tell Mr. Lindner? He tells him that the Younger family is proud and that they plan to move in and be good neighbors.

5. What do Mama and Ruth agree that Walter has finally come into? his manhood

Guidelines for Response

Thinking About Act Three, pages 384–385

1. Students' attitudes may include admiration, relief, respect, surprise, and affection.

2. Students may suggest that Walter changes his mind partly because of his family's horrified reaction to his proposal. Students may also note that Walter, too, views the offer as humiliating: he breaks down emotionally as he acknowledges that taking the money would place him in the role of a subservient black. Some students may suggest that he changes his mind because he does not want to appear weak before Travis, who is in the room. Students might also think that Walter is influenced by the memory of his father and previous generations who struggled for a better life in America.

3. Students may propose that Hansberry would reject Walter's initial view of manhood, one based on material wealth, power, and privilege. They may note that Walter believes being a man means being able to buy pearls for his wife. He refers to Lindner as "The Man," a representative of the powerful white world that excludes him; the implication is that Walter himself is not a man. Students may suggest that accepting this definition of manhood is what almost destroys Walter. Students may note that when Beneatha says that Walter is not a man but a toothless rat, she is linking manhood to self-respect. She later does refer to Walter as a man, after he regains his dignity by rejecting Lindner's offer. Students may point out that this view of manhood, based on self-respect, respect for others, and responsibility to others, seems to be affirmed by Hansberry when Mama and Ruth agree, at the end of the play, that Walter has "finally come into his manhood."

4. One idea that students may come away with is that dreams are essential to the human spirit. Students may report feeling disappointed when, in reaction to "life like it is," Mama is willing to give up her dream of owning a home and Walter is willing to abandon his ideals. Another idea, suggested particularly by Asagai's speech to Beneatha, is that any dream worth having—such as Beneatha's dream of healing, Asagai's dream of independence and progress for Africa, or the entire Younger family's dream of a better life—should not be abandoned because of setbacks, no matter how devastating. None of these dreams is relinquished at the end of the play. A third idea that students may gain is that some dreams are dangerous. Walter's all-consuming dream of wealth and prestige must be sacrificed for his own good and the good of his family.

5. Some students may suggest that the play ends happily because Walter has gained a new sense of manhood and the entire family has grown closer. These students may note that while Walter and Beneatha continue their sibling disputes, their arguing cannot destroy the respect they have developed for each other. These students may also note that Ruth and Mama rejoice in Walter's personal growth and achieve their dream of moving to a new home. Other students may suggest that the ending is not entirely happy, since the Youngers must now cope with hostile neighbors. Students may also point out that the family still does not have much money and that it is uncertain whether Walter's new-found self-respect can survive a return to a menial job.

6. Students may suggest that Walter's acceptance of Lindner's money would have destroyed the family. Students may speculate that Walter would have felt such guilt and self-disgust that he would have become even more difficult to live with. Students might also imagine that the rest of the family would have lost respect for him, which might have forced him to leave.

7. Students may note that the plant symbolizes life and hope in the midst of a discouraging environment. Students may also note that Mama's attitude toward the plant and her retrieval of it at the end of the play suggest the value she places on life.

8. Students may answer that Hughes's poem is an appropriate epigraph for the play because it deals with deferred dreams. They may suggest that all the members of the Younger family have put off their dreams for a long time. Some of their dreams, such as Mama's dream of owning her own home, are in danger of drying up, and others, such as Walter's dream of quick wealth, explode.

9. Students' responses will vary; some may relate the play to their own dreams of wealth, career success, and independence from parents. Encourage students to offer specific examples from the play to illustrate the relationships they see between their own hopes, fears, or dreams and those presented in Hansberry's work.

Connecting Reading and Writing, page 385

Offer students copies of playbills for contemporary plays to be used as models for their analysis of Mama or Walter in assignment 1.

For assignment 3, ask students to select a scene from *A Raisin in the Sun* and to review in that scene Hansberry's use of dialogue, stage directions, and mood development. Students might share their opinions of Hansberry's techniques in a small group discussion prior to writing their own scenes.

For assignment 4, provide samples of newspaper reviews of plays for students to examine.

NAME ______________________ DATE ______________

A Raisin in the Sun, Act Three (page 373)

Test

Part 1 Broad Interpretation

Answer the following essay questions based on your understanding of the play. Write your answers on a separate sheet of paper. *(12 points each)*

1. Do you think that the tremendous change Walter undergoes in the final act is believable? In your answer, consider whether Hansberry provides sufficient motivation for this change.
2. How do the women in the family react to Walter's calling Mr. Lindner? Why do they react this way?
3. Think about Beneatha's argument with Asagai. She accuses him of not having any answers to the important questions in life, such as "What good is anything? Where are we all going? Why are we bothering?" In response, Asagai says, "I live the answer!" What does he mean? Explain your answer.
4. As Mama stands alone in the apartment at the end of the play, "a great heaving thing rises in her." What do you think she is thinking about? Explain your answer.

Part 2 Close Interpretation

A. Think about what Africa and America seem to represent to Beneatha. Then write some of your ideas in the boxes below. *(10 points)*

Africa	America

B. In each of the boxes below, identify something in the play that for one or more of the characters becomes a symbol of hope for the future. *(12 points)*

NAME ______________________ DATE ______________

C. Think about how the conflicts that are introduced in the first act of the play are eased or resolved in the final act. Then, for each of the pairs of characters below, identify at least two events in the play that help to ease the conflict between them. You may refer to an event more than once. *(30 points)*

Ruth and Walter
Ruth and Mama
Walter and Mama
Walter and Beneatha
Mama and Beneatha

A Visit to Grandmother

William Melvin Kelley

page 386

- **Vocabulary Worksheet,** TG page 283
- **Test,** TG pages 285 and 286

Objectives

1. To respond to a short story about how a mother's indulgence of one son affects another sibling.
2. To interpret the effect of dialogue in a short story.
3. To express ideas in a variety of writing formats: journal, dialogue, newspaper advice column, personality profiles, pamphlet, newspaper column, and research report.

Plot Summary

After attending a class reunion, Dr. Charles Dunford, accompanied by his son Chig, visits his mother in her home in the South—the first visit between the doctor and his mother in many years. Instantly, Chig realizes that something is strained in his father's relationship with his mother. At dinner that evening, the grandmother tells a funny and affectionate story about an older son, GL, who obtained a horse fraudulently in a trade, only to have the horse bolt during a buggy ride. Then Dr. Dunford bitterly remarks that his mother always indulged GL, despite his misbehavior, because she loved him more. The mother replies that she tried to give each of her ten children what they needed; GL, not as smart as Charles, needed more attention or he would have gotten into serious trouble. After Dr. Dunford leaves the room in anger, GL himself arrives, late for the meal, asking after his brother with what the narrator describes as "the innocent smile of a five-year-old."

IdeaBank

✤ **Multimodal Activity.** Have students rewrite and then present the story as a one-act play, opening with the arrival of Chig and his father at the grandmother's home. Remind students of the importance of stage directions in telling actors how to look and move. Have students give a dramatic reading of their play for the class, and then prompt the class to discuss how their understanding and appreciation of the story is affected by its translation from narrative to drama—i.e., what is lost and what is gained. ✤

IdeaBank

▲ **Motivation.** As an alternative to the Connecting Writing and Reading activity, have students jot down in their journals examples of situations in which they might have given unequal treatment to friends or family members. Ask them also to make notes about situations in which they think they have received unequal treatment. Then have students read the story and think about this question as they read: Can a parent always give equal treatment to all of his or her children? ▲

InformationBank

Literary Note. Chig Dunford is a central figure in William Melvin Kelley's 1970 novel, *Dunfords Travels Everywheres* [*sic*]. The novel tells the adventures of Harvard-educated Chig as an American tourist in Paris. A parallel story follows the experiences of Chig's alter ego, Carlyle Bedlow, a Harlem street hustler.

IdeaBank

❖ **Cooperative Learning.** Divide the class into small groups to debate whether or not parents should treat all their children in the same manner. One member of each group should act as secretary, recording the arguments, examples, and conclusions offered on each side of the debate. Each group should try to reach a consensus. Have one student from each group report the group's conclusions to the class. ❖

⌘ Connections

Across Literature. For a comparison of different accounts (both fictional and factual) of relationships between parents and children, students may wish to read the story "Two Kinds" (page 198), the excerpt from *Kaffir Boy* (page 222), and the poem "Hiccups" (page 234).

ResourceBank

For the Student. Kelley, William Melvin. *Dancers on the Shore*. (Howard University Library of Contemporary Literature) Washington, D.C.: Howard University Press, 1984.

For the Teacher. Kelley, William Melvin. *Different Drummer*. New York: Doubleday, 1990.

Content Quiz

1. What event does Chig's father travel to Nashville to attend? his college class reunion

2. Who is with Mrs. Dunford when Chig and his father arrive? GL's wife, Aunt Rose

3. What happened when GL took Mrs. Dunford for a buggy ride? The horse ran away with them.

4. How does Dr. Dunford believe his mother felt about him? He thinks she loved him less than she loved GL.

Guidelines for Response

Thinking About the Story, page 392

1. Students may perceive Charles as bitter, stubborn, wounded, and sad. They may emphasize the consistent portrait of GL as a five-year-old; others may identify with Charles's jealousy of him. Students may see the mother as loving, indulgent, smart, or insensitive.

2. Students who support his mother's indulgence of GL may refer to her suspicions that he could have ended up lynched ("swinging"); they may suggest that the mother wanted to protect GL from a life of trouble by allowing him extra attention she felt he needed. Those who disagree with the mother's indulgence of GL may point to the depth and nature of Charles's resentment; his bitterness is so strong that even as an adult, it reduces him to tears.

3. Some students may suggest that Charles's feelings are understandable because they developed when he was young and unable to understand his mother's behavior from a parent's point of view. Those who feel that Charles's view of his mother is wrong may point out her pride in her son when she tells Chig to be "honest like your daddy" or her emotional reaction to Charles's arrival.

4. Some students may suggest that had his mother made the young Charles an ally in her attempts to protect GL, her increased attention and shared confidences may have given him a sense of importance. Other students may suggest that Charles's expression of his feelings and his mother's attempt to explain her actions and intentions may help the two understand each other.

5. Some students might indicate that GL's referral to Charles as a "rascal" (page 391) shows that his perception of Charles reflects GL's own character more than it does Charles's. Some may say that since GL is childish and insensitive, he probably has very little idea of Charles's pain. Students may suggest that GL is in awe of or feels inferior to Charles; he may sense his mother's view of Charles as smarter or more self-sufficient.

6. Students may suggest that while Charles's version would be shaped by his strong emotions, Chig's viewpoint offers the advantage of a naturally curious but unbiased character who is also intelligent and perceptive.

7. Students may note that Mama zealously protects GL due to the dangers faced by African Americans living in the South at the time the story is set. They may also say that without the constant fear experienced by those deprived of their rights, the family might have found better ways of dealing with GL's behavior. Others may suggest that these conflicting relationships transcend setting and are universal problems for families.

8. While this criticism may confirm some students' feelings that they did not get the "whole" story, others may disagree strongly. Students who agree with the criticism may note that no other characters from the town were introduced, that they never had a chance to judge GL for themselves, and that they were not given detailed descriptions of the setting. Students who feel that the story is complete as is may mention that the characters' conversations give insight into the complex family relationships.

Analyzing the Writer's Craft, page 393

From the exchanges between the mother, Aunt Rose, and Chig, students may conclude that the mother prides herself on her independence and continued ability to fulfill her responsibilities as the matriarch of the family; that she values family life when she immediately acts to bring the family together to celebrate Charles's return; that she continues to be aware of GL's true character; and that Aunt Rose fondly supports the mother. Aunt Rose also reveals her discomfort regarding GL's lack of reliability.

From the exchanges between the mother, GL, and Essie, students may note that the mother does not trust GL's honesty or judgment. Her pleasure in GL's reaction to her agreement to ride shows her fondness for her child. GL's assessment of the horse and his insistence that his mother accompany him may indicate to some that his behavior is that of a pleasant but thoughtless child.

Students may note that the vast distance in time and space that separates Charles from his family, coupled with a lack of honesty in any communication they did have, limits their understanding of one another. From the exchange between the mother and Charles, students may feel that Charles's bitter resentment continues to shape his relationship with his mother. Students may also feel that the mother is completely surprised by Charles's reactions to his childhood experiences.

Connecting Reading and Writing, page 393

For the optional assignment 1, you might post copies of an advice column such as "Ann Landers" or "Dear Abby."

If the grammar and composition book you use has a lesson on research reports, you may want to refer to this lesson.

NAME ______________________ DATE ____________

A Visit to Grandmother (page 386)

Vocabulary Worksheet

Essential Vocabulary

engaging *adj*. Tending to draw favorable attention; attractive.
indulgence *n*. A yielding; lack of strictness.

The connotation of a word is the meaning it suggests. Using words correctly involves recognizing their connotations in addition to their definitions. Read the definitions, given above, and the information about connotations, given below. Then, for each word, circle the letter in front of the one sentence that uses the word *incorrectly*.

1. To say that you treat someone with **indulgence** usually suggests that you have some fondness for that person or that you are humoring him or her.

- **a.** On the instructions of the jury, the judge treated the prisoner with **indulgence**.
- **b.** If you treat a puppy with too much **indulgence**, you could end up with chewed slippers and shoes all over the house.
- **c.** Joanne's parents have always treated her with **indulgence**; in fact, they've spoiled her.
- **d.** Uncle Fred's slide show was intensely boring, but it was important to him, so we sat through it with patient **indulgence**.

2. **Engaging** people make you want to be around them. They delight with their charm.

- **a.** I don't know whether I'd trust him with my checkbook, but his cheerfulness certainly makes him **engaging**.
- **b.** He was not the handsomest man in the world or the smartest, but he was unusually **engaging**. Your heart simply warmed to his smile.
- **c.** The novelist had a reputation as an extremely **engaging** conversationalist, but it seemed to me he was interested only in promoting himself and his new book.
- **d.** She was trustworthy, dependable, honest, and, as a result, a thoroughly **engaging** individual.

NAME ______________________ DATE ____________

A Visit to Grandmother (page 386)

Test

Part 1 Broad Interpretation

A. Answer the following essay questions based on your understanding of the story. Write your answers on a separate sheet of paper. (*16 points each*)

1. Which character do you think is more deserving of the reader's sympathy, Charles or his mother? Why?
2. Why might it be significant that the mother, and not GL, stops the runaway horse? Explain your answer.
3. The grandmother makes statements such as "Them white folks'll burn us alive" and "GL could-a ended up swinging." How do you think that ever-present threat influenced her treatment of GL and Charles? Explain your answer.

B. Think about Charles's reasons for going home. In the appropriate boxes below, identify what you think is the most important thing that Charles accomplishes by visiting his home and the most important thing that he fails to accomplish. Then, on the bar below the boxes, make a mark to show how successful you think Charles's visit home is. (*12 points*)

MOST IMPORTANT ACCOMPLISHMENT	MOST IMPORTANT FAILURE

The visit is a complete failure. The visit is a complete success.

C. Think about how you felt about the mother and her two sons at the end of the story. Has she been a good mother? Have the men been good sons? On the bars below, make marks reflecting how successful you think each has been in fulfilling her or his family role. (*6 points*)

The mother has been a terrible mother. The mother has been a perfect mother.

Charles has been a terrible son. Charles has been a perfect son.

GL has been a terrible son. GL has been a perfect son.

Part 2 Close Interpretation

A. Although GL does not appear until the end of the story, the reader learns a great deal about him from the members of his family. In each of the boxes on the left, identify a character trait possessed by GL. In the corresponding box on the right, briefly explain how this trait is revealed by one of the other characters in the course of the story. *(10 points)*

B. Write the letter of the best answer. *(7 points each)*

____ **1.** Which of the following traits does the grandmother reveal by the way that she allows Rose to cook dinner? *(There may be more than one answer.)*

a. Laziness.

b. Craftiness.

c. Helplessness.

d. Independence.

____ **2.** The mother, despite her better judgment, agrees to ride in the buggy behind GL's new horse because she

a. loves GL.

b. has faith in GL's judgment.

c. wants to discourage GL's potentially dangerous behavior.

d. wants to prove to GL that her judgment is superior to his.

C. Think about how dialogue is used in the story to reveal the feelings and traits of the characters and information about the relationships between them. Then read the dialogue below, between the grandmother and Chig. In the box, briefly tell what the grandmother's words reveal about her feelings for her two sons. *(10 points)*

"You be honest, you hear? Promise me. You be honest like your daddy."

"All right. I promise."

"Good. Rose, where's GL at? Where's that thief? He gone again?"

Choices

Nikki Giovanni

Oranges

Gary Soto

page 395

■ **Test,** TG page 289

Objective

To respond to two poems in which speakers make choices that involve compromises.

IdeaBank

▲ **Motivation.** As an alternative to the Connecting Writing and Reading activity, have students copy the following sentence in their journals:

The hardest choice that I have ever made is ______________________.

Have them complete the sentence, explaining why this choice was so difficult to make. Then, as they read the poems, they should think about the choices made by the speakers of the poems. ▲

IdeaBank

✣ **Multimodal Activities**

1. Encourage students to turn "Choices" into a rap song and to perform it for the class.
2. Encourage students to collect reminiscences from friends, family members, neighbors, and so on, about the first date they ever had. Guide students to take notes or tape-record answers to this question: "What do you especially remember about your first date?" ✣

IdeaBank

✱ **Limited English Proficient Students**

1. To help students with "Choices," have them suggest places where punctuation and capitalization might be added and have volunteers read the new version aloud.
2. Encourage students to share their own experiences about dating. Do they think first dates generally are awkward, exciting, or embarrassing? ✱

IdeaBank

✲ **Collaborative Learning.** Ask pairs of students to role-play the speaker and the girl in "Oranges." Ask students to use props and to create impromptu dialogue to convey the feelings and the experiences of the boy's first date. ✲

InformationBank

Literary Note. Paula Giddings, a literary critic and a friend to Nikki Giovanni, has written these views about Giovanni's attitude toward her poems: "It is not important to her that her poems live in greatness, but that they live. That they have the force to pull someone in who may say, 'Yes. I have felt that way. No. I am not alone.' That is their great test. The heart, not the form, is the final arbiter."

"*Black women . . . had to learn to be self-forgiving quickly, for often their exterior exploits were at odds with their interior beliefs.*"

— Maya Angelou, *I Dream a World,* 1989

Tips from the Classroom

In class discussion, create two columns on the board that students can fill with notes. In a column headed "Since I can't . . ." have students list what the speaker in "Choices" cannot do, so that students will understand why "mankind . . . learns to cry." In a column headed "then I . . ." have students list the alternatives chosen by the speaker to help him or her cope with despair.

Donald T. Hollenbeck
Deerfield High School
Deerfield, IL

IdeaBank

❧ **Gifted and Talented Students.** Have students write poems about choices they have in life. Ask them to create cluster diagrams showing choices and obstacles to those choices in order to generate ideas for their poems. Also encourage students to experiment with punctuation and capitalization in their poems. ❧

ResourceBank

For the Student. *Nikki Giovanni*. Verdugo City, Calif.: Pied Piper Productions, 1979. Filmstrip.

Soto, Gary. *Black Hair* (Pitt Poetry Series). Pittsburgh: University of Pittsburgh Press, 1985.

For the Teacher. Giovanni, Nikki. *The Women and the Men*. New York: William Morrow and Company, 1975.

Norris, Ken, ed. *The Insecurity of Art: Essays on Poetics*. Montreal: Vehicule, 1982.

Soto, Gary. *Living Up the Street: Narrative Recollections*. San Francisco: Strawberry Hill, 1985.

———. *Who Will Know Us?* San Francisco: Chronicle Books, 1990.

Guidelines for Response

Thinking About the Poems, page 398

1. Responses will vary. Students may suggest that the speaker in the first poem is flexible, realistic, practical, prudent, insightful, or philosophical. Students may state that the speaker in the second poem is romantic, resourceful, confident, tender, or clever.

2. Some students may provide instances of being unable to do or have what they want, to go where they want, or to express real feelings. These students may mention examples of compromises that they made, times when they settled for less than what they wanted, or feelings they had when they realized their limitations. These students might add that the speaker in "Choices," though she makes compromises, retains honest standards, controlling situations as much as possible. Some students may cite examples that suggest the discrepancy between aspiration and achievement. Other students may offer examples of the predicament of not having enough money to buy a gift for someone they care about.

3. Most students may state that the speaker in "Choices" might have commended the speaker in "Oranges" for finding a way to buy the chocolate rather than disappoint his date and disclose his poverty. Some students may speculate that the speaker in "Choices" might have considered the speaker in "Oranges" lucky to find such a sympathetic, flexible saleslady. Still other students may say that the speaker in "Choices" might have suggested that the speaker in "Oranges" could have persuaded his date to select a nickel chocolate rather than risk being embarrassed.

4. Students may say that the speaker might have persuaded his date to select something else, made a secret arrangement with the saleslady to pay the other nickel later, or explained to his date that he did not have enough money.

⌘ Connections

Across Literature. Other works in this text that explore the choices made by characters include the following:

"Everyday Use," Alice Walker

from *Narrative of the Life*, Frederick Douglass

"Blues Ain't No Mockin Bird," Toni Cade Bambara

"Two Kinds," Amy Tan

"Seventeen Syllables," Hisaye Yamamoto

from *Kaffir Boy*, Mark Mathabane

A Raisin in the Sun, Lorraine Hansberry

"A Visit to Grandmother," William Melvin Kelley

Content Quiz

1. What does the speaker in "Choices" do when unable to express what he or she really feels? practices feeling what can be expressed

2. According to the speaker in "Choices," what distinguishes humans from other mammals? humans cry

3. In what season do the events in "Oranges" occur? winter

4. What does the boy in "Oranges" buy his date in the drugstore? a chocolate

5. How does the boy pay for his date's treat in "Oranges"? with a nickel and an orange

5. Some students might suggest that without the last three lines, the effect would be less powerful because the speaker would appear to be a complacent compromiser rather than an astute observer of the human condition. These students might add that the last three lines convey the poignancy of the speaker's predicament and, by extension, that of all humans. Other students may suggest that without the last three lines, the effect would be even more powerful because the emphasis would not shift from the speaker to humans in general.

6. Students may remark that Giovanni's use of contrast in the poem strikes a balance between the speaker's desires and limitations. Other students may suggest that Soto's use of contrast reinforces the change in the speaker's feeling from loneliness (cold and dark images) to affection (heat and light images).

7. Students may state that the lack of capitalization and punctuation creates interesting rhythms (lines 1–5), fluid transitions (lines 8–9 or 16–17), and a conversational tone throughout. Students also may mention that this omission suggests that the speaker is not rigid but flexible and amenable to compromises.

NAME ______________________________ DATE ______________

Choices (page 395)

Oranges (page 395)

Open-Book Test

Part 1 Broad Interpretation

Answer the following essay questions based on your understanding of the poems. Write your answers on a separate sheet of paper. (*25 points each*)

1. The Chinese writer Lin Yutang says, "A strong determination to get the best out of life, a keen desire to enjoy what one has, and no regrets if one fails: this is the secret of the Chinese genius for contentment." Do you think Giovanni would agree with this view of life? Support your answer with details from the poem "Choices."
2. Why do you think the speaker of "Oranges" did not ask the girl to choose a cheaper chocolate? Explain your answer.
3. How do you think the speaker of "Oranges" felt about his decision after he made it? Explain your answer and support it with details from the poem.

Part 2 Close Interpretation

Think about the values of the speaker that you can infer from each poem. In the middle boxes, note specific things, ideas, and/or feelings that each speaker values in life. In the boxes on the right, write brief notes on how each speaker deals with obstacles to achieving what's valuable. In the box at the bottom, briefly explain whose approach for dealing with obstacles you prefer. (*25 points*)

	What speaker values in life	How speaker deals with obstacles
"Choices"		
"Oranges"		
Which speaker do you think has the better approach for dealing with obstacles, and why?		

Marigolds

Eugenia Collier

page 399

- **Vocabulary Worksheet,** TG pages 293 and 294
- **Test,** TG pages 295 and 296

Objectives

1. To respond to a short story that explores a character's growth through suffering and hardship.
2. To appreciate the use of symbol in a short story.
3. To express ideas in a variety of writing formats: journal, cluster diagram, proposal, word search puzzle, script, sermon, editorial, note, dialogue.

Plot Summary

Grown-up and removed from the dusty shantytown of her childhood, Lizabeth recounts an incident that occurred one summer during the Great Depression when she was fourteen. While her father looked for work and her mother cleaned house for a white family, Lizabeth and her brother Joey entertained themselves—along with other unsupervised neighborhood children. A favorite game was annoying Miss Lottie—an old black woman who lived with her "queer-headed" son, John Burke, in a tumbledown shack. One day, Lizabeth led the gang in throwing rocks at the marigolds in Miss Lottie's garden—the only spot of beauty in their poor neighborhood. Later, she felt ashamed. But after awaking from a fitful sleep, Lizabeth overheard her father's despairing conversation with her mother about his joblessness and the family's poverty. Lizabeth, in an irrational fit of rage, ran back to Miss Lottie's garden in the early morning and destroyed her marigolds.

IdeaBank

▲ Motivation. To help students get started, present specific circumstances involving unhappiness or loss: the death of a pet, illness, a best friend leaving town, failure to accomplish something, or the family breadwinner losing a job. This activity could lead to a group discussion about destructive things that people may do when they are feeling extreme unhappiness: abusing drugs, fighting with other people, destroying property, or running away. Encourage students to offer more constructive ways to deal with situations of unhappiness or loss. ▲

IdeaBank

✱ Limited English Proficient Students
Encourage LEP students to draw a twenty-four-hour timeline of the story, beginning with 6 A.M. the first day and ending at approximately the same time the second day. On the timeline, they should mark the events in the story. Under each event, have them list the names of the characters involved as well as the setting. Pair each LEP student with a classmate who is proficient in English. Ask LEP students to retell the story, using their timelines, to their partners. ✱

InformationBank

Historical Note. The Great Depression began in the fall of 1929 with the stock market crash and the subsequent failure of banks across the United States. In the aftermath, factories closed, businesses went bankrupt, and unemployment soared. Blacks and whites lined up together for bread, milk, and work. However, blacks were particularly hard hit. The percentage of black unemployment was higher than the percentage of white unemployment. Blacks tended to be the first fired and last hired. In addition, blacks had less savings as a buffer than did whites, and black businesses were struck harder, because blacks had less money to spend than whites.

"What is important about any writer's work is the wisdom contained therein and the writer's ability to impart that wisdom in a way that is unforgettable."

— Eugenia Collier,
from *Black Woman Writers,* Mari Evans, ed., 1984

IdeaBank

✏ Self-Assessment. Ask the students to assess whether or not they understand the concept of literary symbolism by performing the following tasks: (1) write a short explanation, in their own words, of what a literary symbol is; (2) briefly analyze what the marigolds in the story symbolize; and (3) analyze a symbol in another short story that they have recently read—for example, the quilts in "Everyday Use." If a student cannot do one of these tasks or isn't confident about his or her answer, invite the student to come to you for help. ✏

⌘ Connections

Across the Language Arts. "Marigolds" contains many examples of figurative language, such as these:

> "Memory is an abstract painting" (metaphor)
>
> "illusive as smoke" (simile)
>
> "tangled together in the multi-colored skein of fourteen-going-on-fifteen" (metaphor)
>
> "days . . . running together . . . like a fresh watercolor painting left out in the rain" (simile)

Use these and other examples to point out how figurative language enriches writing. Encourage students to incorporate similes and metaphors into their own writing. If the grammar or composition book you use has a lesson on figurative language, you may want to refer to this lesson.

Guidelines for Response

Thinking About the Story, page 406

1. Among the emotions students may feel are anger, shame, confusion, sorrow, pity, and compassion.

2. Students may suggest that Lizabeth understands that planting marigolds is Miss Lottie's way of having something beautiful in life, of rising above her squalid circumstances. Lizabeth may, as an adult, have overcome some of her childhood poverty, but she realizes that every life has bleak moments and situations that cannot be controlled. For her, planting marigolds represents trying to deal with these moments, adding hope to life.

3. Students may attribute Lizabeth's behavior to her frustration and inability to cope with the circumstances of her life. Miss Lottie is different and defenseless and therefore an easy target for the children.

4. With the destruction of the marigolds, Lizabeth has discovered her own capacity for cruelty. Students may suggest that she has lost her innocence and is more aware of her own position in life and the difficulties it presents. Many students will note that Lizabeth has also acquired compassion—a characteristic of maturity—because she perceives the poignancy of Miss Lottie's quest for beauty.

5. Students may choose to highlight the following points when discussing the unhappiness of these characters:

> Miss Lottie: her bleak environment, her severely impaired son, her own physical impairments
>
> Lizabeth's father: his inability to find work, his shame in letting his wife support him, his frustration at watching his children run wild
>
> Lizabeth: the "you, who will not come" (as an adult), the frustrations that cause her to destroy the marigolds (as a child)

❓ Content Quiz

1. At the time of the events described in the story, Lizabeth's age is fourteen years.

2./3. After the children throw rocks at her marigolds, Miss Lottie calls her son, John Burke.

4. After hearing a conversation between her father and mother, Lizabeth leaves her home and runs to Miss Lottie's house.

5. At the end, when Lizabeth sees Miss Lottie looking at her, she feels shame, compassion.

6. Students may speculate that the use of flashback allows the narrator to tell the story as an adult who has thought about the experience and realizes its importance. They may also suggest that knowing that the narrator has overcome her early poverty helps the reader understand her character.

7. Students may trace Lizabeth's growing frustration as a reaction to her poverty, her boredom and restlessness, her uncertainty about whether she is an adult or child, the daily absence of her mother, and her father's disappointment in himself.

Analyzing the Writer's Craft, page 407

Students should infer that Miss Lottie is burdened with a son who is severely impaired and potentially violent as well. His disability extends to basic language skills, which may lead students to conclude that Miss Lottie is not only poor but also isolated and lonely.

Students' lists will likely include at least some of the following symbolic meanings:

> To Lizabeth as an adult: hope, beauty, childhood innocence, resilience
>
> To Lizabeth as a child: beauty, aspirations for a better life, cheer as opposed to bleakness
>
> To Miss Lottie: hope, possibilities, refusal to succumb to despair, resilience

Connecting Reading and Writing, page 407

Give students an opportunity to share and/or display their pictures for the class.

Use a copying or mimeograph machine to duplicate word-search puzzles for other members of the class.

To help prepare students for the option to assignment 4, you may want to have them review some of the dialogue in the excerpt from *Kaffir Boy*.

NAME ______________________ DATE ____________

Marigolds (page 399)

Vocabulary Worksheet

Essential Vocabulary

contrition *n*. A feeling of sorrow or regret for wrongdoing.

degradation *n*. A state of corruption and loss of dignity and humanity.

impoverished *adj*. Made poor; robbed of strength or power.

perverse *adj*. Stubbornly contrary, wrong, harmful, or against one's own interests.

poignantly *adv*. Sharply, keenly, or painfully affecting the feelings.

stoicism *n*. Stern control or holding in of emotion.

Useful Words

incongruency *n*. Lack of harmony, consistency, or appropriateness.

placidly *adv*. Calmly, without apparent emotion.

Fill in each set of blanks with the correct word from the word list. (Clue: The boxed letters will spell a two-word place in which marigolds are sometimes grown.)

1. If you can keep a straight face while watching a funny movie or stubbing your toe, you're an expert at this. _ _ _ _ [ ] _ _ _
2. How you might remember a friend you deeply miss. _ _ _ _ _ _ _ _ [ ] _
3. The most vicious villains in the James Bond spy stories are in a state of this. _ _ _ _ [ ] _ _ _ _ _ _
4. It would be surprising to hear someone describe a recent tragedy in his or her life this way. _ _ _ _ _ _ _ [ ]
5. Cutting off your nose to spite your face is an example of this kind of behavior. [ ] _ _ _ _ _ _ _
6. What finding a cabbage in a pear tree would be an example of. _ _ _ [ ] _ _ _ _ _ _ _ _
7. The feeling that a sincere apology contains. _ _ _ [ ] _ _ _ _ _ _
8. Badly eroded and overworked farmland might be described this way. _ _ _ _ _ _ _ _ [ ] _ _ _

NAME ______________________ DATE ____________

Marigolds (page 399)

Vocabulary Worksheet

Essential Vocabulary

futile *adj*. Useless; hopeless; ineffective.

Useful Words

chary *adj*. Not giving freely; sparing.
elude *v*. To escape or avoid through skill or cleverness.
exploit *n*. A feat or achievement.
illusive *adj*. Unreal.
nostalgia *n*. A longing for something far away or long ago.
pallet *n*. A small, crude bed or mattress used on the floor.
revel *v*. To take much pleasure in.
tersely *adv*. Using no more words than are needed to be clear.
verve *n*. Liveliness; spirit; energy.

Use the word list to work the crossword puzzle below.

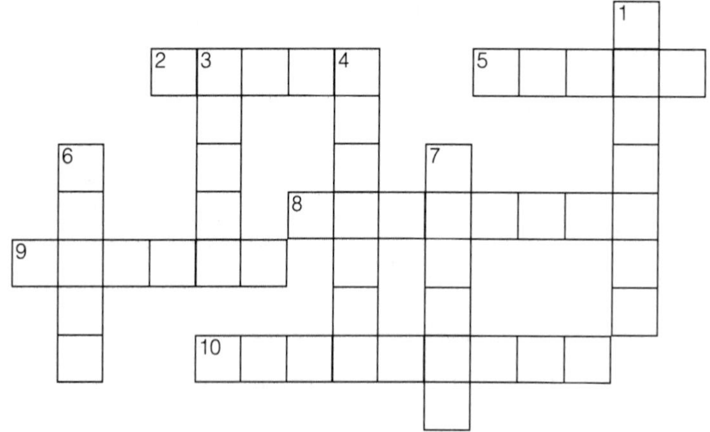

ACROSS

2. This is a quality found in the best racehorses and babysitters.
5. This is like delight. You might do it in victory or in your enemy's defeat.
8. This describes magic tricks and false impressions.
9. This is a great deal better than a bed of nails, but it's not exactly luxurious.
10. This is the feeling you have when you want what you used to have.

DOWN

1. Neighbors who talk like this don't spend a lot of time chatting over the fence.
3. This is what you try to do to "it" while playing tag.
4. Climbing Mt. Everest is this, and so is saving someone's life.
6. People who are hard to please are this with their praise.
7. This describes the search for a needle in a haystack.

NAME ______________________ DATE ______________

Marigolds (page 399)

Test

Part 1 Broad Interpretation

A. Answer the following essay questions based on your understanding of the story. Write your answers on a separate sheet of paper. *(15 points each)*

1. Why do you think Lizabeth destroys Miss Lottie's marigolds? Why do you think she immediately regrets doing it? Explain your answers.
2. The narrator says that the destruction of the marigolds was the "beginning of compassion, and one cannot have both compassion and innocence." How does this statement relate to the idea that Lizabeth's destroying the marigolds signals the end of her childhood and the beginning of her adulthood?
3. The marigold incident signals a change in Lizabeth. Is that also true of Miss Lottie? Explain your answer.

B. Think about the rite of passage Lizabeth undergoes in the story and how it changes her. Then, using your knowledge of the ways in which Lizabeth is changed, check the statements below that describe what you think Lizabeth would be like as an adult. If the statement describes what you think Lizabeth would be like only as a child, leave the box blank. *(15 points)*

	√ ADULT
Protecting her brother from harm	
Thinking of ways to disturb John Burke	
Expecting her parents to always be strong	
Volunteering at a nursing home for senior citizens	
Paying attention to the needs and feelings of others	
Feeling a strong need to prove herself to others her age	
Understanding why her father's problems drive him to tears	
Suggesting to her parents that she help out with their financial situation	

Part 2 Close Interpretation

A. Write **T** if the statement is true. Write **F** if it is false. *(4 points each)*

_____ **1.** Lizabeth's father's unemployment results from his laziness.

_____ **2.** The reason the narrator says John Burke speaks a "strange enchanted language" is that John Burke is from a foreign country.

_____ **3.** Joey thinks his sister's destruction of the marigolds is the greatest thing she's ever done.

_____ **4.** When the narrator says that the marigolds "interfered with the perfect ugliness of the place," she means that the beauty of the marigolds seemed out of place in Miss Lottie's yard.

_____ **5.** When the narrator calls Miss Lottie's house "a monument to decay," she wants the reader to understand that it is next to a graveyard.

_____ **6.** When the narrator says of Miss Lottie "the witch was no longer a witch," she means not that Miss Lottie has changed but that Lizabeth's perception of her has changed.

_____ **7.** The reason Miss Lottie does not plant marigolds again is that she is too crippled with arthritis.

_____ **8.** At the point in the story when the narrator says, "And I too have planted marigolds," she expects the reader to understand that she is referring to marigolds strictly as flowers.

B. Think about what marigolds and dust symbolize in the story. Then, on the chart below, circle all the possible things that each symbol represents in the story. *(4 points each)*

9. MARIGOLDS	**10.** DUST
Hope	Despair
Death	Poverty
Responsibility	Love
Beauty	Freedom
Accomplishment	Barrenness
Poverty	Accomplishment

My City

James Weldon Johnson

The Tropics in New York

Claude McKay

page 408

- **Vocabulary Worksheet,** TG page 299
- **Test,** TG page 300

Objective

To respond to two poems concerning New York City.

IdeaBank

▲ **Motivation.** As an alternative to the Connecting Writing and Reading activity, have students create in their journals cluster diagrams of words associated with New York City. Encourage students who have lived in or visited New York City to share their experiences with the class. Ask students for as many details as they can think of that relate to the city, such as those in the following example:

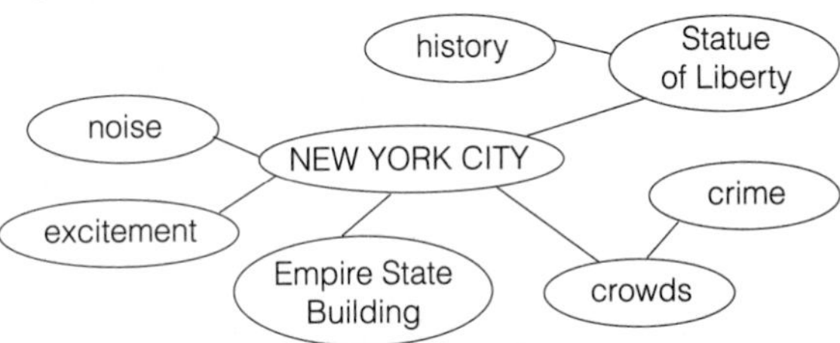

Then have students read the poems and add more details to their cluster diagrams. ▲

IdeaBank

❧ Gifted and Talented Students

1. Have students write a short poem about a place with which they are very familiar. Ask them to include details to help readers form a mental picture of the place. Students should use "My City" and "The Tropics in New York" as models.

2. Ask students to read the poem "Mannahatta" by Walt Whitman. Have students compare that poem with "My City" by writing a dialogue between Whitman and Johnson in which they comment on each other's poems. ❧

InformationBank

Literary Note. James Weldon Johnson's "My City" is a Petrarchan sonnet. The octave, the first eight lines, raises the question: what would the speaker miss most when he or she dies? The octave then presents beautiful experiences of nature that would not be the most painful loss. The sestet presents the answer: the speaker would miss New York City the most. The rhyme scheme varies the form somewhat: *abbacddc*, *efefgg*.

Vlasta Zábranský © 1972 Roháč

InformationBank

Biographical Note. James Weldon Johnson resigned his job as principal of Stanton School in Jacksonville, Florida, and moved to New York City in 1902. Once there, he and his brother, John Rosamond Johnson, collaborated in writing more than two hundred popular songs. While his brother and another partner, Bob Cole, were performing in vaudeville, Johnson enrolled in classes at Columbia University, concentrating on drama and English literature. Although he had begun writing poetry as an undergraduate at Atlanta University, Johnson's poetry was not published until 1913, when his poem entitled "Fifty Years" was published in *The New York Times*. Johnson treasured his time in New York and in his autobiography, *Along This Way* (1933), recalled his sorrow upon leaving the city to serve as United States consul to Venezuela: "New York had been a good godmother to me, almost a fairy godmother, and it gave me a wrench to turn my back on her."

⌘ Connections

Across the Humanities. Have students report on the contributions of the following figures during the Harlem Renaissance: Louis "Satchmo" Armstrong, Paul Robeson, Scott Joplin, and Duke Ellington (music); Bill Robinson (dance); George Washington Carver (science); A. Philip Randolph (labor relations); Ida Wells-Barnett (journalism); Jesse Owens, Jack Johnson, and Joe Louis (sports).

ResourceBank

For the Student. Johnson, James Weldon. *God's Trombones*. (Poet's Series). New York: Penguin U.S.A., 1976.

McKay, Claude. *Gingertown*. Reprint, 1932 ed. (Short Story Index and Reprint Service). Salem, N.H.: Ayer Company Publishers, Inc., 1972.

For the Teacher. Johnson, James Weldon. *The Autobiography of an Ex-Colored Man*. New York: Random House, Inc., 1989.

McKay, Claude. *Selected Poems of Claude McKay*. New York: Harcourt Brace Jovanovich, 1969.

Wintz, Cary D. *Black Culture and the Harlem Renaissance*. Houston: Rice University Press, 1988.

Guidelines for Response

Thinking About the Poems, page 410

1. Some students may say that New York City seems a vital, exciting place. Others may say that Manhattan seems too large and unmanageable, too far removed from nature and simplicity. Still others may come away with ambivalent feelings about New York.

2. Students may notice that the speaker of "The Tropics in New York" is very homesick; New York probably seems impersonal and noisy to him because he misses the natural beauty of home, with its rills, dawns, skies, and hills. Students may feel that the speaker of "My City" has a much more positive view of New York, perhaps from having lived there for a long time. The speaker in "My City" clearly values the city more than a natural environment, for in dying he would miss the city more than the "smell of flowers" or "the singing birds," whereas the speaker in "The Tropics in New York" is hungry for the natural landscape of his youth and "the old, familiar ways."

3. Some students may feel that New York is a large, frightening, crime-ridden place. Some students may have had negative experiences in New York or some other city and may express appreciation for the speaker's perspective in "The Tropics in New York." Others may argue that New York is a wonderful, vibrant place. From firsthand experience or from reading and viewing, they may tell of its diverse population, its many attractions, and its distinguished history. They may agree with the speaker's emphasis on Manhattan's "sights and sounds, her smells, / Her crowds, her throbbing force" (lines 9–10) in "My City."

4. Some students may say that seeing the tropical fruits of home triggers the speaker's nostalgia in "The Tropics in New York." Others may suggest that if the products of home did not cause the speaker's homesickness, something else would and that, given the speaker's love of home, frequent longing for home may be inevitable.

5. Some students may feel that James Weldon Johnson conveys the depth of his feeling by first listing beautiful things in nature that will not be "the keenest loss" (line 3). By doing so, he makes his images of Manhattan, with "Her shining towers, her avenues, her slums" (line 12), more vivid. Some students may feel that Johnson's emphasis on the sensory experience of Manhattan, with her "sights and sounds, her smells" is what most powerfully conveys his feelings. For "The Tropics in New York" some students may mention that the speaker's listing of colorful, exotic fruits best conveys the depth of his homesickness. For other students, the images evoking the speaker's love of home such as "low-singing rills, / And dewy dawns, and mystical blue skies / In benediction over nun-like hills" (lines 6–8) are most powerful.

6. Some students may say that both the immigrants in Marshall's essay and the speaker in McKay's poem love their homelands and feel uneasy in New York City. Other students may add that the immigrants in Marshall's essay seem tough-minded, receive strength from each other and from a shared language, and are determined to gain financial security in America. The speaker in McKay's poem, on the other hand, is an isolated individual, stricken to the heart with longing for his native land.

❓ Content Quiz

1. What will the speaker in "My City" miss most when he or she dies? Manhattan's sights, sounds, and smells

2. Name one detail about Manhattan included in "My City." [Students may name any one.] crowds; throbbing force; subtle spells; shining towers; avenues; slums

3. Name one export from the tropics mentioned in "The Tropics in New York." [Students may name any one.] bananas; ginger-root; cocoa in pods; alligator pears; tangerines; mangoes; grapefruit

4. Name one thing that the speaker in "The Tropics in New York" recalls at the sight of fruit set in a window. [Students may name any one.] fruit trees by rills; dewy dawns; blue skies over hills

5. At the end of the poem, what does the speaker in "The Tropics in New York" do? weeps

"Every race and every nation should be judged by the best it has been able to produce, not by the worst." — James Weldon Johnson,

NAME ______________________ DATE ____________

My City (page 408)

The Tropics in New York (page 408)

Vocabulary Worksheet

Essential Vocabulary

benediction *n.* A blessing.
laden *adj.* Loaded; burdened.
mystical *adj.* Having a spiritual nature.

Read the following story and use context clues to figure out the meanings of the underlined words. Then use these meanings to help you work the exercise below. If you like, you may use a dictionary to check the meaning of a word.

The deep tones of the Reverend Mrs. Ellerson's voice echoed in the still air of the church as her congregation turned to file quietly out. As the organist began to play, the thoughts of the people were on the beauty of the final scripture passage and the wisdom of Rev. Ellerson's sermon. The church was simple but beautiful, and there was a feeling of peace in its strong lines. Outside, the sun must have broken through the clouds because, suddenly, a beam of light poured like the sword of an angel through the clear panes of the front window. At one point it crossed the aisle, and the face of each worshipper lit up as though from within as he or she passed through it. It appeared for one dazzling moment as though the minister's **benediction** had truly and miraculously bestowed grace on each person in the room.

And perhaps it had.

But human nature is human nature. And if the significance of the light was **mystical**, the reaction of the congregation was all too grounded in the practical, the material, even the worldly. As the people passed through the light, hands reached into pockets and into purses **laden** with wallets, lipsticks, change purses, credit cards, combs, and candies—and pulled out sunglasses.

Circle the word that does not belong.

1. benediction	generosity	blessing	dedication	prayer
2. laden	heaped	loaded	burdened	tiresome
3. mystical	spiritual	confusing	unworldly	holy

My City (page 408)
The Tropics in New York (page 408)

Open-Book Test

Part 1 Broad Interpretation

Answer the following essay questions based on your understanding of the poems. Write your answers on a separate sheet of paper. *(20 points each)*

1. What sense of Manhattan do you get from "My City"? Explain your answer.
2. Do you think the emotion expressed in "The Tropics in New York" goes beyond simple homesickness? Explain your answer.
3. Which of the environments described in these two poems seems more appealing to you? Explain your answer.

Part 2 Close Interpretation

A. Each stanza of "The Tropics in New York" conveys a distinct attitude on the part of the speaker. In the boxes on the left, describe the speaker's attitude in each stanza. Choose from the words below or use your own. Then, in the boxes on the right, make notes about how that attitude is conveyed—through colorful words, vivid images, figurative language, or direct expression of emotion. (*30 points*)

reverent ironic intense bright sorrowful disappointed casual
hurt angry approving nostalgic wistful cheerful objective

	Speaker's attitude	How it is conveyed
Stanza 1		
Stanza 2		
Stanza 3		

B. Briefly answer the following questions about "My City." (*10 points*)

What question is asked in the octave, or first eight lines?	What answer is given in the sestet, or last six lines?

from Mississippi Solo

Eddy Harris

page 411

■ **Vocabulary Worksheet,** TG page 303

■ **Test,** TG pages 305 and 306

Objectives

1. To respond to an excerpt from an autobiographical account of a river journey.

2. To practice the reading and thinking techniques of an independent reader.

Plot Summary

In this excerpt from the book about his solo canoe trip down the Mississippi River, Eddy Harris relates his adventures at Natchez, Mississippi. After surviving a sudden, violent downpour, Harris arrives in Natchez, where he meets a variety of characters. Among them are the city attorney, who gives him a tour of Natchez, and a religious zealot traveling down the river in a bicycle-powered rowboat. Harris shares with the zealot a Thanksgiving dinner of rice and canned beef stew.

"April 20: The weather continues sunny and warm."

IdeaBank

❧ Gifted and Talented Students. Encourage students to read portions of other autobiographical works describing solo adventures, such as *Dove* by Robin Lee Graham (Harper and Row, 1972), the story of a 16-year-old boy's solo voyage around the world; and *Woodswoman* by Anne LaBastille (Dutton, 1976), the account of an ecologist's life in the log cabin she built in the Adirondack wilderness. Have students draw comparisons among the personalities, emotions, and experiences of the authors. ❧

IdeaBank

▲ Motivation. Have students copy into their journals the following list of activities that a person might do alone. Ask students to rate each activity according to the degree of courage required and to circle two or three activities they would like to try.

- sail around the world
- hike across the United States
- bicycle from coast to coast
- cross the Sahara Desert on camelback
- orbit the earth in a space capsule
- live for a year on a deserted island ▲

InformationBank

Literary Note. Because of their religious references, the lines below were deleted from page 415, line 26, following the words *wild eyes*:

> "The eyes flared when he told me about the revolution.
>
> " 'It's time,' he said. 'If the country won't turn to Jesus, it's up to me to make them, and if they still won't listen, I've been given the charge to destroy the country, I'm only letting them have one more chance.'
>
> "When he started quoting from the Bible, I knew breakfast had lasted long enough."

IdeaBank

✤ Multimodal Activities

1. Have students create a display of rivercraft: for example, paddlewheelers, flatboats, rowboats, and canoes. The display might include models, drawings, diagrams, and photographs. Have students explain what rivercraft Harris could have encountered and what rivercraft he actually did encounter, based on the information in the selection.

2. A group of students with an interest in art could create a movie poster advertising a documentary film based on *Mississippi Solo*.

3. Suggest that students present as Readers' Theater several scenes from Eddy Harris's adventure. Suitable scenes would be the storm, his encounter with the three women, or either of the scenes with James White, the religious zealot. Students should create appropriate sound effects to suggest such things as the weather and the calliope on the *Delta Queen*. ✤

IdeaBank

✲ **Collaborative Learning.** Have students work in small groups to create travel brochures. Ask them to use specific details from the excerpt from *Mississippi Solo* to attract tourists to a rafting trip down the river, including the sights, sounds, and experiences related by Eddy Harris. Have students work together to illustrate their brochures with photographs, maps, and drawings. ✲

⌘ Connections

Across Literature. Another work in this text that describes a person facing danger alone is "The Legend of Gregorio Cortez" by Américo Paredes (page 6).

Across the Curriculum. Have students create a map showing the route of Harris's trip down the Mississippi River from Lake Itasca, Minnesota, to New Orleans, Louisiana. The map should include important cities along the river and geological points of interest. Alternatively, students might trace the route on an existing map of the United States.

Guidelines for Response

Discussion Questions

1. How do you react to Eddy Harris's journey down the Mississippi?

[Reactions will differ. Some students will be very impressed by Harris's feat and admire him for trying something so difficult; others may feel that his accomplishment was not a very significant one and that it did not benefit anyone other than himself.]

2. Why do you think Harris enjoys his contact with Jim White?

[Students may indicate that although Harris feels that Jim White is a little crazy, he still admires the man and knows that in some ways they are kindred spirits. There is some similarity in their voyages; both men are traveling on the river alone, for reasons that may not be appreciated or shared by many other people. Also, at this point in their travels both men are lonely, which contributes to the comradery they experience. Although their Thanksgiving dinner is a can of beef stew and some rice, it seems opulent because both men are feeling at one with nature and close to the simple things in life.

3. Why do you think Eddy Harris made this journey down the Mississippi?

[Responses may vary. Harris probably wanted to get away from routine life for a while and do something different. He also may have wanted to get close to nature and to prove his physical resourcefulness. Perhaps he wanted to see the country in a slow, meditative, and direct way. Maybe he saw the trip as an opportunity to figure out some things about himself. You might tell students about Huck Finn's trip down the Mississippi, suggesting that perhaps Harris had this archetypal journey in mind.]

4. How would you describe Harris's attitude toward nature? Use examples from the selection to support your ideas.

[Many students will say that Harris has a deep respect for nature and enjoys its variety. As he says early on, "Too many good days, too many bad days—you need some break in the monotony of one to appreciate the other" (page 411). Harris also feels at one with nature, saying that the river is "a comfortable buddy sharing a lazy day" (page 411). Even when he is battling the river during the storm, Harris says, "I was one with this river, and nothing could happen to me" (page 412).]

5. Why do you think Harris includes the street scene with "the three prettiest women in Mississippi" and his brief interaction with Bill?

[Students may suggest that Harris wants to show the different ways that people react to him; he may use these incidents to explore the theme that people react differently to outsiders. The women are haughty and ignore him because he looks weatherbeaten and unkempt; they quite literally won't give him the time of day. In contrast, Bill is friendly and extends himself to help Harris. By including both of these encounters from Natchez, Harris gives a balanced view of the city. Some students may think that Harris includes these incidents merely to give the reader an indication of his experiences in Natchez, not to develop any particular theme.]

ResourceBank

For the Student. Harris, Eddy. *Mississippi Solo: A River Quest*. New York: Lyons & Burford, Publishers, Incorporated, 1982.

❓ Content Quiz

1. By what means of transportation is Eddy Harris traveling on the Mississippi River? canoe
2. During the rainstorm, where does Harris take shelter? in a grove of flooded trees
3. Who gives Harris a tour of the city? the acting city attorney
4. What would be a sign to Jim White that his voyage was finished? if his boat fell apart
5. What holiday did Harris and Jim White celebrate together? Thanksgiving

NAME ______________________________ DATE ______________

from Mississippi Solo (page 411)

Essential Vocabulary

comradery *n.* Loyalty and warm, friendly feeling among companions, associates, etc.
ethereal *adj.* Very light; airy; like the upper regions of space.
intuition *n.* The direct knowing or learning of something without the conscious use of reasoning.
skeptic *n.* A person who doubts religious teachings.
zealot *n.* A person who shows passion and devotion for something, especially to an excessive degree.

Useful Words

askance *adv.* With suspicion.
disperse *v.* To break up and scatter in all directions.
puce *n.* Brownish purple.
taint *v.* To affect with something harmful.

Fill in each blank with the word from the word list that best completes the sentence.

1. It seems to me that somebody could change the horrid color of prune juice. It tastes O.K. but, as far as I'm concerned, there's no excuse for ________________ juice.
2. She suspected me of lying about being a Scot. She looked ________________ at my pants as if not wearing a kilt proved my guilt.
3. Your reputation as an educated person will suffer if your grammar isn't good. Saying "It's a pretty day, ain't it?" will ________________ it.
4. I once had doubts about what I learned in church. Then I was struck by lightning and became a believer. When I became electric, I ceased to be a ________________.
5. I had a good idea about who the criminal was without ever really thinking about it. My suspicion was ________________.
6. I don't like rice puffs; I like oatmeal. I prefer my cereal less ________________.
7. Zelda Sue spends all her time volunteering at the zoo. She doesn't do anything else; she doesn't even talk about anything else. In short, Zelda Sue's a zoo ________________.
8. We shape our clay and apply our glazes and bake our pots together. We have a lot in common and feel toward each other a pottery ________________.
9. All for one and one for all! Even if we stick together, we know things might be bad, but they will be worse if we ________________.

NAME ______________________________ DATE ______________

from Mississippi Solo (page 411)

Test

Part 1 Broad Interpretation

Answer the following essay questions based on your understanding of the selection. Write your answers on a separate sheet of paper. *(15 points each)*

1. Why does Harris's riverside meal with Jim feel like a real Thanksgiving dinner? What does he have to be especially thankful for?
2. Why do you think Harris and Jim are drawn together? What do they have in common?
3. Why do you think Bill, the attorney, helps Harris and shows him around the town? Explain your answer.
4. Harris says, "Too many good days, too many bad days—you need some break in the monotony of one to appreciate the other." How does the day described in the selection help to break the monotony for him? What do you think it helps him to appreciate? Use examples from the selection to support your answers.

Part 2 Close Interpretation

A. Think about how Harris's feelings vary during the course of the day described in the selection. Then, write the letters of the words in the appropriate boxes below to describe how he felt at certain points in the day. A word may be used more than once or not at all. *(5 points each)*

a. angry
b. excited
c. grateful
d. peaceful
e. indifferent
f. pleased
g. annoyed
h. terrified
i. concerned
j. astonished
k. safe
l. welcome
m. outraged
n. offended
o. appreciative

1. When he's in the storm	**2.** When the three women ignore him	**3.** When the attorney helps him	**4.** When he shares dinner with Jim

NAME ______________________________ DATE ______________

B. Write the letter of the best answer. *(5 points each)*

_____ **5.** When Harris says "the voice of the river came out and spoke to me teasingly but with a chill of seriousness down my spine," he means that

a. he noticed that the river made sounds.

b. he felt as if the river were warning him.

c. he had a dream that the river could talk.

d. he could hear the river literally talking to him.

_____ **6.** Harris does not ride on the *Delta Queen* because

a. he doesn't want to ride.

b. he doesn't have any money.

c. the captain discourages him from riding.

d. the captain refuses to let him come on board.

_____ **7.** When Jim and Harris have breakfast in the hotel restaurant, they encounter

a. open rudeness.

b. grudging civility.

c. courtesy, but also curiosity.

d. a warm, enthusiastic welcome.

_____ **8.** After Jim tells Harris about his religious calling, Harris is careful about what he says because

a. he is not religious.

b. he thinks that Jim is fooling him.

c. he believes that Jim will become violent.

d. he feels uneasy about Jim's predictions of disaster and ruin.

The Writer's Message: Shedding Light on Human Life

Below are suggested answers for the chart assigned on page 417 of the student book. For each of the eight other selections in this unit, one or more themes are recorded. Accept other answers if students can support them with evidence from the selections.

Selection	Human nature	Relationships between individuals	Individual in society
Kitchenette Building			The struggle to survive keeps the poor from nurturing their dreams.
Speech to the Young . . .	Wisdom consists in living in the present rather than in the past or the future.		
Horses Graze	Humans lack the dignity, wisdom, and contentment of animals.		
A Raisin in the Sun	Despite setbacks, a person should not give up a dream worth realizing.	Mutual respect helps unite family members motivated by different goals and needs.	The individual must stand up for his or her principles despite pressure from society to abandon them.
A Visit to Grandmother		A parent with the best intentions may unwittingly fail a child.	
Choices	Even when forced to compromise, an individual must live by a personal code.		
Oranges		Tender gestures nurture human relationships.	
Marigolds	Personal unhappiness can erupt in a cruel act.	Compassion comes when someone realizes the suffering he or she has caused.	

Evaluation Guide for Writing Assignment

The well-developed student introduction will meet the following criteria:

- Recommends three selections to teachers
- Provides reasons why the themes of these selections are particularly relevant to teenagers
- Explains the reasons by citing details from the selections and from the experiences of teenagers

Vocabulary Worksheets

Unit 1

From the Poets in the Kitchen (page 53)
1. encompass
2. exhort
3. aesthetic
4. voraciously
5. indiscriminately
6. adversity
7. apprenticeship
8. legacy
9. infuse
10. testimony

Clue = pots and pans

The Way It Is (page 59)
1. commercial
2. inaudible
3. dominant
4. billowed
5. seizure

Everyday Use (page 72)
oppress, recompose, furtive, sidle, clabber

Sweet Potato Pie (page 81)
1. work
2. fad
3. top
4. brick
5. clear
6. right
7. fear
8. form

Unit 2

***from* To Be a Slave** (page 90)
1. evolve
2. inexhaustible
3. susceptible
4. stupor
5. align

***from* Narrative of the Life** (page 96)
1. dregs
2. singular
3. elasticity
4. stupor
5. languishing
6. epoch

As I Grew Older
Any Human to Another (page 101)
1. marrow
2. diverse
3. unsheathed

***from* Letter from Birmingham Jail** (page 108)
1. rabid
2. moratorium
3. oppressor
4. anarchy
5. retaliated
6. paternalistically

November Cotton Flower
A Note of Humility (page 121)
1. assume
2. meager; drought
3. assume; assume
4. drought
5. meager
6. meager; assume

Unit 3

How It Feels to Be Colored Me (page 136)
1. constrict
2. deplore
3. veneer
4. extenuating
5. pigmentation
6. raiment
7. thorax
8. exultingly

Clue = identity

I Have a Dream (page 141)
1. discrimination
2. degenerate
3. languish
4. tribulation
5. segregation
6. militancy
7. redemptive
8. discords
9. manacles

Getting a Job
***from* I Know Why the Caged Bird Sings** (page 147)
1. charade
2. hypocrisy
3. gumption
4. supercilious
5. alien
6. ancestor
7. conveyance
8. aphorism
9. terse
10. aperture

Clue = dog catcher

***from* Barrio Boy** (page 153)
1. promenade
2. formidable
3. boisterous
4. alien
5. reverie
6. indignation
7. menace
8. anchorage

***from* Hunger of Memory** (page 159)
1. a
2. b
3. b
4. a

My Delicate Heart Condition (page 173)
1. underprivileged
2. infirmary
3. revival
4. rheumatic
5. phantom

Unit 4

Two Kinds (page 182)
1. lamented
2. discordant
3. envision
4. fiasco
5. prelude
6. devastate
7. prodigy

Seventeen Syllables (page 188)
1. vernaculars
2. vacillate
3. anaesthetic
4. indiscretion
5. glib
6. repartee
7. garrulous
8. rapt
9. infinitesimal

***from* Kaffir Boy** (page 194)
1. coterie
2. austere
3. inscrutable
4. admonishing
5. mores

***from* Arctic Dreams** (page 204)
1. benign
2. implacable
3. austerity
4. gargantuan
5. estrangement
6. adumbration
7. pervasive
8. fecundity
9. fixation
10. awry

Clue = ice and snow

***from* Notes of a Native Son** (page 209)
1. conundrum
2. rhetoric
3. interloper
4. articulate
5. advent
6. ambiguity
7. bravura
8. relentlessly

***from* American Hunger** (page 215)
1. subjective
2. cynical
3. libation
4. disconsolate
5. translucently
6. lucid
7. reprisal
8. obsession
9. usurp

Unit 5

A Very Old Man with Enormous Wings (page 224)
1. decrepit
2. repose
3. cataclysm
4. conjecture
5. hermetic
6. tribulation
7. terrestrial
8. providential

Clue = Colombia

The Youngest Doll (page 230)
1. frenzied
2. ostentatious
3. impassive
4. exorbitant
5. furtively
6. fixedly
7. stupor

Clue = Rosario

Tenement Room: Chicago Loo-Wit (page 239)
1. butte
2. tenement
3. gaudy
4. destitution

The Form of the Sword (page 250)
1. interlocutor
2. opprobrium
3. vertigo
4. utopian
5. infamy
6. aplomb
7. apodictic

Ode to the Watermelon (page 255)
1. intense
2. embers
3. hemisphere
4. profundity
5. firmament
6. phlegmatic

Unit 6

Kitchenette Building
One wants a Teller in a time like this
Speech to the Young/Speech to the Progress-Toward
Horses Graze (page 262)
1. awful aria; delightful ditty
2. oodles of oblivion; a little alertness
3. forceful folly; weak wisdom
4. admirable affirmation; nasty no
5. giddy giver; solemn snatcher
6. majestic mountain; plain plain
7. involuntary increase; purposeful plunge
8. tranquil trapper; distressed deliverer

A Raisin in the Sun (page 269)
1. assimilationism
2. retrogression
3. graphically
4. indictment
5. resignation
6. disheveled
7. beseechingly
8. vindicated
9. defer

Clue = a grape in the shade

A Visit to Grandmother (page 283)
1. a
2. d

Marigolds (page 293)
1. stoicism
2. poignantly
3. degradation
4. placidly
5. perverse
6. incongruency
7. contrition
8. impoverished

Clue = clay pots

Marigolds (page 294)

Across
2. verve
5. revel
8. illusive
9. pallet
10. nostalgia

Down
1. tersely
3. elude
4. exploit
6. chary
7. futile

My City
The Tropics in New York (page 299)
1. generosity
2. tiresome
3. confusing

***from* Mississippi Solo** (page 303)
1. puce
2. askance
3. taint
4. skeptic
5. intuition
6. ethereal
7. zealot
8. comraderie
9. disperse

Tests

The guidelines for scoring essay questions and graphics are meant to provide help in scoring a range of responses—not to indicate the minimal requirements for a "correct" answer. The introductory statement for each guideline or set of guidelines indicates whether the responses "should" be found in high scoring answers or whether they may "possibly" be found in high-scoring answers.

Answers for objective questions indicate the only correct choice or choices and, where applicable, list additional answers. An answer choice indicated as "possible" is allowable but need not be included for the answer to be considered correct. Such a choice is not in itself a complete answer and if given alone should receive only partial credit. Similarly, a correct answer accompanied by an answer not listed as either correct or possible should be given only partial credit. Multiple answer choices of equal value must all be indicated for full credit. If fewer than all are indicated by the student, only partial credit should be given.

Students should be allowed to use their books for all tests on poetry. Each of these tests is marked **Open-Book Test.** Page numbers after titles of selections refer to pages on which tests appear in the Teacher's Guide. All other page numbers refer to the student book.

Unit 1 CELEBRATING HERITAGE

The Legend of Gregorio Cortez (pages 43 and 44)

Part 1

A. (20 points each: 4 points for usage and mechanics; 4 points for clarity and coherence; 6 points for soundness of idea; 6 points for adequate detail)

1. Answers will vary. Students might point out that Cortez is similar to tall tale heroes in that
   a. some of his virtues and accomplishments are exaggerated, such as when he takes on hundreds of sheriffs at one time. (page 12)
   b. he embodies certain values of his culture, such as working hard, providing for one's family, respecting older people, and preserving the well-being of the community.

   Students might point out that Cortez is unlike tall tale heroes in that
   a. most of his virtues and accomplishments are within the realm of human possibility.
   b. his strength of character is more important than his skills.
2. Answers will vary. Students may name any one of the following contributors:
   a. The bigoted sheriff who shoots Cortez's brother.
   b. Cortez's vaguely defined enemies who poison him.
   c. El Teco, who betrays him. (pages 15–16)
   d. Cortez's strong family loyalty, which draws him into conflict with the law and later motivates him to surrender.

B. (28 points) Answers will vary. A good answer for the second quotation might be similar to the following:
   a. The quotation does support the message of the story.
   b. Cortez is presented from the beginning of the story as a highly skilled person in all areas of his life.
   c. These skills, combined with his physical and moral courage, save his life during his encounters with the Rangers and with the courts.

Part 2

A. (32 points) Answers will vary. A good answer might be similar to the following:
   a. Everyday life: modesty, skill, loyalty, hard work, quietness, honesty, courtesy, shrewdness, endurance, peaceableness, respectfulness.
   b. Crisis: courage, cleverness, loyalty, trickiness, honesty, courtesy, shrewdness, endurance.

***from* When Heaven and Earth Changed Places** (pages 49 and 50)

Part 1 (15 points each: 3 points for usage and mechanics; 3 points for clarity and coherence; 5 points for soundness of idea; 4 points for adequate detail)

1. Answers will vary, depending on the students' interpretation of the concept of heroism. All answers should reveal the students' realization that what Bay Ly's father is asking
   a. requires tremendous courage.
   b. is a way of serving her country.
   c. will be very difficult.

   For some students, these points will support the idea of heroism. For others, heroism may be more closely bound with war and physical courage in battle.
2. Answers will vary but should include points similar to the following:
   a. Almost an entire generation has been killed or has left home.
   b. Bay Ly's position as daughter has been altered by the loss of the family's sons.
   c. The family is able to maintain its meager standard of living only through tremendous effort by both parents.
3. Answers will vary but should reflect students' understanding that it would not have been as intimate because he
   a. would not have spent as much time with her.
   b. would have been more strict with her.
   c. would not have expected as much from her.
   d. would not have shared as many of his thoughts with her.
   e. would not have felt it appropriate to teach her about her responsibility to herself and her nation.

Part 2

A. (22 points) Answers will vary. Possible answers include the following:

a. Behavior expected of women: obedience, quietness, self-sacrifice, not being active outside the home.
b. Behavior of women in Bay Ly's family: courage, strength, willingness to fight.

B. (3 points each)

1. N 2. T 3. N 4. T 5. T

C. (18 points) Graphs will vary but should reflect students' understanding that those things that are *not* terribly important to him are material wealth, the Republicans' political rhetoric, and the communists' political rhetoric.

From the Poets in the Kitchen (pages 55 and 56)

Part 1

A. (16 points each: 3 points for usage and mechanics; 3 points for clarity and coherence; 5 points for soundness of idea; 5 points for adequate detail)

1. Answers will vary. Students might point out that it
   a. gives them a sense of community.
   b. allows them to express themselves.
   c. serves as therapy.
   d. gives them a refuge from an overwhelming world.
2. Answers will vary. Students might mention that
   a. the language of the women is lively, condensed, full of imagery and insight, and often interestingly contradictory.
   b. the women express their creativity through words, as do poets.
   c. the writer believes that poetry is a way of looking at the world as much as it is a way of organizing words on paper.
   d. the writer believes that life is poetry.
3. Answers will vary but students should note that these are African-American writers. Students might mention that the author finds
   a. a sense of shared feelings.
   b. comfort.
   c. a sense of belonging.
   d. an awareness of her heritage.

   Students might point out that many of these things are what the women in the kitchen find in their talk with one another.

B. (1 point each)

4. T 9. T
5. T 10. T
6. N 11. T
7. T 12. N
8. N 13. T

Part 2

A. (18 points) Answers will vary. For the first saying/aphorism, students might say that the saying and the aphorism both seem to suggest that God is not interested in appearances. For the second saying/aphorism, students might say that the saying and the aphorism both concern the power of the spoken word, but the aphorism does not stress the necessity of defending oneself.

B. (3 points each)

1. N (page 33)
2. R
3. R (page 34)
4. N (page 33)
5. R
6. R
7. R
8. N

The Way It Is (page 61)

Part 1

A. (16 points each: 3 points for usage and mechanics; 3 points for clarity and coherence; 6 points for soundness of idea; 4 points for adequate detail)

1. Answers will vary. Possible answers include the following:
   a. The speaker likes herself and believes that she is attractive.
   b. She feels that she is more attractive than white people who have "commercial" beauty.
   c. She feels special in that, while others accept the media image of women's beauty, she has her own sense of beauty.
2. Answers will vary. Possible answers include the following:
   a. The media values white skin, blue eyes, and blonde hair.
   b. The speaker values dark skin and dark hair like her mother has.
   c. The speaker's sense of beauty has helped her self-esteem by making her feel beautiful.
3. Answers will vary. Possible answers include the following:
   a. The speaker is explaining her point of view in a direct way, that is, telling it the way it is.
   b. The speaker sees society's vision of beauty, but expresses a different one.
   c. The speaker accepts herself the way she is.

B. (16 points) Answers will vary. Ways in which the speaker is like her mother include the following:

a. She has dark skin.
b. She has dark hair.
c. She accepts herself and feels that she is attractive.

Ways in which the speaker is different from her mother include the following:

a. The speaker is not as tall or as dark as her mother.
b. She is bonier and more angular.
c. She does not have her mother's Southern accent.
d. She is not as beautiful.

Part 2 (12 points each)

1. a (page 41)
2. b (page 41)
3. a (page 41)

Mother to Son (page 62)

Part 1 (20 points each: 4 points for usage and mechanics; 4 points for clarity and coherence; 6 points for soundness of idea; 6 points for adequate detail)

1. Answers will vary but should reflect students' understanding that the mother is advising her son to persevere and not to give up.
2. Answers will vary but should reflect students' understanding that life for the mother has been difficult, discouraging at times, an ongoing struggle, and a process of carrying on against all odds.
3. Answers will vary. Possible answers include the following:
   a. A crystal stairway would be beautiful, glossy, smooth, appealing, and welcoming.
   b. A crystal stairway exists only in the imagination, so a person who wishes for one is being unrealistic.
   c. The word *crystal* suggests something expensive, glamorous, and delicate, unlike the life the mother has led.
   d. The word *stair* suggests a journey that requires effort, like life.
   e. The metaphor of a crystal stair sets up a clear, easy-to-visualize contrast between what her life has been and what she may have dreamed of.

Part 2

A. (20 points) Answers will vary. Possible answers include the following:

a. My life has included a number of difficult and painful situations.
b. Facing changes in my life.

c. Don't give up; persevere.
d. Carrying on in life even when I didn't know what was ahead.

B. (10 points each)
1. d
2. d

Lineage (pages 65 and 66)

Part 1

A. (15 points each: 3 points for usage and mechanics; 3 points for clarity and coherence; 5 points for soundness of idea; 4 points for adequate detail)

1. Answers will vary but students should include points similar to the following:
   a. The speaker admires and respects the grandmothers.
   b. She believes that she does not measure up to the strength, cheer, and wisdom of the grandmothers.
   c. She wishes that she were more like the grandmothers.
2. Answers will vary but should reflect students' understanding that the grandmothers were strong because
   a. they worked long and hard.
   b. they performed physical labor.
   c. they had a great deal of responsibility.
3. Answers will vary but students should include points similar to the following:
   a. The speaker believes that satisfaction and pleasure can be found in doing one's job well.
   b. She believes that work can be enjoyable.
   c. She thinks that one should take pride in one's work.

B. (15 points) The best answers are:
   a. Energy.
   b. Capability.
   c. Satisfaction in work.
   d. A sense of purpose in life.
   e. Enjoyment.
   f. Common sense.
   g. Rich, full lives.
   h. A connection to nature.

Part 2

A. (10 points each)
1. a
2. a

B. (20 points) Answers will vary. Possible answers include the following:
   a. Line *a*—repeated sound *s*—descriptive words *hissing, rolling, smooth, gentle, soothing.*
   b. Line *b*—repeated sound *gr*—descriptive words *explosive, popping, breaking through, pounding.*
   c. Line *c*—repeated sound *s*—descriptive words *hissing, rolling, smooth, gentle, soothing.*
   d. Line *d*—repeated sound *r*—descriptive words *breaking through, rolling, smooth, gentle, soothing.*

In the last box, answers should reflect students' understanding that alliteration
   a. may suggest certain feelings or ideas.
   b. may suggest the literal sound of the thing being described.
   c. may help to support an image.

Women (page 67)

Part 1

A. (30 points each: 6 points for usage and mechanics; 6 points for clarity and coherence; 10 points for soundness of idea; 8 points for adequate detail)

1. Answers will vary but most students will find support for the following feelings:
   a. Admiration for their strength, determination, and willingness to fight for an education for the speaker's generation.
   b. Respect for their vision of a future for the speaker's generation.
   c. Gratitude for what they have done for the speaker's generation.
2. Answers will vary but should reflect students' understanding that
   a. the mothers are leading a fight for education.
   b. they have to do battle with opposing forces, such as racism, sexism, and poverty.
   c. they strategize to achieve their goals.
   d. they lead their children.
   e. they put themselves at risk for the sake of what they believe.

B. (20 points) Answers will vary. Obstacles include the following:
   a. Racism.
   b. Sexism.
   c. Poverty.
   d. Lack of education.

Qualities that help the mothers overcome the obstacles include: a, b, f, g, possibly also e.

Answers that include *h* (other) should reflect students' understanding that the mothers overcome the obstacles through their capability, independence, and willingness to fight for what they believe is important.

Part 2 (10 points each)
1. c
2. b

Everyday Use (pages 73 and 74)

Part 1

A. (12 points each: 2 points for usage and mechanics; 3 points for clarity and coherence; 4 points for soundness of idea; 3 points for adequate detail)

1. Answers will vary. Most students will point out that Maggie now realizes that
   a. she does not have to live in her sister's shadow.
   b. she has no desire to be like her sister and therefore is free to be her own person.
   c. she has triumphed over her sister for the first time.
   d. her mother loves and values her.

   Some students may say that she smiles at the combination of Dee's African dress with the sunglasses or at her own reflection in Dee's glasses.
2. Answers will vary. Most students will probably say that Maggie should get the quilts because
   a. she appreciates them for the reason that they were made—their usefulness.
   b. the quilts remind her of people she loved and of those who taught her to quilt.
   c. her mother has promised them to her upon her marriage. (page 56)
   d. Dee only wants the quilts because they are worth money and are fashionable.
   e. Dee rejected the quilts when her mother offered them before.

   Some students may say that Dee should get the quilts because she will preserve them.
3. Answers will vary. Students might point out that Hakim-a-barber seems to think that the narrator and Maggie
   a. are "backwards" and quaint.
   b. are very unlike the bright, attractive, and enlightened Dee.

c. are worth visiting only for the sake of pleasing Dee.
4. Answers will vary. Students might suggest that the title
   a. refers, on one level, to Maggie's using the quilts on an everyday basis rather than preserving them as Dee would. (page 56)
   b. might, on a deeper level, refer to Maggie's everyday contact with her heritage, as opposed to Dee's artificial attempts to "rediscover" it.

B. (12 points) Answers will vary. A good answer might be similar to the following model:
   a. Dee: pride, independence, group history, picturesque objects.
   b. Maggie: personal memories and contacts, useful things and skills, people caring for each other.

Part 2

A. (5 points each)
1. a
2. d

B. (30 points) Answers will vary. A good answer might be similar to the following model:
   a. Well educated: Maggie and the narrator are both poorly educated.
   b. Outgoing: Maggie is painfully shy, and the narrator is shy around white people.
   c. Figure: Maggie is very thin, and the narrator is quite large. (page 52)
   d. Feels superior: Maggie thinks of herself as inferior, and the narrator seems to have a balanced view of herself.
   e. Old house: Maggie and the narrator both value the house.
   f. Heritage: Maggie and the narrator both live with and use their heritage.

My Mother Pieced Quilts
My Father's Song (pages 77 and 78)

Part 1 (20 points each: 4 points for usage and mechanics; 4 points for clarity and coherence; 6 points for soundness of idea; 6 points for adequate detail)
1. Answers will vary. Students might suggest that to the speaker the quilts
   a. bring back memories of family life.
   b. preserve moments of family history.
   c. represent the mother's love, skill, and competence.

   In addition, students might suggest that to the mother the quilts
   a. keep the family warm in winter. (lines 1–4)
   b. provide a creative outlet for her talents.
   c. preserve memories of family life.
   d. offer a way of expressing love. (lines 54–55)
2. Answers will vary. Students might suggest that the father
   a. listened to the son.
   b. expressed his emotion freely.
   c. loved his son.
   d. grew things.
   e. was gentle and compassionate.
   f. tried to give his son insight and understanding.
3. Answers will vary. Students might say that both speakers feel
   a. respect and admiration.
   b. love and affection.
   c. gratitude for the attention their parents paid to them.

Part 2

A. (4 points each)
1. Sight, possibly also taste and smell.
2. Sight, touch.
3. Sight, touch.
4. Hearing, possibly also sight.
5. Sight, touch.
6. Sight, touch, possibly also smell.

B. (4 points each) Answers will vary. Among the possibilities are the following:
7. Alliteration: *th*en, *th*em; *th*read, *th*imble; cemented, steel. Assonance: th*e*n, c*e*m*e*nted, th*e*m, thr*ea*d; w*i*th, th*i*mble; st*ee*l n*ee*dle. Consonance: the*n*, ceme*n*ted; ce*m*ented, the*m*, thi*m*ble; cemen*t*ed, s*t*eel; cemente*d*, threa*d*, nee*d*le; stee*l*, need*l*e, thimb*l*e.
8. Alliteration: *r*iver, *r*oaring; *c*urrent, *c*arrying. Assonance: w*e*re, curr*e*nt. Consonance: ca*rr*ying, roa*r*ing; curren*t*, no*t*es; carry*ing*, roar*ing*.
9. Alliteration: None. Assonance: pl*ow*share, m*ou*se; un*ea*rthed, b*u*rrow. Consonance: ha*d*, unearthe*d*.
10. Answers will depend upon phrase chosen.

Sweet Potato Pie (pages 83 and 84)

Part 1 (20 points each: 4 points for usage and mechanics; 4 points for clarity and coherence; 6 points for soundness of idea; 6 points for adequate detail)
1. Answers will vary but students might say that
   a. Charley cares a great deal more about what the people in the hotel think about his brother than what they might think about him.
   b. Charley really doesn't have anything to lose by carrying the bag into the hotel himself.
   c. making Buddy happy is important to Charley and, in this case, that means making sure that Buddy gets the pie.
2. Answers will vary but most students will probably note that
   a. Charley doesn't seem bitter or angry.
   b. Charley seems glad to have helped his brother succeed.
   c. Charley's lost opportunities are heartbreaking, especially since he showed artistic promise.
   d. Charley's lost opportunities are tragic in that they represent the lost opportunities of others who have never had a chance to make all that they could of themselves and their talents.
3. Answers will vary but should reflect students' understanding that
   a. part of the reason that Buddy has had to work so hard and his family has had to make so many sacrifices for his education is that he is black and has had to deal with racism.
   b. Buddy hasn't forgotten how his education was gained and why it had to be gained in that way.
   c. Buddy's feelings while walking through Harlem—he describes Harlem as "home" and "the very heart of Blackness"—show that his blackness is a very important part of his identity.

Part 2

A. (10 points) Answers will vary but should reflect students' understanding that
   a. as a child, Buddy's opportunities resulted mainly from his being the youngest child (luck), not from his being the smartest.
   b. as an adult, Buddy's opportunities result mainly from his having a good education and the resulting well-paying job.

B. (10 points) Answers will vary but should include points similar to the following:
   a. Charley: "country"—the rural, simple, "downhome" life that Buddy left behind.
   b. Buddy: all the good things about his youth, as well as the giving, loving nature of his family.

C. (20 points) Answers will vary. A model answer for Buddy as the protagonist follows.
   a. Protagonist: Buddy.

b. Antagonist: Poverty and the hardships it inflicts; possibly also racism.
c. Buddy changes by developing an understanding of his family and of the position he has attained as he grows older and wiser.
d. The conflict centers on whether or not Buddy can overcome the disadvantages of his childhood environment and "be somebody."
e. The conflict is resolved. The love and assistance of his family enables Buddy to become "somebody" without losing touch with his roots.

Unit 2 OPPOSING INJUSTICE

from To Be a Slave (pages 91 and 92)

Part 1

A. (15 points each: 3 points for usage and mechanics; 3 points for clarity and coherence; 5 points for soundness of idea; 4 points for adequate detail)

1. Answers will vary. Most students will express the opinion that slavery cannot be justified under any circumstances and will offer suggestions such as the following:
   a. The colonists could have paid more—in cash, land, passage, and so on—to encourage more laborers to come of their own free will.
   b. Growth of the colonies could have been limited to what the colonists could do for themselves.
2. Answers will vary but should reflect students' understanding that, in general, all three demonstrated total disregard for the well-being of their captives and seemed to be motivated entirely by greed. Individual arguments for which one was most despicable include the following:
   a. The African chieftain was willing to capture and sell his fellow Africans into slavery. (page 82)
   b. The slave ship captain abused his "cargo" and held them in lower regard than he would cattle. (pages 82–84)
   c. The plantation owner created and maintained the demand for slaves.

   In addition, students should offer and defend an opinion concerning who was most responsible for the continuation of the slave trade. Although arguments could be made in support of any of the three, many students may think that the slave trade would have been significantly endangered if any of the three had refused to participate in the business.

B. (18 points each)

3. Answers will vary widely. Possible answers include the following:
   a. Capture: seeing people attacked and captured or killed by enemies from a neighboring tribe; seeing white people for the first time.
   b. Passage: being taken on a ship, placed in irons, and shut up in a dark, crowded place for weeks; enduring the rough ocean crossing; seeing people starve and die from beatings or disease; seeing babies being killed.
   c. Arrival: not being able to stand or walk right because of being chained for so long; being exhibited and sold like an animal at a market.
4. Answers will vary widely. Possible answers include the following:
   a. Capture: fear for family and friends; fear of the white people and their weapons.
   b. Passage: missing family, friends, and village; missing freedom of movement; fear of starvation, disease, and beatings from the crew; fear that the ship would be destroyed in a storm; possible consequences of not being able to communicate with the whites who controlled his fate.
   c. Arrival: missing family, friends, and village; fear of the strange new white people and their buildings, clothes, and machines; possible consequences of not being able to communicate with the whites who controlled his fate.
5. Answers will vary widely. Possible answers for Capture, Passage, and Arrival include the following:
   a. Physical strength and endurance.
   b. Hatred for captors.
   c. Hope of escaping.
   d. Faith in God (or the gods).
   e. Being able to speak with other captives.

Part 2 (8 points each)

1. a (page 81)
2. b, c

from Narrative of the Life of Frederick Douglass (pages 97 and 98)

Part 1

A. (15 points each: 3 points for usage and mechanics; 3 points for clarity and coherence; 5 points for soundness of idea; 4 points for adequate detail)

1. Answers will vary but could include the following points:
   a. Douglass realizes that crushing a man's spirit makes him a slave and that resisting domination makes a slave a man. (page 88)
   b. This realization is significant because it helps Douglass to survive slavery by giving him hope, pride, purpose, and self-confidence.
2. Answers will vary. Students might point out that Douglass
   a. first goes to his owner to ask for his protection. (page 90)
   b. next goes to friends to ask advice.
   c. then returns to Mr. Covey and takes up his duties.
   d. responds with violence only when all else fails.

   This response to the brutality he suffers reveals Douglass to be a courageous, reasonable, and remarkably patient man.
3. Answers will vary. Possible answers include the following:
   a. The loss of humanity that comes from being oppressed and the loss that comes from oppressing someone.
   b. The cruelties to which one is willing to submit a fellow human being for personal gain.
   c. The brutalities that were committed because human beings were seen as property, not as human beings.

B. (20 points) Answers will vary. A good answer might be similar to the following model:

   a. Points that support the Whately quotation: Mr. Covey is sadistic and sneaky. Master Thomas is willing to send Douglass back because of the money. A point that contradicts the quotation: Douglass remains patient until pushed too far.
   b. Points that support the Maximus quotation: Douglass has a sense of freedom after he resists Mr. Covey. The reputation Douglass gains is, in a sense, that of a free man.
   c. Points that contradict the Dyonysius quotation: Douglass shows higher values and, possibly, intellect than either of the slave owners who rule over him. A point that supports the quotation: As a superior human being, Douglass establishes moral dominance, a kind of rule.

Part 2 (35 points) Answers will vary. Among the possibilities are the following:

   a. Objective: Choice is effective because the event is horrible and dramatic in itself; objective description in this case has more impact than a subjective description of pain.
   b. Subjective: Exaggeration gives the impression of Covey's spying from the slaves' point of view, which is more effective than merely pointing out that Covey constantly spied on his slaves.

c. Subjective: Language choice effectively communicates the intensity of Douglass's emotions.

As I Grew Older
Any Human to Another (page 103 and 104)

Part 1
A. (15 points each: 4 points for usage and mechanics; 4 points for clarity and coherence; 4 points for soundness of idea; 3 points for adequate detail)

1. Answers will vary. Students might suggest that
   a. the wall is racism.
   b. an example might be the denial of an education and a job that offers chances for research and creativity to an intelligent young person with an interest in science.
2. Answers will vary. Students might mention
   a. affirmative action in education and job opportunities.
   b. changing those attitudes that limit opportunities in subtle ways.
3. Answers will vary. For some students the effects of the idea would be good because if people could feel one another's pain
   a. they might be more likely to stop others in society from being hurt.
   b. they might feel psychologically closer to others.

   For other students the effects might be disastrous if people were able to feel but not to alleviate one another's pain because
   a. everybody in society would always be suffering.
   b. psychologically, people might resent always having to feel another's pain.

B. (2 points each)

4. A
5. A (lines 13–19)
6. D
7. A (lines 25–28)
8. D
9. D
10. A
11. D

Part 2
A. (15 points) Answers will vary. A good answer might be similar to the following model:

a. Stanza 1: c, e.
b. Stanza 2: g.
c. Stanza 3: a.
d. Stanza 4: f.
e. Stanza 5: b, h.

B. (24 points) Answers will vary. A good answer might be similar to the following model for "Any Human to Another":

a. Simile or metaphor: "Your every grief/Like a blade/ . . . Must strike me down."
b. Thing described: the grief of another person.
c. Compared to: a sword.
d. Qualities or ideas communicated: sharp, painful, bringing someone low.

***from* Letter from Birmingham Jail** (pages 109 and 110)

Part 1
A. (16 points each: 3 points for usage and mechanics; 3 points for clarity and coherence; 5 points for soundness of idea; 5 points for adequate detail)

1. Answers will vary. However, whether students agree with King or not, they should recognize that King's position is that
   a. unjust laws should be disobeyed as a matter of principle. (page 106)
   b. disobedience is a tool for changing unjust laws.
   c. those who disobey should do so publicly and with a willingness to accept the consequences.
2. Answers will vary. Students might say that King would describe a hero as one who
   a. stands up for what he or she believes is right.
   b. refuses to participate in a discriminatory system.
   c. acts with courage in the face of threats and violence.
3. Answers will vary. However, whether students agree with King or not, they should recognize that King's position is that
   a. injustice is often accepted by the majority so long as things are peaceful.
   b. tension in the community causes the majority to look for a solution. (page 103)
   c. in attempting to eliminate the tension, the majority may show a willingness to eliminate the injustice.

B. (2 points each)

4. D
5. A
6. D
7. D
8. A
9. D
10. A
11. A

Part 2
A. (12 points) Answers will vary. Among the possibilities are the following:

a. The first quotation appeals primarily to the reader's intellect because it outlines, in straightforward language, a series of events.

B. (3 points each)

1. T
2. F
3. F
4. T
5. T
6. F
7. T
8. T

***from* Farewell to Manzanar** (pages 113 and 114)

Part 1
A. (15 points each: 3 points for usage and mechanics; 3 points for clarity and coherence; 5 points for soundness of idea; 4 points for adequate detail)

1. Answers will vary but should reflect students' understanding that while her family worked hard to maintain normal everyday lives, they did suffer. Details from the selection include the following:
   a. They are imprisoned for the "crime" of being of Japanese Americans.
   b. They are forced to live in a very cramped space, after losing most of their worldly possessions.
   c. Their loyalty to their country is repeatedly questioned.
   d. Their freedom of movement and expression is greatly restricted.
   e. They are isolated and excluded from the rest of America.
   f. Upon their release from detention, they are left with the feeling of having no other place or lives to return to.
2. Answers will vary. Possible answers include the following:
   a. People who are deprived of their homes and of most of their freedoms and possessions strive to live as normally as possible.
   b. People who are imprisoned solely because of their heritage still embrace the culture of the society that imprisoned them.
   c. The American government is so blinded by prejudice that it fears treachery from these very American Americans.
3. Answers will vary widely. Possible answers include the following:
   a. Resentful that you and your people are being singled out because of your heritage.
   b. Fearful that this prejudice might lead to other restrictions and even to bodily harm to you and your people.
   c. Anxious that this prejudice might follow you after you leave the camp.

B. (19 points) Answers will vary but should reflect students' understanding that the detainees are

a. proud.
b. orderly.
c. resigned to their fate.
d. determined to make the best of the situation.
e. eager to beautify their surroundings.
f. talented and artistic.
g. comforted by beauty and nature.
h. industrious and determined to lead useful, meaningful lives.

Part 2

A. (6 points each)
1. b (page 113) 2. c (pages 113 and 115) 3. b

B. (3 points each) Answers will vary. Possible answers include:
4. Other accounts of the time.
5. The writer's own memories.
6. The writer's own memories and family stories.
7. The writer's own memories and family stories.
8. The writer's own memories, family stories, and the high school yearbook.
9. Other accounts of the time.

Blues Ain't No Mockin' Bird (pages 117 and 118)

Part 1

A. (16 points each: 3 points for usage and mechanics; 3 points for clarity and coherence; 5 points for soundness of idea; 5 points for adequate detail)
1. Answers will vary. Students might suggest that, for Cathy,
   a. the hammer represents power of many kinds.
   b. the proper use of power is to preserve one's rights and dignity.
2. Answers will vary. Most students will probably think that the reaction is reasonable because
   a. the filmmakers are trespassing on the Cains' property and privacy.
   b. the filmmakers fail to treat the Cains with respect.
   c. the Cains' reaction is fairly mild and no one gets hurt.

   Some students might say that
   a. the filmmakers are working in a good cause.
   b. they don't do anything terrible.
   c. the Cains damage the film.
3. Answers will vary. Students might point out that
   a. Granny's values are based on decent behavior rather than material wealth.
   b. people have routinely behaved rudely to her, and her politeness is a defense against that.
   c. politeness expresses her strength, self-control, and internal dignity.

B. (1 point each)

4. R
5. R
6. D
7. R
8. R
9. D
10. R
11. R
12. D
13. D
14. R

Part 2

A. (21 points) Answers will vary. Among the possibilities are the following:
   a. Granny: dignified, intelligent, proud, righteous, compassionate, powerful, quick to anger, quick-witted.
   b. Granddaddy: dignified, slow to anger, intelligent, proud, righteous, powerful.

B. (10 points each)
1. Answers will vary. Among the possibilities are the following:
   a. One must not cause human suffering while recording it.
   b. Relates to the theme of dealing with people as human beings.
2. Answers will vary. Among the possibilities are the following:
   a. Trespassing and messing with other people's things is rude.
   b. Relates to the theme of showing respect for other people's property.

November Cotton Flower
A Note of Humility (pages 123 and 124)

Part 1

A. (15 points each: 3 points for usage and mechanics; 3 points for clarity and coherence; 5 points for soundness of idea; 4 points for adequate detail)
1. Answers will vary. Students might point out that
   a. the event is unusual. (lines 9–11)
   b. the reaction of the people is inspiring. (line 13)
   c. it is a story that includes a recognition of grim reality, a hint of the supernatural, and a feeling of hope.
2. Answers will vary. Students might point out that
   a. the octet describes a drought, a time when the means to sustain life are difficult to obtain.
   b. the drought could represent any life—such as that of many rural or urban blacks—in which it is difficult to scrape by.
   c. the sestet seems to suggest that people with such a life are, nonetheless, appreciative of beauty and capable of hope.
3. Answers will vary. Students might point out that the people will not be allowed to feel a moment's triumph until
   a. all of their hopes and dreams have been defeated. (line 1)
   b. they have given up trying to get anything for themselves. (line 2)
   c. they can no longer sing. (line 3)
   d. everything they love is dead. (line 5)
   e. they can no longer feel love. (line 7)

B. (14 points) Answers will vary. Among the possibilities for "November Cotton Flower" are the following:
   a. Images: dried crops, dried up stream, dead birds, blooming flower.
   b. Qualities or ideas communicated: harsh, stark, barren, strange and lovely.
   c. Overall feeling: appreciation of beauty, joy, a sense of hope in the most unlikely circumstances.

Among the possibilities for "A Note of Humility" are the following:
   a. Images: stony ground, soundless songs, thorns choking green things.
   b. Qualities or ideas communicated: harsh, stark, barren.

Part 2

A. (3 points each) Note: scoring should depend upon how well the student matches the paraphrase to the corresponding lines in the poem. If an early mistake causes the numbering to be off, but the sequence is followed thereafter, credit should be given accordingly.

1. A
2. F
3. G
4. E
5. B
6. D
7. C

B. (4 points each) Examples may vary. Possible answers include:
8. Yes—ground, sound.
9. Yes—long after our last songs have lost their sound.
10. Yes—we may come back.
11. Yes—when all our hopes, when thorns have choked, when love that moved.
12. No.

The Censors (pages 120 and 130)

Part 1

A. (15 points each: 3 points for usage and mechanics; 3 points for clarity and coherence; 5 points for soundness of idea; 4 points for adequate detail)
1. Answers will vary but should reflect students' understanding that the government is
   a. a dictatorship of some kind.
   b. highly repressive.
   c. firmly established.

2. Answers will vary but should reflect students' understanding that Juan's behavior is caused by a combination of factors including
   a. initially, fear of government action against him, leading him to conform superficially.
   b. later, a natural desire to succeed on his job and in the promotion hierarchy.
   c. finally, an equally natural need to do his job well that is perverted by the circumstances into an obsession that leads to his own death.
3. Answers will vary, but students might mention that
   a. no government can control behavior entirely by force—it's too expensive.
   b. by exploiting natural, ordinarily harmless desires for success and achievement such as Juan's, a government can get cooperation without force.

B. (15 points) Answers will vary widely. Possible answers include the following:
   a. First position: enjoying life, his own life, Mariana's safety, his own safety, Mariana's happiness.
   b. Second position: promotion, achievement, security.
   c. Third position: his job, work well done.
   d. Fourth position: perfection.

Part 2

A. (8 points each)

1. b, c
2. b
3. b, possibly also d
4. d, possibly also a

B. (8 points) Answers will vary widely. Among the phrases students might choose are the following:
   a. You know how hard it is to get anything done these days.
   b. Anyway, we can't complain.
   c. We know you couldn't pass up an opportunity like that overseas.
   d. There seems to be more rain than usual this year.
   e. Weeds are springing up everywhere.
   f. You'd hardly recognize the old place, it's changed so much.
   g. Maybe we'll get a chance to come see you some day.

Unit 3 AFFIRMING IDENTITY

How It Feels to Be Colored Me (page137)

Part 1 (30 points each: 6 points for usage and mechanics; 6 points for clarity and coherence; 9 points for soundness of idea; 9 points for adequate detail)

1. Answers will vary but should reflect students' understanding of the implication that although skin colors may be different, people are pretty much alike on the inside. A possible answer for those who agree is that regardless of skin color,
   a. people have similar physical needs—for food, water, shelter, and so on.
   b. most people have similar emotional needs—for comfort, love, support, and so on.
   c. most people have similar problems—sickness, loneliness, and fears.

   A possible answer for those who disagree is that while the color of a person's skin does not matter, what is inside varies greatly from person to person.
2. Answers will vary. Students who feel that black people would be more likely to appreciate Hurston's views on life might say that
   a. many blacks would relate more directly to her experiences than the average white person.
   b. if blacks and whites are different, in at least some ways, as she implies, then her views on life speak to that difference.

   Students who feel that Hurston's views offer the same thing to both blacks and whites might say that
   a. the sentiment that "the world is to the strong regardless of a little pigmentation more or less" speaks to everyone. (pages 139–140)
   b. the feeling of being in a world where everyone else is different is shared by people of all races.
   c. it is clear that Hurston believes that beneath it all, people are very similar. (page 141)

Part 2 (10 points each)

1. Answers will vary. A possible answer is:
   a. Key word or phrase: "a little pigmentation more or less."
   b. Tone: ironic, tolerant.
2. Answers will vary. A possible answer is:
   a. Key word or phrase: "game." b. Tone: playful.
3. Answers will vary. A possible answer is:
   a. Key word or phrase: "a dark rock surged upon, and overswept."
   b. Tone: self-confident.
4. Answers will vary. A possible answer is:
   a. Key word or phrase: "Great Stuffer of Bags."
   b. Tone: humorous.
   c. Overall feeling: bitterness, almost hopeless resignation.

I Have a Dream (pages 143 and 144)

Part 1

A. (12 points) The best answers are: a, b, c, f, g, h, j, l, n, t, u, v, w, x.

B. (12 points each: 2 points for usage and mechanics; 3 points for clarity and coherence; 4 points for soundness of idea; 3 points for adequate detail)

1. Answers will vary widely, but should demonstrate students' understanding that King's speech was electrifying and profoundly inspiring. Possible answers include the following:
   a. Standing peacefully with all those people, listening to King's words, it made me feel like all of us could accomplish anything we wanted if we tried hard enough. It seemed like the whole world was on our side.
   b. It was very awe-inspiring. I knew history was being made and that I was a part of it. Somehow, being in that crowd and listening to King, I knew that one day I would be telling my grandchildren about it.
2. Answers will vary but should include points similar to the following:
   a. King expected the Civil Rights Act to be passed by Congress.
   b. He listed some very specific goals necessary to realize his dream: nondiscrimination in motels and hotels; elimination of ghettos; elimination of "For Whites Only" signs; rights to vote where there were none, and something meaningful to vote for.
   c. He expected all people to work in a nonviolent manner toward the goal of an integrated society.
3. Answers will vary but should demonstrate students' understanding that King had a positive view of human nature and potential; he clearly felt that the evils of racism could be eradicated by people working together toward that common goal.
4. Answers will vary widely, but students should demonstrate their understanding that although great progress has been made toward civil rights since 1963, discrimination still exists in American society.

Part 2

A. (7 points each)

1. c (page 146)

2. c (page 146)
3. c
4. c, possibly also b
5. a, b (pages 146–148)

B. (5 points) Graphs will vary, but the best answers will find that King's appeal to emotion was very important and his appeal to reason somewhat less so.

Getting a Job
***from* I Know Why the Caged Bird Sings** (pages 149 and150)

Part 1 (20 points each: 4 points for usage and mechanics; 4 points for clarity and coherence; 6 points for soundness of idea; 6 points for adequate detail)

1. Answers will vary. Students might point out that Marguerite learns
   a. that determination can pay off.
   b. about the practical realities of life in a racist world.
   c. about the joy of achievement.
   d. that victories must be not only won but also protected.
   e. that victories can change one's life in unexpected ways.
2. Answers will vary. Students might point out that Marguerite
   a. has already had to eliminate several other options and is attracted to the uniform.
   b. is challenged by her mother's reaction.
   c. feels that she can prove something about and to herself by getting the job despite the obstacles.
3. Answers will vary. Students might describe Marguerite's mother using such terms as
   a. intelligent.
   b. optimistic.
   c. supportive.
   d. full of common sense.

Part 2

A. (20 points) Answers will vary but should include points similar to the following:
   a. At first she views the encounter as a scene in a drama that was written long ago by whites. She and the receptionist assumed the roles that their ancestors handed down to them. She decides that the encounter doesn't really have anything to do with her as an individual.
   b. Now she rejects her previous thoughts as nonsense. The encounter has everything to do with who she is and who the receptionist is. She can't just dismiss it.

B. (20 points) Answers will vary. Students should include points similar to the following:
   a. Confidence: she identifies possible jobs based on whether she wants them rather than whether she can do them.
   b. Pride: the idea that the job is unavailable to her because of race is enough to make her determined to get it.
   c. Poise: rather than allow the receptionist to disconcert her, she manages to disconcert the receptionist.
   d. Imagination: she is able to view the exchange with the receptionist in terms of a drama.
   e. Determination: she does not give up until she achieves her goal.

***from* Barrio Boy** (pages 155 and 156)

Part 1

A. (12 points each: 2 points for usage and mechanics; 3 points for clarity and coherence; 4 points for soundness of idea; 3 points for adequate detail)

1. Answers will vary but should reflect students' understanding that
   a. although there are things that Galarza as a child misses about Mexico, he seems to be relatively happy in his new country.
   b. he thinks of America as a land of opportunity, especially in terms of education.
   c. his view of America doesn't seem to have changed much as he has matured. He doesn't say that he sees things differently now and doesn't speak disparagingly of America.
2. Answers will vary but should include points similar to the following:
   a. The lessons in life concern tolerance, fellowship, identity, patriotism, democracy, and self-respect.
   b. These lessons are taught through example. Miss Hopley stops the singing at the flag salute, and all of the teachers treat the students with respect and tolerance for their national differences.
   c. These lessons are also taught through a system of rewards and punishments. Miss Ryan announces the accomplishments of individual children to the entire class, and Miss Hopley punishes those who engage in name-calling.
3. Answers will vary but should reflect students' understanding that
   a. many problems that Galarza dealt with are those typical of any child trying to adjust to a strange place.
   b. immigrant children today still have to find a way to fit in without losing their cultural identity.

   In addition, students who think that life is easier for immigrant children today might mention that
   a. there are many more agencies specializing in the problems of immigrants today.
   b. some states have even instituted bilingual laws, making language differences less of a problem for some immigrants.

   Students who don't think that things are easier today might point out that
   a. crime is a greater problem today than it was then, and the highest levels of crime usually are found in poor neighborhoods, where many new immigrants are likely to live.
   b. drugs and gangs—also most prevalent in poor neighborhoods—pose greater problems for youths today than they did then.
4. Answers will vary but should reflect students' understanding that
   a. the theme has to do with the difficulty of feeling a sense of unity in a nation of immigrants.
   b. the theme has to do with finding a common point among diverse groups.
   c. the selection suggests that the school serves as the common ground for all of the children; at school they are treated the same, and the same things are expected of them, while after school they split off to their own neighborhoods and ethnic customs, and even trade discriminatory insults.

B. (10 points) Answers will vary but most students will find that
   a. accepting his new self-image was easiest.
   b. winning acceptance by his peers was fairly easy.
   c. learning English, learning new customs, and letting go of old customs was fairly difficult.

Part 2

A. (6 points each)
1. d (page 160) 2. c (page 160) 3. d

B. (24 points) Answers will vary. For the first quotation, students should include points similar to the following:
   a. Mazatlán: friendly, congenial, casual, warm.
   b. Sacramento: orderly, formal, businesslike, cold, unfriendly.

For the second quotation, students should include points similar to the following:

a. Mazatlán: neighborly, casual, tolerant, with a sense of community.
b. Sacramento: private, self-centered, with a sense of isolation and alienation.

***from* Hunger of Memory** (pages 161 and 162)

Part 1
A. (20 points each: 4 points for usage and mechanics; 4 points for clarity and coherence; 6 points for soundness of idea; 6 points for adequate detail)
1. Answers will vary but students might say that Rodriguez would
   a. pay less attention to the lists other people made.
   b. pay more attention to what he enjoyed reading and less to what was "important" to read.
   c. try to know himself better in order to bring his own point of view to his reading.
   d. not disregard a book because he believed it was for children.
   e. not assume that the meaning of a book could be summarized in one sentence.
   f. not try to read books that he couldn't understand.
2. Answers will vary. Students might point out that Rodriguez
   a. is insecure about his own choices.
   b. yearns to be learned and believes that learned people become that way entirely from the books they read.
   c. seems to view the lists as representing both a path to and a certification of a higher state of being.
3. Answers will vary but might include points similar to the following:
   a. Reading with a point of view implies that the reader is a unique individual with attitudes gained from his or her experience. This approach aids in evaluating what is read.
   b. Reading to acquire a point of view implies that the reader is inexperienced, and cannot evaluate what is read.
   In addition, students should include a personal response regarding the value of reading widely before establishing a point of view. They might say that it is
   a. advisable because reading can provide a range of experiences.
   b. inadvisable because everything that is read may be accepted.

B. (18 points) The best answers are as follows:
   a. Reading is a pleasure: B.
   b. A reader must bring something: A. (page 171)
   c. Extensive reading: B.
   d. The harder a book: C.
   e. The real meaning: C. (page 170)
   f. Finishing a book: C.
   g. Experiencing a story: A.
   h. Little value: A.
   i. It is possible: A.

Part 2 (22 points) Answers will vary. A good answer might be similar to the following model:
   a. Technique: revealing his thoughts as a child.
   b. Qualities conveyed: naivete, literal-mindedness, persistence, a sense of frustration and inadequacy.

High Horse's Courting (pages 165 and 166)

Part 1
A. (16 points each: 3 points for usage and mechanics; 3 points for clarity and coherence; 5 points for soundness of idea; 5 points for adequate detail)
1. Answers will vary. In describing High Horse, students might use such terms as
   a. sweet, good-natured. This makes the reader like him and want to enjoy his story.
   b. determined, passionate, sincere. This leads to his taking the great lengths that make so much of the story funny. (page 177)
   c. uncool. His willingness to risk making a fool of himself gets him into silly situations.
2. Answers will vary. Most students will probably say that the story's main purpose is to entertain. In support of this idea they might mention that
   a. the tone of the story is conversational and humorous.
   b. the story is funny.
   c. while certain values are revealed, they are not explored or emphasized to any greater degree than in the average story.
3. Answers will vary. Students might mention that the culture seems to value
   a. male courage.
   b. male determination and resourcefulness.
   c. female timidity.
   d. friendship. (page 178)
   e. respect for parents.

B. (16 points) Answers will vary. Among the possibilities are the following:
   a. High Horse: the girl.
   b. The girl: High Horse, prestige.
   c. The girl's father: a good husband for his daughter. (page 179)
   d. Red Deer: to help his friend.

Part 2 (6 points each) Possible answers include the following:
1. Verbal irony.
2. Exaggerated language, description of comic behavior.
3. Exaggerated language, description of comic behavior.
4. Description of comic behavior.
5. Description of comic behavior, exaggerated language.
6. Description of comic behavior, verbal irony.

The Secret Lion (pages 169 and 170)

Part 1
A. (15 points each: 3 points for usage and mechanics; 3 points for clarity and coherence; 5 points for soundness of idea; 4 points for adequate detail)
1. Answers will vary. Possible answers include the following:
   a. His youth.
   b. His innocence.
   c. The ball.
   d. "Heaven."
   e. Swimming in the creek.
   In addition, the who or what that took these things away might include the following:
   a. Nature.
   b. Life.
   c. Adults.
2. Answers will vary but should reflect students' understanding that
   a. the grinding ball is seen as perfect by the boys.
   b. the boy has enough experience with his mother (the adult world) to know that she will think it is just a piece of junk.
   In addition, most students will feel the difference is accounted for by the difference between the wonderment of children and the practicality of adults.
3. Answers will vary but should reflect students' understanding that the boy seems to feel that
   a. he is abandoned by the teachers.
   b. the girls have changed.
   c. there are words that he wants to know about but that he cannot ask about.
   In addition, students should understand that the boy is dealing with changes and difficulties typical of adolescence.

B. (3 points each)
4. YES

5. YES
6. NO
7. NO
8. YES

Part 2

A. (5 points each)
1. a, b
2. c

B. (30 points) Answers will vary. Descriptive terms might include:
   a. Description: forbidden, secret, dirt, water, privacy, and sewage. Effect: It gave him a place for privacy, independence, rebellion, but taught him that these freedoms had costs.
   b. Description: unfamiliar, impersonal, and backward. Effect: It made him feel isolated and abandoned, and it made him more weary of adults, girls, and himself.
   c. Description: beautiful, green, water, unlike anything he had seen, an adult secret. Effect: It opened a new world to him, an idyllic place, but then nature and the adult world took it back.

My Delicate Heart Condition (pages 175 and 176)

Part 1

A. (15 points each: 3 points for usage and mechanics; 3 points for clarity and coherence; 5 points for soundness of idea; 4 points for adequate detail)
1. Answers will vary but should reflect students' understanding that the battle Harriet loses with the Fly family is a test of nerves. Possible answers include the following:
   a. Harriet will no longer challenge herself to sit through daring performances by the Fly family.
   b. After Harriet learns that she is underprivileged, she believes that she risks heart failure if she becomes frightened.
   c. Harriet discovers the sensitive side of her personality.
2. Answers will vary but should reflect students' understanding that learning she is underprivileged changes her. Possible answers include:
   a. She feels frightened because she believes she has been unknowingly endangering herself.
   b. She is worried because she believes she needs to change her behavior to protect her heart.
   c. She feels solemn and serious because she thinks she bears a new responsibility to take care of her heart.
   d. She feels special because she thinks she is different from the other kids at school.
3. Possible answers include the following:
   a. The new Harriet is sensitive and compassionate, looks out for others, and is willing to admit her mistakes. The old Harriet was at times a bully who had fun at the expense of others.
   b. The old Harriet was self-confident, independent, daring, adventurous, fun, and she constantly challenged herself. The new Harriet is weak, vulnerable, and less fun to be with.

B. (15 points) Things that are important to Harriet before her camp experience include: b, c, d, g, l. Things that are important after include: a, e, h, j, k.

Part 2 (8 points each)
1. a, possibly also b (ms 188-190)
2. d, possibly also a,b
3. c (ms 191)
4. c,d (ms 191)
5. d

Unit 4 EXPLORING CULTURAL CONFLICTS

Two Kinds (pages 183 and 184)

Part 1

A. (12 points each: 2 points for usage and mechanics; 3 points for clarity and coherence; 4 points for soundness of idea; 3 points for adequate detail)
1. Answers will vary but should include a point similar to any of the following:
   a. The narrator has conflicting feelings about her mother that are reflected in the two contrasting songs.
   b. The two songs express the narrator's different experiences in dealing with her mother's desire for her to be a prodigy.
   c. The two songs communicate the narrator's inner struggle with her desires to succeed, to please her mother, and to accept herself.
2. Possible reasons that the narrator feels strong include the following:
   a. She expresses her true feelings for the first time.
   b. She defies her mother, who possesses enormous strength of will.

   Possible reasons that she feels frightened include the following:
   a. She has never openly defied her mother before.
   b. She realizes that her anger is causing her to say hurtful things.
   c. She realizes that she is capable of causing her mother deep pain.
3. Answers will vary but should reflect students' understanding that the mother wants her daughter to have the successful life that seems to be possible in America. Things the mother hopes being a prodigy will achieve for her daughter include:
   a. Fame.
   b. Financial security.
   c. The American dream of a better life.
   d. The opportunity to be the best at something.
   e. An opportunity to outdo Waverly.
   f. Knowledge, discipline, and obedience.

   Things the mother hopes it will achieve for herself include:
   a. Pride in her successful daughter.
   b. An opportunity to outdo Auntie Lindo.
   c. The American dream of a better life.
   d. Financial security.
4. Answers will vary. Possible answers include the following:
   a. It is not possible to learn to be a prodigy, since a prodigy shows remarkable—almost miraculous—talent or ability. The mother's expectations place unrealistic demands and a great deal of pressure on her daughter.
   b. It is possible to learn to be a prodigy if one cultivates his or her inborn talent through discipline and hard work. To be a prodigy does require talent, but it is not necessarily unreasonable to expect that someone could develop that talent by working at it with determination and devotion.

B. (12 points) Answers will vary widely. Possible answers include:
   a. At the beginning of the piano lessons, to the mother the piano means hope and the opportunity for the daughter to succeed.
   b. At the beginning of the piano lessons, to the daughter the piano means responsibility and the obligation to fulfill her mother's wishes.
   c. When the mother gives the piano to the daughter, to the mother it means that she has never given up her belief that her daughter could be a prodigy.
   d. When the mother gives the piano to the daughter, to the

daughter it means that she has been forgiven for disappointing her mother.

Part 2

A. (4 points each)
1. N (page 199)
2. N
3. R (page 200)
4. N
5. R

B. (6 points each)
6. d, possibly also c
7. a (page 204)

C. (8 points) Students should circle the second sentence and indicate that the narrator is compared to the Christ child.

Seventeen Syllables (pages 189 and190)

Part 1 (15 points each: 3 points for usage and mechanics; 3 points for clarity and coherence; 5 points for soundness of idea; 4 points for adequate detail)

1. Answers will vary. In response to the first question, students might point out that Mrs. Hayashi
   a. feels trapped in a relationship that does not allow her to pursue her deepest interests.
   b. feels that her life could be fuller if she did not have to consider the needs and limitations of her husband.
   c. loves her daughter and wants Rosie's life to be fuller than her own.
   d. does not see romance as the problem (she does not ask Rosie not to fall in love), but marriage itself.

   Students might say that Rosie says yes because
   a. it is easier for her at this point than saying no.
   b. she tends to say yes, because it is easier, even when she means no.
   c. she realizes that, at this highly emotional moment, they cannot discuss the matter calmly.
   d. she will not feel bound by the promise she is making.
2. Answers will vary. Students who find Mr. Hayashi's behavior justifiable may point out that
   a. he resents the fact that since Mrs. Hayashi became a poet, she often ignores him.
   b. he is unable to share Mrs. Hayashi's excitement about haiku and cannot understand why she enjoys writing poetry.
   c. he feels socially and intellectually inferior to his wife.
   d. he feels intimidated by the haiku editor.

   Students who find his behavior unjustifiable may point out that
   a. Mrs. Hayashi has done nothing cruel to him and does not deserve the hostility and destructiveness of his action.
   b. he does not even try to discuss his feelings with his wife.
   c. it is not his wife's fault that he is incapable of understanding her needs.
   d. his wife has not neglected her duties as a wife and mother.
   e. he goes over the boundaries of justifiable behavior when he acts so rudely, destructively, and cruelly.
3. Answers will vary. Students might suggest that Rosie
   a. is too worried and confused to deal with what she knows will be a painful revelation.
   b. does not want to know something worrisome about things she cannot affect.
   c. wants to be able to concentrate her emotions on her new, fragile romance.
4. Answers will vary. Possible answers include the following:
   a. The story of Rosie's mother, while tragic, would not have the immediate, urgent quality that it has if it did not also affect Rosie's dawning romantic interest.
   b. The mother's isolation is increased by the contrast between her own cynicism and Rosie's budding romantic hope.
   c. The story of Rosie and Jesus is complicated and made more poignant by the fact that while Rosie's life is expanding due to a relationship, her mother's life is being constricted by a relationship.
   d. The mother's negative experience spoils Rosie's pleasure of first love.

Part 2

A. (4 points each)
1. d
2. c
3. d (page 214)
4. b (page 216)
5. d

B. (20 points) Answers will vary but might include points similar to the following:
   a. Crippled, emotionally or physically: Mr. Hayashi, Mrs. Hayano.
   b. Difficulty interacting with people: Mr. Hayashi, Mrs. Hayano.
   c. Interactions with their families limited: Mr. Hayashi, Mrs. Hayano.
   d. Physically or emotionally changed: Mrs. Hayashi, Mrs. Hayano.
   e. Another similarity: Both Mrs. Hayashi and Mr. Hayano are interested in haiku and other intellectual pursuits.

***from* Kaffir Boy** (pages 195 and 196)

Part 1

A. (12 points each: 2 points for usage and mechanics; 3 points for clarity and coherence; 4 points for soundness of idea; 3 points for adequate detail)
1. Answers will vary, but most students will probably find that Mathabane's mother is the most important factor. Support for this idea includes the following:
   a. She goes through all the frustration to get the papers he needs to enroll in school, and she is willing to make whatever sacrifices are necessary to keep him there.
   b. She physically forces him to go to school against his will.
   c. She stands up to his father at great danger to herself.
   d. She forces him to understand why it is so important that he go to school.
2. Answers will vary but should reflect students' understanding that
   a. the mother's views help to explain why it is sensible. From her point of view, education is the only hope her son has for a better future; therefore, he should be given the chance. She believes that even if education can't completely free him from the chains of apartheid, it can enable him to live a better life within the system.
   b. the father's views help to explain why it might not seem sensible. From his point of view, there is nothing to be gained through education and much to lose. He believes that education cannot open the doors that apartheid closes to blacks, that a "white man's" education will separate his son from his tribal past, and that the financial sacrifices necessary for gaining an education will endanger the family's ability to survive.
3. Answers will vary but should reflect students' knowledge that the government hampers Mathabane's ability by
   a. underfunding schools for blacks.
   b. making admissions requirements difficult to meet.
   c. maintaining apartheid.
   d. imposing conditions that make education for blacks seem meaningless.

   In addition, students should address the issue of whom the government serves and why, by including points similar to the following:
   a. The government attempts to serve the interests of its white citizens.

b. Many South African whites want their government to discriminate against blacks because they are afraid of blacks, they are unwilling to share their power and give up their preferred status, they believe themselves superior to blacks, and they do not want their way of life to change.

4. Answers will vary widely. Many students will probably express a greater appreciation for
   a. the power that education gives a person.
   b. the American belief that education is a basic right.

B. (8 points each)

5. Answers will vary but should include points similar to the following:
   a. His mother supports by getting the necessary papers, taking him to the school, enrolling him against his will, standing up to his father, explaining to him how important education is.
   b. Motivations: love for him, desire for him to have a better life, desire to change the system, need to stand up for what she believes in.
6. Answers will vary but should include points similar to the following:
   a. His father opposes by refusing to allow him to go, reacting to his going with violence against the family, refusing to financially support his education.
   b. Motivations: selfishness; desire to be the "man" of the family, belief that education is worthless, desire to maintain tribal ways, desire to survive.
7. Answers will vary but should include points similar to the following:
   a. The strange woman supports by relating the story of her son as an example, encouraging his mother's efforts.
   b. Motivations: guilt over her son's fate, desire for others not to share her son's fate.
8. Answers will vary but should include points similar to the following:
   a. The principal supports by encouraging the mother's efforts, bending the admissions rules, threatening him, serving as an educator, serving as a role model.
   b. Motivations: belief that education is important, desire for blacks to have greater power in South Africa.

C. (8 points) Graphs will vary but should reflect students' understanding that while most of the things listed do complicate the issue, those things that do *not* include the following:
   a. Religious beliefs.
   b. Mathabane's ability to learn.

Part 2 (12 points) Answers will vary widely. Possible answers include the following:
   a. Mother: disrespectful, headstrong, independent, bitter, regretful.
   b. Grandmother: traditional, respectful, conventional, dependent.

Hiccups (page 200)

Part 1 (15 points each: 3 points for usage and mechanics; 3 points for clarity and coherence; 5 points for soundness of idea; 4 points for adequate detail)

1. Answers will vary, but students might mention that the speaker feels that his mother
   a. was too strict.
   b. emphasized some of the wrong values.
   c. restricted his life unnecessarily.

   In addition, the best answers will recognize a self-mocking tone in the poem and see in it affection and perhaps even some gratitude toward the mother.
2. Answers will vary. Students who feel the attitudes would be harmful might say that the mother
   a. created a negative atmosphere, which could undermine a child's confidence.
   b. pressured her son to conform and to achieve, perhaps causing anxiety and stress.
   c. limited her son's acquaintances and activities, perhaps depriving him of rich experiences.
   d. may have kept her son from developing pride in his heritage.

   Students who do not feel that the attitudes would be harmful might point out that
   a. most of the things mentioned are minor.
   b. the tone of the poem suggests that the speaker himself doesn't think they amount to "calamity" and "disasters."
3. Answers will vary. Most students will note that the son has probably grown up
   a. well-mannered.
   b. well educated.
   c. socially acceptable.
4. Answers will vary, but students could include points similar to the following:
   a. Most of the poem could apply to almost any mother and child.
   b. The desire to make a child socially acceptable is understandable and, if not overdone, a good thing.
   c. That desire, when exercised by a member of a minority or oppressed group, can become encouragement to accept the oppression.
   d. Conformity in an oppressive society can be self-destructive.

Part 2 (40 points) Answers will vary. Possible answers include the following:
   a. Well-mannered—lines 11–33, lines 54–55.
   b. Well-educated—lines 38–41.
   c. Socially acceptable—lines 42–50, lines 66–76.
   d. Conformist—lines 77–92.

***from* Arctic Dreams** (pages 205 and 206)

Part 1 (25 points each: 4 points for usage and mechanics; 5 points for clarity and coherence; 8 points for soundness of idea; 8 points for adequate detail)

1. Answers will vary. Students might point out that
   a. Lopez dreams of finding a way for humans to live in harmony with the environment of the Arctic.
   b. one way that individuals might fulfill the dream of not having lived in vain is by endeavoring to make the first dream come true. (page 245)
2. Answers will vary but should reflect students' understanding that Lopez feels that
   a. the Arctic is a fragile, complex environment that is susceptible to being destroyed by human exploitation. (page 244)
   b. the Arctic has a dangerous and harsh climate that makes human habitation very problematic.
   c. humans must be aware of the effect they have on the Arctic and the effect the Arctic has on them.

Part 2

A. (10 points each)

1. Answers will vary. Possible answers include the following:
   a. Senses: sight, touch.
   b. Figurative language: "small as a kite."
2. Answers will vary. Possible answers might include the following:
   a. Sense: sight
   b. Figurative language: "like the window light in a Vermeer painting."

B. (10 points) Answers will vary. A possible answer might include the following points:

a. Examples of precise use of language: corolla of a flower, intimacy . . . sought, begins to notice, monotonic, wolf spider lunges, shred . . . lies inert, sudden and unexpected sight.
b. Feeling: wonderment at the intricacies of nature.

C. (20 points) Answers will vary. A good answer might be similar to the following model:
a. The dogsledder: local people living in harmony with the land.
b. The military men: invaders or outsiders.
c. The steaks: affluence of the outsiders; the upsetting of the natural order.
d. The dogsledder's reaction: local people's suspicion of invaders; an attempt to get away from outsiders.
e. The dogs' reaction: how animals and the land can be permanently altered by contact with outsiders.

from Notes of a Native Son (pages 211 and 212)

Part 1

A. (15 points each: 3 points for usage and mechanics; 3 points for clarity and coherence; 5 points for soundness of idea; 4 points for adequate detail)

1. Answers will vary, but students should recognize that Baldwin wants to be an honest person and a good writer. Most students will probably say that he succeeded because
   a. in his writing, he gets at a deeper understanding of himself and his experiences.
   b. he does so in a straightforward, honest manner.
   c. his writing is graceful, clear, and vivid.
   d. he is humble about his abilities as a writer, lacking arrogance or egotism.
   e. he displays great concern for humanity.
2. Answers will vary. Students might suggest that Baldwin was looking for
   a. a sense of belonging.
   b. a better understanding of his own feelings and experiences.
   c. models of behavior and achievement.
   d. pride in the accomplishments of people with whom he might identify.
3. Answers will vary. However, students should reveal an understanding that Baldwin believes each American is responsible for these conditions. Many students will probably agree with that position, pointing out that
   a. each citizen of any country bears a certain responsibility for what that country is and does.
   b. improvement can occur only when the people of the country work for and demand it.
   c. small improvements can be effected by even the youngest or the most powerless.

   Some students may say that the government bears primary responsibility for the conditions facing minorities and that individual citizens have little or no power.

B. (15 points) Answers will vary. A good answer for the fourth quotation might be similar to the following model:
a. Baldwin means that one must think about one's own experiences, explore one's own feelings, and decide on certain standards of right and wrong, using those standards to guide one's actions and writing.
b. This would be a good inspirational sign because it would remind a person to keep his or her personal code in mind and not be swayed by other people's values and goals.

Part 2

A. (6 points each)
1. a (page 250) 2. d (page 251) 3. c, d (page 253)

B. (22 points) Answers will vary but should include points similar to the following:
a. Baldwin was drawn to white American culture in some ways, but he was excluded from it because of his race.
b. Baldwin saw African-American culture as impoverished.
c. This conflict left him in limbo and forced him to make his own meaning, clarifying his position in society before he could write about it.

from American Hunger (pages 217 and 218)

Part 1

A. (15 points each: 3 points for usage and mechanics; 3 points for clarity and coherence; 5 points for soundness of idea; 4 points for adequate detail)

1. Answers will vary widely. Students might say that he discovers
   a. he has chosen a pattern of relating to the world that keeps him isolated. (page 258)
   b. in order to meet his ultimate goal of being a writer, he must devote himself to being a careful observer.
   c. being a good writer requires that he reject emotional attachments, because they would interfere with his ability to be objective about the world.
2. Answers will vary, but students might include points similar to the following:
   a. Poverty: hampered by forcing him to worry constantly about the basic necessities for survival; may have helped by inducing him to work harder at learning to write so that hecould make a living at it.
   b. Lack of support from friends and family: hampered by making writing a lonely, less rewarding experience; may have helped by adding to his sense of isolation, thereby playing a part in his becoming a more introspective, sensitive writer.
   c. Lack of a formal or advanced education: hampered by denying him an easier route to learning how to write well; may have helped by forcing him to develop his own style and way of writing.
3. Answers will vary, but most students will find that there was no way for people to know that Wright would develop into a gifted writer. Support for this idea includes the following points:
   a. Wright didn't let others know what he really felt.
   b. He didn't talk about his reading and writing with others.
   c. He showed no signs of having any deep emotions or desires.
   d. His verbal reactions to others were slow and showed little, if any, sign of his intelligence or abilities.

B. (15 points) Answers will vary but should include points similar to the following:
a. Physical hunger: suffered from malnutrition; constantly tried to get enough food to gain weight. (page 258)
b. Mental hunger: wanted a job, the opportunity to write, and knowledge through reading.
c. Emotional hunger: wanted meaningful relationships with others and wanted to express his emotions openly instead of repressing them.

Part 2 (10 points each) Answers will vary. Among the possibilities are the following:
1. Qualities and feelings suggested: perfectionism, determination, possibly insecurity.
2. Qualities and feelings suggested: willingness to work hard, love of writing.
3. Qualities and feelings suggested: joy in creation, ambition for excellence.
4. Qualities and feelings suggested: despair, sense of inadequacy, respect for excellence.

Unit 5 ENGAGING THE IMAGINATION

A Very Old Man with Enormous Wings (pages 225 and 226)

Part 1 (15 points each: 3 points for usage and mechanics; 3 points for clarity and coherence; 5 points for soundness of idea; 4 points for adequate detail)

1. Answers will vary. Students who think the winged man is an angel might point out that
   a. he changes the lives of his hosts for the better.
   b. he performs miracles.
   Students who think he is not an angel might point out that
   a. the changes he makes in his hosts' lives are entirely material; the people are not better in any other way for his being there.
   b. his miracles probably don't count in a world where a lot of strange things happen anyway.
2. Answers will vary. Students might suggest that the people they know would be
   a. skeptical, suspecting some sort of trick.
   b. convinced that the wings had been grafted on by medical science.
   c. unlikely to conclude, as the people in the story do, that they are seeing an angel.
   d. likely to react, as the people in the story do, with curiosity, hostility, and lack of sensitivity.
3. Answers will vary. Students might suggest that the winged man represents
   a. the unknown and unexplainable.
   b. an ideal religion worn and battered by modern life.
4. Answers will vary. Students might point out that García Márquez's style could be said to satisfy Moore's description because he
   a. creates a world of the imagination where fantastic things can and do happen.
   b. grounds that world with realistic characters, motivations, and dialogue.

Part 2

A. (16 points) Answers will vary, but students will probably say that plot and setting would be affected least and characterization and tone affected most.

B. (4 points each) Answers will vary. Possible answers:

1. Realistic detail.
2. Ironic tone.
3. Bizarre events, unusual humor.
4. Ironic tone.
5. Unusual humor.
6. Realistic detail, ironic tone.

The Youngest Doll (pages 231 and 232)

Part 1 (15 points each: 3 points for usage and mechanics, 4 points for clarity and coherence; 4 points for soundness of idea; 4 points for adequate detail)

1. Answers will vary widely. Students might describe the world portrayed as total fantasy; others might imagine a fairly realistic setting in which seemingly normal human activities are interrupted by bizarre acts of nature. Make sure students' answers contain references to specifics.
2. Allow for variant answers. Students will most likely identify the following reasons for their feelings of sympathy:
   a. The aunt: She suffers the physical pain of the prawn's bite; she is an invalid for many years; she could have been cured but for the doctor's greed; one assumes that her reason for remaining a maiden aunt is her affliction, which greatly impairs her lifesytle.
   b. The young doctor: He might be viewed as a victim of his father's greed, which he came to accept without question; he married the youngest niece without knowing the significance of the doll.
   c. The youngest niece: Although she does not suffer the physical pain that her aunt did, she is victimized by her husband, who seems to have married her simply for reasons of social status; she is forced to sit on the balcony each day and to suffer the company of her husband's patients.
3. Answers will vary but will likely reflect one of the following ideas:
   a. Those who insist on greed pay for it.
   b. Two wrongs don't make a right.
   c. Money and social status do not make up for shallowness of character.
4. Answers will vary but should reflect students' understanding that the view of marriage is rather negative. Support for this idea includes the following points:
   a. The niece's marriage has nothing to do with love. She is motivated by curiosity, while the young doctor is motivated by a desire for social status.
   b. Over the course of her marriage, the niece grows more and more doll-like and less and less human. This is true both physically and in the way she is treated by her husband.
   c. By the end of the story, the niece has lost all of her humanity and is nothing more than a doll.

Part 2

A. (15 points) Answers will vary but should include points similar to the following:

a. Middle class: overly concerned with wealth, social prestige, and appearances, hypocritical; lacking in true emotions; lacking in concern for others, especially women.
b. Aristocracy: morally weak; incapable of self-determination; holding a low opinion of women.

B. (5 points each)

1. c
2. b
3. b, possibly c

C. (5 points each) Answers will vary widely. Possible answers include the following:

First quotation

a. Underlined terms: *bathed in the river, heavy rains, soft feeling of melting snow, head nestled among the black rocks' reverberations, slamming of salty foam, sound of waves, her hair had poured out to sea, sharp bite, screaming, writhing in pain.*
b. Mood: mysteriousness, tranquillity mixed with harshness, horror (at end).

Second quotation

a. Underlined terms: *took her off, square house, cement block, made her sit out on the balcony, high society, motionless inside her cubicle of heat, suspect, husband's silhouette . . . made of paper, soul as well.*
b. Mood: frustration, anger, suspicion.

What I Have Been Doing Lately (page 236)

Part 1 (35 points each: 7 points for usage and mechanics; 7 points for clarity and coherence; 11 points for soundness of idea; 10 points for adequate detail)

1. Answers will vary but should include points similar to the following:
   a. Events happen without cause or explanation.
   b. Events can reverse themselves, sometimes at the wish of the narrator.
   c. Contradictions are unimportant.

d. Nothing is surprising.
e. Time expands and contracts.

2. Answers will vary. Some students might point out that
   a. the question is usually a conventional, polite thing to ask.
   b. it can be quite annoying to have to answer that kind of question when one knows the inquirer has no interest in the answer.
   c. the idea of giving a bizarre response to this kind of question may seem appealing.

   Other students might suggest that the question is a convenient trigger for the imagination, an opportunity to exercise a free-associating mind.

Part 2 (30 points) Answers will vary. For the usual account, students might furnish answers similar to the following:

a. Events described: ordinary things such as getting or losing a job, taking a vacation, projects at school.
b. Diction used: simple, straightforward.
c. Communicated: some simple, usually not very interesting, facts.

For this account, students might furnish answers such as the following:

a. Events described: bizarre events such as seeing monkeys, crossing rivers, falling down holes.
b. Diction used: simple, straightforward.
c. Communicated: some feelings, a strange atmosphere, perhaps a sense of humor.

Tenement Room: Chicago (page 241)

Part 1 (30 points each: 6 points for usage and mechanics; 6 points for clarity and coherence; 9 points for soundness of idea; 9 points for adequate detail)

1. Answers will vary. Students might say that the speaker feels
   a. compassion for the weariness and suffering.
   b. distaste for the filth.
   c. bitterness about a world that creates and condones such circumstances.
2. Answers will vary. Most students will probably say that the poem does communicate the weariness of poverty. Among the words and images that may be cited are the following:
   a. "The day creeps / Slowly / From the tired room."
   b. "A cringing bed, age-weary."
   c. "Exhausted / The room sleeps dreamlessly."
   d. Such verbs as *lounge*, *drooping*, and *slumps*.

Part 2 (40 points) Answers will vary. A good answer might be similar to the following model:

a. Underlined words and phrases: crippled, drooping, spiritless as wounded soldiers, cringing, age-weary, corseted, squats, flabby, slumps, punished, defeated.
b. The person would have led a very hard life, characterized by poverty, illness, lack of love, and neglect by society.
c. The room would have led a life of neglect, seldom or never being maintained or repaired by its owner and lived in by people who were unable or unwilling to care for it.

Loo-Wit (page 242)

Part 1 (29 points each: 5 points for usage and mechanics; 6 points for clarity and coherence; 9 points for soundness of idea; 9 points for adequate detail)

1. Answers will vary. Students might point out that she is responding to people who
   a. damage her.
   b. treat her disrespectfully.
   c. rob her of her dignity.
2. Answers will vary. Students might suggest that evidences of the culture might include
   a. the name given to the volcano.
   b. the attitude toward nature.
   c. certain personifying images, such as that of "shaking the sky like a blanket about her."

Part 2 (7 points each) Possible answers are:

1. Spews out lava or ash.
2. Bushes grew near the top.
3. Strip mining, farming, other development.
4. The volcano remained dormant.
5. Logging.
6. The volcano erupts.

Rhythms
Prayer to the Pacific (page 245)

Part 1 (20 points each: 4 points for usage and mechanics; 4 points for clarity and coherence; 6 points for soundness of idea; 6 points for adequate detail)

1. Answers will vary. Most students will probably say that the most significant change occurs at line 15 because after that point,
   a. the images are of nature rather than human life.
   b. the images are of things coming together rather than coming apart
   c. the movements depicted are smooth and slow.
   d. the words form one long sentence that slows the rhythm of the language itself.
2. Answers will vary widely. In proposing a subject, students might refer to the images of
   a. the "criminal of love," which could suggest a person whose love was not approved by parents, the community, or society as a whole.
   b. the child dropping out of a tree, which could suggest either a family and the fun that a family has or a younger child spying on the criminal of love, perhaps an older sibling.
   c. the ship leaving, which could suggest someone going on a journey.
   d. the cars tearing away, which could suggest a car chase or a busy metropolitan area.
   e. nature, which could suggest a quiet, peaceful rural scene.
3. Answers will vary. Students might suggest that the speaker seeks and finds
   a. some part of his or her heritage.
   b. a connection with the ocean that is described in myth.
   c. a connection with the Chinese culture. (lines 9–10)
   d. rain clouds to bring rain to her homeland

Part 2 (40 points) Answers will vary widely. A model answer might be the following:

a. Image: "Four round stones in my pocket I carry back the ocean / to suck and to taste." (line 15)
b. Communicates an overall feeling of leaving the ocean but taking some of it with you.

The Form of the Sword (pages 251 and 252)

Part 1

A. (14 points each: 3 points for usage and mechanics; 3 points for clarity and coherence; 4 points for soundness of idea; 4 points for adequate detail)

1. Answers will vary, but students should recognize that the Englishman feels that
   a. he behaved like a coward.
   b. he betrayed a man who saved his life.
   c. he betrayed a cause he claimed to believe in.

Answers will vary as to whether he is despicable. However, good answers should recognize that the acts he committed are usually thought of as despicable.

2. Answers will vary. As to whether the punishments are similar, answers could include the following points:
   a. In each case the guilty man is forced to live with a constant reminder of his terrible deed.
   b. Cain's act is made known by his mark, but Moon's act is his own secret.

   As to whether the punishment fits the crime, possible answers include the following:
   a. Yes—Moon suffers his entire life for his crimes.
   b. No—Moon deserves to die for causing the death of the man who saved his life.
3. Answers will vary, but students should recognize that the author uses this form to build the suspense of the story. In addition, students should recognize some of the following as foreshadowing:
   a. The shape of the scar and Moon's name.
   b. The Englishman's drinking bouts. (page 298)
   c. His receiving no mail. (page 298)
   d. His saying that men who died in the civil war were "not the most unfortunate ones." (page 299)

B. (28 points) Answers should reflect students' understanding of the following:
   a. Frame characters: the frame narrator and the Englishman.
   b. Frame setting: South America.
   c. The secret is revealed in the frame.
   d. Central characters: the central narrator (revealed to be John Vincent Moon) and the fighter for Irish independence.
   e. Central setting: Ireland.

Part 2

A. (10 points each)
1. b (page 299)
2. b, d, possibly also c

B. (10 points) Answers will vary, but most students will find that all of the elements are at least somewhat important, with the possible exception of insights about life.

Ode to the Watermelon (page 256)

Part 1

A. (20 points each: 4 points for usage and mechanics; 4 points for clarity and coherence; 6 points for soundness of idea; 6 points for adequate detail)
1. Answers will vary but students should recognize that the watermelon is wonderful, primarily because it is cool and wet. Some other wonderful things about the watermelon include the following:
   a. It is round.
   b. It is star-filled.
   c. It is green, white, and red.
   d. It is sweet and pure.
2. Answers will vary. Possible answers include the following: fatigue; scorched shoes; glare; dustiness; feet feeling as though tortured by thorns and hot stones; thirst felt in the teeth, lips, and tongue; being weighed down with the heat like an oven.
3. Answers will vary but should reflect students' understanding that poetic descriptions are not to be taken literally and, therefore, with absolute seriousness.

Part 2

A. (20 points) Answers will vary. Possible answers include the following:
   a. "The tree of intense/summer"—sight, possibly also touch.
   b. "The green whale of summer"—sight.
   c. "firmament of coolness"—touch.
   d. "dissolves into/wild rivers, sugar,/delight!"—taste.

B. (4 points each)
1. S (page 302)
2. S (page 302)
3. W (page 303)
4. W
5. S

Unit 6 EXAMINING LIFE EXPERIENCES

Kitchenette Building (page 263)

Part 1 (15 points each: 3 points for usage and mechanics; 3 points for clarity and coherence; 5 points for soundness of idea; 4 points for adequate detail)
1. Answers will vary but should include points similar to the following:
   a. The "we" is the people who live in the kitchenette building.
   b. They are urban poor.
   c. Their primary concern is day-to-day survival—fixing dinner, getting along with each other, getting into the bathroom, coming up with the rent.
   d. They have little time or energy for leisure.
   e. They are physically tired and emotionally worn out by the demands of life.
2. Answers will vary but might include points similar to the following:
   a. They are poor, have little power in society, and have no reason to believe that their situation will change. Since disappointment is already an important factor in their lives, they don't see any reason to set themselves up for more disappointment by dreaming of things that they aren't likely to get.
   b. They have no time or energy to dream.
   c. Dreams might make them even more unhappy with the reality of their lives. If they don't think about alternatives, their lives may not seem quite so bad.
   d. Dreams require risk taking. Their lives are already marginal, and taking risks could hamper their ability to pay the rent or put food on the table.
3. Answers will vary but might include points similar to the following:
   a. The assurance that the risk is worth taking. This might come through the example of "one of their own" daring to dream and actually realizing his or her dream.
   b. Aid from outside sources. A government program or private agency might provide the resources necessary to realize a dream or to make dreaming less risky to survival.

Part 2 (55 points) Answers will vary but should include points similar to the following:
   a. Hearing/people: strong sounds; the everyday sounds of life in the building.
   b. Hearing/dream: giddy sounds; fluttering sounds; musical sounds; an aria.
   c. Smell/people: cooking smells of onions and fried potatoes; the stench of garbage.
   d. Smell/dream: clean, fresh smells.
   e. Sight/people: grayness and lack of color; garbage lying in the halls; waiting in line for the bathroom.
   f. Sight/dream: white and violet; floating up above the people's lives.
   g. Taste/people: greasy tastes of inexpensive foods.

h. Taste/dream: clean, fresh, light tastes.
i. Touch/people: dryness; lukewarm; heaviness; numbness.
j. Touch/dream: lightness; warmth.

One wants a Teller in a time like this (page 264)

Part 1 (15 points each: 3 points for usage and mechanics; 3 points for clarity and coherence; 5 points for soundness of idea; 4 points for adequate detail)

1. Answers will vary but should include points similar to the following:
   a. The speaker is probably comforted by home, traditions, and close relationships with people.
   b. The speaker finds comfort in these things because they are usually consistent and reliable and they provide a good foundation for dealing with those things in life that aren't.
2. Answers will vary but the best answers will reflect students' understanding that
   a. "time" in the poem refers to an age, era, or other extended period of time.
   b. the use of the word *in* suggests an extended period of time, one that has more to do with feeling than with actual time.
   c. the use of the word *at* would suggest a short period of time, one associated with a particular event, such as a death or an emergency.
3. Answers will vary but students might say that those who would relate best to the poem would probably
   a. be old enough to have exercised individual freedom of choice and discovered that it is not always as wonderful as it appears to be in childhood.
   b. be having difficulties in life in making choices or facing conflicts.
   c. have once experienced a "home," or safe place where a "Teller" made most of the decisions and showed the correct path to follow.
4. Answers will vary but the Teller should be someone who
   a. has some degree of control over the student's life.
   b. feels certain—or gives the impression of feeling certain—about how to live one's life.
   c. is loving.

Part 2 (40 points) Answers will vary widely. Possible answers include: adult, questioning, lonely, caring, religious, fearful, needy, lost, uncertain, overwhelmed.

Speech to the Young / Speech to the Progress-Toward (page 265)

Part 1

A. (18 points each: 3 points for usage and mechanics; 3 points for clarity and coherence; 6 points for soundness of idea; 6 points for adequate detail)

1. Answers will vary but most students will say that it means
   a. to live in the present.
   b. to not worry about the past or the future.
2. Answers will vary but students might say that the speaker asks that the young
   a. remain true to themselves and not be unduly influenced by others.
   b. stand up and defend right principles.
   c. lead full lives, making every moment count.
   d. be positive and optimistic.
3. Answers will vary but might include points similar to the following:
   a. It might be easy if one was wealthy and had little to risk by not thinking about where the next meal would come from, or if a person had no children depending on him or her.
   b. It might be difficult if a person was unemployed and needed to find a job, or if a person wanted to achieve some goal that would require a great deal of planning and preparation.

B. (6 points) The best answer is: c.

Part 2 (40 points) Answers will vary widely. Students might note words such as the following: negative, selfish, pessimistic, mean-spirited, bitter, angry.
Possible answers for the remaining boxes include the following:
a. Down-keeper: anyone who attempts to keep people from achieving goals or bettering themselves, such as a high school counselor who tells a motivated young woman that she doesn't have what it takes to be a scientist.
b. Sun-slapper: anyone whose attitude toward life is negative, such as the character Eeyore in the *Winnie-the-Pooh* series.
c. Self-soiler: anyone whose actions toward himself or herself are harmful or hateful, such as one who takes drugs.
d. Harmony-husher: anyone who attempts to create discord among others, such as a person who spreads rumors.

Horses Graze (page 266)

Part 1 (20 points each: 4 points for usage and mechanics; 4 points for clarity and coherence; 6 points for soundness of idea; 6 points for adequate detail)

1. Answers will vary but students might say that horses' sanity comes from their knowledge that
   a. the uncomplicated life is best.
   b. the world is really a lovely place.
   c. living in the present increases one's satisfaction with life.
   d. taking on more than one needs to survive only complicates one's life.
2. Answers will vary but students might say that, by nature, humans
   a. are too busy.
   b. unnecessarily complicate their lives.
   c. take themselves and their lives much too seriously.
   d. live for tomorrow, thereby losing out on today.
   e. inevitably strive for what they do not have and do not need.
3. Answers will vary but students might say that life would be more
   a. relaxed and unhurried.
   b. rewarding.
   c. enjoyable.

Part 2 (40 points) Answers will vary. Possible answers include the following:
a. Horses' simplicity is contrasted with people's needless complexity; horses "eat / eat / eat," and "they lift their clean calm eyes and they lie down / and love the world," while people do *not* realize that "creature feet may press / only a few earth inches at a time" and that "earth is anywhere earth."
b. Horses' contentment is contrasted with people's dissatisfaction; horses "do not wish that they were otherwhere," while people engage in "follies," "inflation," and "the knocks and nettles of administration" trying to get somewhere or make something happen.

A Raisin in the Sun, Act One (pages 271 and 272)

Part 1

A. (40 points) Answers will vary but might include points similar to the following:

a. Mama dreams of owning her own home; it is important to her because she sees "home" as the idea that holds her family together and gives them dignity; she will probably "sag."
b. Walter dreams of owning a liquor store; it is important to him because he wants to do something meaningful that will bring him a better life and the respect of others; he will probably "explode."
c. Ruth dreams of having a better home; it is important to her because she hates the way her family now lives; she will probably "sag."
d. Beneatha dreams of becoming a doctor; it is important to her because she wants a better life and she wants to be independent; she will probably "explode."

B. (10 points each: 2 points for usage and mechanics; 2 points for clarity and coherence; 3 points for soundness of idea; 3 points for adequate detail)

1. Answers will vary widely. Reasons for each dream's being worthwhile include the following:
   a. Mama and Ruth's dream is practical and will improve all of their lives without much risk involved.
   b. Walter's dream is worthwhile because it may make the family financially secure and give him the sense of self-worth and self-respect that he sorely needs.
   c. Beneatha's dream is worthwhile because becoming a doctor will put her in a position where she can help herself, her family, and others.
2. Answers will vary but should reflect students' understanding that
   a. the immediate reason their dreams have been deferred is that they are poor; without money, their dreams cannot be realized.
   b. furthermore, their dreams have been deferred because of the negative effects of American racism and the legacy of slavery.
3. Answers will vary but should reflect students' understanding that
   a. the term "ghetto-itus" is used as if it were a disease.
   b. the symptoms of the disease—poverty and cramped living conditions—have begun to take their toll on the family.

Part 2 (30 points) Answers will vary but should include points similar to the following:

a. Ruth and Walter: Ruth is tired of listening to Walter complain about his life, and she is tired of living in a "rat trap" of an apartment. Walter is tired of dreaming about being rich and powerful. He wants to do something to change his life, but Ruth will not support him or even listen to him. Travis and the baby that Ruth is carrying also complicate their relationship.
b. Ruth and Mama: Mama spoils Travis and interferes with Ruth's supervision of him. Ruth wants to have an abortion; Mama doesn't want her to.
c. Ruth and Beneatha: Ruth, who feels hopelessly mired in poverty, can't understand why Beneatha doesn't see wealth as a desirable quality in a mate. Beneatha has set higher goals for herself; she wants more out of life than Ruth, and money is not her only aim.
d. Walter and Mama: Walter wants Mama to listen to him and to let him make the decisions in the family. Mama doesn't understand Walter's frustrations; as far as she is concerned, he has a nice family and a good job and he ought to be thankful. She doesn't realize that he needs to feel more in control of his life. Walter also cannot be "his father's son" and give his pregnant wife the support she needs because he is so depressed about his life and marriage. This makes Mama disgusted with him.
e. Walter and Beneatha: Walter is annoyed that Beneatha does not appreciate all that the family does so that she can go to school. He also thinks that she should set her goals lower, as other women do. Beneatha thinks that Walter is a fool, with no ambition and no respect or appreciation for her goals.
f. Mama and Beneatha: Mama doesn't understand Beneatha's attempts to "find herself" and won't tolerate Beneatha's contempt for religion. Beneatha wants to control her own life, and she resents Mama's old-fashioned ways, interference in her life, and insistence on the importance of God.

A Raisin in the Sun, Act Two (pages 275 and 276)

Part 1 (13 points each: 2 points for usage and mechanics; 3 points for clarity and coherence; 4 points for soundness of idea; 4 points for adequate detail)

1. Answers will vary widely. Students who judge Walter sympathetically might say that
   a. he doesn't lose the money—his friend steals it from him.
   b. he may have been foolish for entrusting Willy with the money, but that is no excuse for Mama's behavior.
   c. he is devastated by the loss and notes that the "money was made of my father's flesh."
   d. he was just getting back on his feet and now his hopes are shattered.

   Those who judge Walter harshly might say that
   a. he is a fool for entrusting the money to Willy, whom Ruth has always recognized as a loser.
   b. he had no right to risk his sister's share of the money.
   c. he loses everything because his dreams are extravagant.
   d. he disappoints Mama after she entrusts him with the money.
2. Answers will vary widely. Possible answers include the following:
   a. Walter. He loses not only the money but all of his dreams, his mother's trust, what remains of his wife's respect for him, and the possibility of providing a better life for his son.
   b. Beneatha. The money that would have paid for her schooling—her dream—is lost.
   c. Ruth. The revival of her marriage may not occur, the future of her unborn child is once again questionable, her hopes for Travis's future are dashed, and the family's ability to keep up payments on the new house may be imperiled.
   d. Mama. Her hopes for her children's futures are shattered: Beneatha may not go to medical school, and Walter has proven untrustworthy.
3. Answers will vary. Students might say that she needs him to say it because
   a. she feels guilty about having frustrated his dreams.
   b. she wants him to be happy with what she sees as best for all of them.
   c. she loves him and doesn't want him to be angry with her.
   d. she wants to be reassured that her difficult decision was the right one.
4. Answers will vary but might include points similar to the following:
   a. Walter is no longer desperate for money.
   b. Walter thinks that his investment is going to pay off.
   c. Walter has great pride in his race and in his own integrity.

Part 2

A. (6 points each)

1. d 2. b 3. b

B. (2 points each) The best answers are:

4. Light.	9. Dark.	14. Light.
5. Dark.	10. Dark.	15. Light.
6. Dark.	11. Dark.	16. Dark.

7. Light.
8. Dark.
12. Light.
13. Light.
17. Light.
18. Dark.

George is a fool, she shouldn't date him; Beneatha's taking pride in Walter's transformation in the final act.

A Raisin in the Sun, Act Three (pages 279 and 280)

Part 1 (12 points each: 2 points for usage and mechanics; 3 points for clarity and coherence; 4 points for soundness of idea; 3 points for adequate detail)

1. Answers will vary. Most students will think that it is believable because of reasons such as the following:
   a. Travis's presence when Mr. Lindner returns plays an important part in Walter's transformation, and Walter's desire for Travis to look up to him is well-established earlier in the play.
   b. Walter delivers his speech to Mr. Lindner in a halting manner, indicating that he is struggling with his conscience and that he is unsure of what he is saying.
   c. Walter's actions in the final act are not completely out of character; his pride in his race has already been established, in the Ocomogosiay episode and in the scene in which Mr. Lindner first visits the family.
   d. Walter's call to Mr. Lindner is made at a time of extreme duress and disappointment.

   Students who think it isn't believable could point out that Walter's overwhelming desire for money over anything else has been well-established by
   a. his saying in Act One that money "is life."
   b. his taking his sister's share of the money.
2. Answers will vary but should include points similar to the following:
   a. The women react with absolute repulsion and disbelief.
   b. They react this way because they cannot believe that Walter would humiliate himself by playing the role of the subservient African American.
3. Answers will vary but students might say that he means that
   a. he is not going to sit down and simply work out a theoretical answer.
   b. he is engaged in working out answers to the questions through his actions.
4. Answers will vary but students might say that she is
   a. remembering her husband and the life and dreams they shared in the apartment.
   b. thinking about how hard it is to leave her home now that she finally can leave.

Part 2

A. (10 points) Answers will vary widely but might include points similar to the following:
   a. Africa: hope, identity, pride, the past, dignity, individual expression, intensity, action, heritage, dreams.
   b. America: despair, domination, racism, but also hope.

B. (12 points) Answers will vary but could include any of the following: the insurance check, the new home, Mama's plant, Africa, the new baby, education, the liquor store, the African independence movement, the gardening tools and hat given to Mama.

C. (30 points) Answers will vary but might include points similar to the following:
   a. Ruth and Walter: Mama's giving Walter the rest of the money; Walter's turning down Mr. Lindner the second time.
   b. Ruth and Mama: Mama's buying the new house; Mama's giving Walter the rest of the money.
   c. Walter and Mama: Mama's giving Walter the rest of the money; Walter's turning down Mr. Lindner the second time.
   d. Walter and Beneatha: the Ocomogosiay episode; Walter's turning down Mr. Lindner the second time.
   e. Mama and Beneatha: Mama's telling Beneatha that if

A Visit to Grandmother (pages 285 and 286)

Part 1

A. (16 points each: 3 points for usage and mechanics; 3 points for clarity and coherence; 5 points for soundness of idea; 5 points for adequate detail)

1. Answers will vary. Students who choose Charles might say that
   a. he has been afraid his whole life that his mother might not love him.
   b. he may even hate himself because he feels that his mother was unable to love him.
   c. he courageously decides to find out as an adult whether or not this perception of his mother's feelings is true.
   d. his emotional needs were not met when he was a child.
   e. he has made something of himself with almost no help from his family.
   f. his homecoming is a terrifying, bittersweet experience for him.

   Students who choose the mother might say that she
   a. has raised ten children to the best of her ability.
   b. has tried to meet the individual needs of her children.
   c. welcomes Charles even though he has neglected her.
   d. is shocked to learn that Charles felt unloved.
   e. upon hearing what Charles has to say, seems deeply saddened, not only for herself but for Charles.
2. Answers will vary but should reflect students' understanding that
   a. although GL is a grown man and is the one who gets them into the crisis, he turns to his mother to save them, and it is she who eventually handles the situation.
   b. the incident shows why the mother has felt it necessary to treat GL more indulgently than her other children.
3. Answers will vary but students might include points similar to the following:
   a. There was little margin for error for a black person in that region at that time.
   b. GL's irresponsibility could have been punished by death.
   c. Under these circumstances, fairness had to become a secondary consideration for the mother.
   d. Charles was shortchanged because he wasn't in any such danger.

B. (12 points) Answers will vary widely. Students might indicate that
   a. his most important accomplishment is confronting and expressing feelings toward his mother that have been troubling him his whole life.
   b. his most important failure is being unable to deal with his mother's expressions of love for him in a mature and constructive manner.
   c. the visit is neither a complete failure nor a complete success.

C. (6 points) Answers will vary widely depending on students' personal views of each character. The best answers will indicate that none of the characters have been completely terrible or perfect.

Part 2

A. (10 points) Answers will vary widely. Possible answers include the following:
   a. Immaturity: The grandmother tells the story about GL and the horse in which GL demonstrates this trait.
   b. Irresponsibility: Rose tells the others about how GL once took off to Chicago to see Joe Louis fight without telling anyone beforehand.

B. (7 points each)
1. d, possibly also b (page 388)
2. a

C. (10 points) Answers will vary but could include points similar to the following:
a. The grandmother regards Charles as an honest man.
b. She knows that GL is untrustworthy.
c. She doesn't seem to mind GL's crafty behavior, however.

Choices
Oranges (page 289)

Part 1 (25 points each: 4 points for usage and mechanics; 5 points for clarity and coherence; 8 points for soundness of idea; 8 points for adequate detail)

1. Answers will vary. Some students may say that Giovanni would agree with this view of life. In support, they might point out that "Choices"
   a. has a strong underlying message that one should try for each of the positive things mentioned—doing what one wants, having what one wants, going where one needs to go, and expressing what one feels.
   b. clearly advises enjoying what one has or can achieve.
   c. advises one to accept the idea of sorrow as a natural consequence of life's disappointments but does not suggest that this sorrow is a reason for regretting one's choices.

   Some students may say that Giovanni would not agree with this view of life. In support, they might point out that "Choices"
   a. focuses on accepting compromises, or settling for less. (lines 28–32)
   b. conveys a message about coming to terms with limitations.
2. Answers will vary. Students might say that the speaker
   a. did not want to spoil the moment.
   b. wanted the experience of giving freely.
   c. did not want to tarnish his image in the girl's eyes.
   d. wanted the moment to be concerned with love, not money.
3. Answers will vary. Most students will probably say that the speaker did not regret his choice because
   a. the generous gesture was preserved with its meaning intact.
   b. the image of the orange as a fire indicates that the speaker felt warmed by the experience, probably because of the saleslady's gesture as well as the girl's happiness with the chocolate.

Part 2 (25 points) Answers will vary. Possible answers include the following:
a. "Choices": What speaker values in life—freedom, individuality, independence, integrity, and assertiveness; How speaker deals with obstacles—isn't defeated or discouraged by obstacles, faces limitations positively, makes compromises, and doesn't give up.
b. "Oranges": What speaker values in life—relationships, making someone else happy, sharing, and giving; How speaker deals with obstacles—relies on his own resourcefulness to get something and trusts other people to help.

Some students may prefer the approach of the speaker in "Choices" because making compromises is more applicable to a variety of situations in life. Others may prefer the approach of the speaker in "Oranges" because his or her resourcefulness involves less compromise and may accomplish goals that making compromises would have limited.

Marigolds (pages 295 and 296)

Part 1

A. (15 points each: 3 points for usage and mechanics; 3 points for clarity and coherence; 5 points for soundness of idea; 4 points for adequate detail)
1. Answers will vary widely, but should include points similar to the following:
   a. Lizabeth herself isn't sure of her motives for destroying the marigolds.
   b. She is in a state of emotional confusion brought to a head by overhearing her father's crying.
   c. She feels scared and lonely.
   d. She is driven to lash out by doing something destructive.

   In addition, students should include points similar to the following:
   a. Lizabeth immediately regrets doing it because she suddenly realizes how much her action will hurt Miss Lottie.
   b. She doesn't like the guilt that her action makes her feel.
2. Answers will vary but should demonstrate students' understanding that
   a. Lizabeth's awareness of the impact of her action on Miss Lottie comes from her emerging adult sense of reality, just as her destruction of the marigolds has come from her childish lack of caring.
   b. compassion is a quality that requires one to know about pain and suffering—things that the innocent know nothing of.
3. Answers will vary but should reflect students' understanding that, after the marigold incident, Miss Lottie never plants marigolds again. Most students will find that this change symbolizes a more profound change in Miss Lottie's attitude toward her life.

B. (15 points) The best answers are:
a. Protecting her brother from harm.
b. Volunteering at a nursing home for senior citizens.
c. Paying attention to the needs and feelings of others.
d. Understanding why her father's problems drive him to tears.
e. Suggesting to her parents that she help out with their financial situation.

Part 2

A. (4 points each)
1. F
2. F (page 402)
3. F
4. T (page 402)
5. F (page 402)
6. T
7. F
8. F

B. (4 points each)
9. The best answers are: hope, beauty, accomplishment.
10. The best answers are: despair, poverty, barrenness.

My City
The Tropics in New York (page 300)

Part 1 (20 points each: 4 points for usage and mechanics; 4 points for clarity and coherence; 6 points for soundness of idea; 6 points for adequate detail)
1. Answers will vary. Students might describe the city using such terms as
   a. crowded. b. full of life. c. diverse.
2. Answers will vary. Students might point out that the speaker
   a. seems profoundly uprooted.
   b. longs for a lost life and a lost culture.
   c. reflects the sense of loss and alienation a person can feel when transplanted to a different culture. (lines 11–12)
3. Answers will vary, depending on the environment the student

chooses. Students who choose New York might mention the
a. sense of action and vitality. (lines 10–11)
b. diversity.
Students who choose the tropics might mention the
a. sense of peace and serenity. (lines 6–8)
b. natural beauty.

Part 2

A. (30 points) Answers will vary. Among the possibilities are the following:
a. Stanza 1: bright, approving; colorful words, vivid images.
b. Stanza 2: almost reverent; vivid images, figurative language.
c. Stanza 3: extremely homesick, sorrowful; vivid images, direct expression of emotion.

B. (10 points) Wording will vary. Among the possibilities are the following:
a. Question: What am I going to miss most when it's time for me to die?
b. Answer: Manhattan.

from **Mississippi Solo** (pages 305–306)

Part 1

A. (15 points each: 3 points for usage and mechanics; 3 points for clarity and coherence; 5 points for soundness of idea; 4 points for adequate detail)

1. Answers will vary but might include points similar to the following:
   a. The journey down the river has stripped away Harris's trivial concerns, and he appreciates the opportunity simply to share a meal with another person.
   b. The river experience has made Harris more thankful for the simple concerns of life and survival.
   c. Given the isolation of traveling down the river, Harris is grateful for human contact.
   d. Having felt like an outcast in the town, Harris is thankful that he's spending the holiday with someone who shares his experience.
2. Answers will vary but students might point out that Harris and Jim are both
   a. traveling alone down the river.
   b. regarded as strange by the townspeople.
   c. outsiders.
   d. in need of human contact.
3. Answers will vary widely, but students might point out that
   a. Harris looks as if he needs help.
   b. Bill is a kind, compassionate person.
   c. Bill is killing time, apparently putting off going home to his wife and visiting in-laws.
   d. Bill is proud of Natchez and wants to make a good impression on this visitor.
   e. Bill enjoys showing people the sights of Natchez.
   f. Bill is acting city attorney and enjoys this sense of responsibility.
4. Answers will vary, but students should include points similar to the following:
   a. Harris is surprised by a spectacular storm during which he feels a special closeness to the river and comes to appreciate nature even more.
   b. Harris encounters a variety of people. The unpleasant encounter—with the women who will not talk to him—makes the pleasant encounters—with the Queen's captain, Bill, and Jim—all the more special.
   c. Harris celebrates Thanksgiving in an unusual way. The simple meal he eats with Jim on a sandbar reminds him, in a way that no traditional Thanksgiving has ever done, of all he has to be thankful for.

Part 2

A. (5 points each)
1. The best answers are: b, i, possibly also f.
2. The best answers are: a, g, n.
3. The best answers are: c, f, l, o.
4. The best answers are: c, d, f, possibly also l, o.

B. (5 points each)
5. b (page 412)
6. c (page 413)
7. c (page 415)
8. d